I0825364

LINCOLN'S SPEECHWRITER

LINCOLN'S SPEECHWRITER

John Hay and the Friendship That Inspired American Eloquence

JAN CIGLIANO HARTMAN

A POST HILL PRESS BOOK
ISBN: 979-8-89565-280-0
ISBN (eBook): 979-8-89565-281-7

Lincoln's Speechwriter:
John Hay and the Friendship That Inspired American Eloquence

Cover design by Cody Corcoran
Cover illustration by C.F. Payne

This is a work of nonfiction. All people, locations, events, and situations are portrayed to the best of the author's memory.

Post Hill Press
New York • Nashville
posthillpress.com

Published in the United States of America
1 2 3 4 5 6 7 8 9 10

For George, My Beloved

TABLE OF CONTENTS

PREFACE

This book is the product of dozens of years of archival research, writing, editing, and rewriting. As I pen this, I feel a professional kinship with Elizabeth Winkler, a journalist, book critic, and author of *Shakespeare Was a Woman and Other Heresies: How Doubting the Bard Became the Biggest Taboo in Literature.* Winkler has been chastised for her groundbreaking scholarship. "Among Shakespeare scholars," Winkler states, "the Shakespeare authorship question...does not exist; that is, it is not permitted."[1] Winkler continues, "the dusty Shakespeare establishment—almost entirely male—was not pleased to have English literature's supreme genius co-opted by female scholars and declared a feminist." Carol Symes, Harvard-educated professor of history and theater at University of Illinois, argues that negating new knowledge is immoral, much worse than the dishonored discovery. "It's unethical for a group of scholars to be confronted with perfectly plausible questions and some plausible evidence and to refuse to consider it."[2] Richard Waugaman, a clinical psychiatrist and Shakespeare scholar, argues, "There are many cognitive errors that ensue from overconfidence in one's beliefs.... First, we mistake beliefs for facts." Groupthink, Waugaman says, occurs when a group—such as Shakespeare or Lincoln scholars—"maintains cohesion, agreeing not to question unproven core assumptions and excluding anyone who deviates from group doctrine." Similar to Lincoln, Waugaman continues, "Shakespeare has been revered so much by so many people for so long that it is deeply disconcerting to be told we may have been admiring the wrong man."[3]

Every Lincoln historian who has read a draft of this book—a narrative that cautiously interweaves evidence supporting the claim that John Hay was President Abraham Lincoln's speechwriter—has declared that it is bunk, unprovable, indefensible, wrong. Most Lincoln historians, in fact, refused to read the entire manuscript, simply contesting the claim and the knowledge without considering the literary and factual evidence presented. They know better considering their many years of reading and researching Lincoln, they say. "Students of Lincoln," Gabor Boritt has argued, "have a difficult time separating themselves from their subject."[4] This self-revealing statement from the lips of a Lincoln historian is prophetic.

Let's begin.

I came to know John Hay working on the history of Euclid Avenue in Cleveland, Ohio. Hay captured my attention as a fascinating figure, yet his biographical record appeared to be superficial. His full story remained untold. Embarking on a cradle-to-grave biography of Hay—which I have since laid to rest—I immersed myself in the John Hay papers at Brown University, the Library of Congress, the Massachusetts Historical Society, the Houghton Library at Harvard University, the Huntington Library in California, and others.

As all historians do, I have marshaled the facts of Hay's life, arranging and interpreting those facts to give them meaning, offering new insight into Hay's character and the themes that guided him. I was excited to read Hay's college bluebooks and speeches, which had not been viewed since his children deposited them in the Special Collections of the John Hay Library at Brown in 1939, revealing Hay's distinct literary voice and beginning to see the glimmer between Hay's eloquent rhyme and rhythm patterns and that of President Lincoln's major speeches and letters. Entering Lincoln's world through the door of Hay scholarship, I had a unique perspective on Hay's contribution to Lincoln's prose.

Relying entirely on the historical record, I chronicle in the following pages the archival record of Hay's college essays, debates, and oratories; his diaries, letters, speeches, photographs, and official documents; and also the knowledge that emanates from statements of fact, descriptions of actions, photographs and illustrations, and informed judgments that are balanced against critical evidence to resolve previously unanswered questions.[5] I have tapped multiple genres of historical documentation, such as behavior and speech or material changes in expression, which bear witness to John Hay's role under President Lincoln.

The archival record is invaluable. Human memory, Lincoln and Hay claimed, was faulty. It was not to be trusted. "Biographers," said Lincoln, "are not only misleading but false."[6] When Hay and fellow Lincoln assistant John Nicolay were at work on the ten-volume *Abraham Lincoln* biography during the 1870s and 1880s—the first authorized history of the sixteenth president, which was sanctioned by Robert Lincoln—they relied entirely on written documentation at the time it occurred. They recognized the danger of reminiscences. In 1885, Hay wrote to *Century* publisher, Richard Watson Gilder, asking, "Can you remember things?" "No," he wrote, a redundancy to his own question. "I have to rely exclusively on documents. I would not trust my recollection in the slightest matter of historical interest—yet every newspaper is full of long stories—in the utmost detail—telling us all about the great men and deeds of the past." Still, he concluded, "I, who knew them all, have not a word to say."[7]

In addition to the archival record, I am indebted to the scholars who have dedicated themselves to the important work of researching and writing about John Hay and Abraham Lincoln. William Roscoe Thayer, William Tyler Dennett, and Michael Burlingame are foremost. Major references of Abraham Lincoln and his known writing compiled by Roy P. Basler, Nicolay and Hay, and Burlingame were also invaluable sources.

The body of historical background created by Lincoln scholars offered a deep understanding of Lincoln's life, oratory, and rhetoric: Garry Wills and his Pulitzer Prize-winning *Lincoln at Gettysburg: The Words that Remade America;* David Zarefsky's *Abraham Lincoln: In His Own Words;* Douglas L. Wilson's insightful *Lincoln's Sword: The Presidency and the Power of Words;* Ronald C. White Jr.'s *The Eloquent President, Lincoln's Greatest Speech,* and *Lincoln in Private;* Doris Kearns Goodwin's *Team of Rivals;* Gabor Boritt's *The Gettysburg Gospel;* and, Michael Burlingame's ground-breaking *Abraham Lincoln: A Life.*

The discovery of Hay's contribution to Lincoln's major messages, speeches, and letters is based on the written record of Hay's diary and his anonymous and pseudo-anonymous press filings. It is based on an evaluation of Hay's speeches and poetry during his college years at Brown and while working with Lincoln before his presidency, establishing Hay's literary voice and poetic patterns. It is also based on major changes in Lincoln's oratory once Hay was working with him. A close reading of Hay's diary became a key source of documentation. Hay's Civil War diaries offered telltale signs when the two men began working together and the details of Lincoln's and Hay's personal conversations and times together in Washington, DC, confiding thoughts, ideas, and convictions. Begun at the outset of the war, Hay recorded in his private journal his conversations with President Lincoln at the time they occurred, offering evidence of Hay's daily proximity to the president and Lincoln's thoughts. This also provided the basis of Hay's anonymous journalism that advocated Lincoln's policies, plans, and personal beliefs.

The one known instance that Hay revealed his material contribution to Lincoln's oratory—notably, the Gettysburg Address—was cited in the 1933 memoir by Jean Jules Jusserand, French ambassador to the United States during Theodore Roosevelt's presidency, when John Hay was Secretary of State. Jusserand remembered that the highlight of an evening at the home of John and Clara Hay, which also included Teddy and Edith Roosevelt, was Hay displaying some rare items in his library. The high point was the autographed manuscript of Lincoln's Gettysburg Address, which President Lincoln gave to Hay soon after he delivered the speech in November 1863. In the leather folio, Hay also shared "some proofs revised by him [Hay], for, far from being an improvisation, every word had been carefully weighed."[8]

Hay's scrapbooks have offered further evidence. Here he pasted his anonymous and pseudo-anonymous newspaper columns, as well as several of Abraham Lincoln's speeches and documents, believed to be given to Hay by the president in gratitude for Hay's material contributions to the works, including the Springfield Farewell speech, the Gettysburg Address, the Second Inaugural, and the Meditation on Divine Will, among others. Ronald C. White Jr. has described his "first encounter with a Lincoln fragment" when he held the "single, blue-lined sheet of paper" that Hay had inscribed as the "Meditation" at the John Hay Library at Brown. Professor White was in search of antecedents to Lincoln's second inaugural. At the Hay Library, he found it in the "Meditation," a lyrical, even mystical poem that survived in Hay's personal papers archived at Brown, Hay's alma mater.[9] It was Hay who named the fragment "Meditation" a decade after Lincoln's death. Rather than finding the epistle in a drawer as he packed up the slain president's papers, which he maintained in the 1890 Lincoln biography, I believe Hay possessed it much earlier, at the time of its creation, for the same reason that other Lincoln documents were in Hay's possession: President Lincoln gave John Hay the original document in which Hay had made a mark. In all of Lincoln's private notes and fragments transcribed and published by White in *Lincoln in Private,* only the "Meditation" departs from Lincoln's characteristic plain, matter-of-fact prose lacking any hint of poetry.[10] It is also the one fragment not found in Lincoln's papers.

Beyond the archival record, on-site surveys of the places where Hay lived, influential places of family, nature, and culture, brought to life references that Hay made in his own writing as well as those that appeared in his temperament. I examined the historic house where Hay was born and spent the early years of life in Salem, Indiana; I stood along the Mississippi River in Warsaw, Illinois, where John Hay spent hundreds of hours absorbing the majesty and power of this vital aquatic highway, where he listened to the dialogue of dock workers and communed with nature; I walked the streets of Pittsfield, Illinois, enjoying the privilege to examine the private house where he lived with his uncle Milton Hay during his middle and high school years; I studied the historic Brown University campus and Providence Athenaeum in Rhode Island, the place of Hay's transformative college days; I walked the streets of Springfield, Illinois, where Hay walked with Abraham Lincoln in the days between June 1859 and February 1861; and in Washington, DC, the nation's capital, I came to understand the place that had changed immeasurably since the early 1860s, while admiring the preservation of such influential landmarks as the White House, the Capitol building, the Seventh Street market corridor, the house where Lincoln died, even the refurbished Willard Hotel.

Both Hay and Nicolay condemned retrospective accounts of Abraham Lincoln, which appeared after his death. Human memory, Hay argued, failed by the very nature of its existence: self-interest. "When Nicolay and I came to Washington, we thought we should have great advantage in personal conversation with Lincoln's contemporaries in regard to the important events of his time," Hay said. "We ascertained after a very short experience that no confidence whatever could be placed in the memories of even the most intelligent and most honorable men when it came to narrating their relations with Lincoln."[11] Hay and Nicolay dismissed early biographies by Ida Tarbell and William O. Stoddard, an occasional private secretary to the President. "Every old dead-beat politician in the country is coming forward to protest that he was the depository of Lincoln's innermost secrets and the engineer of his campaign."[12]

Ironically, it was Hay and Nicolay and their expansive *Abraham Lincoln* biography in 1890 that established the foundation of future Lincoln scholarship. The work exalted the president's singular place in American history, repressed details that might diminish his singular influence—including Hay's contribution to Lincoln's oratory—and solidified his omnipresence. From that time forward, the image of Abraham Lincoln's omnipotence, carrying out every responsibility of his presidency, continued.

INTRODUCTION

Prevailing views of John Hay generally reference early twentieth-century biographies of him by William Roscoe Thayer and Tyler Dennett. Since then, Michael Burlingame's historical research and publications have proven the most formative in developing a fuller, more complex portrait. The foremost Lincoln historian today, Burlingame has relied on first-person accounts of Hay during the Lincoln presidency. Galusha Grow, Speaker of the House from 1861–1863, for example, explained that "Lincoln was very much attached" to Hay "and often spoke [to Grow] in high terms of his ability and trustworthiness." Congressman Grow knew of "no person in whom the great President reposed more confidence and to whom he confided secrets of State as well as his own personal affairs with such great freedom."[13]

Journalist John Russell Young, who frequently visited the Executive Mansion, portrayed Hay as "exceedingly handsome" and "a comely young man with [a] peach-blossom face."[14] A contemporary of Hay, who rose to become Librarian of Congress, 1897–99, Young described Hay as "brilliant," "chivalrous," "poetic," "independent," though socially "reserved," and "always graceful, composed, polite, and equal to the complexities of any situation [that] might arise." His speech, said Young, was "smooth, low-toned, quick in comprehension, sententious, reserved."[15] One Civil War journalist described Hay as "almost foppishly dressed, with by no means a low down opinion of himself, either physically or mentally, with plenty of self-confidence for anybody's use."[16] Similarly, modern historian Adam Goodheart portrayed Hay in his book *1861* as "urbane, satirical," in contrast to the "dour, Germanic Nicolay," Lincoln's official secretary.[17]

In the nineteenth century, part-time journalist Thomas Coke "T. C." Evans, the agent for photographer Mathew Brady's studio, said that Hay appeared "to possess…a silent power of work, doing a great deal and saying little about it," while "his talk was apt, varied, refined, and of a markedly literary quality." Evans, who occasionally wrote for the *New York World,* had befriended Hay on the Lincoln train to Washington, DC, in February 1861. His characterization of Hay's working style, which involved long days of discrete work, portrayed Lincoln's aide to a tee. Then, and in later years, Hay spoke little about the actual work he did for the president.

Michael Burlingame and John R. Turner Ettlinger, the editors of *Inside the Lincoln White House,* wrote that "the relationship between Lincoln and Hay resembled that between earlier wartime father-and-son surrogates George Washington and Alexander Hamilton...showing as Hamilton did in similar offices, the tact and common sense which were to serve him as they served Hamilton in wider spheres of public duty."[18] Hamilton was President Washington's speechwriter during his second administration.

Honing in on Hay's contribution to Lincoln's letters and speeches, Burlingame states, "It is impossible to identify precisely other correspondence that Hay wrote for the president, but informed guesses can be made." Burlingame points to Hay's three medium-sized notebooks: "In the scrapbooks of his own writings, Hay pasted newspaper clippings of three letters bearing Lincoln's signature: to G. B. Loomis, 12 May 1864; to John Phillips, 21 November 1864; and to Lydia Bixby, also 21 November 1864. It seems likely that Hay wrote these letters for Lincoln to sign, or else he would not have preserved them in scrapbooks of his own compositions." Teasing out Burlingame's evidence that Hay "preserved them in scrapbooks of his own composition," Hay also preserved his handwritten manuscripts of the Gettysburg Address and the Second Inaugural. Short of attributing Hay's speechwriting, Burlingame has focused on the Bixby letter. "The most noteworthy of Hay's ghostwriting is the celebrated Bixby letter.... Stylistic considerations, along with Hay's statements to friends and the evidence of his scrapbooks, suggest that Hay is the author of that prose poem that is widely regarded as Lincoln's epistolary masterpiece, often ranked with the Gettysburg Address and the Second Inaugural address." Burlingame concludes with this unexplained statement: "He may have been a ghostwriter for political leaders even before he reached the White House." Is Burlingame claiming that Hay was also the ghostwriter for the president?[19]

By contrast to Burlingame's archival characterization of Hay, Daniel Mark Epstein, in *Lincoln's Men: The President and His Private Secretaries,* relied on secondary sources. Epstein editorialized Hay as "at once nonchalant and assertive, a man-about-town air of superiority and rakish humor."[20] While acknowledging Hay the poet, Epstein, along with Patricia O'Toole in

The Five of Hearts and David Herbert Donald in *Lincoln,* claimed that Hay owed his place in Lincoln's administration to the insistence of Nicolay.[21] The archival record indicates otherwise: Lincoln chose to bring Hay to Washington, just as he had Nicolay; the only question was how to pay for a second personal secretary (Hay) when there was only one official place on the Executive Mansion staff (Nicolay). White has also portrayed Hay, in *The Eloquent President,* as the junior to Nicolay, the senior presidential aide.[22] This depiction blurs the reality that Hay and Nicolay had different functions and offered Lincoln different services. Erroneous characterizations repeated by several historians have created the impression that Hay was an accessory to Nicolay. Actually, he was an essential, right-hand aide to President Lincoln.

"The twenty-four-year-old poet had become as important to the president as the president was to Hay, as remarkable as that seems," Epstein wrote of Hay and Lincoln's relationship in spring 1865, signifying that the wordsmith Hay was actually essential to Lincoln's presidency. Historians Ted Widmer and Joshua Zeitz both tell the story of a dream John Hay had just before dying in 1905, by way of demonstrating Hay's role as the president's ghostwriter: "In 1905, just before he died, Hay had a dream of seeing Lincoln in the White House. Lincoln handed him two letters to answer, as if there were still unfinished business between him and the American people."[23]

Doris Kearns Goodwin and Donald portrayed Hay as Lincoln's confidant and companion, a fact that is brought to life in the following pages.[24] Goodwin understood that Hay had an inside seat on Lincoln's action, moods, anxieties, and notes, all of which Hay chronicled in his diary.[25] Several Lincoln historians, including White, Donald, and Jon Meacham have described Hay as Lincoln's diarist and Hay and Nicolay as the president's biographers.[26] All true. Yet the Hay–Lincoln relationship runs deeper.

Douglas L. Wilson writes in *Lincoln's Sword* that Hay "quickly became a trusted aide. Intelligent, loyal, and discreet, Hay's powers of observation and ready wit made him an ideal companion for a beleaguered president to whom it became increasingly important to see the humor in things and find occasions to indulge his innate sense of fun." Wilson continues, "Hay's letters and diary are such a mine of inside information on Lincoln's private sayings and personal views." Wilson concludes, "Hay had another asset that made him valuable to this particular president—his special affinity for wordplay and literature." Wilson unveiled Hay's unique talent, though stopped short of stating why his wordplay and literature was indispensable to Lincoln.[27]

Warren Zimmerman, in *The First Great Triumph: How Five Americans Made Their Country a World Power,* came as close as any Hay chronicler to understand the full relationship between Hay and the president. Highlighting Hay's "knack for rhyming," Zimmerman notes that in the Executive Mansion, as the White House was then called, "Hay's duties included reading letters written to the president, drafting answers to them." Confirming this, Hay confided to Robert Lincoln, who informed Nicholas Murray Butler that "it was the custom of John Hay to write in the name of Lincoln all letters of a non-political kind."[28] Zimmerman substantiated this statement when he wrote, "the young man won Lincoln's trust; soon the president was signing the letters Hay had drafted for him without reading them." Describing the kernel of their bond, Zimmerman said, "They had in common a sense of irony and humor and a talent for storytelling," claiming that Hay helped Lincoln with "speechmaking."[29]

The Making of the Presidential Speechwriter

From the very beginning, the US president's speechwriter, a term that originated during 1825–1835, remained an informal and often invisible role during the first century of the Union. Biographer Ron Chernow has documented Alexander Hamilton as General George Washington's speechwriter. When President Washington contemplated retiring after his first term, he asked James Madison to draft a farewell address, which Washington edited during his second term. Four year later, he handed the Madison draft to Hamilton. "The result," said Robert Schlesinger in *White House Ghosts,* "was the first and one of the best presidential farewell addresses."[30]

The role of presidential speechwriter was unofficial in Lincoln's time, one of several duties required of a private secretary, as it had been during the presidencies of George Washington down to Woodrow Wilson, who actually wrote most of his own speeches on a typewriter. The first official "literary clerk" was Judson Welliver, who ghosted for Warren Harding and Calvin Coolidge. Yet then, as today, the private secretary in the Civil War White House bore close resemblances to characteristics of contemporary presidential speechwriters, from personal access to a repartee and an innate sympathy with the principal. John Hay stood at Lincoln's side, and also in Lincoln's shadow, his ego and persona integrated into the public voice and public persona of the president.

An unpublished fact is that President John Adams was likely assisted by his wife, Abigail, and eldest son, John Quincy, who edited at least 124 known addresses that President Adams then edited during 1825–1829, according to the editor in chief of the Adams Project at the Massachusetts Historical Society.[31] President Andrew Jackson, 1829–1837, worked with former newspaperman Amos Kendall to draft his written and spoken public statements. Kendall, according to Schlesinger, "smoothed out Jackson's thoughts and dictation." Through repetition, they arrived "at a formulation that suited the president"—a similar process that Lincoln and Hay developed. James K. Polk was assisted by Secretary of the Navy George Bancroft, a historian and also a beautiful writer, who Andrew Johnson commandeered for messages to Congress. [32]

During the presidencies of Warren Harding, 1920–1923, then Calvin Coolidge, 1923–1925, Judson Welliver, a well-known reporter for the *Sioux City Journal, Des Moines Leader,* and the editorial page of the *Washington Star,* was the first White House staff member whose job was to aid the president in drafting his remarks. Schlesinger mentions that Welliver was both speechwriter and press handler for Harding, as was Hay for Lincoln. Welliver was also the first official speechwriter.[33] Clark Clifford managed Harry S. Truman's speechwriting in his first term, 1945–1950.[34] Later, Franklin Delano Roosevelt worked with several policy advisors, including Raymond Moley.[35]

One of the most noteworthy speechwriters in modern times is Ted Sorensen, presidential counselor and speechwriter to John F. Kennedy. Sorensen confirmed the stresses of the executive office, explaining that President Kennedy lacked the time to plan and draft with full consideration all the statements required of him. Ultimately, he depended on Sorensen to do much of the heavy lifting. Sorensen explained in his memoir, *Counselor: A Life at the Edge of History,* that President Kennedy "never pretended…that he had time to draft personally every word of every speech he was required to make virtually every week and ultimately virtually every day. Many historians have it wrong. He did not dictate first drafts for him to polish. Our collaboration was not a secret; nor was it without historical precedent.… The debate among journalists and historians over who wrote a particular passage or speech wrongly puts the emphasis on the student, not the teacher."[36] Another notable speechwriter during this era was Richard Goodwin, briefly for Kennedy, then for Lyndon Baines Johnson, and for Robert F. Kennedy during his aborted campaign for president.

Lincoln scholars have essentially claimed that Lincoln was the only president in American history who wrote all of his speeches. Acknowledging William Seward's limited suggestions for Lincoln's First Inaugural address, the Lincoln establishment steadfastly maintains that the president did all his own writing. At the time of Lincoln's presidency, the speechwriter was a familiar role in the Executive Mansion, as it had been since Washington's day. It simply wasn't on the official payroll or formal executive staff.

With a master of fine arts from Brown University in hand in June 1858, Brown's class poet John Hay carried his literary acumen into public life, reaching wider audiences and speaking to graver subjects.[37] In May 1859, the Illinois native arrived in the state capital of Springfield to study law in the Logan & Hay office, which was shared with Abraham Lincoln. Within months, the collaboration between the politician, Lincoln, and the writer, Hay, took shape. In time, the functional relationship deepened into a unique friendship. It was Lincoln's Cooper Union speech in February 1860, when uses of such refined literary devices as alliteration, repetition, and parallel structure appeared for the first time in Lincoln's political writing. The Cooper Union speech revealed Hay's early ghostwriting for Lincoln. It was a speech that raised Lincoln's national profile and launched his successful presidential campaign.

Hay's press writings during the 1860–1861 presidential transition period in Springfield voiced Lincoln's thinking. It signified Hay's proximity to the president-elect. As Lincoln's journalist, Hay was privy to Lincoln's convictions and intended future actions. Lincoln admired Hay for his classical education and gifted rhetoric. And while his own storytelling lightened the thickest air and flattered his harshest critic, he lacked Hay's literary intelligence born out of his college education. Hay offered Lincoln literary depth, classical knowledge of the ages, and an absolute loyalty that no one in his inner circle equaled.

In Washington, DC, Hay accompanied Lincoln virtually everywhere. He moved easily through the high offices of government. He was privy to breaking news of statesmen and generals as well as to the telegraph office in the War Department. Lincoln and Hay owned important similarities of wit, rhyme, and intelligence. Still, Hay's poetry and philosophical depth transported Lincoln's folksy speech to artful prose and audible rhyme. Their shared regard for democratic government and civic duty demanded precise and inspiring communication during the days of civil war.

Lincoln communicated ideas and thoughts that Hay drafted into dozens of speeches and hundreds of letters, messages, and newspaper articles. Their hours together—working, talking, walking, and riding on horseback, as mentor and apprentice, as collaborators, and with every new day as genuine friends—grew into a rare rapport. Lincoln's spiritual wisdom informed Hay, and Hay's brilliant mind and eloquence inspired the president to shape his thoughts to a higher, wider, and even deeper level. The words, phrases, and messages they produced could not have been created by one without the other, or with anyone else. Hay's work as Lincoln's journalist, scribe, poet, and speechwriter evolved from Lincoln's direction.

Gary Wills explained in *Lincoln at Gettysburg* that "Lincoln's desire for honest literary discussion" drew him to "[become] ever more intimated with Hay." Reflecting upon their creative process, the word "poetry" stood foremost. It derived from the ancient Greek word *poiesis,* signaling the act of making. In the classical tradition in which Hay was taught, poetry didn't refer to the writing of verse. Instead, it was the act of making, of bringing something into being that didn't before exist. This is exactly what Lincoln and Hay accomplished together.

John Hay had listened hundreds of times to Lincoln tell stories rich in historical context and moral parable. Mastering the president's speaking style, Hay internalized Lincoln's tendency toward reflection, idealism, and principle. Shaping the words that Lincoln wrote and spoke, Hay enhanced it with verse, mythology, classic rhetoric, and Romantic impressions of the war, exalting the duty done. His cadence and love of poetic couplet, alliteration, and Greek literature were some of the main literary techniques in Lincoln's landmark speeches. Refining American eloquence, Lincoln and Hay developed a literature that was greater than either of them. It was a literature based on principle, engaged with hope, projected in poetry.

"Lincoln treated Hay with the affection of a father," said Brooks Adams, a historian and political scientist. He also promoted Hay's stature and future potential when he brought him to the nation's capital and gave him a central seat in the Civil War White House. By a stroke of nature, Hay became the closest person to President Lincoln. He was twenty-two years old at the start of Lincoln's presidency, a fledgling young man, as yet unformed and inexperienced. While some members of Congress and the president's Cabinet regarded Hay as immature, Lincoln knew differently. He entrusted Hay with sensitive and privileged information. He also tempered Hay's tendency to skate on the edge of intemperance when provoked, recognizing the young man's pitchiness simply as the dark side of a quick wit.

Naturally, the question of why the discovery of John Hay's contribution to Abraham Lincoln's speeches, messages, and correspondence is introduced now. The college writings of John Hay at Brown University, 1855–1858, played an important part in my understanding. These essays and blue books had not been read until my research, since they were deposited in the Brown archives over eighty years ago. They demonstrated Hay's characteristic style of rhyme, cadence, tempo, and tone, his brilliant fabrication of words, his love of alliteration, polarities, and parallel structure, and his classical training in ancient Greek and Latin texts. These stylistic patterns provided the source of the poetic prose of Abraham Lincoln's prepared speeches. It was an extraordinary transformation that first appeared in Lincoln's February 1860 Cooper Union speech, launching the Republican campaign that culminated with his election to the sixteenth presidency.

Revising historical myth is unsettling, even blatantly damning, for many established Lincoln historians, especially if the subject is a folk hero as great as Abraham Lincoln. W. A. Dunning, a late president of the American Historical Association, reminded the historians and scholars who gathered for his annual message on December 29, 1913, in Charleston, that "the province of history is to ascertain and present in their causal sequence such phenomena of the past as exerted an unmistakable influence on the development of...social and political life." Yet in many cases, he reminded his colleagues (mostly men), the "influence on the sequence of human affairs has been exercised, not by what really happened, but by what men erroneously believed to have happened."

Make no mistake: Lincoln fired the ideological torch and moral vision of his presidency as he drafted and dictated notes and memos to John Hay, many of which Hay chronicled in his diaries. Hay transformed these notes and conversations into authoritative newspaper columns or spoken prose that gave voice to the nation's leader. The words flowed from a pen that had mastered literature and the literary techniques of ancient Greece, the epic Renaissance, and eighteenth-century English poets. Hay advanced verbal persuasion to an art form on multiple platforms at Brown, and put it into public service as Lincoln's private wordsmith, elevating it to a keystone of the Lincoln presidency.

John Hay had both the literary gift and classical education in rhetoric, Greek and Latin literature and languages, and a recitative vocabulary that the self-educated Lincoln simply lacked. Lincoln's strength lay in recognizing that he had in his very suite the expertise of a just and civil individual who transformed his ideas and principles into refined prose, turning sweeping visions and maxims into durable truths.

From his youth in Indiana and Illinois, to his classical education in private schools at an early age, to his education at Brown University and then law in Springfield, in the shared office of Milton Hay, his uncle, and Abraham Lincoln, the narrative of Hay's grounding in literature, poetry, and eloquent writing unfolds in the pages that follow.

Chapter 1

1840 AMERICA

The day was Friday, October 8, 1840, the second birthday of John Hay. Fog swept across the flat farmlands surrounding the small village of Salem, the seat of Washington County in Indiana. The inland town on the stagecoach route lay twenty-five miles north of the Ohio River and the Kentucky border, slave country. The family of Charles and Helen Hay and their four children: Edward, the oldest, Leonard, Mary, and John, the youngest, resided in a former one-room schoolhouse. Flush against the dirt road, it stood on South College Street, two blocks west of the center of town, known as Courthouse Square.

The red-brick structure was small, 450 square feet and built in 1824. Charles Hay, a doctor, had bought the building for his family's home in 1837. By 1840, seven people lived in the one-room house and its open living area on the ground level. The children's sleeping loft was above. By day, natural direct light streamed in through the front door and two large windows. At night, candles and the fireplaces at each end of the room illuminated the space. Their housekeeper, a free woman of color twenty-six to thirty-five years old, lived with the Hay family.[38]

On this day, John Hay might have lain in bed awaiting the sound of his parents' steps. Precocious, he could have awakened with a special sense about his day, anxious for one of his parents to climb the ladder to the loft, to wake him and his sister, Mary, three-and-a-half years old, his older brothers, Leonard, five-and-a-half, and Edward, a month shy of his seventh birthday.

Slight in build and petite in height, John more than made up for his small size and young age by his quick mind and bright personality. Layers of wool blankets kept his small body warm in the pre-dawn chill, the air in the uninsulated rough-hewn timbers that framed the gabled wooden ceiling. The minutes awaiting his mother or father may have felt like hours to John. Finally, Dr. Hay approached his daughter and three sons, kneeling across the loft floor. First he went to Edward, the eldest. Since the night before, the feverish boy slept in his own cot, separated from the other children. Perhaps he was sickened by one of the rampant contagious diseases—cholera, typhoid, or influenza—taking millions of American lives during the 1830s and 1840s. Salem was hit especially hard in 1832 and 1849, when cholera killed hundreds. Across the two decades, lethal bacteria seeped into fresh water sources and wells.[39]

Charles Hay leaned down to Edward's forehead. It was ice cold. He knelt down and embraced his son of six years and 334 days, his stocky thumb on the radial artery of the tiny wrist. No pulse. Edward was dead. The doctor's firstborn child was gone. Two-year-old John lay frigid with fear. The heaviest blow of his young life left emotional scars from the mortal shock. This should have been the joyful start to his third year. What happened? What did he do wrong? Edward's death must be his fault. After all, he was awake when tragedy struck. As child psychologists have since discovered, young children create false connections between an alarming event, such as fire or death, and what they were doing. John was awake on the morning when his eldest brother died.

A silent, deafening grief filled the Hay home that day. Leonard, Mary, and John stayed close with one another, afraid of their parents' sorrow, a stranger they had not previously known. They kept clear of their parents' curtained bed corner, the small area in the great room, draped by dark muslin, where Edward's body lay in rest. Sadness hung on every ray of sun, every particle of dust. Their mother, four months pregnant, groaned into her moist handkerchief, always at her lips or eyes. By late afternoon, Dr. Hay, with the help of a neighbor, had finished shoveling the black Indiana clay soil for his son's grave in the village cemetery. Salem's one burying ground for residents, all Christians, was the town's only resting place since its founding in 1814.

The cause of Edward's death remains unknown. His burial headstone Is the one known document of his death:

Edward Leonard Hay
Born November 9, 1832; Died October 8, 1840.

The first child of Charles and Helen Hay, Edward was born fourteen months after their marriage. He was named for Helen's oldest brother, Edward A. Leonard, who had died in January 1832.

The tragedy debuted for John Hay a painstaking awareness of his small world. The heaviest blow of this young life left emotional scars that stayed with him throughout life. The tragedy gave John a new awareness of himself, a perception both wonderfully sensitive and painfully fearful: he could influence critical events that might have devastating ends. It was an anxiety that tapped his inner psyche and brought him a foreboding of disaster and death until his own life ended in 1905.

John Milton Hay was the fourth child and third son of Charles and Helen Hay. He was named for his paternal grandfather, John Hay, and his father's younger brother Milton (1817–1893), who was a pivotal figure in John's early life, a mentor really. After Edward's death, John and his siblings, Leonard (1834–1904) and Mary (1836–1914), were later joined by brother Charles (1841–1916) and sister Helen (1844–1873).[40]

The Hays created a world of education, intelligence, and strong abolitionist sentiment for their children, loathing slavery, the institution that permitted owning and manipulating another human being, regardless of skin color.

Charles and Helen came to know John as a fast learner, a sweet and charming boy, with a constitution prone to nervous illness and hypochondria, traits that marked his personality. Perhaps unaware of the profound imprint his oldest brother's death had on John, his parents nurtured John's educational development. They understood he was different from their other four children. Even before they had celebrated his first birthday, John's parents noticed he did things faster. Before his tenth birthday, he made precocious remarks and observations. He asked penetrating questions that adults were unable to answer. He simply did things other kids didn't or couldn't do.[41] He was a gifted child, his mind "genetically programmed to work faster than most, to absorb more than most, and to need more than most," in the words of Marylou Kelly Streznewski, author of *Gifted Grownups: The Mixed Blessing of Extraordinary Potential*.[42]

John Hay came into a world of astonishing change and growth. Until the age of twenty, his life paralleled a period of dramatic nation-building in America. Extraordinary advances in industry and mechanization boosted production and reduced the time and distance of travel and communication. The country's geographic expansion during the half-century before had tripled the country's land area. Wealthy southern white supremacists, who dominated the White House between 1800 and 1841, uprooted Native American communities from long-held settlements, forcing them to far Western lands. In 1833, the state of Georgia had forced Cherokee people out to Oklahoma territory, leaving in its wake the bloody Trail of Tears. And arrivals in America's ports from Britain, Europe, and Asia had added almost one million foreign born to the US population during the half-century between 1790 and 1840. The flow of immigrants continued to accelerate, more than doubling during the rest of the nineteenth century.

Steam engines propelled vessels and vehicles; bridges connected lands and voids; railroads traversed long distances at high speed and carried large volumes of people and parcels; sanitized running water protected against waterborne disease and hydrated thousands from a single source; photography recorded and commemorated; and wires transferred news and power. In March 1838, for example, the luxury passenger steamship *Sirius* launched the first transatlantic steamship line. Her inaugural passage from Liverpool into New York Harbor, a voyage of eighteen days, clocked an average speed of eight knots, making the sailing packet's forty-day passage between America and England obsolete.

A surging commerce in coal-fired railroads in the continental United States had doubled the miles laid down over the past two decades, reaching 2,816 miles from north to south, east to west and beyond to the Pacific frontier by 1840. Britain, with roughly the same population as America, had less than half the length of railroad tracks. Britain relied on an agricultural economy and an ancient culture whose roots were so deep that Brits traveled and relocated little. In America, by contrast, personal upheaval and resettlement were commonplace during the nineteenth century. Individuals and multiple generations of one extended family journeyed long distances to unknown lands at great expense and turmoil. Their quest was for liberty and prosperity.

Innovation shaped John Hay's world. It also shaped his character. This is a story about American character and its heritage. The impetus of innovations shaped his learning, his words, his works. He was a fast and deep learner. His intuitive wit assimilated and also projected innovation and creativity.

Chapter 2

"I AM NOTHING BUT AN AMERICAN"

The first ancestors I ever heard of were a Scotchman who was
half English and a German woman who was half French.
My mother was from New England and my father was
from the South. In this bewilderment,
I can confess that I am nothing but an American.[43]

The Hay clan of America descended from an eighteenth-century Scottish soldier, known to be a man of education and standing. He left Scotland to serve during the early years of the eighteenth century in the Rhineland-Palatinate army in western Germany. Here, he married a woman from Alsatia. Among their four sons, their second boy, Johann Adam Hay, known as Adam and born about 1735 near Zweibrucken, Germany, was the father of the John Hay branch in America.

The family sailed to British America about 1760, settling in Northampton County, Pennsylvania, an area with other Scottish immigrants.[44] Adam Hay was then twenty-five years old. Soon after, he left his parents and the Lehigh Valley to endure weeks of grueling travel on horseback along unmapped mud trails, rocky terrain, freezing rain, and rushing rapids. He settled in Berkeley County, Virginia (now part of West Virginia), at the base of the Shenandoah Valley bordering the Potomac River.

This land on the northern edges of the Shenandoah, renowned for its beautiful sulfur baths of Berkeley Springs, was then part of Fairfax County,

Virginia.[45] A young engineer by the name of George Washington, age sixteen, had completed the first survey of the Fairfax lands, a territory becoming part of the newly founded state of West Virginia. Putting down roots in this remote and rugged territory, Adam Hay married Anna Maria Boyer in 1770.[46] They had nine children. Their third, John Hay, was born on February 13, 1775, a few months before the outbreak of the Revolutionary War. He was our subject's paternal grandfather and namesake. Yet the baby's father, a passionate British American revolutionary, was absent for the baby's birth. Major Adam Hay had earlier left his Berkeley home to prepare for war against Britain, under the command of General George Washington and Virginia's Lieutenant Governor Alexander Hamilton, revolutionaries consumed with unceasing military and naval preparations, along with others in Pennsylvania, New Jersey, Delaware, and the New England states. Adam may have first laid eyes on his son at the war's end sometime in 1783.[47]

The childhood of John Hay, son of Adam and Anna Hay, growing up in the heart of bountiful farmland, was shadowed by the abject poverty of western Virginia's slaves, a way of life he came to abhor. In his eighteenth year, 1793, he left his father and mother, leaving behind a strict home life at the hand of his father and the shame of living openly in the country's most populous slave state. Virginia's enslaved population was more than double the number in South Carolina, the second-most populous.[48] John Hay was just one among hundreds, even thousands at this time, who embodied the growing dissonant sentiment between South and North, slavery and antislavery, simmering more than six decades before the Civil War.

From Virginia, he traveled by horseback to Kentucky, which Congress had made an independent state the year before. He settled in Lexington. A young farmer, he cultivated the fertile soil, earning a subsistence living by the strength of his hands. In time, he also learned the art of brickmaking, entering a profitable building trade in the fast-growing region, and invested in speculative property that proved especially profitable.

Within his first year there, John Hay married Jemima Coulter of Lexington (1781–1843). Together, they had six children in their first sixteen years of marriage—sons Charles, Nathaniel, and Theodore, and daughters Elizabeth, Maria, and Elma. For this antislavery couple, their household had no slaves and no free persons of color, a common choice for many abolitionist families in a slave-holding state. [49] During the next eleven years, John and Jemima Hay added five children to their family with the birth of daughters Julia Ann and Deniza, and sons John, Milton, and Joseph.[50]

Lexington's active center of western trade was a terminus of foreign imports, a producer of manufactured cotton, flax, and hemp cloth and home to 4,326 people in 1810. It was also known "as the most elegant and fashionable city in the West," producing such luxuries as fine fabrics and polished doorknobs.[51] The urban center catered to Fayette County's slave-owning gentry, the stewards of cotton plantations and textile mills. Surrounding the downtown were grand plantations splaying across the bluegrass region's black soil and heavily forested countryside. The families of Todd, Clay, Davis, and Breckinridge formed the foundation of Lexington's nineteenth-century hierarchical society, richly endowing the educational and cultural centers, notably Transylvania University and the private Lexington Lyceum club. Among them were Robert and Elizabeth Todd, whose beguiling and witty daughter Mary, the future wife of Abraham Lincoln, dined and danced at the same affairs as Jefferson Davis, the future president of the Confederate States of America. And there was Henry Clay, the legendary abolitionist who served as a US senator, as speaker of the House, and as secretary of state to John Quincy Adams.[52]

The rural patchwork of smaller farms and factories outlying the great plantations was the backbone of Lexington's prosperous economy. The landscape, viewed from above, portrayed the complicated circumstances that governed Lexington's social and political fabric. For every wealthy landowner, hundreds of workers, many enslaved, labored in the fields. The inequalities were glaring. This region was home to some of the most impoverished people in Kentucky. Working the land of both the large and smaller farms and factories were one thousand Black slaves, 20 percent of Kentucky's populace. And while the senior John Hay chose Lexington to leave behind Virginia's dominant slave culture, Lexington was home to Kentucky's most concentrated slave population.[53]

Even Henry Clay, an outspoken opponent of slavery's extension, personally owned forty-seven slaves who tilled the tobacco and hemp fields on his 600-acre Ashland plantation. Next door lived John and Jemima Hay and their eleven children, who eventually came to own two male slaves by 1830. Slavery, embedded in the Southern economy, was not so much a preference for the Hays as it was a necessity for securing household help.

During this time, John and Jemima Hay's eldest son and our subject's father, Charles Hay (born February 7, 1801), was grooming himself as a young scholar and also a principled citizen. His free-spirited pedigree for knowledge earned him a place in Transylvania University's medical college.

A revered institution of higher learning, Transylvania was the place where leading Kentucky families in politics, business, and the military sent their sons for a refined classicaldducationon. Charles Hay's privilege of progeny as the eldest son was denied to his two older sisters, Catherine and Mary. For Charles, his life unfolded to an advanced education and esteemed profession. His large frame and prominent forehead projected over wide, deep-set eyes and thick-matted hair. He appeared less the scholar than a man who worked with his hands instead of his mind. Mannered and industrious, he found kinship with the medical scholarship at Transylvania. Here, the bluegrass region's preeminent schools of medicine, law, and divinity clustered under the same roof of Old Morrison Hall, as did the college of arts and sciences.

Charles Hay, MD, ca. October 1831, Salem, Indiana. Courtesy of John Hay collection, John Hay Library, Brown University.

In May 1829, his medical certificate in hand and promising to obey the word and principles of the Hippocratic Oath, Charles, twenty-eight years old, departed Lexington within days of his graduation. He dreamt of living in a Free Soil state where slavery was outlawed. He crossed the Ohio River and headed north to the non-slave territory of Salem, Indiana, traveling 112 miles from his family's home, a journey of several days. The village of Salem was home to 800 people, sparsely settled around the county courthouse square.

"I arrived here yesterday safe in every respect except that my mare's back was somewhat sore," he wrote his father on June 9, 1829. His horse, under the burdensome load of Charles Hay's heavy packs, took lame the second day out on the road.

"I have been kindly received by those persons here that I brought letters to," Charles reported home. One friendly acquaintance was John Hay Farnham, a New England-trained attorney.

"The town is well built," Charles said, "handsome and healthy as well as the country around it."[54]

The seat of Washington County and a community dependent on its agricultural economy, Salem was surrounded by dense stands of forests and verdant farmland. The agricultural economy took root in wheat and cotton crops, supported by a spinning mill and two brickmaking factories. Charles decided to set up his medical and pharmacological practice in a shop he rented near the public square within three days of arriving. As two doctors were already established in Salem, Hay opened an apothecary. Because the business absorbed most of his cash, he lived sparsely in his shop, keeping his mare in a pasture on the outskirts of town and taking meals at a nearby tavern. "I am treated with the utmost kindness, hospitality, and friendship by the citizens of this place," he wrote his younger sister Elisabeth. "I have nothing to wish for but business."[55]

Within days, he soon gained some measure of notoriety across the region's medical community when Salem's two physicians came to consult him about a difficult case. A troubling situation, Dr. Hay's university education and the reputation of his medical apothecary drew the provincially trained doctors to him. John "Scott" Tilford, twenty-nine, a Salem native, suffered from a baffling and fast-growing facial growth. To Charles Hay, it appeared to be a tumor "of a scrupulous character of very considerable size and violence in its symptoms." He examined Tilford over a two-week period.[56] Every day, the disease spread. Dr. Hay understood the fatal nature of the malignancy. Persuaded "to inform his friends of the improbability of success in the case," Charles told his sister Elisabeth that he believed the best he could do was alleviate Tilford's suffering. He offered no promise about an optimistic outcome, remaining forthright with Tilford and his family that the illness was fatal and fast-moving.

Tilford's father was grateful for Hay's candor, thanking him for the honest if hopeless prognosis. No other doctor was so candid. The metastatic tumor was vicious. It spread to Tilford's throat, neck, and his entire face. Remarkably, he survived more than three months after Charles Hay began treating him. Tilford's case drew wide interest nationally for its "greater notoriety than any that has ever occurred in this country," Dr. Hay wrote to his brother Nathaniel on the day of Scott Tilford's funeral, September 17, 1829.[57]

The Tilford case enhanced Salem's respect for Charles Hay.[58] Yet his own practice was slow to flourish. Residents in the small town held to familiar customs, choosing who they did business with based on habit and political inclinations. Shadowing the entrenched standing of Dr. Bradley and Dr. Newland, both of whom enjoyed independent means and indulged their patients with free services, Dr. Hay recognized that biases against native-born Southerners like himself played a role in his struggling practice.

Indiana was experiencing an influx of New England Yankee newcomers, a people who disparaged the growing number of Kentucky transplants, of whom Charles Hay was one. Discouraged by his prospects, he wrote letter after letter to his family, repeating "my practice is about as it was when I wrote you last," a monotonous drumbeat. Charles Hay was similar to thousands of young men who struck out on their own to establish a livelihood or profession in a fledgling western town. Arriving in the free state of Indiana and the rural town of Salem, Dr. Hay soon discovered that Salem's time had not yet arrived. He also disagreed with Salem's effort to expel "free Negroes," as they were called, from Indiana. His closest friends were lawyer John Farnham and his wife, Evelyn Leonard Farnham. They, too, were transplants, having relocated from their native New England.[59] Both liberal-minded and educated, the Farnhams and Hay shared a trusted friendship that in due course changed their lives.

Charles had captured the attentions of the single ladies in town. This college-educated bachelor, age twenty-nine, was thought to be quite a good catch. He, however, did not share their curiosity. He settled into his practice, satisfying himself with three good libraries, one with an impressive medical collection. He was soon distracted by a newcomer in town: Evelyn Leonard Farnham's younger sister, Helen (1804–1900), who had arrived for a visit. The bright and gentle twenty-seven-year-old Helen, then living with her parents in Bristol, Rhode Island, had enjoyed a fine education in a local private school for women. Evelyn Farnham was anxious to introduce her sister to Charles Hay, her husband's best friend. During the days of October 1830, Helen Leonard's arrival set in motion a peevish rearrangement of the town's female pecking order. "The young ladies became splenetic as soon as she arrived," Charles, amused, told his sister Deniza Hay. Salem's young ladies certainly had good reason: Helen Leonard fast captured the affections of Salem's young physician. "She is far better educated than any of them," he confided to Deniza, and "besides she is witty and a little sarcastic withal."

Helen Leonard Hay, ca. October 1831, Salem, Indiana. Courtesy of John Hay collection, John Hay Library, Brown University.

Charles and Helen, born three years apart on the same date of February 7—Charles in 1801 and Helen in 1804—soon became engaged. They married a year after meeting. Once decided, the couple was anxious to wed and consummate their vows. Yet Salem's county court was in session. The courthouse schedule was clogged. In a day when premarital relations were forbidden, or at least discouraged, Charles Hay avoided a scandal by eloping with Helen. They traveled almost two hundred miles north to Albany, Indiana, joined by seven friends across a train journey of fourteen hours. Albany's Presbyterian minister, Reverend Wells, officiated the nuptials at seven o'clock in the morning of October 12, 1831, just nine minutes after sunrise. Following the hour-long service, Dr. and Mrs. Hay celebrated with their friends over a sit-down breakfast, setting out on the day-long return to Salem. They came into the small town depot just before midnight, a half-moon lighting the eastern sky.

"I am married and happy," Charles wrote sister Elizabeth five days later. "We moved into our own house today."[60]

Helen Leonard Hay, a seventh-generation American who hailed from the Eastern Seaboard, was grounded in a seafaring culture where women led the town's civic life and ran its businesses while the leading men, shippers and whalers, were away for long stretches, months and even years. The New England economy at the time of her father and grandfather fostered a structure in which women governed and men left on trade ships for long periods. Throughout Helen's youth, her father, David Augustus Leonard, was present, working as a minister and postmaster. Her mother, Mary Pierce of Assonet, Massachusetts, the daughter of a master mariner, found a landlubber of a husband in David Leonard. In Assonet, Helen Leonard was born on February 7, 1804, one of five daughters and three sons.

Few details of Helen's early life in Assonet and Bristol survive. In a day when a common woman's personal history went unrecorded, except the place and date of her birth, all that is known of Helen's youth was that she was "well-educated" and little else. The private school was unnamed and her accomplishments were not mentioned. Helen Leonard was a woman with a resilient constitution. John Hay, our subject, admired his mother's big heart and a strong will. Her optimistic spirit inspired her husband and her children. She lived until the age of eighty-nine, a remarkable age in late-nineteenth-century America.

Helen's father, David Leonard, offered clues to his daughter's character. He was highly educated and literary, natural gifts reflected in grandson John

Hay, Charles and Helen's middle son. A child of the Revolutionary War era, David Leonard was the son of a master mariner. In the fall of 1788, a year after the United States of America had adopted its Constitution, David Augustus Leonard at age seventeen entered the College of Rhode Island, renamed Brown University in 1804.[61] Brown's entire campus existed in one large building, similar to most colleges of the time. College Edifice, later known as University Hall, stood upon College Hill, high above the working waterfront of commercial Providence. The all-purpose building, a sprawling, four-story, red brick structure dominating the College Green, was home to student rooms, the chapel, refectory, and classrooms. Students entered University Hall's north and south entrances as they mounted the dark, narrow stairways to their third- and fourth-floor residential rooms. The central front doors led into the chapel, where students and faculty came together in morning, midday, and evening prayers. From the chapel, they entered the common room where they ate together and engaged in instructions and recitations. Four large fireplaces heated the building and sixty-five windows gave light and air in a day long before electric light and automated ventilation. The naturally lit basement level housed the living and working quarters for butlers and housekeepers, who cooked and laundered for faculty and students. Upstairs in the third- and fourth-floor lofts, students slept in small rooms furnished with a bed, a desk, and a table for the water pitcher and waste basin—no plumbing and no running water.

David Leonard entered the Baptist ministry in December 1794, age twenty-one, promising himself to God's service and God's grace. He soon turned to evangelism and preaching Baptist theology. The facile orator, also politically inclined, campaigned for President Thomas Jefferson during his re-election campaign. Leonard answered an invitation by Bristol County's Republican Party to deliver the keynote speech on behalf of the incumbent. His natural literary finesse heralded the wisdom of the Louisiana Purchase as Jefferson's coup d'etat.

President Jefferson recognized Leonard's contribution to bringing home the vote in Bristol, appointing him the town's postmaster, a term he held for eleven years. Unfettered by laws excluding federal employees from private investment, Leonard also delved into private businesses, serving on the board of the Bristol Insurance Company and publisher of the *Bristol Republican,* the local Republican newspaper.

Daughter Helen Leonard Hay, now in Salem, Indiana, bequeathed son John the birthright of her father's poetry and oratory.

Learned and knowledgeable, in fact cultivated with rare secondary educations, John Hay's father and also maternal grandfather established the foundation for his life of scholarship. Grandfather Leonard's powerful voice and his parent's own spirited intelligence tendered a literary flair that heightened John Hay's personal talents.

Chapter 3

ILLINOIS HEARTLAND

In 1833, Salem and Indiana generally were hit hard by the cholera epidemic. Dr. Hay's medical practice was under siege, his own endurance tried. Helen Hay's days as the mother of the infant Edward involved sleepless hours and moments of unimaginable fear. The disease swept the country, devastating small farm towns in the Ohio and Mississippi valleys, infested from North to South. Infectious bacteria had arrived in the intestines of two passengers on the *Voyageur*, a ship landing in Montreal, Quebec, in June 1832, having departed Cork, Ireland, during a peak cholera epidemic, contaminating waterways feeding into the St. Lawrence River and The Great Lakes, coursing south to the Erie Canal and Ohio and Mississippi Rivers. Another transatlantic ship originating in Europe and reaching the port of New Orleans in October 1832, infiltrated the Mississippi River valley from the south. Cholera killed thousands in New Orleans, St. Louis, Lexington, and New York City, reaching its long fingers into the families of the farming borderland regions of Indiana, Illinois, Ohio, and Kentucky.[62]

"We have had between 60 and 70 deaths in town" during the first six weeks, Charles Hay wrote his brother Nathaniel. He observed the epidemic's fast-moving devastation, beginning with imperceptible symptoms of "a mild, watery purging which scarcely gives the patient any concern," he said. "So delusive is this watery diarrhea that the patient can scarcely be persuaded that any danger attends it." Cholera victims were dehydrated by the disease's diarrhea, dry-heaving until they lost consciousness, bodies parched. Until the cramp seized, it was too late to help. The pace was exhausting. "I was the only physician for several days when the disease was raging," Charles Hay wrote. He "from house to house on horseback through the town in order to attend the numerous cases occurring every hour through the night and day."

Exhausted, he traveled unpaved miles each day, sleeping when and where he could find a clean bed. During the first week of July 1833, the most disruptive period, "thirty-five young women fell, carrying them off in from four to ten hours most generally after the attack."[63] Terror of the killer bacteria crept into every home. On the Fourth of July, traditionally a day of celebration, "every store, factory, and workshop…was shut up except the coffin makers." Charles Hay, however, remained untouched by the disease.

The house where John Hay was born on October 8, 1838, Salem, Indiana. Built 1824, as a school building; purchased by Charles and Helen Hay, 1837, which they sold in 1841 when the family moved to Warsaw, Illinois. Courtesy of John Hay collection, John Hay Library, Brown University.

The day's medical authorities blamed cholera's spread on the filthy living conditions of slave colonies and Irish immigrants. Denying its infectious properties, they pointed to people with either Black skin or brogue accents. They relied for evidence on bias and ignorance rather than objective biological research. In truth, drinking water was the source.

Families, farms, hospitals, and industry all dumped their waste into streams and cesspools, flushing the waterborne microbe, *Vibrio cholerae,* into connecting rivers, lakes, and shallow underground wells. Syphoned drinking water infected thousands of communities. In a day when scientific knowledge had yet to discover the real source, uninformed sanitation practices seeped through the country's waterways, killing thousands. Cholera claimed the lives of Helen Hay's older sister, Evelyn Farnham, and also John Farnham, their brother-in-law and Charles Hay's closest friend.

The Farnhams died within twelve days of one another in July 1833, leaving their five children orphaned and homeless. Helen and Charles took in two of the Farnham children, who stayed with them for more than a year, until their aunt, Charlotte Farnham of Boston, brought them into her home. The Hays also adopted a seven-year-old Black girl, now freed from slavery, who had lost both parents during the summer of 1833. The Hays gave her money "and a suit of freedom clothes," said Charles Hay. She helped Helen look after their six-month-old son, Edward.[64] Helen's brother, Augustus, also lived with them while he was schooled in Salem.

Helen shouldered most of the responsibility for the expanded household. "You may reasonably suppose that our family is large enough for one lady to superintend in the character of Mrs.," Charles wrote to his brother, "Mrs. of the drawing room, superintendent of the wardrobe and kitchen." Helen was also ten weeks' pregnant with their second child, Augustus "Leonard" Hay, born on December 2, 1834.

Charles Hay's medical practice often felt hopeless. Compounding the loss of life was his modest income, Salem's business prospects failed to fulfill his original hopes. He longed for more money, acquiring a partial ownership in a printing press in February 1835, the weekly *Western Annotation,* the first Salem news outlet. He also bought some farmland, then in 1837 he speculated on an investment in undeveloped acreage adjacent to Salem's town line. "I thought for once I would act upon father's maxim: 'If you never venture you will never make everything,'" he wrote his youngest brother, Addison.[65] Yet the financial success Charles Hay had envisioned failed to materialize.

Year after year, Salem's shaky business climate dashed Dr. Hay's hopes of any reward. Cotton and wheat crops were shattered by desolating frosts, oversupplied market prices, and the Ohio River flooding as winter snows melted to drown out farms, houses, and businesses. The town's economy struggled.[66] "Bankruptcy prevails to an alarming extent and many of our most substantial citizens will most likely be overwhelmed in ruin before the times change," he told brother Milton Hay in January 1841. This period was a dark time for the Hay family, just three months after the death of their oldest son, Edward. To make matters worse, Charles's investment in the Salem newspaper had failed to find an active readership in this farming town.

During these years, Dr. Hay's central joy was his wife and growing family of Mary, Leonard, John, and baby Charles. Two-year-old John was a singular bright light. Charles told brother Joseph, John "is now toddling all over the house and is beginning to say some words."

Our subject, John Hay, began life bursting with precocious tendencies. "A better grown, more thrifty and forward boy has not been seen here lately," Charles wrote Milton around the time of John's second birthday. John's silken, platinum white baby hair was striking. While Dr. Hay's work continued to be a disappointment, his family was a joy. "I met the most perfect of wives and mothers," he confided to Milton, "I have always wished to found a family [and to] leave behind me children...with whom intelligence, honor, and thrift would be matters of instinct and tradition." [67] That he accomplished.

Family and education lay at the heart of Charles Hay's close relationship with his brother Milton Hay, sixteen years younger. "A taste for learning, industry, and a good constitution are what alone are necessary to make a man intelligent as ever learned," Charles explained to Milton in the months leading up to his younger brother's study of law in the Springfield office of Abraham Lincoln and John T. Stuart, 1838–1841. [68]

Charles Hay, disillusioned with Salem, looked to towns where commerce was supported by an established infrastructure, such as "a water course where [it] is a favorable point of trade," he said. Charles Hay looked for a place where "the population is intelligent and enterprising" and "a suitable location for steamboat landing, steamboat building, and all other building."[69] Charles and Helen Hay also favored a place where their children—Leonard, seven; Mary, four; John, three; and infant Charlie—had access to a classical education. Their ambitions were lofty, if limited by the westernmost states of the day, where everything was younger, more rustic, and less developed.

After eleven years in Salem, the Hays pushed westward toward the boundaries of continental settlement. They were among thousands of Americans in the pre- and post-Civil War decades who took heart in the idea that they could create a better life by moving to a place inventing itself.[70] In 1841, they moved themselves and all their worldly possessions four hundred miles west to Warsaw, Illinois, a frontier farming town of four hundred people, where they joined in the town's prospering future.

Founded in 1814 and home to Fort Edwards military camp, Warsaw enjoyed the advantages of looking out upon three states, two navigable rivers, and five towns. Laid out on seven-and-a-half acres, the town was originally known as Spunky Point, referring to its connection with the force of the Des Moines River rapids that fueled the town's life spring. It bordered the eastern banks of the Mississippi River Valley, the rolling prairie land of rich red and black soil stretching vast distances. With thinly forested stands of woods, these parts of Illinois in Warsaw's Hancock County held thick veins of coal composite, deep into the earth at seven hundred feet, a resource that brought prosperity to the town in the second half of the nineteenth century.[71]

John Hay was three years old when his family moved from southern Indiana to western Illinois. Over the years, as the boy grew to adolescence and adulthood, he drew inspiration from Warsaw's dynamic environment, nature clashing with commerce. This was the dramatic wilderness the future poet reimagined in his 1871 *Pike County Ballads,* a best-seller of its time, lyricizing Hay's sensorial impressions.

The Warsaw of John Hay's boyhood was a quiet village of scattered houses and small neighboring farmsteads strung along the beds of Mississippi River tributaries. The winding aquatic thoroughfare, running north to south from Chicago to St. Louis and New Orleans, fed commerce while irrigating the surrounding agricultural fields. From a bird's-eye view, Warsaw splayed out in a scene of orchards, frame fences marking borderlands, lush agricultural meadows, and numerous narrow creeks and waterways—the Bay, McGee, Six Mile, Honey, Pigeon, and McCraney's. Warsaw lay at the juncture of Iowa, Missouri, and Illinois, where the Illinois and Mississippi rivers met on the Des Moines tributary. The Mississippi's rolling waters, winding through the high bluffs of Warsaw, had first attracted the Sauk and Fox tribe to the fertile land. Long before the Hays arrived, White settlers pushed out the native Algonquin-speaking peoples, banishing them from their soil and lifeblood, tearing down their bark houses. In their place, the colonists built farms of eighty to over 300 acres, producing spring and summer crops of oats, wheat, and corn.

Trade took place in neighborhood exchanges, where farmers loaded a flatboat with beeswax, honey, tallow, peltries, and bushels of wheat or corn, and sawn clapboards. Barges carried people, carts, carriages, and provisions across the river.[72] A railroad bridge that spanned the Mississippi connected Keokuk, Missouri, with Hamilton, Illinois, five miles above Warsaw. Local steam-boat commerce opened trade to the southern ports of St. Louis, Cincinnati, and New Orleans.[73]

John Hay, ca. age three. Courtesy of John Hay collection, John Hay Library, Brown University.

In summer, tall grasses blanketed the prairie. The stalks "coarse in appearance, and soon assumed a yellow color, waving in the wind like a ripe crop of corn," said Basil Hall in *The Prairies of Illinois,* amassing a bounty of natural fibers.[74] Farmers planted groves of sweet-scented fruit and nut trees, which also stood as barriers to the stiff winds and snow sweeping across the flat and open countryside in winter.

Young John lolled away hours along Warsaw's riverfront docks. He was mesmerized by the bawdy scenes and dialect of the steamboat laborers, few of whom probably spoke to the slender boy. He gazed down upon the docks, listening to the curious dialect and common slang of the boat hand. "The great river was the scene of my early dreams," Hay recalled in later years. "The boys of my day led an amphibious life in and near its waters in the summer time, and in the winter its dazzling ice bridge, of incomparable beauty and purity, was our favorite playground."[75]

The riverbed's riveting life captured John Hay's poetic imagination, as it did for Samuel L. Clemens, the son of homesteading pioneers in Hannibal, Missouri, across the Mississippi from Warsaw. In Hannibal, the future Mark Twain's parents scratched a bare living, cherishing their one copy of Shakespeare on the shelf, a beacon for the future wordsmith.

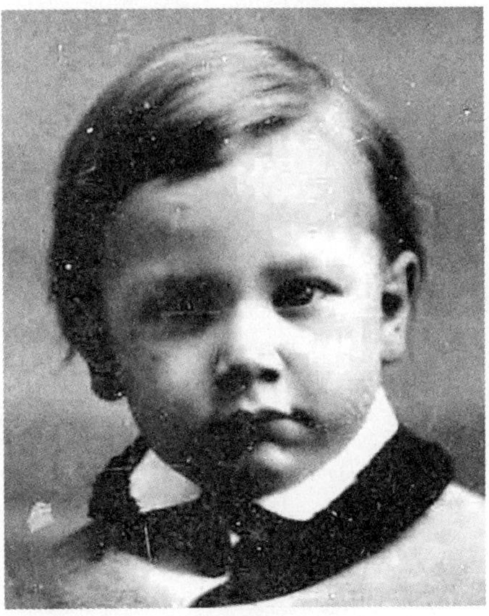

John Hay, ca. age four, Warsaw, Illinois. Courtesy of John Hay collection, John Hay Library, Brown University.

Chapter 4

THE GIFTED CHILD

Warsaw, Iowa. (Illinois side of river); Henry Lewis, illustrator, 1854–57, multi-stone lithograph with hand coloring; published by C.H. Muller, *Das Illustrierte Mississippithal* (The Valley of the Mississippi Illustrated).

The stern Charles Hay appeared larger than life to young John. He was a formidable figure in the boy's life. Charles and Helen Hay had been educated in the classical tradition, a rarity in early nineteenth-century America, especially among the agricultural plains of western Illinois where they now lived. Their own knowledge enabled them to recognize that John was different, naturally brilliant. The boy respected his father, even feared his methodical demeanor. He inherited his grounded sense of duty from Dr. Hay, who many days awakened before dawn to answer the emergency of a farmer or a woman in labor. His mother, in contrast, was sweet and honorable with a feisty wit and optimistic outlook. John adored her. She inspired his honesty, his directness, and his general goodwill.

John's love for learning came from both. "I have still a greater thirst after knowledge than anything else," Charles Hay had written to his brother Addison. "[I] desire more pleasure from its acquisition than from that of money."[76] This, son John especially shared. With his siblings, he understood his father was an esteemed physician in the Warsaw region.

The Hay family's first house in Warsaw, Illinois, 1841. Courtesy of John Hay collection, John Hay Library, Brown University.

Helen and Charles Hay created a home life by their personal actions, rather than irate words. Dr. Hay explained the three principles he hoped would guide his children through life: "Lex: Order, system. Lux: Intelligence. Pax: Gentleness and forbearance with another."[77] These, John Hay later inscribed on the stairway of his own house in Cleveland in the 1870s and 1880s, by then the father of four. The Hay children understood the value of rigor, intellect, and tolerance, values that John clung to throughout his life, passing onto his own children. In the days of John's youth in western Illinois, the educated values that Charles and Helen Hay imprinted on their children were generally unknown to Warsaw's farmers, merchants, and flatboat captains, who were bound to subsistence and hard work, a world of modest education and fundamental cultural traditions.

Beyond his parents, John Hay's ideology about life began to develop between the ages of ten to twelve as he sat along the banks of the Mississippi River. Here, he became sensitive to his surroundings. From then on, whether in the midst of pastoral serenity, urban vibrancy, alpine majesty, land or sea, he drew inspiration from place. The environment in which he stood elevated him to new heights of inspiration or threw him down to the depths of despair, taking him to a dark place. Sensitivity to place, Hay described years later in a newspaper column: "Cities and communities have their peculiarities and proclivities as well as individuals," he wrote in 1862 from Washington, DC, "these distinguishing characteristics are as interesting as surprising."[78]

Looking out to the river's rushing waters and the toiling boatmen, among them the ruddy roustabouts and plying farmers, John watched and recorded, on paper and in his mind, the power of the men, their coarse manners and strapping bodies. He was captivated by the routine of the working waterfront. Notebook in hand, he lay on the tangled grass covering Warsaw's great bluff, chronicling what he saw and heard. There was nothing pretty about dock life on the Mississippi—rough, dirty, and physical, self-organized by tribal brotherhoods and banded gangs. Yet young Hay was spellbound by the vulgar dialect of the riverboat pilots. He listened, mesmerized by the commercial agents and flatboat dealers bellowing orders to the crews working the wharves and flatboats. Many days he stayed long enough to watch the pinkish orange sunsets melt into the horizon.[79]

The language of the Mississippi riverfront, a dialect all its own, infatuated Hay's ear. It sounded so free and picturesque to his unrestrained imagination.[80] "Mark 'twain!," the dock hand yelled out to the flatboat pilot, who measured the water's depth at twelve feet, or two fathoms, barking orders to drop the anchor and cleat the dock lines. The boat hands numbered free Blacks who mixed with mostly German and Irish immigrants. Loading and unloading the flatboats in spring's pouring rains, summer's stinking heat, and winter's freezing ice storms, they worked together in harmony. Weather notwithstanding, boat commerce moved as long as the river flowed.

Young Hay's poetic sensibilities honed as he observed the raw grit of riverboat life. His wavy brown hair and dewy eyes, whether laughing with joy or crying with sorrow, John's observations milked a tender emotional intelligence. Drawing together low and high, he also read his Latin and Greek studies by the evening light of the fireplace and hand-dripped beeswax candles.

He didn't need his parent's prodding.[81] John's ease with rhyme and verse might have reminded his mother of her father's own lyrical poems. Recalling David Leonard's instantaneous wit, spilling out in a moment of humor or gloom, Helen Hay might have remembered how his poetry captured the spirit of local lore.

On one morning, John's younger brother, Charles E. "Charlie" Hay, sat idly in front of the new family house, alone on a log in the street, he explained to historian William Roscoe Thayer decades later. John came along. He sat down beside Charlie on the log, their arms and legs touching, side by side. John had walked over from the wild forest along the river banks.

"I have seen the end of the world," he told Charlie.

"What did you see there?"

"Nothing," he replied, "only trees and flowers and some birds."[82]

The budding naturalist experienced a spiritual awakening. He visualized the end of time. Rather than an apocalypse, he saw flowers and birds. John's vision was lyrical, poignant. A glimmer of his future literary genius, John captured the purity of nature in the expressiveness of his words before the age of twelve.

This day and throughout his boyhood, the Mississippi's incomparable beauty pulled young Hay to its shores and onto its waters. In future years, when the young adult came home from college or from his work in Washington, DC, he continued to wander along the steep riverbed. He gazed out, always seeing something different and new in the light, the clouds, the wind, air, and river. On the east bank of Warsaw, looking north, he saw a developed countryside; on the west bank, he fixed his eyes upon territory that made up the state of Missouri, observing endless miles vanishing into the horizon of unsettled and sparsely built land. He could no longer locate encampments of Native Americans, whom the government had transplanted from Warsaw's soil to lands in Missouri, west of the Mississippi.

Back in the spring of 1845, when John was seven, the long fingers of continental expansion began claiming Western lands. Newly inaugurated president James Polk commenced an aggressive campaign of territorial annexation, so swift that his inaugural Bible had barely cooled from the swearing-in. He held firm to Jeffersonian ideals of an agricultural economy as well as Southern demands for more lands to grow cotton. In March 1845, the president acquired the state of Florida from Spain. Nine months later, he ordered the military to surround and confront the Republic of Texas, an independent nation covering an enormous land area the size of Egypt. Mexico accused Polk of an act of aggression, declaring the Republic of Texas to be rebel territory. Polk replied by threatening Mexico with war if it obstructed America's claim. The outbreak of the Mexican–American War in 1846 played out over seventeen months, claiming the lives of almost thirty thousand Mexicans and Americans. In the end, the Treaty of Guadalupe Hidalgo drew the international border with Mexico along the Rio Grande, handing Polk a 1.2 million-square-mile region the size of Western Europe, embracing all of California, Nevada, and Utah, most of Arizona and Colorado, and parts of New Mexico, Texas, Oklahoma, Kansas, and Wyoming.[83]

By the age of eleven in the late 1840s, the precocious and well-read John Hay grew to appreciate the importance of land, water, and location. He understood the Mississippi was something more than beautiful. It was the vital highway carrying commerce to southern and northern markets. It was the coursing aquatic highway for western Illinois. He seemed to grasp the value in the drive of nation-building and the energy of expansion, an understanding that appeared a few years later in his Brown college essays. The vitality of the growing nation and expanding economy clashed with societal tensions arising from the influx of immigrants settling in Illinois and Missouri, peoples whose ways of living and speaking were unfamiliar, so different from their rural neighbors. The ever-present encroachment of slavery into Western lands also provoked a sharp backlash, unprecedented rebukes from antislavery advocates.

Hay absorbed the inflamed tensions permeating the social order of communities, human relations, and national politics. For a sensitive boy with a high aptitude, the tightening grip of slavery, foreign immigration, and the rising industrial nation—touching every life—raised his awareness about the huge divides in the rights of different individuals, whether those of Black skin, of foreign birth, or female persons. He witnessed the rise of heated protests giving voice to unjust practices by the government. The expansion of slavery instigated the loudest outcries. Yet slavery was not the only untreated malady in American life: women's lack of voting rights was another gathering force.

For solitude, John resorted to nature, a particularly intoxicating lure for him. The beauty of the Mississippi and the visceral draw of bawdy riverboat life seduced him time and again, drawing him to the fields overlooking the riverbanks and the falls of Warsaw.[84]

Sometime during this period, when John was ten or eleven, a knock on the front door announced an unexpected visitor. Dr. Hay opened it to an educated German man, calling to ask him for "assistance in forming a class for the study of German." Charles Hay remembered, "John listened with a great deal of interest." He whispered to his father, "I would like very much to study German." Dr. Hay agreed and the boy became a student with his father and other men. John memorized his lessons before the evening sessions, inevitably stretching into his bedtime. At the end of a long school day, a bit tuckered out, he occasionally nodded off. His father's firm hand roused him, John rising clear and alert to recite the German phrases as well as the best of them.[85]

John Hay's appetite for knowledge was virtually boundless. In poetry, prose, literature, history, and journalism, his acquisitive mind collected and stored vast volumes of information: he memorized and virtually catalogued in his mind thousands of verses from the great classics, and in their respective original languages of English, German, French, and Spanish. So complete was his recall, he quoted in a flash-second passages from the *Odyssey*, *Beowulf*, *Madame Bovary*, and others. His vocabulary, too, amassed a baffling quantity of words. John's talent for applying his wealth of knowledge enabled him to think with clarity and distinction. He wrote in the same fashion, with exceptional beauty, readily citing historical moments and passages from a favorite poem or play. His own prose, written in his clear, rounded script, often required minor editing. Yet when it did, his editors in later years took cover. John's petulant streak was uncompromising. Stinging, his impressive array of profanity was designed to cut to the quick: he swore like a stevedore and most effectively in French.

More than religion, more than gamesmanship, and even beyond sensual pleasures, the acquisition of knowledge remained the transcendent passion throughout John's life. He absorbed information from people, places, literature, and experience. Yet different from many, he was favored by the influence of some exceptional people. These included Milton Hay, his uncle, as well as his Brown University professors, Abraham Lincoln, and in the 1870s his father-in-law, Amasa Stone.

First learning to read at home, John afterwards attended a one-room schoolhouse in Warsaw. Later, when he was about eight years old in 1846, he told his father that he was bored with his classes and wished to go to school with his older brother Leonard, age twelve. His parents admitted that their bright son needed better schooling, turning the very next week to send him off with Leonard to the classroom of Rev. Stephen Childs, an Episcopal clergyman. Here, John began his study of the classics in Latin and Greek.[86] This early stimulation encouraged him to read classical literature in the ancient texts.

John's youthful poetry, however naïve, was recognized by *Warsaw Signal* editor Sharpe, the family's former neighbor. Sharpe published the ten-year-old boy's rhymes on occasion in the weekly newspaper. John addressed them to playmates Annie and Hebe, real or imagined as they may have been, a privilege of poetic license.

About 1848, when John was ten years old, his parents built a two-story brick residence, essentially a square block of a house enhanced by a two-story porch and pavilion on the front. Dr. Hay hired a local mason to lay the foundations and the walls. He topped the second-floor roof with a cupola, historically known as a widow's walk, originally built for the wives of sailors who climbed above the attic to look out over the seaway for their long-gone husbands, hoping one day to see their ships coming into home port. In Warsaw, the cupola was decorative rather than functional. Three stories above the street, it turned heads in a town of mostly farmers, worldly enough to acknowledge that architectural ornament was a suggestion of prosperity.

Dr. Hay's medical practice had grown in Warsaw's vibrant economy. He had accumulated a modest level of capital. Two decades later, during the post-Civil War years, the Hays added fluted wooden columns to the pavilion, decorating the front of the house facing the public street. Their neighbors looked a good deal like themselves, mostly families with young and teenaged children. One was a professional lawyer, others included three merchants with retail businesses, and another was a mason, the latter just as Charles Hay's father and younger brother were in Springfield.

Summers were a happy time for the Hay children, a playful time for the three boys and two girls. Enjoying the life of leisure away from school, they were free of the farming duties and heavy chores that occupied many of Warsaw's youth. John, Leonard, and Charlie Hay played in the fields on the outskirts of town, countryside grown high with rush, sedge, and blue joint grass. The buzzing of bees pollinating on wild daisies, asters, and sunflowers fused with a musty scent of dry reeds. "The happiest days of the year to us who dwelt on the northern bluffs of the river," John said, "were those that brought us, in the loud puffing and whistling steamers of the olden time, to the Mecca of our rural fancies, the bright and busy metropolis of St. Louis."

Indeed, St. Louis, New Orleans, and St. Augustine were fairylands to these boys, faraway places calling up fantastic visions of exotic French women and Spanish swash-bucklers.

In winter, play also unfolded in the great outdoors. "We built snow forts and called them the Alamo," John recalled. "We sang rude songs of the cane-brake and the cornfield."[87] Unlike modern winter festivities, in John Hay's boyhood of the late 1840s and early 1850s, traditional holidays were simple affairs celebrated by one special meal with family and friends and the giving of alms to those who were less privileged. The first painted Christmas card of 1846, by British illustrator John C. Horseley, portrayed just this: a colorful and convivial family scene of plump men and well-loved women who drank with good cheer and gave alms to those in need. No Santa and no gifts.[88]

The Hay family's second house in Warsaw, Illinois, ca. 1850. Courtesy of John Hay collection, John Hay Library, Brown University.

The continental union connecting huge swaths of territory continued to expand, sharpening the blistering debate about slavery's spread. The United States Congress, sitting hundreds of miles east in the swamplands of the District of Columbia, was deeply divided on the issue. Debates between Southern and Northern senators and congressmen were filled with passion, vitriol, and spite, magnifying stark differences between the proponents and opponents of the extension of enslaved people into newly annexed territory. The dispute dragged on for six years, finally culminating in the Kansas–Nebraska Act of May 30, 1854, opening new Western lands to the spread of slavery, from Missouri across to California. The legislation spiked pro-slavery and antislavery passions, which eventually culminated in the Civil War almost seven years later.[89]

In the small western town of Warsaw, the Hay family held firm to the belief that slavery was immoral and wrong. They also believed it was illegal. Its extension corroded fledgling communities and territories. It limited the rights of humans and introduced an archaic labor system into free economies. Charles and Helen Hay explained to their children that the federal government had the responsibility to abolish it. John and his brothers and sisters were certain this was true, as if the scriptures ordained it. Word of a bill to abolish slavery, if only in the District of Columbia, put forth Abraham Lincoln, the young US Congressman from Illinois, drew interest from the Hays. The lawmaker represented their antislavery beliefs.[90]

The Hay dinner table resounded with lively discussion about the day's experiences. Charles and Helen encouraged their five children to speak openly. They were joined by five boarders who lived in the house and took their meals with the family. The mix of different views and experiences offered the Hay children, ages six to fourteen, an unusual mix of life that was otherwise unfamiliar to them.[91]

For John, the horror of oppression was very personal. It was dreadfully familiar.

One day, he had stepped down the wooden stairs to the cellar, possibly on an errand for his mother or father. There, he felt the cool air and smelled the earthy scent of the fresh dirt floor. The rawness gave him a homey feeling.

Then came a voice.

"Little Master, for the love of God, bring me a drink of water."

John was shocked.

"The ghost spoke," he told brother Charlie. Frightened, he ran upstairs to his bedroom, two flights up. The next evening at dinner, Dr. Hay told his family that officers from Missouri had overtaken three runaway slaves nearby. The slaves had resisted arrest. One was captured and taken back. One was fired upon and killed. The third had been badly wounded but escaped. He left bloody tracks in the woods.

"I saw him staring at me across the supper table," Charlie remembered of John. But he said nothing.

"After the meal," Charlie said, "[John] told...father about the voice he heard in the basement." Dr. Hay and his son "went down to investigate, and on a pile of kindling wood was the appearance of someone having used this for a bed." What they found were the traces of a slave running for his freedom, an innocent's trespass. "There was a stain of blood shed there nearly eighteen inches in diameter. This was probably the blood shed by the runaway slave who had escaped capture."

Shaken, John had stood within touching distance of the man, his black skin veiled by the dark of the cellar. It wasn't a ghost at all who spoke to him. He was a runaway slave, a man frantic for the fear of captivity. His wounds bleeding from the bullet and his mouth parched dry, the fugitive trembled in terror in the unknown house. He had escaped slavery for a life of freedom. Leaving early that morning, likely before dawn, he fled from the safe haven of the Hay cellar. Never knowing the slave's fate, the "ghost" left John with a horror of the institution, though he never knew anything of the slave's fate.[92] Chilled by the memory, he never forgot the plight of the runaway's distress.

Politicians, the press, even poets expounded antislavery ideals. John Hay consumed every word he laid his hands on.[93] He read, he listened, he absorbed the facts and the nuances of the question and the rising advocacy of abolition. The literature—newspapers, broadsides, pamphlets, fiction, and plays—portrayed the immoral institution's despair, the cruelty and inhumanity. Henry Wadsworth Longfellow's widely published *Poems of Slavery* (1842) drew attention to the gruesome, brutal life, especially his six-stanza "Slave in the Dismal Swamp." The poem contrasted the heartbreaking misery of the enslaved against the pleasure of the free.[94] Charles Dickens's *American Notes*, also published in 1842 after his cross-Atlantic tour to the States, shamelessly decried Americans' unremitting attachment to Africans' servitude. (His native England had banned slavery in 1833.) Abolitionist Harriet Beecher Stowe, too, fueled a backlash against the grip of Black bondage with *Uncle Tom's Cabin* (1852), the bestselling novel of the nineteenth century and the second bestselling book of all time. Stowe touched a deep nerve that stretched across regions and cultures. It enraged abolitionist sentiment.

By his twelfth birthday, John Hay understood the wrongs and realities of human bondage. Within his small town of Warsaw and even within his own family and home, he experienced the friction between slaveholders and those who opposed slavery. He listened to those who agitated for its expansion into Western territories. He shared his parents' beliefs about slavery's tragedy. In the decade to come, he formed his own ideas about the divisive power slavery etched into American politics, government, and everyday life.

He continued to read, to absorb knowledge from different times and cultures.

Chapter 5

A CLASSICAL EDUCATION

By the age of twelve, John Hay had read six books of Virgil and some of Homer's *Odyssey*, grasping the rhythmic and dialectical patterns of the original Greek text. With his knack for verse and a tongue for languages, he was now fluent in German, speaking effortlessly with Warsaw's immigrant community. Transported from their native rural regions, several German families clustered on farms ringing the town's village square.[95]

John's sharp intelligence soon advanced him beyond the other students in the local Episcopal classroom. He studied Greek in school and Latin with his father and older brother Leonard at home. By 1850, his parents recognized that John was ready for a more progressive curriculum than what Mr. Child's school in Warsaw offered. He required a place that challenged him.[96] Dr. Hay had expressed this same view when he counseled his own younger brothers when they were John's age. "Omit no opportunity of gaining knowledge in any way when you have a chance," Charles Hay said.[97]

Charles and Helen desired a level of instruction that exceeded the standards, and frankly the capacity, of what Warsaw offered. For John, this meant leaving home. His parents' commitment to their son's developing intelligence led them to decide that he must live away for a better education. They arranged for him to live with his uncle Milton Hay, Dr. Hay's younger brother and an attorney in Pittsfield, Illinois, 100 miles away. Here, Pittsfield was home to the private Thompson Academy, the domain of Irish schoolmaster John D. Thompson, a well-regarded educator whose pedagogy offered private instruction in the classics of literature, languages, mathematics, and the sciences.[98]

By late summer 1851, John said goodbye to his parents, to brothers Leonard and Charlie and sisters Mary and Helen. He piled his bags onto the rear platform of a four-horse road coach. Saying farewell to Leonard, his best friend four years older, left a void for the tender twelve-year-old. His passage across twenty hours of rugged roads transported him to his new life in Pittsfield.

Greetings card, John Callcott Horsley, 1843, England. Museum no. MSL.3293-1987. © Victoria and Albert Museum, London.

Greeting card for "A Merry Christmas and A Happy New Year."
Courtesy of Victoria & Albert Museum, 1843.

Here, he arrived in the seat of Pike County and its circuit courthouse. John's Uncle Milton, thirty-four, met the coach in the central square.[99] Respected throughout the state, the young attorney had settled in Pittsfield ten years before. He had built an estimable law practice that served the tri-state region of Iowa, Missouri, and Illinois. The year before, Milton Hay, a bachelor living in a single room in the local residence hotel, had married Pittsfield native Catherine Forbes, age twenty-two.[100] A few months before John arrived, their daughter, Katy, was born. They resided in one of the finest houses on Washington Street, Pittsfield's main road.[101] The two-story red brick Greek Revival residence stood a few blocks from the bustling courthouse square, an easy walk for Milton.

John's time with Milton Hay became a pivotal turning point for the boy, on the cusp of adolescence. Milton Hay's reputation in Pittsfield, seventy miles west of the Springfield state capital, galvanized his emerging law practice. He had a wide circle of acquaintances, thanks to his collegial manner with clients, colleagues, and neighbors—and especially with his nephew. Milton's ease with John grew into an important relationship for both, well into John's college years. Unlike his father, whose discipline made him appear larger than life to the boy, Milton was more akin to an indulgent big brother, as Charles Hay was to Milton.

Uncle Milton felt empathy for his nephew's dislocation, himself at fifteen having left his own home in Lexington, Kentucky, when his parents moved to Springfield in 1833. Four years later, 1837, Springfield became the state capital, a dusty place of unpaved streets and a sprawling rural cluster of log cabins and shabby frame houses.[102]

In Springfield, teenaged Milton watched as his father, the senior John Hay, grew to be respected as a man of reliable and honest character.[103] A farmer, a brick mason, and a speculator, the senior John Hay had had a modest education, yet the limitations of his own life didn't stop three of his five sons from pursuing advanced professional educations. He raised two future doctors and a future attorney, reflecting the elastic social mobility of White Americans during the early nineteenth century.

When the Hays had relocated to Springfield in 1833, they reunited with former Lexington neighbor John Todd Stuart, a lawyer elected to the state legislature where he served beside Abraham Lincoln, the husband of Stuart's cousin Mary Todd, also of Lexington. Legend has it that when Lincoln asked Stuart's advice about pursuing the law, Stuart advised him to do it, loaned him the books, acted as his preceptor, then invited him to join his thriving practice when Lincoln passed the bar in April 1837. The legendary log-splitter arrived in Springfield with his possessions in two saddlebags on a borrowed horse.[104]

Milton Hay had set his sights on a career in the law within a few years of his family's arriving in Springfield.[105] He met Lincoln through his father's business association with the lawyer, who was the senior John Hay's legal counsel in property cases. "The first time I saw Lincoln to know him," Milton said, "must have been I think in some murder trial—his rawness, awkwardness and uncultivated manner were most apparent." Milton, age twenty-one, approached Lincoln, thirty, to "go into his office and read law there." Lincoln agreed. The year was 1839. Wishing to study at night and seeing that Lincoln boarded in an apartment hotel, Milton suggested they board together and put up a bed in the lawyer's one-room office.[106] "This suited him exactly," Milton said, "and we slept together all the time I was with him." In that day, men sleeping together in the same bed was nothing more than practical economy.

Milton methodically read *Blackstone's Commentaries,* also accepting occasional work from Lincoln. With law partner Stuart periodically away in Washington, DC, for several weeks at a time, fulfilling his terms as a US congressman, Lincoln worked solo while he gained a reputation as a shrewd tactician in the courtroom.[107] He fielded a prosperous law practice. "[He] was a new man at the bar [and] was expected to make a strong speech in the case, and that expectation was not disappointed," Milton said.[108] An Illinois congressman during the 1839–1840 session, Lincoln also distinguished himself at the Illinois statehouse, his political rhetoric overshadowing more established politicians.[109] He won people over through his court arguments, his story-telling, and his ability to yield to the key arguments of his opponents.

Working side by side and living in tandem, a confidence developed between Milton Hay and Abraham Lincoln, extending well beyond the principles of law. Hay had an intimate view of Lincoln's political ascension, in both Illinois and the national Whig Party, which was advocating for a protective tariff and federal subsidies for the nation's developing infrastructure of roads and rails. Milton also had a front-row seat on the dramatic turmoil stirring Lincoln's engagement to Mary Todd, the vivacious daughter of a wealthy slave-holding plantation family. Lincoln and Todd had first met in December 1839, in the Springfield home of Mary's sister, Elizabeth Edwards. They were engaged a year later, yet Lincoln canceled their wedding set for January 1, 1841.[110]

Milton later confided to John that "the explanation of [Lincoln's] morbidity about his contemplated marriage" stemmed from the fact that he "had entered into the engagement in all probability before he had discovered the unstable and capricious temper of the woman he proposed to make his wife." "Embezzlement" was the word Milton chose to describe Mary's courtship with Lincoln. As drawn as Lincoln was to Mary's mind, conversation, and sex appeal, he despised her sharp tongue and uncontrollable temper. "His distrust was of her not of himself," Milton recalled. When Lincoln discovered her volatile nature during their engagement, "it became a question of whether to back out or go on," Milton said. "Wrestling with this, he became morbid and half crazed."[111] Duty-bound, Lincoln married the besotted Mary Todd in November 1842, almost two years after the original wedding date.

Starting his law practice in Pittsfield, Illinois, Milton Hay may well have been influenced by Lincoln, who had represented several cases at Pittsfield's Pike County courthouse. Lincoln knew the county seat to be alive with business start-ups, offering a well-spring for an endless stream of contract cases. Everything was fresh and raw in the town's primitive environment, fueled by the court scene. Lincoln may have also thought about the advantages of an affiliate lawyer such as Milton Hay in Pittsfield, especially competent.

Pittsfield's courthouse scene clamored during court week. Attorneys arrived from all quarters of the state and as far away as Chicago. "The very character of this simple litigation drew the lawyer into the street, and neighborhood, and into close and active intercourse with all classes of his fellow men," Milton explained.[112] The law was as much a social and political engagement as it was legal. "There was scarcely a day or hour when a knot of men might not have been seen near the door of some leading store, or about the steps of the court house eagerly [discussing] a current political topic," Milton said. The lawyers surrounded themselves with pioneers, farmers, and fledgling shopkeepers, their horses intermingling and harnessed around the common public watering hole.

Lincoln's cases in the Pike County courthouse numbered nearly 550 filings of legal documents. From Springfield, he rode more than sixty miles on horseback across the flat Illinois prairie, land both stunning for the bountiful expanses of crops in the rich prairie loam and also numbingly flat, infinite vistas of dead level terrain. Across the thirteen years between 1839 and 1852, Abraham Lincoln adjudicated thirty-four cases in Pittsfield.[113] Biannual court sessions lasting ten weeks each found Lincoln in Pittsfield much of the year, sparing him little time with his family. In Pittsfield, he likely saw Milton Hay on a regular basis, perhaps even staying as a guest in the Hay home, which included young John. Lincoln's friendship with Milton Hay appeared a fixture in the life of each man, enduring throughout the political firebrand's widening national presence.[114]

Abraham Lincoln's reputation for legal repartee and sharp rhetorical skills earned him a brisk business representing the fast-growing railroad, bridge, and river-barge companies and combinations. He took on the most difficult cases, intricate deals involving complex legal arrangements between merging regional lines. Mounting conflicts between lines, builders, and investors produced a flourishing practice. Lincoln's rising income supported a comfortable life in Springfield for his growing family and household.[115]

Yet tragedy was never far from Lincoln's side. His three-year-old son, Eddie, died of pulmonary tuberculosis in February 1850, throwing Mary Todd Lincoln into weeks of mourning, bedridden and unable to eat. According to Doris Kearns Goodwin, Eddie's death, just one month before his fourth birthday, "left an indelible scar on her psyche—deepening her mood, magnifying her weaknesses, and increasing her fears. . . . stories of 'hysterical outbursts' against her husband, rumors that she chased him through the yard with a knife, drove him from the house with a broomstick, smashed his head with a chunk of wood."[116] In response to Mary's deranged episodes, Lincoln turned to silence and remote outings, walking with his children, spending long days in his office, expanding his itinerant law practice, and eventually reigniting his political career. Had he married "a woman of more angelic temperament," Milton Hay speculated, "he, doubtless, would have remained at home more and been less inclined to mingle with people outside."[117]

Life in Pittsfield with Uncle Milton, Aunt Catherine, and baby Katy offered John some memorable associations. For one, there was of course Abraham Lincoln, a regular presence. Another was the publisher of the *Pittsfield Free Press*, Zachariah Garbutt and his wife, Phimelia, who lived nearby. Intrigued by the newspaper life, John, thirteen, developed a friendship with Garbutt's foster son and also the on-press printer, John "George" Nicolay, nineteen.

The slim, German-born Nicolay hailed from the tiny village of Essingen Daun Rhineland-Pfalz, part of the Rhineland-Palatinate collective, also the native home of Hay's own ancestors. Nicolay had immigrated to America with his parents and two older brothers at the age of five. The boy's mother, Helena Mueller Nicolay, died the year after they arrived, leaving Nicolay's father and his three sons bereft. They eventually settled near Pittsfield, in the small town of White Hall. Seven years later, Nicolay's father, Johann Jacob Nicolay, also died. George, fourteen, was an orphan. Without home or work, he answered the *Free Press* call for a printer's devil, an assistant. "Wanted, an intelligent boy, from 14 to 17 years of age, who can read and write, to learn the Printing Business." Nicolay walked the twenty-five miles to Pittsfield for his interview. The next morning, publisher Garbutt handed him the job.

The publisher and his wife were also immigrants to America, originating from Yorkshire, England. A childless couple, they took a liking to the Bavarian teenager, bringing him into their home as his foster parents. Nicolay had lived in the shadow of death, poverty, and illness throughout his entire life. His gray eyes, long, slender face, and aquiline nose and high forehead portrayed the mask of the young man's sadness. Through the Garbutts and Milton Hay, the Bavarian-American bonded with the younger boy from Warsaw. For reasons beyond differences of age and circumstance, it was their mutual passion for writing and story-telling that drew John Hay and George Nicolay together.

George left the Garbutts's home to strike off on his own at the age of eighteen, renting a room with another local printer in Pittsfield's Dillingham Hotel, a rooming house run by Thomas Worthington. It was this very place that Milton Hay had lived as a bachelor before his 1850 marriage.[118] In 1854, Nicolay, twenty-two, succeeded Garbutt as the *Free Press* editor when the owner died of smallpox.

In school during the day at Thompson's Academy, Hay was described as "chock full of fun and devilment that hurt nobody." Though his academic records are not known to have survived, John's literary passion ran straight to Shakespeare, he said. He was smitten. "In thousands of barns in my own native land, Pike County," Hay said, "the ingenuous youth of that region are grappling the bloody dagger of *Macbeth* or adding the terrors of idiocy to the madness of *Hamlet*." He concluded, "the miracle that we all find in Shakespeare is [that] he is the greatest poet and the greatest playwright both who ever lived."[119] Certainly a truth he was reminded of in future years when reading Shakespeare with Abraham Lincoln.

John completed his primary education at Thompson's Academy by spring 1853. Starting that fall, Charles and Helen Hay enrolled him, now fourteen, with his older brother, Leonard, nineteen, at the Illinois State University (which became Concordia College). Saying goodbye to Uncle Milton, John moved to Springfield with Leonard. The boys roomed with their widowed grandfather, the senior John Hay, who lived comfortably in the family residence at Second Avenue and West Jefferson Street, just three blocks from the old state Capitol building. Across the twenty years since he had arrived in Springfield, the senior John Hay (and his wife, Jemima, who had died in April 1843) had invested in several parcels of land in town, and also north and south of the state capital. Land was considered a sound investment, long held as an article of faith.

The Hay home also included Charles and Milton Hay's unmarried sisters Maria, Elma, Deniza, and Elisabeth, and their bachelor uncle, Nathaniel, fondly known as Nat. A successful landowner himself, Nat Hay distinguished himself as the largest stakeholder in the thirty-five-acre Bullock's Addition just north of town.[120] He amused the boys with his tricks, gladly helping them in the evening with their school studies.

Illinois State held classes in the Mechanics' Union School during this time, when the university was building a new campus across town. Among the growing number of instructors was a Rev. Richard V. Dodge, a Yale graduate who taught mathematics and languages. Dodge admired John and Leonard Hay's natural gifts for learning, admitting "that he had never taught smarter boys than these two brothers—especially John."

Grasping the importance of a secondary education, and this in a day when many youth had no access to upper school, Charles Hay was thankful for his sons' accomplishments. "They seem to be wholly absorbed in their studies," he wrote to sister Elisabeth.[121] Among the class, the instructors chose Leonard Hay, John Hay, and N. Lawson to "deliver an original oration," a declamation, at the close of the first-year winter exercises in February 1854.[122] The semiannual exhibition by selected students was adorned with youthful pomp. It was a moment of pride for the extended Hay family. Grandfather Hay beamed. Charles Hay lamented his absence. "How I would have been pleased to have witnessed the examination exercises," he said. "I hope they sustained the honor of their name both in Springfield and elsewhere." Yet he gave no slack for the laurels of his sons, impressing on them that their future "onward and upward" demanded "both temporal and spiritual goals." Charles Hay was especially happy that John and Leonard "are both together," in the home of his father, sisters, and brother.[123] This very month, though, sadness fell over the Hay family. Nat died in early February 1854 at age fifty-three, perhaps stricken by the heart disease that had killed his mother, Jemima Hay, eleven years before.

John Hay's poetic development appeared to rise during these days in Springfield. Poetry, he said, "is one of the noblest faculties of our nature, and should be cultivated to its fullest extent." Explaining that the poet's thoughts are different from others, John said that they rise above commonplace concerns of the everyday world. "The imagination soars above the ark and gloomy real, to mingle with the bright and ever glorious idea creations." Speaking with kindred spirits of the past, he worshipped Milton, Byron, Moore, and Burns. Studying Latin, Greek, and rhetoric, he read the odes of Horace and Homer's *Iliad.* On Friday evenings, John joined his teenage buddies, who debated original essays.[124]

John and Leonard advanced to the sophomore class of Illinois State in fall 1854, having passed their monthly examinations and public presentations.[125] By the summer of 1855, the university—really a prep school—declared John, known to be "a bright, jolly, spirited boy with literary inclinations," fit for college.[126] In the Hay family, college signified Brown University in Providence, Rhode Island, the alma mater of his maternal grandfather, David Leonard.[127] Charles and Helen Hay could afford the tuition of just one child; John was the choice, the brightest of the Hay children.

Chapter 6

BROWN UNIVERSITY

In 1855, the year Brown University accepted John Hay as a student, fewer than 1 percent of college-age men, and far fewer women, attended college. Antebellum America witnessed the founding of over 150 colleges and universities during the first half of the nineteenth century, a cultural explosion reflecting the country's rising prosperity and burgeoning industrial economy. Most colleges were organized as same-sex institutions. Educators of the day believed that males and females required different curriculum, differentiating their manners of cultivation. Only fifteen American colleges and universities were coeducational at the time. Considered liberal or even extreme in their admissions practices, these included Oberlin, Antioch, Bates, and the University of Iowa, the country's only public coed university.

The intent of higher education in the 1850s was to refine predominantly young White men for the clergy, politics, and academia. Business and enterprise had a minor place in the college classroom. Most boys entered college in their mid-teens, as did John Hay, devoting their days to lectures and recitations and learning Latin, Greek, moral philosophy, mathematics, and science. The mid-nineteenth-century campus espoused a spiritual element as much as educational, and most were founded to promote a particular religious faith, such as Brown's Baptist roots. They were sanctuaries for the pursuit of scholarly knowledge and moral guidance.

Brown was founded in 1764, the seventh oldest institution of higher learning in the United States. It remained a college solely for young men until 1891. Following in the footsteps of his maternal grandfather, Leonard, John

Hay was just six weeks shy of his seventeenth birthday when he departed his family home in Warsaw to travel alone more than one thousand miles to Providence, Rhode Island.

The provincial capital of Rhode Island at the head of Narragansett Bay, Providence was one of the oldest cities in the country. Rhode Island was one of the original thirteen Colonies, founded in 1636 by Roger Williams, a Baptist theologian and religious exile. Rhode Island's religious plurality and independent thinking offered a fertile climate to foster Christian and Jewish faiths, as well as advanced education. The busy river port fostered wealth through seagoing trades, shipbuilding, traditional crafts, and the textile industry. Post-revolutionary war prosperity replaced eighteenth-century wooden houses with ornate brick townhouses and mansions, many standing around the Brown campus.

Like thousands of young men and women before him, Hay left home and his family to travel without companionship for more than one hundred hours, all for the lofty aim of continuing his classical education. In a day before national and even many regional railroad conglomerates, Hay purchased a one-way ticket on a dozen routes, all connecting with the next, making changes in the early hours before dawn and taking meals between trains at local taverns near the rail station. Traveling in noisy, third-class cars for a week or more, ingesting airborne soot and seeping fumes from coal engines, grated by the screeching of rough wheels on the rails, the teenager probably endured sleepless nights and shrill days.[128] In all, the excitement of the journey and the thrill of a new life at Brown boosted John's spirits. "I had a whirling, bustling time on the way here, but at last arrived without any accident on Tuesday evening safe & sound," he wrote his family, "except my eyes, mouth and ears were full of cinders & dust."[129]

He stepped from the train on a pleasant day in early autumn, the mercury having reached the mid-70s by noon. New England's second largest city teemed with a population seven times larger than Springfield, and twenty times the size of his hometown of Warsaw. Attuned to the nuances of place, Hay felt invigorated by the city, the bustling of the riverfront, the smell of the aged wooden buildings. A single suitcase in hand, John walked up the steep hill to the Brown campus, rising upon College Green, the ridge forming Providence's highest point. His first assignment was to pass the entrance examination and secure admittance to the school, justifying his journey and his parents' ambitions. Different from today's college admissions process stretching out over several months before the start of the school year, admission of applicants to college in the 1850s and '60s was decided once they arrived, a day or two before the formal commencement exercises. The oral examination by the head of school and one or two professors determined the destiny of each prospective student.

The morning of September 5, 1855, John Hay appeared before Rev. Barnas Sears, the scholar soon to be inducted as Brown's fifth president. Among the nation's leading Baptist educators, Rev. Sears was joined by professor of Latin language and literature, John Larkin Lincoln, recently returned from Germany and his classic work on Roman historian Titus Livius (59 BC–AD 17). Professor Lincoln's amiable nature steadied Hay's nerves. "Although we were studying a dead language, no classroom was more alive than his," said recent Brown graduate James Angell, then himself a young professor at the college.

Students affectionately recalled Lincoln's nervous gait, a rhythmic tap. A coveted few also remembered the invitations to join the professor and a few other students in his chambers for evening talks. Here, students such as Angell and Hay listened to eminent university teachers from Harvard University and Union College who taught classics, admiring their precise executions of Greek and Latin texts. The privilege to read ancient literature with esteemed scholars helped to perfect Hay's own facility with the metrical and syntactic demands of ancient Greek verse.

On September 5, John Hay understood that his matriculation was not a foregone conclusion. He stood before the president and professor, the fifty-first of seventy-seven students to be examined. Before the test, each boy signed the oath to obey the laws of the school. "I, having read the Laws of Brown University, do herby promise to obey them and all laws enacted by the corporation of the same or by their authority, so long as I remain a member of said institution."[130]

Standing 5' 5" and weighing a trace over 100 pounds, Hay looked every bit like his rustic origins. He had no way of knowing that his greased-down hair and the wide ribbon bow at his neck betrayed his provincial roots. Well mannered, John presented himself to the Baptist cleric, a serious scholar of demanding spirit and wholesome ego. Sears inspected the boy, challenging his knowledge and aptitude in order to determine his suitability for Brown. Presenting himself to the venerable don draped in his academic robe and trimmed with tufted white sideburns, John drew on his prodigious knowledge, a draconian challenge in arithmetic, algebra, geography, English grammar, Greek and Latin grammar and poetic structure, as well as Caesar's commentaries, the Aeneid of Virgil, and Six Orations of Cicero.[131] He had prepared. He knew his stuff. He passed with flying colors. On the completion of the exam, Rev. Sears admitted John Hay with academic standing to the sophomore class. Seven days later, Sears advanced Hay to the junior class, to complete a master of arts degree in three years, by summer 1858.[132]

Milton Hay, John Hay's uncle, Springfield, Illinois. John Hay papers, OV 40, Manuscript Division, Library of Congress.

John Hay joined the formal commencement procession, the most sacred event of the year, the ceremonial rite of passage inducting the incoming students, draped in their black robes. They marched in step behind a brass band. Descending College Hill, they strode through the lively market square and into the First Baptist Meeting House (1775). This sacred sanctuary was the very place where John's grandfather, David A. Leonard, had marched in his own commencement when he entered the college in 1788. The "old church," as the Meeting House was known, revealed in its elegance certain ambitions by the Baptist congregation.[133] Designed by local architect Joseph Brown, First Baptist seated a full house of 1,500. On this pleasant September day, natural light reflected off the Waterford chandelier, while the university's chancellor politely memorialized the retirement of Francis Wayland as president. He then turned to Barnas Sears. Reverend Sears stepped out of the pulpit and officially addressed the Fellows of Brown University for the first time as their new president.

Brown Corporation chair John Carter Brown and the Corporation had chosen Reverend Sears for his gentle yet firm manner, his nonpartisan thinking, and his trusted dedication to the college's interest and students' welfare.[134] Successor to President Wayland's controversial curriculum, which the Corporation believed to be overly broad and lenient with electives, Sears offered a classical approach designed to elevate scholarly standards and Brown's credentials.[135] His respect among the scholarly New England community was matched by his officious manner as administrator, vilifying the boys' natural inclinations for carnal merriment. Where the teenage males saw fun, Sears saw weakness. Known as a gentleman "who had the *suaviter in mado* as well as the *fortiter in re,*" Sears gave the impression of a gentle leader. Yet he was firm in action and conventional in thought during a time of pitch-forward change in Brown's educational culture.[136]

John Hay was entering a whole new world in this bastion of White Christian males, a society draped with heavy Baptist undertones. Conservative religious ideals joined with scholarly investigation.[137] Prevailing racial theories in America in the mid-nineteenth century projected a self-defined, hierarchical structure that were peculiarly masculine and especially Anglo Saxon.[138] John, while comfortably White and male, was an outlier in Brown's sacred environment. Impossibly cute, he had an impish streak peeping out between his loose religious beliefs and sharp tongue, unfamiliar as he was with all the time-honored rituals of the academy. He was now living amid tradition and history, nothing like his Illinois education. Brown was old and Providence was even older. The urbane and bustling city of commerce and governance was steeped in almost two centuries of heritage. He had never known anything like it. The daily practice of prayers, classes, and private study felt like a dream. In Brown, John found something magical.

He was coming home to the New England campus of his birthright. It was the home of his grandfather and also his mother, Helen Leonard Hay, who was born just thirty miles from Providence, in Assonet, Massachusetts. Living now in the native place of his grandfather and mother, this was also his heritage.

John Hay, age fifteen, one month before his sixteenth birthday, upon entering Brown University, daguerreotype, September 1855. Courtesy of John Hay collection, John Hay Library, Brown University.

On the morning of Tuesday, September 11, 1855, six days after the commencement exercises, a day still warm and humid with a trace of morning showers, President Sears welcomed all of Brown's 225 students in the Manning Hall chapel. Together, they prayed.

On the Brown campus of Hay's time, all scholars slept, ate, studied, and worshiped in four buildings on College Hill: Manning Hall (1835), presenting a stately facade of Doric columns on College Green and housing the Chapel and the modest twenty-eight-thousand-volume library; Rhode Island Hall (1840), an austere Egyptian revival facade leading to a classical interior of lecture and specimen rooms for the study of geology and physiology; and two brick student dormitories, University Hall and Hope College, mirror images of one another, their long and horizontal facades taking in the light of morning and the setting sun at evening.[139] In University

Hall's commons, the students and faculty took most meals together, each class having its own table and faculty proctor at the head. By all accounts, the lively conversation more than made up for the plain and meager fare. "Occasionally it became so boisterous," one student remembered, that the otherwise good-natured steward brought "down his big bread-knife with a loud resounding whack."[140]

Brown was the most influential Baptist institution of higher learning in America.[141] Prayers in morning, midday, and evening were compulsory, summoned by the chapel gong. The boys' discipline and moral guidance remained firmly in the president's hands. The entire college of dons and students attended chapel on the second floor of Manning, Rev. Sears presiding, the central figure on the platform before the student body, flanked by four professors on each side. Scholars who missed prayers or recitation were penalized with demerits on their academic record. Indifference to religious rituals lowered grades. The sanctioned protocol dictated that underclassmen entered the chapel after upperclassmen. In fact, the university prohibited younger scholars from entering before their elders, whether the chapel, the dining hall, or a meeting room. Removing their hats upon arrival, scholars were required to do the same when passing a fellow, a trustee, an officer, or steward of the college.[142]

The university's ten professors, including President Sears, were academics of national standing. Yet the school's small staff required that each professor periodically sleep in Hope College or University Hall, serving as proctors to the boys' dormitories. Here, without spouses or families, they adhered to celibacy while they monitored the students. For this, Brown paid modest annual salaries of $1,200 to $2,000, approximately $36,000 to $70,000 today. The Brown dormitories were a primitive fare, without public, piped water, and no plumbing of any kind. No water closets, no showers, and no bathtubs. Hay and other boys without butlers slogged a heavy wooden pail of well water up one, two, or three flights of stairs to their sleeping rooms. On the following day, they came down with their own waste and dirty bathing water.[143]

Hay's own class of 1858 numbered fifty-four scholars, thirty of whom were studying toward a master of arts and twelve for a bachelor's degree. The professors tutored them in philosophy, chemistry, history, Latin, Greek, rhetoric, English literature, modern languages, and mathematics. Across Brown's four classes, three in four students hailed from the Eastern Seaboard.[144] Among the incoming class of 1858, only two came from Illinois, John Hay of Warsaw and William E. Norris of Pittsfield. Norris, however, was dismissed the second year, having an overindulgent appetite for Providence's taverns and billiard halls.

John Hay arguably walked a fine line between serious study and good fun. The strict religious code was new to him. Yet he seemed content with this different life. "My room is a comfortable and conveniently furnished on the second floor of the college," he wrote his family. His roommate, William L. Stone, "a young man from the state of New York, steady, studious and a good scholar," seemed a good fit for the sociable Hay, who loved the raw side of life. "I stand a chance of doing a good deal of hard study this winter," he said, referring to the example set by Stone. Out of reach were Springfield's wayward temptations, "too agreeable for my own good," he admitted. "It is not hell as in Springfield," he said. And besides, "I am acquainted with no one in the city & I have no inducements to leave the college."[145] Yet.

In Brown, John Hay discovered a place that matched his intellectual stamina. "The life here suits me exactly," he wrote his parents in November of his first term. He worked hard and his grades fared well, though not up to his accustomed exceptionalism. "The prescribed studies are about as much as I can attend to," he said. And, having entered the junior class later than the others, he had "several studies to make up" before he was on a par with his classmates. In his first term, September 6, 1855 to January 25, 1856, John's classes in chemistry with George I. Chace was a favorite. Professor Chace's groundbreaking research combining chemistry, physiology, and the arts demonstrated the interdependent relationship between mental and bodily functions. The class was tough, requiring a "good deal of hard study," said John, with recitations following his lectures. Yet Hay and other students admired the don for his social finesse. On occasion, Professor Chace invited a small number of four or five boys to his Benefit Street house for an informal evening of dessert and talk, John Hay among them. He admired Chace as a man of science, inspiring his superb performance that earned him a 19.5 average for the term (just below a perfect 20.0).[146]

Another favorite was James B. Angell, the professor of modern languages. A man of genuine kindness, Professor Angell's deep-set eyes, thin face, and sharply pointed beard bespoke youthful good humor. The boys cherished his instruction and companionship. He was the oldest son of a tavern-keeper and farmer in nearby South Scituate, twenty miles from Providence, similar in background and ambition to thousands of young men at mid-century seeking to raise their standing in life, leaving their family farms for higher education, a life of scholarship. Having graduated from Brown six years before with highest honors, the young English professor felt a kinship with Hay, sharing a love of literature, the classics, and journalism.[147]

The ambitious boy was anxious to know, to grow into the Brown culture. Dinner-table discussions among his classmates and the don who dined with them favored lively dialogues on the likes of Carlyle, Shelley, Coleridge, Macaulay, and Emerson. Conversations easily turned to debate.[148] John had never discussed literary giants and exciting new books over a meal. The dinner table was alive with intellect and ideas. Many of the New England boys who had attended prep school, such as Andover, Exeter, or Choate, were accustomed to the elevated discourse. Not John. It was new. It was exciting. He loved the intellectual challenge, the literary stimulation.

Inquisitive, Hay indulged his own independent inquiry in Brown's library, small by the standards of Yale or Harvard. For him, though, the library felt like a gift from heaven, "one of the greatest advantages of an eastern college," he told his family. The university had accumulated books in the ancients, classics, history, and literature, a bountiful collection that a young western college had neither the time nor funds to compile. *Beowulf* topped the list of books that John Hay checked out from the Brown library, the first in fact, memorialized by his small, tight signature on the lending ledger for Saturday, September 29, 1855. He discovered the perfect weekend conquest, absorbing the longest and greatest Anglo-Saxon poem, pitting the chieftain Hrothgar, who aided Beowulf in confronting Grendel in sixth-century Denmark.

The following weekend, his signature in the library's ledger appeared larger, more certain. He borrowed Herbert Spencer's *Principles of Psychology*, published that year. Spencer demonstrated a physiological basis for psychology, an iconoclastic counterpoint to Brown's deeply Baptist environment, maintaining that the human mind could be discovered through general biology and classified through a systematic developmental perspective for an individual, a species, and a race. In sharp contrast to the deistic theology of President Sears, Spencer maintained that human culture, human language, and even human morality were explained through scientific investigation. John Hay, a deist, discovered in Spencer a new resolve about life in nature and the sciences.

The Brown library, much like the Mississippi riverfront, exposed him to ideas radically different from his own world. Here, among the stacks of books, John found new ways to challenge his knowledge on the ancients and the moderns. Privately, he recognized the limitations of his Illinois education, expressing his concern to his mother that he might not obtain the highest achievement at Brown. "I think I can *graduate* in time, but will not stand high." Hay thirsted to do better, feeling his intellect inferior to his classmates. "You & Pa may be assured that whatever time I remain here," he said, "I am determined to show you that your generous kindness has not been misapplied or ungratefully received."

Stunned to learn from the registrar by late fall "that I stand in the first class of honor, my average standing being 18 in 20," John rushed to tell his parents. This was a proud moment for the Illinois boy.[149] In this amazing place, he pushed to do better. While other students, such as Norris of Pittsfield, failed to live up to Brown's expectations, John Hay applied himself both in the classroom and evening's private study.

Studious, he was known by some friends and faculty to be "reticent and shy." Others thought him "jolly and loquacious," valuing his innate gift for turning a good tale. He enjoyed a sound reputation "as a punster and impromptu poet." In an instant, seemingly without thought, he made up a poem or recalled verse from Shelley or Shakespeare, or a paragraph in the original Greek text from the *Iliad*.[150] Brown roommate William L. Stone remembered that the Theta Delta Chi fraternity, the seventh secret society on campus, competed for Hay's allegiance during the fraternity rush in September 1855. (The fifty years between 1855 and Stone's 1905 declaration may have added some improvised facts to his memory). Having won Hay's commitment, Theta Delta Chi elected him into their number on September 14, 1855, initiating him the next day. A supper at the local pub and brewery, What Cheer, taken to mean "greetings, friend," followed the rite of passage.

"Speech, speech, speech," toastmaster Burdge called on Hay.

A classmate called out from the gallery, "We don't want anything dry."

John shot back, "Hay that is green can never be dry."

This zesty moment sealed John Hay's reputation as the class's literary prodigy.

The next morning, roommate Stone reenacted "the horror of the members of the rival fraternities when they saw Hay come into chapel...wearing the [Theta Delta Chi] shield," probably a cloth pendant. That moment, President Sears stood impatient at his usual post, scorning the commotion in the student gallery, his sharp brow and penetrating eyes trained on the boys, his spectacles sliding down to the precipice of his sharp nose. "A universal and audible howl went up from the opposition, which evoked a corresponding cheer from our side," Stone said. Theta Delta Chi triumphed in its duel to secure Hay. "The triumph was complete and Dr. [Sears], was constrained to stand some moments until the commotion had subsided before offering up his interrupted orisons."[151]

The Greek fraternities, and also the two literary debate societies—the Philermenians and the United Brothers—made up the heart of Brown's student community, private groups beyond the peering eyes of the professors.[152] In fact, Brown's authorities had disapproved of the secret societies from their first appearance in the 1830s and well down to the late nineteenth century. They opposed the clannish nature, the intrigue, and the peculiar behavior provoked by the society's odd group customs. Theta Delta Chi was the latest to appear in 1853.[153] The debate societies, instead, were as old as Brown, an extension of its lively intellectual culture. The first among them was the Philermenian Society, known as the Phils, and it was soon joined by the United Brothers Society. Hay joined the Phils on November 3, 1855, along with thirty-two others.

President Sears, a former Phil himself, welcomed the new members in their room on the top floor of Hope College. Across the hall was the United Brothers threshold. Hay's love for debate and rhetoric ensured his loyalty to the Phils throughout his three years at Brown, a crucial time for debate societies nationwide, which were slowly being crowded out by a growing number of Greek letter fraternities.[154]

The appearance on campus of poet Oliver Wendell Holmes Sr. in November, and William Thackeray in December, cast something of a mystical influence on Hay. In the presence of these great literary figures and in an intimate venue, the blossoming poet felt he was witnessing Janus at the gates of knowledge.[155] Hay was also among a few students who met privately with Mr. Holmes, an exceptional source of wisdom.

Winter snowfalls brought the jaunty jingle of sleigh bells around Providence. On Christmas day 1855, the university suspended classes, allowing boys who lived nearby to go home to their families. Not a part of mid-century Christmas, though, were the modern-day garlanded trees, joyous carols, personal gifts, and Santa Claus. The day was celebrated with a large meal. John apparently stayed on campus with schoolmates, instead traveling home at the end of the January term, a holiday of three weeks, most of which he spent on trains to and from Warsaw.

Returning to Brown in mid-February, John stepped from the train to the icy station platform.[156] Despite the bone-chilling cold, he was happy and confident. "I have commenced this term well," he wrote Milton Hay on March 30, 1856, acknowledging receipt of the bank draft from his uncle (who contributed financially to John's education). Classes in Latin, Greek, physics and rhetoric, he admitted, "are all pretty difficult." He relished the challenge, the grueling study and recitations that demanded exact verbal reproduction of the text.[157] In Latin and physics, John earned high marks. His Greek and rhetoric professors rated Hay's performance exemplary, near perfect.[158]

Some nervous pride filled his words telling Uncle Milton that President Sears and the faculty had invited him to open the university's Spring Exhibition with the keynote speech. It was his second term at Brown when John Hay, seventeen, distinguished himself for his rhetorical talent. Planned for Saturday, May 3, 1856, he told Uncle Milton, "My time will be completely taken up, leaving me little leisure for reading." Chattering on in his characteristic self-deprecating manner, hinting at his anxiety about living up to the honor of the fêted event, John was absent from classes for a full three weeks before the address.[159] He suffered what was a lifelong condition affecting his stomach and intestines, likely stemming from a nervous condition. He had never worked with the intensity he did at Brown.

The day of the Spring Exhibition opened mild, a soft fog hanging low over Narragansett Bay, the warm air misting upon the ocean's chilly waters. Warmer days in late April coated the campus with spring blooms of daffodils, forsythia, and magnolias. No stranger to public speaking since the age of seven, Hay was familiar with ceremonial recitals. He took care to dress in the formal attire of Brown University, setting aside his school-day clothes of black jacket and trousers, slipping into an evening coat for the public exercise.[160] With his time at Brown, John's attire reflected the natty dress of New England men.

Beyond the speech itself, which Hay had committed to memory, he dreaded the audience of Brown professors and the distinguished Corporation members. When the moment arrived, John spoke with the measured tempo of a poet, the somber resonance of a preacher. Opening his tribute to "Indian Traditions," he had chosen "the far-off voices of a dying nation," a sensitive subject for the day and one many Americans regarded as taboo. He spoke from the heart, honoring the plight of Native Americans who had been violently removed from their lands, their homes, and the natural environment that fed, clothed, and sustained them.

> The immortal past of the Indian do not wholly die.
> So should their memory live,
> grown in the hearts of all the coming ages,
> twined with the records which preserve to us
> the loves, the emotions & the simple religion
> of these rude children of the forest.

The infamous Trail of Tears displacement, occurring in 1838, the year of John's birth, uprooted the Cherokee Nation from its homelands east of the Mississippi River, pushing them overland along a bloodstained route that ended in Oklahoma territory.

Coming of age along the banks of the Mississippi, gazing for hours across the river to the shores of Missouri and Iowa, John had witnessed the fast-paced nation-building that consumed lands previously occupied by the "rude children of the forest." He described "rude" to mean rough, raw, primitive, and uncouth, rather than ill-mannered, indecent, or unpleasant.

> "Each heart that is made better or…wiser by their influence," he said, "each mind that is lighted with a true philanthropy of their contemplation, may blot a page in the red record of their wrongs."[161]

Forgiveness, he said, came to anyone who acknowledged both the wrongs done to these people, and the long-underrated contributions the natives made to advance American civilization.

President Sears commended the literary performance.[162] John Hay had once more risen above his ranks to secure the admiration of Brown's headmaster and also the Class of '56 orator, Richard Olney, future US Secretary of State, 1895–1897.[163] "This young gentleman delivered an admirable address," Olney said to the *Providence Journal,* speaking "on the importance of carrying literary culture into professional life." Hay held true to Olney's sentiment when in future years he found paid work that applied his poetry.

The time preparing for the May exhibition brought reflection to Hay's thoughts about civilization and the acts of violence of people against people. He thought about the news of the murderous attacks between free-state settlers and pro-slavery forces in Kansas in the wake of the repeal of the

Missouri Compromise and the 1854 passage of the Kansas–Nebraska Act, permitting settlers to decide whether slavery was lawful or not. A relatively unknown Illinois politician, Abraham Lincoln, had declaimed "the monstrous injustice of slavery" in an 1854 speech in Peoria: Slavery had been prohibited in new territory since the Declaration of Independence.[164]

Hay, too, referred to the abuse of slaveholders and colonial imperialists, when he wrote in a Brown blue-book essay:

> While they who have labored
> to crush the spirit of freedom from the souls of men
> & have used the life & happiness of a perishing people
> to building memorials of their grandeur…
> become the scoff of the nations.

Standing up for freedom, fighting for the right, Hay concluded:

> our labors if successful
> shall be hallowed by the praises of men
> and the approval of heaven;
> & if we fail, should cheer us with the triumphant consciousness that,
> "Gods in his heaven
> All's right with the world."

Invoking the words of Robert Browning, Hay's descriptions of "perishing people" and "hallowed by the praise of men" revealed words that appeared later in President Lincoln's address at Gettysburg.

In the Brown library, open four hours daily before the midday meal,[165] Hay continued to consume literary works. From Wordsworth, especially, he learned that a poet was affected more than others by the voids in life, as if absence had a life of its own. Choosing works by Turner and Thierry, as well as the *Foreign Quarterly Review* and *Northern British Review*, he learned that in history lay inspiration and an understanding of the future, "for from experience arises prophecy, & from the shining deeds which the past ages have placed among the stars we may cast the horoscope of coming time," he wrote in a spring 1856 history essay.[166]

Hay delved into the world of words as many times throughout the week as he could manage. He poured through books as he wandered through the stacks, taking home others to read alone in his room. His independent study equipped him to carry off a paper for his rhetoric class on "The Saxon Conquest and the Norman contrasted in respect of their influence upon the Languages and the Literature of the Conquered Place."[167] His sweeping knowledge, from modern literature to ancient history, reflected the knowledge of a serious scholar.

Embracing the didactic debates with the Philermenian society, Hay joined with Daniel B. Pond of Massachusetts, an upperclassman who shared his abolitionist moral views and who had earlier read with Ralph Waldo Emerson, Nathaniel Hawthorne, and Henry David Thoreau. Together, they argued in favor of the question of whether "the course of the president on the Kansas question has been unconstitutional."[168] Hay and Pond persuaded their opponents that the spread of slavery into newly annexed territory was illegal. On another occasion, the duo upheld the opposition on the question of whether "prose writers have done more for the English language than poets." Drawing on their discerning literary knowledge, Hay and Pond developed a persuasive argument that claimed the greater influence of poets on English dialect.

At the close of Hay's first year of college, his academic performance reflected his aptitude for the classics, earning a 19.4 and 18.9 in Latin and Greek, respectively, on a perfect scale of 20, as well as an 18.8 in rhetoric and an impressive 19.2 in physiology. The inner scientist revealed the amateur naturalist's kinship with his world.

Chapter 7

BROWN POET LAUREATE

Settling into his second year at Brown in 1856, eighteen-year-old John Hay joined with other dorm mates in University Hall to protest unannounced evening visits to students' room by hovering proctors, monitoring the boys' rooms for the alcohol that President Sears feared. Fifteen boys, including Hay, packed up and moved over to Hope College, Brown's oldest residential dorm on the opposite end of College Green.[169] Built as a gift from Nicolas Brown Jr., it was named for his sister, Hope. The forty-eight rooms offered superior lodgings, including coal-burning fireplaces. Hope's water, drawn from the more sanitary southern well on Campus Green, freed the boys from the bacteria-infested water of the north well, known for breeding epidemic outbreaks in University Hall residents.[170]

Hay's parents agreed to a private room for their son, accepting his desire for solitary contemplation. A room of one's own was a luxury in nineteenth-century America, a place to withdraw in private. Emerson's *Nature* had made an impression on Hay. His parents also paid for a servant to make his bed and carry and change his water and waste each day. The cost of seven dollars a term, or $210 today, seemed a good value, affording him more time for his studies. The irony in the Hope system was that the servants were the spies. Brown monitored every student room.

In spite of the comfort and privacy of his lodgings, Hay's health plunged during the winter months of 1856–57, likely depression, manifest in hypochondria. He was absent a full four weeks of classes, one in five days of the term. His class standing dropped as the demerits rose, failing to attend the lecture theater and Manning Chapel twice a day. Brown's academic standards did not yield to Hay's tender constitution, regardless of his brilliant mind.

Deep snows and the bitter cold of December 1856 also curbed Hay's frequent visits to the university library, but not his appetite for literature. Worse than the freezing drifts were two very long weeks without mail from home, halted by treacherous roads across the country, east to west. Hay sated his loneliness by immersing himself in his daily declamations. Encouraged by literature professor Dunn, John worked to enrich his understanding of the source and power of poetry. Repeating rhyme, tempo, and timbre, he memorized Shakespeare and other favorites, including Scott, Chaucer, and Wordsworth. He studied what the great poets said and how they affected their audience. Even in his juvenile love poems, Hay channeled the dramatic voices of the eminent writers. Brown offered Hay the critical platform to refine his voice, style, and rhetorical talent. The foundations of his intellect developed under the tutelage of the university's dons as he perfected his oratorical persuasiveness.

By spring of 1857, the second term of his second year, Hay began testing the boundaries of authority. Brilliant and adolescent, John was acting perfectly normal for once. He was exploring the fun side of life, unmonitored by his parents or Uncle Milton. He was part of a scuffle that left one student expelled and three temporarily suspended. He began smoking hashish, a habit he continued for several years.[171] He was also lightly fined for keeping Longfellow's *Poets of Europe* in his rooms beyond the allowed rental. Careful to mind the library's rules, Hay turned his literary choices to German literature, including Thomas Roscoe, the lyric poetry of Johann Wolfgang Goethe, George Henry Lewes's monumental *Life of Goethe*, and Weimar classicist Friedrich Schiller. These works apparently didn't tempt him to trespass the library's due dates.

The Phils offered John invariable pleasure. His spirits rallied as he joined with two other boys to argue in favor of the question of whether "political excitements are beneficial to Republican governments." Indeed they are, said brother Hay. The mental gymnastics of debate brought him personal delight. He triumphed in the logical leaps and oral feats, also earning high marks in French and German literature.[172] Hay loved rhetorical debate and he was good, which he also liked. The term's debates took up national political controversies that addressed the southern secession crisis and the divided nation. In the nation's capital, Democrat and Southern sympathizer James Buchanan had taken over the presidency on March 4, 1857. Since his election, Buchanan had urged the Supreme Court for a ruling on *Dred Scott v. Sandford.* Chief Justice Taney, a southern Maryland native, announced the court's decision just two days after Buchanan's inauguration.

Shocking the nation, the majority ruled a decisive 7–2 vote that Dredd Scott, a Black man, was not a citizen and had no constitutional rights: neither to vote, to be counted as a person, nor to be free. In one sweep, the Supreme Court declared the Missouri Compromise of 1820 unconstitutional, reversing the balance of power in Congress between slave-owning and free states. Seven justices had overturned the revolutionary law prohibiting slavery in the unorganized territories of Iowa, Kansas, South and North Dakota, Montana, Minnesota, Wyoming, Colorado, and Nebraska.

The political implosion sent a groundswell through the nation's financial markets, tumbling railroad securities and Western land futures. The country's political landscape shifted as the slavery question rose to define America's future. Would slavery extend into the new Western territories? Would it fail there, yet survive in the Southern states? What did the future hold? Who would decide and how? Brown's Phils debated the issue. "According to the true construction of the Constitution," they stated, "colored men are citizens of the United States." Hay argued in favor of the statement with his fellow Phils on April 18, 1857. Within moments, the opposition was silenced. "After a short discussion," the minutes stated, the question was "decided in the affirmative by a unanimous vote."[173] Citizenship was a legal and political right for all people, regardless of the color of their skin. Hay's argument reflected the prevailing beliefs of the Republican Party, the Whigs having virtually collapsed by 1856.

Hay was recognizing the power of oratory, balancing words, wit, and wisdom. He was discovering that persuasion lay in the soundness of the argument and also the verse—the effect the speech had on the audience. He was gaining the idea of the musicality of words to impress the mind and heart of the listener.

In another Phil debate, mounting a compelling argument that favored secession by the Southern slave-holding states to ultimately end slavery, Hay's line of reasoning forecast both the horrific Civil War as well as its prophetic outcome. This was more than three years before the first shot was fired on Fort Sumter.[174] His rhetoric decided the question for the Phils that, yes, secession of the slave states from the Union would hasten the extinction of slavery. Young Hay harnessed his understanding of society and politics to build a convincing case. He stitched together a precise choice of words, a compelling line of argument, and a dash of surprise. Brown was refining young Hay's use of language and rhetoric to address complex, even troubling issues.[175]

Settling down to serious study as 1857's autumn light dimmed to the neutral grays of winter, Hay began to read epic works of history. Through books, he met the leaders and thinkers that had propelled transformation across the European continent and beyond. He expanded his awareness about great military and religious events. He read Protestant historian Jean-Henri Merle d'Aubigné's *History of the Reformation of the Sixteenth Century*, an exhaustive, two-volume work on the Reformation—from Scotland's Haldane to Germany's Martin Luther, to the chaotic Reformation in France. Hay studied the role of the country's leaders, good and bad, and the gains and crushing defeats brought on by civil war.

In Joseph François Michaud's six-volume *Histoire des Croisades* (1840), a historical epic, Hay followed the author on his dangerous trek to the lands of Syria and Egypt, risking his life documenting the crusades of European Christians, Michaud gave voice to the national pride of the European crusaders and the inspiration of their cause, offering Hay a model for his and George Nicolay's future multivolume biography of Abraham Lincoln.[176]

Beyond Brown, the Providence Athenaeum navigated literary life in Providence and Rhode Island. Joining esteemed writers, the teenage Hay was lucky to be among the self-selected circle. Months after arriving at Brown in early 1856, John had become an Athenaeum stockholder, a freedom and an honor for the first-year student. He was the only Brown student among the 570 shareholders. Providence society rarely opened its doors to students before their senior year, when scholars were considered sufficiently mature to reflect the university's character, in the view of President Sears.[177] John Hay's immersion in the old city's literary community reflected a privilege and the Athenaeum's respect for his literary knowledge. Spending hours at a time in one of the two large reading rooms on the ground floor, Hay treasured the open-stack library above, natural light streaming in through large multipaned windows.[178]

The Athenaeum had originated from Benjamin Franklin's idea for creating a public library owned by a joint stock association. Founded in 1753, the Providence Library Company united with the Providence Athenaeum (est. 1831) in 1836. Having high ambitions for the library, the stockholders retained eminent classical architect William Strickland of Philadelphia to design their new home. The library's elegant Grecian Doric order gracing Benefit Street near the Brown campus was Strickland's only work in New England. Providence bookseller and publisher George H. Whitney was the Athenaeum's source for contemporary works of literature. Whitney no doubt was acquainted with Hay from his visits to the bookshop, surely even introducing the young scholar to the Athenaeum's members. Whitney owned share 545, and Hay, 546. [179] Their successive stock numbers was a sound clue to the influential connection.

The annual premium of five dollars, or $150 today, gave every owner access to any book. Especially sought after were the much talked about first editions of leading works. In fall 1855, Whitney had introduced Walt Whitman's *Leaves of Grass* and Catharine Beecher's authoritative *Letters to the People on Health and Happiness* for domestic well-being. He also brought the Athenaeum's abolitionists a stark portrait of slave and freedman in Frederick Douglass's *My Bondage and My Freedom,* and Henry David Longfellow's tender epic poem of Native American legends, in *The Song of Hiawatha,* published that year by Boston's Ticknor & Fields, later to become John Hay's publisher.

In 1856, Whitney introduced the Athenaeum to Robert Browning's breakthrough book of poetry, *Men and Women,* and Frederick Law Olmsted's personal observation of slavery and the farming economy of the Southern states, in *A Journey in the Seaboard Slave States,* exposing the underbelly of the South's autocracy. (Olmsted's book was published one year before he and Calvert Vaux began the landscape design for Central Park in New York City.) Hay's introduction to Olmsted was a powerful tonic: he was six years Hay's senior and not classically educated. Olmsted had published a book and was now designing America's great urban parkland before the age of twenty-five. A farmer from Staten Island, a wanderer and journalist, he was enjoying incredible success with an ambitious publisher who leveraged the secession crisis to raise Olmsted's specter. Hay might have gained inspiration from Olmsted's personal journey. He, too, had big dreams.[180]

Finding a home in the Providence Athenaeum, Hay relished reading and assimilating the stimulating new literature of slavery, art, history, biography, and drama. Here, he also fell into intimate friendships with two older women.[181] Sarah Helen Power Whitman and Nora Perry, poets, essayists, and pillars of the Athenaeum's inner circle, garnered the young man's creative esteem. Whitman, fifty-five, daughter of the wealthy Power shipping family and widow of John W. Whitman, co-editor of the *Boston Spectator and Ladies' Album,* became a devout spiritualist after her husband's death. Romantically involved with Edgar Allen Poe, her short-lived affair with Poe ended after the novelist's betrayal.[182]

John Hay, thirty-five years Sarah Whitman's junior, was a breath of fresh air for this solitary woman. He admired her literary soul. Even her iridescent personality dancing with flashes of hot and cool, near and far, enchanted him. "I am so variable that I should inevitably disappoint you if you hoped to find in me tomorrow the same aspect which one knew today," Whitman had once confided to an oppressed Poe.[183] Her sorrowful eyes gave the impression of a fascinating woman in a constant state of grief. Mrs. Whitman appealed to Hay's inner sorrow, a deep-seated kinship with his own soul. They were also bound by a mutual joy in the spirit, sitting silently in the misty hot-air séances in her home, a haven for the literati of liberal thinkers. So taken was he by Sarah Whitman, Hay gave her a photographic portrait of himself, the wistful poet.[184] He also composed a poem for her, "an offering" he called it, writing a soliloquy portraying the joy and despair of life and love, a sorrow-filled fantasy aroused by a moment of passionate reverie.

Titled "In the Mist," he never gave it to her. The final stanzas bear witness to Hay's characteristic rhyme pattern, the anapestic tetrameter of Byron, Poe, and Greek and Hebraic texts. "In the Mist" also displayed Hay's fondness for alliteration and the universal polarities of life-death and time-space.

> The world with its burden of woe & of crime
> Rolls on through the twilight of gathering years,
> While she twines round her brow the dim trophies
> of time,
> And joins in the thunderous chime of the spheres.
> No wail from the earth breaks the calm of the sky
> Unheeded we live & unheeded we die.
> Then why should we sing of a home in the skies,
> Or mourn in the dusk of the spirits eclipse.
> When a pledge of joy lurks in the challenging eyes
> And the love dew is sparkling on budding red lips?
>
> Within the white joy of Love's sheltering arms!
> Launch the Boat! Set the sails! & adown the still stream,
> We will glide with the mystical float of a dream.

Ah, vain the endeavor! Along the dim river.
The voice of the ages low whispers 'In vain,'
Death sits at the helm & our shallop forever
Drives into the night, through the mist and the rain."

He held onto the poem for months. At last, after he had left Brown, he posted it in January 1859, sending it instead to Nora Perry.

Perry was a mainstay of the Athenaeum's lair. Just two years older, the petite, dark-haired woman with opal-shaped eyes that cast a thoughtful glance, her beautifully tailored dresses giving the impression of a woman of means, confident and gentle. Nora admired John's sense of fairness, his sympathy, his clever repartee. Fiercely independent at a young age, she preferred boys to the company of girls—a tomboy who loved *Arabian Nights.* Her warmest female friendships were with writers themselves, such as Sarah Whitman and Harriet Prescott Spofford of Boston.

John Hay also discovered novels of Gustave Flaubert, Washington Irving, William Thackeray, Elizabeth Gaskell, Wilkie Collins, Charles Dickens, and Henrik Ibsen as the light dimmed on the late autumn days of 1857. He experienced the power of narrative, stories of influence and principle. *Fraser's* and *Blackwood's* periodicals, too, London-based competitors, garnered his interest for first-edition poems by Carlisle, Thackeray, and Ainsworth.

On September 4, 1857, the start of his final year at Brown, Hay entered the Master of Arts program, which continued through January 21, 1858. His work in philosophy and history commanded a near-perfect average grade of 19.64. Outstanding.[185]

As early as the start of his last semester, John began feeling low about his passing time in academia. A universally dark time of year of little sun and short days, John Hay reflected that the budding friendship with nineteen-year-old Hannah Angell, the sister of Professor Angell, was also waning. She had completed her private schooling in Providence, returning to the family's home in the hills near Scituate. Encouraged by Hannah's welcome, John visited frequently. They walked arm in arm along the dirt road bordering the banks of the Ponangansett River, protected by overarching elms and maples. Crossing the wooden bridge to the other side, John engraved "**H. A.**" in the post, and added "**Y.**" to her initials.[186] **H**annah **A**ngel plus **Y** spelled HAY. A proposal? If so, Hannah did not reply.

During his final term at Brown, Spring 1858, Hay filled his days in the Brown library and Providence Athenaeum. He saw a good deal of Nora, who invigorated his poetic sensibilities. She liked his verse, and she read hers to him. By all appearances, theirs was a platonic relationship founded in a love of literature.[187] The harmless flirtation was good fun. He sent her poems of love and death. Her open, stark personality intensified John's passionate verse while heightening his odd preoccupation with death. "I have wandered this winter in the valley of the shadow of death," he wrote Perry, paraphrasing Psalm 23, verse 4. "All the universe, God, earth, and heaven have been to me but vague and gloomy phantasms."[188] Hay's sympathetic connection with place often led him down a dark, murky road of mourning and pity. Poetry was the outlet of his despair.

John's investigations in the Brown library led him to the songs and poetry of Pierre-Jean de Béranger, France's prolific songwriter—its *chansonnier*.[189] Béranger's witty and sparkling folk songs stimulated Hay's musical voice. The Parisian's influential lyrics had triggered the revolution of 1830, helping the ascent of Louis Philippe I to the throne.[190] Hay was exhilarated to think that one man's verses transformed history. Similar to his own vernacular ballads, Béranger wrote songs for the common people, the sailors and laborers. And, as Hay later discovered himself in his own *Pike County Ballads* (1871), the *chanson* stirred John's literary freedom and placed the entire dictionary of words at his disposal, four-fifths of which were forbidden in formal, academic poetry.

By the close of the spring 1858 term, Hay piled up an impressive semester of work in philosophy, history, and physical engineering, a 19.65 average for his Master's classes. He stood seventh in the class of 1858. Among the thirty-three scholars, ten were set to pursue the ministry; seven the law; seven private industry; five medicine; four teaching; and two diplomacy. Only eleven of the men, a third of the class, entered the Union army during the Civil War. Remarkably, as officers, not one lost his life or was seriously injured.

On the Sunday before graduation, John wrote Hannah Angell. He longed for Hannah to attend the graduation ceremony, her presence softening the routine of the prepared speeches. "Will we have the pleasure of seeing you on the tenth?" he asked. "It will be too correct to be ridiculous & too dull to be amusing. Still," he said, "my ruling motive in hoping you will be there is entirely selfish."[191] He wished for her to witness his performance of the class poem.

Thursday, June 10, 1858, graduation day, opened overcast. The skies cleared at the morning chime, exactly at 10:15 a.m., summoning the senior class to form its procession in front of Rhode Island Hall. Proceeding in step, walking in numbered order into the Manning Hall chapel, the scholars opened with a prayer and musical interlude. President Sears delivered the opening address.

He was joined on the podium by the seven students in his class who had achieved the highest academic standing: Joseph Henry Gilmore, valedictorian and future Baptist minister; Arnold Greene, forthcoming Rhode Island Supreme Court justice; Eliab Washburn Coy, future lawyer and professor; Samuel Thurber, soon to be a high school teacher; Lyman Beecher Tefft, also an imminent Baptist minister; William Brown Phillips, the future Swarthmore classics professor; and John Hay, grateful to depart Brown with high standing, relieved to have graduated at all. Following addresses by his six classmates, Brown's 1858 class poet stood to deliver his poem.

Brown University, College Green with University Hall (right) and Manning Hall (left). Author's photo.

Hay's "Erato" echoed the terse drama of the crusades and the reformation, celebrating Greeks, Trojans, Romans, and life at Brown. In the weeks before, feeling anxious from the devilment of the epic poem, he drafted, edited, and rewrote "the fearful incubus," he said, inflicting "such acute Iambic torture." Part ode and part lampoon, the rhythm was iambic pentameter and the rhyme scheme ABAB, astonishingly clever for a teenager.

The *Providence Journal* claimed that the "brilliant performance" was "enlivened by passages of keen wit and pleasing humor," giving way to streams of impassioned tears and deafening applause throughout his delivery. "Marked by a fertility of conception, a depth of sensibility, and a power of poetic expression," the *Journal* raved in the hyperbole of mid-nineteenth-century journalism, "which we have rarely heard equaled, and never surpassed, at any of our literary anniversaries."[192] One stanza alone, the final verse, highlighted John Hay's poetic preferences for parallel structure, life's polarities, and the iambic rhyme pattern.

Our words may not float down the surging ages,
As Hindoo lamps adown the sacred stream;
We may not stand sublime on history's pages,
The bright ideals of future's dream;
Yet we may all strive for the goal assigned us,
Glad if we win and happy if we fail;
Work calmly on, nor care to leave behind us
The lurid glory of the meteor's trail.
As we go forth the smiling world before us
Shouts to our youth the old inspiring tune;
The same blue sky of God is bending o'er us,
The green earth sparkles in the joy of June.
Where'er afar the beck of fate shall call us,
'Mid winter's boreal chill or summer's blaze,
Fond memory's chain of flower shall still enthrall us,
Wreathed by the spirits of these vanished days.
Our hearts shall bear them safe through life's
commotion,
Their fading gleam shall light us to our graves;
As in the shell, the memories of ocean,
Murmur forever of the sounding waves."

Professors, classmates, and assembled friends and families applauded Hay's soliloquy. Professor Dunn, professor of literature, rose to his feet, embracing John after the ceremony. Joyous to be free from "Erato's clutches," Hay walked away "in overflowing spirit." Years later, William Dean Howells admired "Erato" for Hay's "graceful handling of a familiar measure," but, he said, "it was more than commonly representative of the poet's own thinking and feeling. "[193]

The term ended on July 8, 1858. Hay prepared to depart Providence and Brown University for the last time. In his Hope College room, he took up a sheet of writing paper. He picked up his pen and ink bottle to write the storyline of his inner voice. "In these last hours, I cherish these vanishing treasures & close my eyes to the joys that lie beyond the western hills," he wrote to Hannah. He paused as he recognized the truth about his unknown future in western Illinois. "When the time comes, I shall be ready to go," he admitted.[194] John Hay set down his pen, sealed the envelope, and doused the candle flame. He sat alone in the darkness of sleepy old Hope.

John Hay, official graduation photograph, Brown University, Providence, Rhode Island, June 1858. Courtesy of John Hay collection, John Hay Library, Brown University.

Chapter 8

RETURN TO ILLINOIS

As he prepared for his passage home, John reflected on the differences between Providence and the life awaiting him in Warsaw. "From scenes that I hold dearest, to scenes that deserve a warmer love," he said, comparing life in Rhode Island's vibrant capital and that of his provincial Illinois hometown. The vision of Providence's literary life was winning out over the parochial rural west. Besotted, Hay reckoned with his future. "A life, not new, but strange from long absence, calls upon me now and I shall accept calmly if not joyfully the challenge of fate."[195]

His trunk packed, his room in a confusion that signaled a life moving on, John Hay stepped away from Brown's ivy walls. With languorous strides, he padded a slow-paced beat down College Hill, crossing the narrow river bridge to the train depot. The university's campus disappeared behind him, the distance with each pace producing a looming unease that spread like a chill off Narragansett Bay. At the station, Hay stepped onto the steaming train headed for Boston, then westward through Pennsylvania, Ohio, Indiana, and finally Illinois.

Departing the 200-year-old port city of Providence and a population greater than 50,000, Hay soon arrived in Warsaw, a young town of 2,800 people, a village of dirt roads and rural countryside. "Who knows but I may find rest & peace in the tumult of the West, and feel an inner calm—ascending in the outward roar," he said. "At least the future cannot blot out the past," and what a ride it was. Traveling alone, the slender young man appeared younger than his years, his delicate manner betraying his natural intellect, the heavy-eyed youth sitting quietly. On the long journey, Hay began reading legal texts, preparing himself for the intended law study with Uncle Milton in Springfield. Certainly, the life of a lawyer was an admirable calling of scholarly merit and financial reward. He read William Blackstone's *Commentaries,* shadowing the likes of John Jay and John Adams. Blackstone had a profound influence on every lawyer in the day, *Commentaries,* the only authoritative law school. In antebellum America, lawyers were just beginning to build a body of living law precedents to create a foundation of legal cases with local and federal rulings. Yet even as the courts were becoming somewhat less dependent on Blackstone for reference, *Commentaries* remained the core curriculum for law students like Hay, the bible of the law, the singular text for legal preparation.

It was not surprising that Hay found romantic references in the legal treatises. Never at a loss for "a powerful antidote to sentiment," he said, "yesterday my eye fell on *Hawk vs. Corri* and straightway a tragedy flashed before my mind, and passion and jealousy & hate and despair occupied the thoughts that should have been devoted to the delicate relations of real estate."[196] Interesting that Blackstone's text was open to interpretation. When Hay's thoughts turned to love, his psyche was at rest.

During the decade approaching 1860, the world witnessed groundbreaking advances in transportation and communications. Vast distances and strange lands seemingly pressed closer as the speed of travel and the transmission of information gained momentum. In August 1858 alone, the first transatlantic telegraph cable laid on the floor of the Atlantic Ocean opened instantaneous communication between North America and Europe, a radical innovation that allowed news to be transferred in a few minutes, rather than the painfully long intervals of several days, the norm for the past century or more. Transatlantic passages between New York and Liverpool, too, advanced four times faster in the three years when John Hay was at Brown University, a giant leap forward from the earlier sailing packet's thirty-seven days and hourly crawl of four knots. Now, the newly christened Cunard iron-hulled paddler running between England and northeastern America pushed through rough and high seas at thirteen knots and ten days. The fast pace of life at mid-century emerged amid an explosion in the nation's population, a near doubling within the span of John's life, from 16 million in 1838 to approximately 29 million by 1858. The stark face of this growth beheld the inevitable expansion of enslaved Blacks, a twofold rise to 3.8 million during these twenty years. Publicly, the press and politics gorged on the chasm between North and South, Black and White, slavery and abolition. The secession crisis mounted.

The March 1857 Supreme Court ruling on *Dred Scott*, permitting the opening of Western territories to slavery, prompted dozens of southern farmers to move westward with their chattels in search of fertile and what appeared to be infinite expanses of virgin soil. By expanding slavery into the Western territories, the Northern states were weakening their political clout in the nation. The turmoil deepened the divide between Southern, mostly slave-owning Democrats and Northern, predominantly abolitionist Republicans.

Across the 1,200 miles that Hay traveled between Providence and Warsaw, the country's independent rail lines had also consolidated during his college days to create a national system of interconnecting lines. His one-way transit, in 1855 a dozen days and twelve connections, was now in 1858 only six days and a half-dozen transfers, thanks to advances in railroad technology. John's journey home felt like luxury compared with the discomfort and endurance just three years before. He stopped for several hours to change trains in three of the nation's largest cities of Boston, New York, and Chicago, where the streets surrounding the depots had grown crowded with urbanization, strewn with poverty and the deafening noise of carriages, horse-drawn streetcars, and bellowing hawkers. Stale air heavy with the acrid odor of burnt coal and roads soiled by the waste of horses were the stuff of urban life in pre-Civil War America. Hay felt unnerved by the squalor.

The nation was also growing bigger, noisier, grimier, more divisive. Streaming into America's international ports along the Eastern Seaboard and New Orleans were an unprecedented number of foreign immigrants—29.4 million in 1858 alone, almost double the 16.2 million in 1838, the year of John's birth. Yet equally remarkable, a startling one half of the nation's people now lived west of the Appalachian Mountains, flat and open territory of sprawling farms and tiny villages.

Before the last leg of his journey, John stopped in Springfield for a visit with his sixty-five-year old Grandfather Hay, a familiar occasion on his westward passage. Greeting him was also his aunts Elizabeth, Maria, Elma, and Deniza. The unmarried sisters looked after their widowed father with Irish-born servant Margaret Grogan and carriage skinnery Robert Thompson.[197] Springfield, in step with the uplift of the industrializing nation, had refashioned itself in recent years from a small backwater of muddy roads to a fledgling city that grew by one thousand residents each year. Arriving in Warsaw, Charles and Helen Hay embraced their son, the young man just two months shy of his twentieth birthday, the sanctioned Master of Arts degree in hand. John clung to his family's reassurance, his foundation.

Yet the homecoming was a most difficult transition. The Ivy-league graduate slipped into a funk. It was one of John's many bouts with melancholy throughout life. "I am not living now but merely existing in that slow lazy kind of a way that seems so appropriate to a person who sees his hopes dying steadily & all that he once treasured gliding from his grasp, now nerveless and wasteful," he said. Feeling eerily distant from Providence, "it is not a pleasant thing to feel each night that the setting sun has seen [me] farther from all [I] love & desire than the dawning did; to know that [my] intellect is losing its edge," he wrote Hannah, "to look around [me] & see a well-nigh uninterrupted waste of spiritual desolation, & to feel…that [I am] sinking slowly into the slough of barbarism."[198]

Brown had changed him. Warsaw's once serene, majestic plains that the boy had admired years before now conjured mostly contempt from his lips. He felt stuck out in the middle of nowhere.[199] He clung to the memory of what he called "those flush days" at Brown and the Providence Athenaeum, "when every sand in the glass had a tint of gold & the gray wings of Time flashed like rainbows in the sunshine, when even melancholy was transfigured by the atmosphere that surrounded me, & shone with a tender light like sunset clouds in the effulgence of evening."[200]

Even two months anon, on September 1, 1858, commencement day at Brown, John awoke with a sense of yearning. He detested the hollowness of his Warsaw life, pitching into bittersweet memories of his own commencement in 1855. It felt like yesterday. He recalled the ritualized processional into First Baptist Church—"our awkward ministerial squad"—the pairings of the procession, the decorous attire—"neckties that stun"—and the speakers who opened the first terms with august words of wisdom. "Stupid as the whole affair undoubtedly was," he said, "in my distempered brain it appeared far more so." John claimed to favor the fantasy of a narcotic high to that of Brown's rituals. "My imagination rested with the delight which none but a hashish-eating sensualist can know."[201] Now, in rural Illinois, he felt an overwhelming sense of loss, defeat really.

John's protracted moping grew tiresome for his father, a pragmatic man whose own life was one of perpetual industry and progress. A month after John's return, Dr. Hay began exploring employment options for his son.

"I am somewhat undecided as to what course I will advise him to pursue," Charles wrote Milton Hay, who had moved his law practice the previous year from Pittsfield to Springfield, enticed by opportunity and leaving behind personal tragedy. In 1857, Milton's wife, Catherine Forbes Hay, had died, as did their two children, Katy, seven, and Mary, five. Their infant son, Charles, named for John Hay's father, had died in infancy at thirteen months. How this all came to pass remains unclear. Inviting Milton to join his Springfield practice as his partner, Stephen Trigg Logan, a former law partner of Abraham Lincoln and among the state's reputable lawyers, was perhaps influenced by Lincoln. This was a welcome change for Milton.

Charles Hay explained John's aimless wandering to Milton, expressing both frustration for the young man's laziness and compassion for his son's love of nature. "He is restless and wishes to know his destiny, although he expects me to decide for him entirely." John had suggested to his father that he might "return as a resident graduate to Brown, read extensively and write for eastern periodicals, until a time an opening appeared for taking a higher position somewhere." Irritated, Charles told Milton, "the purse is not full and will not be shortly." He didn't have a bank account to support an impoverished writer. Charles was anxious for his son to move forward "I feel that I would do wrong not to encourage him to acquire a profession at once."[202]

Dr. Hay wondered about a career as a schoolmaster in Warsaw. His wife, Helen, promptly struck it down. Charles Hay admitted that John's ego was probably too big for life in a village schoolroom. "[It] would [not] suit his self-esteem," he said. He also dismissed the idea of placing him in a law office in Warsaw. He didn't want "him to remain at all in Warsaw." Instead, his parents gave wide berth to John's possibilities. "Some of his friends urge him to turn his attention immediately to the law," Charles told Milton, while some Providence friends "advise him to turn his attention at once and wholly to literature."[203] Unnamed, perhaps Helen Whitman or even George Whitney, the bookseller, urged John to embrace his literary bent.

In the end, with John's best interests in mind, Charles Hay and Milton Hay decided that John should study law with Milton in Springfield. "Upon what terms can he enter your office and spend twelve months as a student?" Charles asked. Following in the footsteps of many young men in a day before university law schools, John studied legal treatises under the guidance of an experienced attorney, often a friend or, in his case, a family member. Milton, who had overseen a good deal of John's education, was now set to mentor him in the law.

Unknown at the time, within the year, the decision launched the destiny that established John Hay in the heart of America's presidential drama, Abraham Lincoln at its center.

As the snows of winter melted in early spring 1859, the Mississippi River around Warsaw rose high with fresh water and rushing torrents. John felt the pull of adventure. He withstood the temptation no more. Weeks before he was set to push off for Springfield, he departed the riverfront docks of Warsaw to drift down the Mississippi for a time, "before I trim my sails to catch the breeze that ripples the waters of practical life," he said. He prepared "for work by a course of loafing." The river, "more than beautiful at this season," summoned John to revel in the spontaneity of the raw, dynamic environment. "I could lean forever over the guards and gaze at the inscrutable depths of the tawny flood," he said. For fourteen days, he basked in the river's bawdy life and nature's bounty of white dogwoods, pink redbuds, and wild plum trees bursting with young blooms. Looking upward to the heavens, to the blue and infinite sky, soft breezes caressed his cheeks, the wild woods fragrant with the memory of a vanishing world.

His idling revived his spirits. He described the passage as a lofty "Ishmaelitish wandering," in the spirit of the fourteenth-century Central Asian roamer Timur and his estranged brother-in-law Amir Husain, who were outcast in misfortune, embarking on a romantic and bitter voyage. Glorifying his own journey, John imagined his voyage in epic terms, quoting a favorite passage from Psalm 23:4: "I have wandered this winter in the valley of the shadow death."[204] He felt his demons chase after him while he "conversed with wild imaginings in the gloom of the forests," sitting for hours on the brim of the magnificent Mississippi, magnetized by its infinite and swift flow, "the unquiet murmur of its whispering ripples."

Charles and Helen Hay had allowed John nine months to pass under his languorous feet after college graduation. It was time enough. He must channel his knowledge, focus his intellect, and move on. They fixed the date and destination, establishing the particulars of his engagement—as they had done so many times in the past.[205] He chided his parents that they "were spoiling a potentially good preacher to make a third-class lawyer."[206] Could he appreciate the forbearance his parents had afforded him, their gifted son?

On May 14, 1859, John Hay embarked on his new life, ferrying across the Mississippi to Hannibal, Missouri, then boarding the train to Springfield. A day tossing about on the river and rutted rails, he arrived the same day, a Saturday, a mild spring day, the mercury registering temperatures in the high 60s. Torrential rains soaked the flat planes surrounding the town, a horizon of endless fields of corn. Uncle Milton, forty-three, met his twenty-year-old nephew at the station depot.[207] John's return to Milton's life was a blessing of companionship for both. A lifetime counselor to his nephew, Milton reunited with the one living person whom he had nurtured. They lived in the Springfield residence of the widowed senior John Hay, Milton's father and John's grandfather. John treasured the companionship of the family home in the old merchant district, just four blocks from the law and court district. Milton and John shared a room and a bed.[208]

John's sensitivity to place was shaken by Springfield's smaller and simpler society than Providence. Even in the capital of Illinois, it was no match for his nostalgia after living in the urbanity of two centuries of heritage, the colorful ethnic mix, a third of the residents hailing from abroad. "I am stranded at last, on the dreary wastes of Springfield," he wrote a Brown classmate.[209] Yet even in this wasteland, a city he looked upon as "combining the meanness of the North with barbarians of the South," he was at home with his uncle and grandfather.[210]

Momentous changes in Illinois's political landscape were at play during the year before, shifts that affected Milton Hay's law office and eventually John Hay's life. In June 1858, the Illinois Republican State Convention had met in Springfield, nominating Abraham Lincoln as its candidate for the United States Senate campaign. He was to stand against pro-slavery Democrat Stephen Douglas, the incumbent. On June 16, 1858, the day Lincoln accepted the nomination by his fellow Illinois Republicans, he framed the Senate campaign's central issue within the context of the national debate on slavery. He distinguished between the existing institution of slavery and the recently sanctioned extension into Western territories. Famously remembered as the House Divided speech, with the biblical reference "a house divided against itself cannot stand," the speech unveiled the nonabolitionist Lincoln. Like the Founding Fathers before him, Lincoln was unable to find a middle ground between bondage and freedom for Black people. He hated slavery. He believed it was morally wrong to enslave one person by another. Yet in 1858, the political conservative averred that the Declaration of Independence did not mean that "*all* men were equal in all respects," such as the color of their skin. It did mean, however, that all men were promised life, liberty, and the pursuit of happiness.[211]

Lincoln, similarly to other leading politicians of the day, supported the separation of Black people and White people. He stressed his opposition to the Dred Scott decision, reminding his Springfield audience in the house divided speech that the Supreme Court opinion in *Dred Scott* actually froze out popular sovereignty in the Western territories, a belief that Douglas vehemently opposed. If American slaves were not American citizens, Lincoln said, popular sovereignty did not exist. It was folly. Hundreds of letters protesting the speech's disturbing phrases, and pleading for Lincoln to withdraw his statements, poured into his Springfield law office. Lincoln refused. "If I had to draw a pen across my record and erase my whole life from sight," he replied, "I would choose that speech and leave it to the world unerased."[212] Throwing dry kindling into the blaze, Lincoln's advocacy for the civil rights of all people, Black and White, exploded into a national bonfire.

The Republican Lincoln was lesser known than the pro-slavery Douglas, both in Illinois and also nationally. In the November 1858 Senate elections, Douglas triumphed, winning the Illinois seat over Lincoln. Yet while Douglas went to Washington, Lincoln's constitutional stand on human equality remained in the public mind, fertilizing the soil of future national debate. This was the birth of America's modern political system. Lincoln had raised the specter about the interpretation of human rights and the law of property.

Stephen Logan and Milton Hay housed the Logan & Hay law office in prime real estate on the top floor of a three-story brick commercial building overlooking the Illinois State Capitol. They shared the space and their small library with Lincoln, who occupied a small and dimly lit area at the back of the building. Logan & Hay's spacious chambers, streaming with eastern light, engaged a couple of clerks and apprentices, appearing almost lavish next to Lincoln's threadbare interior, home to his growing law practice. "The furniture, somewhat dilapidated," recalled a former law clerk of Lincoln, "consisted of one small desk and a table, a sofa or lounge with a raised head at one end, and a half-dozen plain wooden chairs."[213] The shared law library, stacked with the foundational basics of Blackstone, Kent, Chitty, Black and others, was augmented by the Illinois State Capitol's law library across the street, open day and night to law students and Springfield's lawyers.

John Hay read under Milton's tutelage. Other apprentices joined him, including Brown classmate Charles B. Brown, who was reading under David Davis, the presiding judge of the Illinois Eighth Circuit and a friend of

Lincoln. Davis studied in a corner of the space occupied by Lincoln, who also proctored Elmer E. Ellsworth of Chicago and George Nicolay, the Pittsfield newspaper publisher, now twenty-seven. Nicolay had sold the *Free Press* in 1857, having accepted Ozias M. Hatch's offer to serve as his principal clerk when Hatch was elected as Illinois Secretary of State.[214] Nicolay's decision to study the law reflected his interest in securing a profession. Hay and Nicolay's brief acquaintance in Pittsfield in the early 1850s rekindled now as they studied law in the adjoining space.

Each day, Hay, Brown, Ellsworth, and Nicolay devoured the legal dissertations for hours, easily distracted by abrupt outbursts of animated parleys and political debates from Lincoln's corner, sometimes infused with his friendly storytelling.[215]

Twenty-one-year-old Hay's infectious good looks turned heads as he walked down Springfield's narrow sidewalks, fetching the attentions of young women. He demurred. His swinging gait and the elegant ballet of his "well-shaped hands," said his sister-in-law, captivated passersby, his "long, loose overcoat, flying open, his hands thrust into the pockets."[216] Hay slowly began to feel invigorated in Springfield. Having placed himself in the literary swirl of Providence, he now found himself standing near the inner circle of the Illinois politician who was framing the national debate on slavery.

Chapter 9

AT LINCOLN'S SIDE

At the moment that Abraham Lincoln's political specter was on the rise, John Hay entered this world, arriving in Springfield in May 1859. Shortly before Hay moved to Springfield, the Illinois Republican Caucus nominated Lincoln as its presidential candidate, one of several Republican hopefuls. The nomination churned up mixed feelings in Lincoln, whose bitter loss of the US Senate seat to Stephen Douglas in 1858 had discouraged him about yet another campaign.[217]

Abraham Lincoln, forty-nine, had struggled for everything he had gained in life. When he met John Hay in the spring of 1859, several years after he had undoubtedly seen the boy of twelve or thirteen at the home of Milton Hay in Pittsfield, Lincoln now recognized a fiercely intelligent young man. Less than half his age and endowed with what appeared to be an effortless life in comparison to his own, Lincoln appeared to admire Hay's intelligence, humor, and quick wit, struck as he was by the Ivy League graduate's grasp of literature and history.

Lincoln found a kinship in Hay's literary soul. The young man's brilliant recitations of Biblical verse, Shakespearean dialogue, and Homer's *Odyssey* charmed the less formally educated lawyer. Lincoln's own love of Burns and of Shakespeare—*King Lear* was his favorite—produced a riveting display of wisdom and humor for the law offices of Milton Hay and Abraham Lincoln. Few others affected Lincoln in the way that Hay seemed to. Hay's reservoir of amusing stories moved the older man to outbursts of laughter. And, the sadness of each man's inner soul inherently formed a natural bond, both prone to melancholy and depression.

The early days of Abraham Lincoln and John Hay's relationship were not recorded. Circumstantial clues shape the outlines of when and how Hay began collaborating with Lincoln. Within the combined law offices of Hay & Logan and Lincoln & Herndon, young associates studying law found themselves drawn into the infectious display of Hay's wit and Lincoln's political life. "I never knew a law student to be so capable to comprehend a question so quickly as John Hay," Shelby M. Cullom said, the Illinois state congressman at the time. "Mr. Lincoln knew him very well...before either of them came to Washington."[218]

Physically, Lincoln and Hay were opposites. Lincoln's thin, square-shouldered, 6' 4" presence towered almost a foot over John Hay's modest 5' 5" frame. Lincoln's sallow complexion, the high forehead framing an unkempt mop of dark hair, compared awkwardly to Hay's humble good looks, his silken and wavy brown hair, and the large brown eyes that revealed his thoughtful spirit.[219]

"I was only fifteen years old," Robert Todd ("Bob") Lincoln recalled of meeting John Hay in 1859. Young Lincoln felt "fortunate enough to be allowed to see something of him." He also admired Hay's success at Brown. His "liking for [Hay] became very great," recalled Jason Emerson.[220] Yet Robert Lincoln lacked Hay's natural genius for languages, history, and verse, himself recently failing his entrance examination to Harvard. Instead, he went off to Phillips Academy at Exeter to prepare for the Ivy League college.

Despite Hay's intellectual gifts, he began the new year of January 1, 1860, blanketed in gloom. Privately, he felt no promise about his future prospects. He held little hope about the life of a common western lawyer. "There is nothing romantic about the career of a second rate lawyer in a country town," he told his brother Charlie in late January. "My life is and shall be from this time forth and forever more (Amen!) very quiet and commonplace." Stealing a pun from poet Charles Lamb, Hay concluded his daymare as, "my first best cause least understood." Brought low by sensing the loss of fertile outlets to express his literary soul, the inner poet, as he had known at Brown and in Providence, Hay mourned western Illinois's arid literary climate. His heart reeled with a desire to do more, to be finer, to live larger. Springfield society was wanting. Even his legal studies with Uncle Milton didn't satisfy his intellectual energy.

"The consciousness that I am not what I was, that much of ambition, much of enthusiasm, much of vague hope that formerly shot athwart the shadows of my life, are gone," he wrote Hannah Angell in Rhode Island at this time. "I contrast my past with my present, and my moderate aims, and I feel a strange and sad self-pity."[221] Hay sensed that his brilliant life in Providence was gone forever. "How can anyone leave Scituate for Springfield?," he asked redundantly.[222]

Yet in the midst of this atmosphere, Hay appeared to experience a life-changing transformation during the early months of 1860. Between late January and mid-February 1860, he underwent an astonishing self-realization. From feelings of desperation on New Year's Day, by early February, Hay spoke about his future with optimism. Something had uplifted him. For one thing, he had created his own literary circle. For another, he began to participate in the political fervor of Lincoln's fledgling presidential campaign. "I feel for a moment as a pilgrim might have felt, in the days when angels walked with men," Hay said, sensing the cataclysmic shift around him. As if watching "the desolate sands empurpled and glorified with a fleeting flash of spiritual wings," he felt the excitement of Lincoln's candidacy taking shape in the early spring days of 1860.

Apparently, sometime in January, candidate Lincoln latched onto Hay's literary intelligence. "The office became the rendezvous of several young men of the town who were making some feeble efforts towards literary culture," Milton Hay said. "Lincoln was fond of mixing in."[223] There may be a clue here signaling the start of the working relationship between Lincoln and Hay.

Lincoln's Cooper Union speech of February 27, 1860, fully prepared and written in advance, was "a superb performance," claimed David Herbert Donald.[224] This one speech crystallized the candidate's views on equality—"let us have faith that *right* makes *might*, and in that faith, let us, to the end, *dare* to do our *duty* as we understand it." The poetic rhyme of "right" and "might" and "dare" and "duty" undoubtedly reflect a new contribution to Lincoln's voice by Hay. The speech set his political light ablaze, establishing his national reputation. Lincoln spoke directly to the heart of Northern abolitionists' sentiment, arguing unequivocally that *all* peoples, regardless of the color of their skin, were equal and free.

The speech also marked a line in the sand of Lincoln oratory. At seven thousand words, the oratory was long. Yet, a new conciseness in his arguments blended with a new literary flare in selected phrases, bringing an unprecedented power and refinement to Lincoln's prose. A few selections portray Lincoln's new voice.

As those fathers marked it, so let it be again marked
...this Republicans contend, *and with this...they will*
be content....
Human action can be modified...but human nature can-
not be changed.

[Addressing the southern states]:

You will rule *or* ruin
you will destroy the Union; and then, you say, the great
crime of having destroyed it will be upon us!
Neither let us be slandered...nor frightened
Let us have faith that right *makes* might,

Lincoln scholar Harold Holzer claimed that the Cooper Union address was "Lincoln's watershed,... Here the politician known as frontier debater and chronic jokester introduced a new oratorical style."[225] John Hay's contribution appears to be the source of this new oratorical style. It was probably Hay's first collaboration ghostwriting for Lincoln on a prepared speech.

Lincoln's respect for the power of words underpinned his understanding about effective public speaking. He believed that words shaped public opinion. He had long and frequently published opinions and editorials in the press, mostly the *Illinois State Journal* of Springfield and the *Lincoln Clarion* of Missouri. And while his intimate knowledge of dialectical speech patterns was not widely understood, it was exceptional.[226] "You can count from one to one hundred quite distinctly in about forty seconds. In doing this, two hundred and eighty-three distinct sounds or syllables are uttered, being seven to each sound," Lincoln said in his February 1860 lecture entitled "Discoveries, Inventions, and Improvements," addressing the "the great inventions of the world." Printing, or publishing, he added, "is the better half of writing." It was this, he concluded, that seeded discovery, invention, and improvements.

The idealist in Lincoln prized the purity of words to communicate thoughts, principles, actions, and intent. Before him, Virginia conservative Thomas Jefferson, in 1787, spoke of priceless value of "the fourth estate" in a democracy, the free press. Jefferson was certainly not the first nor last national leader to cherish this vital platform of views, news, and oversight. "Were it left to me to decide whether we should have a government without newspapers or newspapers without a government, I should not hesitate a moment to prefer the latter."[227] Thankfully, Abraham Lincoln did not have to choose between government and newspapers. Instead, during most of his presidential campaign and presidency, his two principal aides were seasoned in the published word: John Hay, who had an exceptional talent for eloquent writing and poetry, and George Nicolay, who had literally grown up on the press floor. There was no mistaking Lincoln's intent when he selected Hay and Nicolay as his campaign lieutenants.

Abraham Lincoln's animated debates with his political advisors buoyed Hay during his time also reading tedious legal treatises.[228] Blistering excitement ignited in Springfield's Republican circles in the wake of Lincoln's Cooper Union speech, hundreds of invitations swamped the Lincoln law office, requesting him to speak throughout Illinois and along the northeast coast. John Hay became so captivated by the groundswell surrounding Lincoln that in May 1860 he began sending poems of a political bent to the Springfield press, both Republican and Democrat papers. He signed these "J. H."

The first partisan poem he published on May 4, 1860, satirized the pro-slavery platform of the Democratic Party and especially its presidential candidate, Stephen Douglas.[229] Hay's three short rhymes, known as songsters in the nineteenth century, presented the volatile issues of the day in verse. They were titled "New Nursery Ballads for Good Little Democrats." First published in an unidentified newspaper (perhaps the *Missouri Democrat*), Hay took aim at the comic-tragedy of Douglas's about-face during his Senate campaign against Lincoln in 1858, when he reversed his support for the Supreme Court's *Dred Scott* decision to bring home the votes. With more whimsy than gravity, the rhyme and tempo echo the precision and economy of words that marked Hay's political verse.

> *Nursery Ballad I*
> Sing a song of Charleston!
> A bottle full of Rye!
> All the Douglas delegates
> Knocked into pi!
> For when the vote was opened
> The south began to sing,
> 'Your little Squatter Sovereign
> Shan't be our King!

Nursery Ballad II
Hi diddle diddle! The Dred Scott riddle!
The Delegates scatter like loons!
The Little Dug swears to see the sport,
And the southerners count their spoons.

Nursery Ballad III
There was a little senator,
Who wasn't very wise.
He jumped into convention,
And scratched out both his eyes.
And when he found his eyes were out,
With all his might and main,
He bolted off to Baltimore
To scratch them in again.[230]

Always seeking an outlet of his own, Hay needed a muse. Lincoln gave him a focus. Hay listened to Lincoln tell stories, rich in historical context. The politician's rough, uneducated, innate intelligence offered a sharp yet ultimately interesting juxtaposition to Hay's polished, classical education and scholarly knowledge. Hay was a valuable companion for Lincoln, who told the older man about things that fascinated him. Lincoln, in turn, understood that John was a rare talent. In addition, Hay, the natural wit, offered an anecdote to the older man's depression. Hay was a glimmer of light. The politician's ideals and vision matched Hay's distinctive eloquence.

Turning the pages of hopeless love poems of recent years, Hay dipped his pen into pro-Lincoln editorials and columns in the press. He soon recovered some of the intellectual energy and literary depth he had yearned for since Providence. By day, he wrote legal declarations and petitions for his studies with Hay & Logan. By night, he wrote pro-Lincoln poetry and columns.

The week leading up to the start of the Republican National Convention in May 1860, Hay boasted to his old flame, Hannah, "I am fitting myself for a place in the Corps *diplomatique* of Lincoln's administration." His shameless name-dropping was actually the work of a spurned admirer, spiting Hannah for her six months of silence, intimating there was no saying what might have occurred in the meantime. Quite a lot, in fact. Hay admitted that his "insanity has not yet changed its form from rhyme to politics...

unless Lincoln is nominated at Chicago" this month. Clearly fascinated with the politician, Hay's mention of "rhyme to politics" suggested he was contributing to Lincoln's campaign speeches.

The days as warm as summer before the opening gong of the Republican nominating convention in Chicago, ten thousand Republican delegates poured into the country's ninth largest city on May 16, 1860, clogging Chicago's streets and over-filling hotel rooms with 12,000 bodies. The delegates amassed fully 10 percent of the city's population of 112,000. So large was the expected attendance at the three-day nominating convention, May 16–18, 1860, Chicago scrambled to build a meeting space large enough to hold the assembled mass. At the eleventh hour, the National Committee erected a sprawling wooden wigwam, knowing full well the fire hazards and risk for loss of life. Delegates jammed in, hooting campaign cheers and waving colorful banners. Pro-slavery Democrats countered with their own partisan headlines, reviling Republicans' loathing of slavery's extension into the new Western territories. Even while the splintered Democratic National Convention, meeting three separate times that summer, didn't have a delegate-voted candidate, Stephen Douglas of Illinois and John C. Breckinridge of Kentucky stood as the Democrats on the national ballot.

In Chicago, the Republican National Committee adopted a platform embracing the pillars of Lincoln's "house divided" speech and the original principles of equality stated in the Declaration of Independence. The platform called to ban slavery from Western territories. Yet it fell short, loyal abolitionists believed, by pledging not to interfere with slavery in the South. Respecting the tradition that public office sought the man, not otherwise, Abraham Lincoln sent friends David Davis, Ward Hill Lamon, and Leonard Swett to the convention. George Nicolay was also in Chicago to monitor delegate voting, having published an influential portrait of Lincoln in the *Pike County Journal.*[231] Lincoln stayed home in Springfield with Hay by his side, receiving telegraph wires of breaking news. The headlines flashed the alarming shift of allegiances among the five candidates: William Seward, the US senator from New York; Ohio governor Salmon P. Chase; Missouri congressman Edward Bates; Simon Cameron, the US senator from Pennsylvania; and, Lincoln. Hay sat with Lincoln through the hours of May 18, monitoring the three rounds of voting for the nomination. They watched as the telegraph wire operator wrote down each word, recording each round of voting. On the third and final ballot, the dark horse candidate was declared. Abraham Lincoln was the Republican Party's choice for president. Shocked, the victor was no less surprised than his strongest opponent, William Seward, who had been favored to win. Seward had jeered Lincoln's candidacy before the convention. Now, he stood in his shadow.

John Hay rejoiced. "The hearty western populace burst forth in the wildest manifestations of joy," he wrote from Springfield. "Lincoln banners, decked in every style of rude splendor, fluttered in the high west wind." The town's church bells tolled and bright banners flew from the brick building blocks around Capital Square, fluttering in the western wind while spirited crowds assembled around the Illinois State Capitol rotunda. They cheered Lincoln's astounding victory. The crowd moved on to the residence of the Republican candidate, "the illustrious nominee," Hay said. "Soon the tall, gaunt form of the future anchor of the republic appeared in his doorway, and in a few good-humored and dignified words he thanked them for their kind manifestations of regard," Hay reported.[232] On this glorious day, as Hay did in many future press columns, he wrote about Lincoln in a mesmerizing way, a portrayal that reflected Lincoln's own self-appraisal. Hay gave public voice to the high regard Lincoln had of himself.

Within days, *Providence Journal* editor, James B. Angell, Hay's former Brown professor, invited him to write a special report on Lincoln's nomination. Hay was flattered. The thought that his college professors and the city's literati might read the piece and see his name in print swelled his pride. He was back in the game. Providence still remembered him. Writing from the land of Lincoln, the state of Illinois, Hay painted the backdrop of the plain western soul and Springfield's quiet pride as she "bears her honors as coolly as if rockets and cannons were no novelty in the backwoods." He called on a homily to the familiar saying, as Illinois votes so votes the country. In his last words, he said, "the nation has honored the honest man whom we have so long delighted to honor."[233]

The official Republican delegation traveled straight-away from Chicago after the convention closed. Pulling into the Springfield depot on the Great Western Railroad the next day of May 19, they came to deliver the party's formal declaration in person to Abraham Lincoln, the Republican nominee for president of the United States. From the train platform, Hay watched history in the making. The men stepped from the train through the engine's billowing steam. He welcomed them, walking with the delegates to their hotel and then on to the statehouse, surrounded by a large crowd. They were serenaded by "round after round of rousing, electrifying western cheers."[234] Carl Schurz, the well-regarded German-American, was among the speakers who saluted Lincoln's accession. During the coming months, Schurz, a native Bavarian, rallied a large block of the German immigrant vote for Lincoln.[235]

After the evening's supper, Hay walked with the National Committee members to the Lincoln residence. They gathered in the large parlor for the official declaration by convention chair, George Ashmun of Massachusetts.[236] Lincoln read a brief "letter of acceptance," his prepared remarks in hand, tendering his "profoundest thanks for the high honor" and imploring the help of the Divine Providence. Lincoln added an emotional reflection of his new reality. Accepting the nomination, he also expressed humility for the task before him. "Deeply and even painfully sensible of the great responsibility which is inseparable from this high honor," Lincoln said, reading from the letter written in Hay's hand and signed "Abraham Lincoln"—rather than "A. Lincoln," the traditional manner Lincoln signed correspondence. The unfamiliar signature, really a minor stylistic glitch, may reveal the fact that Lincoln did not sign this statement, nor even write it. The oversight may well have been by Hay, having drafted the speech as he did frequently in the months and years to come. [237]

Long into the evening, triumphant revelers partied until midnight, illuminating Springfield's main streets with candlelight. Bonfires blazed in public squares and home-made rockets broke the splendor of the starlit May sky.[238] Hay closed his *Providence Journal* piece of May 26, 1860, his voice idealistic and strong, "Abraham Lincoln will receive thousands of votes that never were Republican before."[239] His predication proved true.

Lincoln promptly handed the reins of his prosperous law practice to his junior partner, William Henry Herndon, a humorless and heavy-drinking man.[240] The Republican candidate moved into the scarcely-used governor's office in the statehouse. (The Illinois governor occupied the space on the rare occasions when the Illinois legislature was in session.) The 15-by-12-foot office, a modest size by contemporary standards, accommodated a sofa, a table, a desk, a few armchairs, and a dozen people.[241]

With his campaign office settled, Lincoln now needed staff. "I wish I could find some young man to help me with my correspondence," he told Illinois Secretary of State Ozias M. Hatch, an enterprising businessman and politician. "It is getting so heavy I can't handle it." Hatch recommended John "George" Nicolay as "entirely trustworthy," praise that Lincoln himself understood from his own experience with the young man who studied law under his guidance.[242] On June 7, 1860, Lincoln engaged Nicolay as his private campaign secretary and offered him $75 a month.[243]

About the same time, Milton Hay recommended his nephew John Hay to the committee covering Lincoln's extra expenses. The young man of "great literary talent and great tact," he said, could help with the avalanche of the candidate's mail pouring into the Hay and Lincoln law offices.[244] Lincoln's engagement of Hay and Nicolay occurred roughly about the same time, according to a source close to Hay, though biographer Michael Burlingame has suggested that Lincoln asked Nicolay first and then Hay. The historical record of the timing remains unclear.[245]

If judged by appearances alone, Nicolay frankly lacked the appearance of a politician's right-hand man. His thin, long face and dark Van Dyke beard gave him the likeness of a billy goat. "Although plain of appearance," Hay's sister-in-law later recalled, "Nicolay was attractive from his intellectual acquirements." In truth, Nicolay was somewhat awkward with people, perhaps a throwback to his orphan days. Lincoln, of course, knew both men well, having relied on their aid and loyalty months before his nomination. During the campaign's long days, the three worked in the close quarters of the statehouse, bonding under the stress of correspondence, meetings with politicians and newspapermen, and the daily crush of uninvited advisors and office seekers.

The Republican national committee urged Lincoln to abide protocol and not stump for his own election that summer, a request he complied. He met with hundreds of visitors in his makeshift office, masterminding ideas to pitch to the local, state, and national press. One influential ally was Horace Greeley, publisher of the *New York Tribune,* the daily newspaper with the nation's largest readership. It was a platform known to shape public opinion. Hay warmheartedly called the columns of the *Tribune* the "Gospel according to St. Horace."[246] Greeley did in fact see himself as somewhat of a kingpin of policy that swung votes.[247] His conservative politics and first-rate journalism made the *Tribune* a potent Republican broadside, a legacy it held for fifty years. For the paper's allegiances, Greeley and his successor, Whitelaw Reid, expected payback from the president in the currency of inside scoops and official high appointments. Sometimes the sitting president paid out and sometimes not. Lincoln did not.

Even if he didn't reward Greeley for his Republican allegiance, Lincoln valued Greeley's counsel and, more so, the media coverage in his influential paper. Lincoln relied on the press to educate and influence public opinion in a day when nearly nine out of ten urban dailies were affiliated with one party. Hay, too, with Nicolay, shared Lincoln's regard for journalists and journalism to influence what people knew and how they thought about it. More than fifty years before radio aired breaking news in real time and a century before television became universal in American households, print journalism was the main source of information and editorial opinion.

Milton Hay's June 1860 marriage to Mary Logan, the daughter of his law partner, offered the childless widow a new happiness. For Hay, his uncle's honeymoon liberated him from his legal studies. He seized the opportunity to begin writing a weekly political column for the *Missouri Democrat* of St. Louis, an assignment he continued through Lincoln's inauguration. His pen name, Ecarte, defined by its Latin definition "to distance oneself," may have represented the outlier's independence in Hay. On assignment, he wrote from Springfield on local, regional, and national politics, also sending in an occasional political poem. For additional exposure, he also sent poetry to the *Daily Democrat* of Chicago, among other papers.

Hay's press filings revealed the poet's fascination with dialect, ballads written in the vernacular language of the Mississippi riverboat dock. "Poor Little Dug," for one, a campaign jingle for the *Daily State Journal* of Springfield, Hay called "a new nigger song to an old nigger tune," poking fun at Democrat candidate Stephen Douglas and praising Abraham Lincoln's virtues. Drawing from the day's stereotypical lexicon of the White man, Hay fell into racial slang to grip Republicans' hatred for Douglas and his pro-slavery principles. [248] He gave voice to the radical wing of the Democratic Party who opposed Douglas, known as "Locofocos." In his ballad, Hay dramatized the Locofocos pushing Douglas overboard in an ironic twist that echoed their own mutiny from the Democratic Party.

> Dere was a little man and his name was Stevy Dug,
> To de White House he longed for to go—
> But he hadn't any votes through de whole of de Souf,
> In de place where votes ought to grow—
>
> ...He shivered and he shook in de cold North blast,
> And de wind from de Souf dat blew;
> But de Locofoco ship hove him over board at last,
> So his friends had to all heave-to."

Drawing on the dialect of his youth, Hay's doggerel elevated his poetic ballads from rancorous fun to dead-serious political protest against slavery. It was a potent style he returned to a decade later in the *Pike County Ballads*.

> A POLITICAL EARTHQUAKE!
> THE PRAIRIES ON FIRE FOR LINCOLN!
> THE BIGGEST DEMONSTRATION EVER HELD IN THE WEST!

Hay's, a.k.a. Ecarte's, typically measured voice broke free in superlatives when he described the immense Springfield rally of August 8, 1860. The first public appearance of Lincoln since his nomination offered a rare glimpse of the Republican candidate. The moment Lincoln stepped out onto the front steps of his family's residence that day, all the demanding groundwork by Hay and Nicolay was justified. Strikingly handsome, hearty, and with an air of calm confidence, the tall, hatless figure in a strapping white summer suit, drew the photographer's lens on the man of the hour, Hay and Nicolay standing close by.[249] A lightning rod of enthusiasm swept through the massive crowd.

"All Springfield is speaking in horse whispers," Hay wrote in the *Missouri Democrat* on August 9, 1860, portraying the scene of cheering Republicans parched by the steamy summer heat. Hay acknowledged to his readers, "It was certainly the greatest political demonstration that our State has ever seen." Extending over a sinuous track of two miles, the brilliant march of "blazing lights and glittering uniforms, [was] like a beautiful serpent of fire."

Roman candles held by the campaigners lighted their way. Disciplined parade battalions guided the disorderly mass, muddled crusaders drunk with joy. Hay contrasted the congenial Republican gathering to the Democrats' "rowdy plebeianism," as if "dirt and Democracy were somehow inseparable" in a Douglas gathering. Impossibly, the Democrats could not agree on a presidential ticket. By contrast the "intense decency and tremendous cohesion" of the Lincoln demonstration was a model of order and civility, said Hay.[250]

That evening, Lincoln delivered a crisp and concise speech. It was nothing like the meandering arguments he had delivered during the 1858 debates with Stephen Douglas. The brief oratory characterized a new style of speaking for Lincoln, Hay said. Especially when he addressed an important constituency such as the Springfield rally, Lincoln read from a prepared speech. Hay concluded his passionate repartee in the *Missouri Democrat* by quoting Walt Whitman to describe the candidate's performance :

> I will not say it was this, I will not allege it was that—
> I will swear it was glorious!"[251]

"Rally Photograph," Lincoln Home, Springfield, Illinois, August 8, 1860. Courtesy of The Huntington Library.

Chapter 10

FINDING HIS MUSE

The days of late summer and early autumn of 1860 mirrored the country's own fractured union, an America deeply divided by partisan politics and sectional divisions. Unusual climatic disturbances in the Atlantic Ocean swept in six powerful hurricanes, bringing torrential rains and destruction along the Gulf Coast of Louisiana and Texas. Cyclones also erupted without notice, exploding abruptly out of eerie clear skies and starry nights. Turmoil was literally in the air and everywhere in society.

Hay asked *Providence Journal* readers to turn their attention further west "from the midst of the smoke of the prairie-fires" to Illinois, where there was "a fight waging such as they never saw before." Known for its Republican majority in the north, from Chicago to Freeport, the state historically voted Democratic in the southern reaches, from Springfield to the Kentucky and Missouri borders.[252] "This year," Hay wrote on August 23, 1860, "there is a minister of the gospel who has buckled on his armor and gone forth to meet the foe, and is astonishingly successful." He was demonstrably enthusiastic about Lincoln, as well as his own campaign lingo. The Republican candidate had captured Hay's soul. Buoyed by the promise of Lincoln's bid for the presidency, the young man campaigned for him in the press, writing speeches for him when Lincoln asked, and drafting letters for his signature day after day.[253]

Reporting from Springfield on October 11, writing as Ecarte, Hay wrote of Lincoln's primary wins in Pennsylvania, Indiana, and Ohio. He recreated images of celebration and revelry: "The quiet October air was frightened with rockets and pyrotechnics," magnificent displays of fireworks. The large procession forming on Springfield's Capitol Square marched to the stirring tunes of the band. Through illuminated streets, heralders walked on to the Lincoln residence. Fifteen cheers erupted the night's silence. Illinois Senator Lyman Trumbull, inside with the Republican candidate, stepped outside, announcing that he was to speak rather than Lincoln. "Excusing him on account of his engagement to make a speech on the 4th of March next."[254] Hopeful of Lincoln's election, Trumbull referred to the presidential inaugural speech. The reference sent shockwaves through the mass. The campaigners went wild. Trumbull counseled restraint, at least until the general election on November 6.

Next up was Stephen Logan, Milton Hay's law partner and father-in-law. "We only need wait till November to ratify the election," shouted Logan. Roaring into his own brim-fire, Logan offered sincere congratulations to his fellow attorney Lincoln. "This was a glorious political lovefeast," Hay said, closing his October 11 column.[255]

The unresolved issues miring the presidential election of 1860 were in part shaped by Americans' unease with a fast-changing culture. No one was untouched. Restlessness was a condition known to every person and family, a general if unacknowledged feeling of the day. The pace of new inventions and the latest norms affected every corner of life. The face of the American worker had changed dramatically over the past two decades under the shift from a country dominated by farmers to a growing number of industrial workers. Newfangled occupations appeared with advances in the way Americans produced, bought, and sold, and in the way products were brought to market: the grocer, surveyor, gardener, butcher, cabinet-maker, clerk, and engineer. The fabric of the American workforce and economy transformed with unprecedented speed.

The shifting sands were further disturbed by the arrival of Charles Darwin's hugely influential book *On the Origin of Species,* published in 1859. Darwin's controversial theory displaced the deity and good works in the lineup to evolution, instead explaining that populations evolved over generations through natural embryonic selection. *On the Origin* played directly into the debate between the presidential candidates about race and slaves, ethnicity and immigrants, and the meaning of "life, liberty and the pursuit of happiness." Darwin's book was joined by John Stuart Mill's essay "On Liberty," originally published in London and reaching American bookstores in 1860. Mill repudiated the tyranny of governments to ensure the liberty of citizens, advancing constitutional checks on authority. Restraint on absolute governmental control and unchecked evolution fueled controversy about limitations on government, immigration, and whether to limit or extend slavery.

The national debate on slavery pitted Democratic candidate Stephen Douglas against Republican Abraham Lincoln. Each challenged the other on principles of morality and liberty. The candidate field was mired in acrimony, including Southerner John C. Breckinridge of Kentucky and constitutional unionist John Bell of Tennessee. By late autumn 1860, Hay had set aside his legal studies to devote all his days to Lincoln's campaign. The Illinois governor's office was his home and office with Nicolay. They often worked well into the night. With freshening breezes and cold nights, the heat of the race took the bite off the Midwestern chill of late October.

On the morning of the presidential election of November 6, 1860, torrential downpours and high winds engulfed Springfield and much of the West and Northeast, yet failed to deter voters from the polls. Over 81 percent of the eligible all-male, all-White electorate voted.

Hay accompanied Lincoln on his walk to the statehouse. (Mary Lincoln, a disenfranchised woman, remained at home.) From there, Illinois Secretary of State Hatch escorted Lincoln and Hay to the polls to cast their votes. "The dense crowd immediately began to shout with that wild abandon that characterizes the impulsive heart of the west," Hay wrote in the *Providence Journal.* "There was something infinitely delightful to the people in the spectacle of a man, great in character and in circumstance," as Lincoln ignored the dignity of his own position and became one among the people.[256]

His vote cast, Lincoln returned to his small room in the statehouse, surrounded by Illinois party men, receiving breaking news on the telegraph wires. Among close friends, said Hay, Lincoln appeared "the ear of the nation and the hub of the solar system." When the "magnificent roll of Republican thunder…came echoing out from New York and Pennsylvania," the two largest electoral states, all measure of propriety let loose. Inside and out, every person in sight rejoiced in the glory of imminent victory.

Lincoln walked with Hay into the Capitol's Representatives Hall. He "was received with a strange outburst of enthusiasm which never for an instant grew disrespectful." By nightfall, Lincoln knew he was to be the country's first Republican president, even as he polled the lowest popular vote in United States history, capturing 1.9 million votes and less than 40 percent of the total. His Democrat opponent, Stephen Douglas, secured 1.4 million votes and 13 percent of the total, carrying only the state of Missouri in the Electoral College. Lincoln won eighteen of the nation's thirty-three states, followed by Breckinridge with eleven states and Bell with three.

Lincoln held a clear majority in the Electoral College, 180 out of the 303 electorates. He carried every Free Soil state in the Union except New Jersey. He had succeeded in navigating a clear and principled course that had cut through the deeply divided Democratic platform. A "peculiar warmth" embraced Springfield and the old statehouse, Hay wrote. It was an ardor that reflected "the recognition by the world of the great soul that they have honored and loved for many years." John Hay revealed in this one statement the emotion of his regard for Abraham Lincoln. Magically, he found himself in the center of Lincoln's world. "Honor" was the word he had repeated again and again during the presidential season as Lincoln ascended from Republican nominee to president-elect.[257]

With Lincoln's election to the presidency, John Hay felt gratitude, even humility, having fulfilled a mission for the candidate. Now, as Lincoln prepared to depart Springfield for the nation's capital and the Executive Mansion in a matter of weeks, John Hay prepared to complete his legal studies and sit for the Illinois bar examination. He expected soon to accept an entry-level position in the law office of Logan & Hay. In his new work, as many times before, he depended on the generosity of his uncle Milton Hay.

Lincoln spoke not a word in public during the weeks following his election. Yet his views, even his very own words, were widely published through the anonymous writings of John Hay in the St. Louis-based *Missouri Democrat,* the *New York World,* and the *New York Tribune.* Editorials appearing in the Springfield *Illinois State Journal* by Lincoln himself, which he had written in decades past, as well as editorials by Hay and the *Journal's* publisher, broadcast the president-elect's positions.[258] Otherwise, Lincoln made no formal speeches until soon before his inauguration. He depended on John Hay and the Republican press to speak for him.

Within days of Lincoln's election to the presidency, Hay and Nicolay moved out of the Illinois governor's statehouse office and set up a 20-by-20-foot furnished office in downtown Springfield's Johnson's Building. Located on the city's main east–west street of West Washington, the space offered "quite a good room," said Nicolay. Lincoln worked from home, hoping for some privacy from the barrage of uninvited callers.[259] Nicolay served as the president-elect's chief private secretary, replying to relevant correspondence and making a bed for himself in the new office. Hay, on the other hand, prepared for his bar exam, remaining close by in Milton Hay's law office and witnessing the swelling pile of incoming mail for Lincoln. The president-elect's attempt to keep up with hundreds of daily letters and telegraphs proved hopeless. His box overflowed with requests and petitions from party organizers.

Sitting one January day with the Illinois Supreme Court justices, Lincoln brought mail with him to read, casually reaching "into his capacious coat pocket, and [bringing] up a handful of letters...to look over them," Hay reported in the *Missouri Democrat* on January 9, 1861. Hay's familiarity with Lincoln's daily habits and the smallest of impulses was testimony to his continuing proximity to the president-elect. "He reads letters constantly—at home—in the street—among his friends. I believe he is strongly tempted in church."[260]

As late as December 1860, Hay and Nicolay knew virtually nothing about Lincoln's plans for them in Washington, or if he had any plans for them at all. The president-elect was consumed with developing national policy and putting together a Cabinet. He finally yielded charge of his correspondence to his two aides. Lincoln dictated as Hay and Nicolay jotted down notes, the précis for each secretary's daily output of seventy-five letters or more.

It was Nicolay who Lincoln tapped as the official private secretary to the president, the one official position on the Executive Mansion staff for an administrative aide. Nineteenth-century presidents had small personal staffs, most without professional training in national politics.[261] Yet there was a certain irony that Nicolay, twenty-nine, 5' 10" and every bit of 130 pounds, was now the official gatekeeper to the President of the United States. The thin Bavarian immigrant, whose early poverty had bred poor health and an acerbic manner, soon would ruffle the feathers of congressmen in Washington.

There was no official place on the White House staff for Hay. Lincoln paused about what to do, even as he prized his literary value. "We can't take all Illinois with us down to Washington," Lincoln was believed to have grumbled to his financial backers. Milton Hay stepped in and promised to take care of his nephew's expenses during his first six months in the nation's capital, according to early Hay biographer William Roscoe Thayer. It was one more contribution by Uncle Milton to advance his nephew's prospects. Milton Hay's generosity gave Lincoln the breathing room to arrange an official government appointment and salary for Hay, offering John the golden chance to serve the president of the United States. "Well, let Hay come," Lincoln was known to have said.[262] In Abraham Lincoln, John had a muse for his writing. Hay had paid work for his literary bent.

Rising tensions between Northern and Southern states, between unionists and secessionists, proslavery and antislavery advocates, and even between agricultural and commercial entrepreneurs demanded that Lincoln make no missteps in the expression of his principles and policies. He could ill afford any misunderstandings or failed nuances, no off-the-cuff blunders. Extreme sentiments of the different factions were already enflaming the winds of war. Lincoln recognized the force that inflammatory statements had on shaping public opinion. Misleading news and deceptive declarations were a menace to "'the irrepressible conflict at the point of the bayonet,'" Lincoln argued, yet all of them "mean nothing without definition."[263]

Hay's unique ability to craft just the right words went to the heart of Lincoln's understanding about the complex public relations job that lay before him. The president-elect recognized the weight of expressing himself and the policies of his administration with precise words and phrases. Drawn to Hay by his knowledge of classical literature and his achievement in poetry, Lincoln, a gifted storyteller himself, soon came to depend on his private wordsmith, a beguiling young man who turned a clever phrase with ease.

"He has higher ambitions," said Charles Hay of his son. "I hope his ambition will always be well directed."[264] With his aspirations, his desire to serve, and his resilient sense of duty, John was a patriotic Republican committed to the cause of the moment. He prepared to serve the new president. His father mused, "The poet is born but the orator is made by ultimatum."[265] John Hay and Abraham Lincoln personified that wise maxim.

Chapter 11

DEXTERITY UNDER PRESSURE

During the ninety days between Abraham Lincoln's election on November 3, 1860, and the start of his train passage to Washington, DC, on February 11, 1861, the president-elect prepared to take the reins of the nation by steadily increasing his leadership of the Republican Party.[266]

It was a time riddled with grave risks. On December 20, 1860, South Carolina seceded, declaring that "the United States of America is hereby dissolved." No previous act was so devastating to the existence of the nation, less than a century old. The House of Representatives officially "regretted" the Southern discontent, recommending remedies to "preserve the peace and the perpetuity of the Union."[267] The president-elect remained unwavering in his trust in the Union, holding fast to the legal foundation of the Constitution and unwilling to compromise his resolve that slavery's extension must be stopped. "The instant you do, they have us under again," he told an Illinois representative. "All our labor is lost, and sooner or later must be done over."[268]

Since its creation, the nation's capital had been mostly governed by wealthy Southerners—ten of the previous fifteen presidents hailed from Southern states—and now as secession gained momentum, Confederates set their sights on Washington, DC, as the capital of the new confederacy. Lincoln thought otherwise. Supported by the Republican Party, the president-elect gained confidence in his authority.[269] Even in the face of the mounting threats to the Union and requests from conservative Republicans for Lincoln to announce his views, he was not to be dissuaded from the hard-fought principles that guided his governance.[270]

New York Tribune publisher Horace Greeley shared Lincoln's conviction as he boarded the train steaming out of New York City on his way to Springfield in January 1861. Greeley came to urge Lincoln to appoint Salmon P. Chase and Schuyler Colfax to his Cabinet. Both rivals in the presidential campaign and the Republican Party, Lincoln agreed.[271] Also influencing Lincoln was New York Republican kingpin Thurlow Weed, who championed archrival William H. Seward of New York for secretary of state, the most senior position in the president's Cabinet. Lincoln was steadfast about constructing a Cabinet of rivals, as Goodwin eloquently portrayed in *Team of Rivals*. The president-elect imagined that adversaries could offer the best advice during a difficult time with Southern Democrats.[272]

John Hay opened the new year of 1861 penning an ode commemorating Garibaldi's recent fight to unify Italy. As his thoughts imagined Garibaldi's bold unification of Italy, the untitled poem celebrated Lincoln's campaign to reunify the United States, a battle Hay had faith was certain to end in victory. The unpublished stanzas reveal the poet's languorous style, tempo, and rhyme, and his characteristic alliteration.

So ring out the sorrow
That cumbered the past,
And ring in the morrow
With joys that shall last.
Ring for the New Year!
Merrily ring!
Music to welcome
Our brave young king!
. . .
In Freedom's calm, majestic power,
Our good old ship at anchor lies,
Nor fear the clouds that darkly lower
Over the red Southeastern skies.
She feels her timbers staunch and true
As when of old she ploughed the seas,
Over the wash of eastern waves—
Over the wild Atlantic sea—
Still is the sob of struggling slaves,
And loud the anthem of the free.

...
Still let us hope the better time
When the spent shafts of faction fall,
As in the Union's golden prime,
And love for one be love for all.
When Union rings from shore to shore,
And Party's sordid clamors cease,
And Freedom's spirits hovers o'er
To bless us with eternal peace!

And when that blissful day shall come,
Saint Louis! 'twill be thine to hear
The voice of Trade's deep echoing hum
Grow loud and far from year to year,
Till crowned with honor all thine own,
Beneath the Union's flag unfurled—
Thou sittest on thine Iron Throne
Queen of the mighty Western World

Hay also reported that Lincoln condemned Buchanan's final annual message to Congress of December 1860, in which he stated the federal government had no claim preventing states from seceding. Opposing this, Hay projected Lincoln's view that a state had no right to secede, writing under his pen name Ecarte in the *Illinois Daily State Journal* on January 22, 1861. "A State cannot secede from the others and become independent of them, at its own will," Hay said. The idea of an indivisible Union goes back beyond the Constitution, beyond the articles of Confederation, beyond the Declaration of Independence," previewing themes that Lincoln brought to life a month later in his speech at Philadelphia's Independence Hall, and also in his First Inaugural address. "The 'articles of confederation' declared the supremacy of the Government. The Constitution is the bond between the people," Hay explained.[273]

John Hay spoke with pride when he talked about his work for Lincoln and his closeness to him. Preparing for life in the White House, he predicted, "I shall be so busy with the business of the mythical being called 'the public' that I shall have little time for private cares." His self-esteem rose as he spoke about his growing admiration for Lincoln. "I am beginning to respect him more than formerly." Perhaps a sign of his youthful hubris, some historians have regarded this statement as disrespectful. Especially problematic for Hay's critics was his description of Lincoln as "the Cincinnatus of the prairie," referring to the ancient Republican Roman farmer and dictator who became the model of Roman virtue.[274] Certainly, youthful pride narrowed his judgment, while literary classics expanded his encyclopedic mind. Hay revered Lincoln, perhaps more than anyone else during the sixteenth president's life. The analogy of Lincoln to Cincinnatus was shrewd, rather than belittling.

Days like the early winter months of 1861 happen in every life, yet the meaning for John Hay emerged imperceptibly. As gray skies and snowfalls tapered to sun and rain, temperatures rose to melt the thick ice, and sleighs gave way to carriages. On February 4, 1861, a Monday, the Supreme Court of Illinois conferred the authority to practice law on John Hay.[275] He had passed the bar exam.

That very day, 650 miles southeast of Springfield in Montgomery, Alabama, seven Southern states declared the birth of the Confederate States of America. Devastating. Trespassing the laws of the Union was equally a slap to the essence of Lincoln's House Divided speech of June 16, 1858, when Lincoln said:

> A house divided against itself cannot stand.
>
> I believe this government cannot endure, permanently, half slave and half free.
>
> I do not expect the Union to be dissolved—I do not expect the house to fall—but I do expect it will cease to be divided.[276]

A divided Union was exactly the nation Lincoln was stepping forward to govern.

Soon after, John Hay received his formal invitation from the governor of Illinois to join the president-elect's special train on its twelve-day journey to the nation's capital:

> Sir, You are respectfully invited to participate in the courtesies
> extended to Hon. Abraham Lincoln, President elect,
> by the several Rail Road Companies
> from Springfield to Washington.[277]

Word of Hay's presidential appointment had reached Providence. Brown's 1858 class poet was joining the Lincoln White House.[278] He was to be among Lincoln's official family.

As Hay packed his trunk, he penned a piece about the presidential transition for the *New York World*, January 28, 1861. "The progress of the President-elect [is] fortunate in its influence upon the tone of public feeling in the Union," he wrote as he praised Lincoln's unifying defense against the tide of Southern secession.[279] Yet Hay remained silent about Lincoln's anxieties over the divided nation, its people frightened by the creeping pall of civil war.

Republican friends had dreamed up the special train tour for the president-elect, a media spectacle campaigning their man in twenty-one cities across 1,904 miles in the major conservative strongholds along his journey to the nation's capital. They had organized celebratory stops in Indianapolis, Columbus, Cleveland, Buffalo, New York, Albany, Harrisburg, Philadelphia, and others, offering Lincoln a forum with party loyalists and an opportunity to air his views directly to the people and the Republican press.[280]

Seventeen-year-old Robert Lincoln returned home from Harvard just in time, joining his father, mother, and two younger brothers on their move to Washington. His brief farewell to Springfield, where he began his college preparation at Illinois State University, turned all the more pleasant with his reunion with John Hay, who shared Lincoln's openly ambitious mind, ironically a place his eldest son was unable to tap. Robert didn't resent Hay's natural rapport with his father, now or in the years to come, instead enjoying his good cheer. Arm in arm on the eve of their departure, the two young men made their rounds through Springfield's neighborhoods, "to make their adieux." Robert donned his smart new plug hat, his first, using it to shoo Hay along when he lingered over partings with lady friends. He rarely passed up a chance to flirt.[281]

The morning of Abraham Lincoln's historic departure from Springfield, John Hay rose early in Grandfather Hay's house. He stepped through the foggy dawn to meet the president-elect's suite at the train depot, raindrops trickling from the building's shabby eaves. Even at this early hour, one thousand well-wishers surrounded the president-elect, appearing saddened by "the gloom of parting with neighbors and friends." Pale and quivering with emotion as he shook each hand, Lincoln bade "farewell to the community in...which he has lived for a quarter of a century," Hay recorded in his diary.[282]

"The stormy morning" described the mood of the moment, Hay wrote as Ecarte in the *New York World*. Lincoln's leave-taking was sad to the bone, the weather seeming only "to add gloom and depression to their spirits."[283] Abruptly, the incoming rush of the steam train charging into the station and the pitch of the bells ringing broke up the Lincoln party. They scattered into the four-car train. Just as the conductor rang the gong to signal their departure, the president-elect stepped forward on the platform of his private car. He raised his hand to ask for a moment. The conductor stopped. Lincoln spoke:

> My friends, no one, not in my situation, can appreciate my feeling of sadness at this parting.

He paused to reflect on the enormity of these words:

> I now leave, not knowing when or whether ever I may return,
>
> with a task before me greater than that which rested upon Washington.

Calling on President George Washington's inspirational guidance, he summoned the deity's will:

> Without the assistance of that Divine Being who ever attended him,
>
> I cannot succeed.
>
> With that assistance, I cannot fail.[284]

The slow, deliberate couplets and parallel structure echoed the solemnity of the moment. The alliteration and measure of time impregnated Lincoln's words and phrases with a steady rhythm:

> Trusting to Him, who can go with me, and remain with you,
>
> and be everywhere for good, let us confidently hope that all will yet be well.
>
> To His care commending you,
>
> as I hope in your prayers you will commend me,
>
> I bid you an affectionate farewell.[285]

Lincoln's dependence on God's will gave biblical consequence to the life-and-death polarity in his words. The short speech, eloquent, even poetic, offered a fluid and complete expression. It was extraordinary.

"Masterful," "succinct," "lyrical," and "poetic," said David Zarefsky, scholar of American historical rhetoric, describing the effect of Lincoln's landmark speech.[286] "His finest poetry so far," stated Gabor Boritt in *The Gettysburg Gospel.*[287] The writer "possessed a rare facility with the spoken and written word that amounted to a formidable literary talent," said Douglas L. Wilson in *Lincoln's Sword.* "We have known Mr. Lincoln for many years," said Edward D. Baker, editor of the Springfield *Illinois State Journal* editor, yet never "have we heard him…ever utter an address which seemed to us so full of simple and touching eloquence."[288] Perfectly symmetrical, the climax of the verse arose in line 5, framed by four lines on each side:

> Let us confidently hope that all will yet be well.

Lincoln's Springfield speech signaled a poetic eloquence that rose higher and finer than his Cooper Union speech a year before. The parallel sentence structure, White said, "became a pattern that was coupled with an almost metered cadence" in future speeches.

The Springfield address marked a pivotal transition in Lincoln's oratory. It replaced the down-to-earth phrases, the circular and winding, long sentences bare of imagery that had previously characterized the country lawyer's oratory. In its place appeared lyrical verse expressing Lincoln's inspirational ideas, projected with masterful lyricism. Lincoln's previous oratory quite plainly was "lacking distinction of phrase," historian Vernon Louis Parrington said. [289]

Why, now, did Lincoln's oratory change, branching out into measured eloquence? White has maintained that the Springfield address was "delivered extemporaneously" and "was not prepared."[290] Yet in all probability, the drafted address was memorized by Lincoln before he gave verbal expression to the words. The evidence of perfect symmetry, parallel verse, and trained poetry in the words and structure exhibited the hand of John Hay.

"He bade farewell to his friends and neighbors, asking their prayers to the God 'without Whose aid I cannot succeed, and with which I cannot fail,'" John Hay later recalled.[291] *New York World* reporter Henry Villard, who had covered the Springfield departure and also Lincoln for the past six weeks, wrote about the emotional farewell: "Towards the conclusion of his remarks himself and audience were moved to tears." Followed by loud applause and cries to Lincoln, "We will pray for you," the president-elect departed. "In the gray winter twilight, from the platform of a car at the Springfield station, the journey was struck," said Hay.[292]

To Lincoln's friend and security guard Ward Hill Lamon, the speech struck a final note, according to Lincoln historian Ted Widmer.[293] "He knew that he would not return," says Widmer. Indeed, he never saw Springfield again.

Lincoln entered his private car, "abstracted, sad, thoughtful," Hay said. [294] The engineer opened the throttle full-out upon reaching the flat Illinois planes. Pitching eastward through prairies that turned into quagmires of putrid ponds along the rail tracks, the train traveled at twenty miles per hour, driven by the powerful Rogers locomotive. Lincoln settled in to reconstruct his Farewell Address, "partly by [his] own hand and partly by" dictating to Nicolay. He also "may have used Hay's notes," Borritt said.[295] Traces of Hay's handwriting are evident in the original document in the Library of Congress, notably the middle sentences. John Hay also had a copy of the address, which Lincoln undoubtedly used to commit the speech to memory.[296] Underway, Lincoln rallied, making notes for other speeches at a spirited pace. The president-elect's ideas and thoughts "filled the sheets" of his large pad. The two secretaries took notes and made copies.[297]

Twenty guests traveled with Lincoln to Washington, including his wife, Mary, and their three sons, Robert, Willie, and Tad. Counselors, aides, bodyguards, and the president-elect's personal physician were among the suite. The dozen reporters on board filled the nation's press with news of the journey and Lincoln's speechmaking, wiring their columns to the home office at station stops. The lot of young journalists included the likes of Henry Villard, twenty-five, of the *New York Herald*; Joseph Howard, twenty-seven, of the *New York Times;* Henry M. Smith, thirty, of the *Chicago Tribune*; Uriah Hunt Painter, twenty-three, of the *Philadelphia Inquirer*; and five correspondents for the *Associated Press*.

Nicolay introduced Thomas Cole Evans of the *New York World* to Lincoln. Gazing at Lincoln from behind his gold-rimmed spectacles, the journalist Evans was captivated by the president-elect's eyes: "A sad look in them and a humorous one also, and depth and mystery, and boundless tenderness and compassion." Of Hay, who Evans saw often in Washington, he described him as "almost beardless, an almost boyish countenance." John Hay's apparent reticence was puzzling to those who didn't know him. His silence made others feel uncomfortable, disquieted by his manner. And, similar to Lincoln's melancholy, Evans saw "a touch of sadness in [Hay's] temperament," a gloom well-known to people close to him.[298] Hay was not widely understood nor really liked by some of Lincoln's senior advisors, notably William Seward and Salmon Chase.

The second day of the train journey, February 12, 1861, marked the president-elect's fifty-second birthday. Steaming down the rails from Indianapolis to Cincinnati, Hay reported that Lincoln had "shaken off the despondency" of his leave-taking. He now "looks and talks like himself," Hay said. This day's Cincinnati correspondent, the pen name Hay used for this report to the *New York World*, characterized the president-elect as full of "good humor, wit and geniality,"[299] a portrait Lincoln might have liked.

In Cleveland, bowing and waving from his horse-drawn carriage along a magnificent two-mile stretch of Euclid Avenue, Lincoln stopped to bend down to a little girl, pretty but buck-toothed—she was Flora Stone, daughter of Amasa and Julia Stone, Cleveland's wealthiest family. Amasa Stone, a railroad entrepreneur, would soon advise Lincoln during the war. The very young Miss Flora Stone presented him with a small bouquet of flowers. The president-elect replied with a kiss on the ten-year-old's cheek. If Flora had been standing next to her older sister, Clara, John Hay might have caught his first glimpse of his future wife, Clara Louise Stone. "The whole party has very pleasant recollections of Cleveland," Nicolay wrote to his fiancée, a memory that Hay surely remembered on his wedding day in February 1874, celebrated from the Stone's Euclid Avenue mansion.[300]

In Columbus, Ohio, however, Lincoln bungled an address to the Ohio State Legislature that the *New York Herald* and *New York Daily News* reporters framed as "a most lamentable degree of ignorance."[301] It was more than clumsy oratory. It was an embarrassment for Lincoln's patrons. His unrehearsed and ad-libbed speech produced a messy combination of loosely shaped policy and ill-framed statements. The *Baltimore Sun,* an unlikely ally, called Lincoln a clown. The *Cincinnati Daily Commercial,* a friend, lauding his sincerity, questioned why he could not "in his own plain way tell the truth."[302] Even his strongest supporters stirred with nervous disappointment. *New York Herald* reporter Villard despaired that Lincoln's speeches during this passage "strengthened my doubts as to the capacity for the high office he was to fill."[303] Young James A. Garfield also felt distress.

Charles Francis Adams Sr., the one surviving son of President John Quincy Adams and among the most prominent of Republican loyalists, confided his own concern to Richard Henry Dana on February 18. Lincoln's "speeches have fallen like a wet blanket here," he said. The powerful Massachusetts congressman, known familiarly as "the Archbishop of Antislavery," was not one to disappoint. Adams's soul wept for the nation and the Republican Party. The president-elect was making a fool of himself and the party with his botched, ad-lib oratory. "They put to flight all notions of greatness," he admitted. Writing in his diary, Adams despaired the president-elect's discouraging public appearances during the train campaign, a passage instead designed to fortify and boost his leadership. Lincoln's oratorical missteps did just the opposite. "In this lottery we may have drawn a blank," Adams confided privately. The president-elect's public statements, Adams said, "betray a person unconscious of his own position as well as of the nature of the contest around him." The Republican Party was beginning to have grave concerns about the future head of state. "I confess I am gloomy about him," Adams admitted.[304]

John Bigelow, the wealthy Republican pillar who stood a strapping 6' 3" in his bare feet—every inch the match to Lincoln's lean 6' 4"—was also sanguine about the recent "forensic performances," he said on February 21. [305] William Seward, who was traveling with Lincoln, confided that the idea of having to coach Lincoln made him "more depressed than he had been previously during the whole Winter." For decades, the conservative press, Whig and Republican alike, had been friendly to Lincoln. Not so now. His unprepared remarks cost him early capital with Republican loyalists and the fourth estate. His missteps of judgment when speaking about Union and antislavery policy handed fodder to the country's partisan press.[306] The opposition widely aired the president-elect's verbal gaffes.[307]

On the special train, Lincoln and his advisors read the damning criticism. A few days after, in New York City, Lincoln spoke not one word. Arriving on a pleasant afternoon in late February, thousands of people gathered. The city noise fell silent when the omnibuses and other vehicles were turned off. There was "an unusual hush in that busy part of the city" on Broadway," said Walt Whitman, on the occasion of his first meeting with Lincoln. Two or three shabby carriages drew up to the posh Astor House hotel, the tall figure of the president-elect stepping out and pausing on the sidewalk. He looked up to the building's granite walls, stretching his arms and legs, turning to acknowledge the vast crowd. Lincoln did not speak.[308] Instead, the president-elect's advisors and speechwriter were drafting his prepared, written statement for Philadelphia, the hallowed ground of the Declaration of Independence.

Eleven days into the journey, as Lincoln's train drew closer to Washington, the president-elect and his team felt weary, yet invigorated by the "religious fervor in the welcome everywhere extended" to Lincoln, Hay recalled.[309] Intelligence from Washington, however, warned of a plan to assassinate the president-elect as he passed through Baltimore on February 23. Baltimore was filled with secessionists. It had a history of political violence. The evidence of malice was certain.[310] "There may be trouble in Baltimore," Hay wrote to a friend. "If so, we will not go to Washington, unless in long, narrow boxes."[311] Hay, Nicolay, and Robert Lincoln packed revolvers under their coats in concealed harnesses.[312]

Hay assisted Lincoln at a sustained pace, writing correspondence and drafts of messages and speeches. "I have had no time to think calmly since we left Springfield," he wrote a friend.[313] The duty was infectious if demanding. "Very laborious and exciting," he said of the Springfield-to-Washington passage.

In Philadelphia, on the bitter cold morning of February 22, 1861, Abraham Lincoln unfurled the American flag of thirty-four stars in the clear light of the rising sun, raising the majestic colors in front of Independence Hall. Inside the hall just minutes before, he had regained his oratorical footing with a short, prepared speech that previewed themes that ten days later, March 4, he would emphasize in his First Inaugural address.

> All the political sentiments I entertain have been drawn,
>
> so far as I have been able to draw them,
>
> from the sentiments which originated and were given to the world
>
> from this hall in which we stand.
>
> I have never had a feeling politically that did not spring from the sentiments
>
> embodied in the Declaration of Independence.
>
> I have often pondered over the dangers which were incurred

by the men who assembled here
and adopted that Declaration of Independence.

I have pondered over the toils that were endured
by the officers and soldiers of the army,
who achieved that Independence.
I have often inquired of myself, what great principle or idea it was
that kept this Confederacy so long together.
It was not the mere matter of the separation of the colonies from the mother land;
but something in the Declaration giving liberty,
Not alone to the people of this country
but the hope to the world for all future time.

It was that which gave promise
that in due time the weights should be lifted
From the shoulders of all men
and that all should have an equal chance
This is the sentiment embodied in that Declaration of Independence."

It was in these first two hundred words—succinct and metaphorical, echoing the poetic cadence and alliteration of the Springfield speech—Abraham Lincoln emphasized the Declaration of Independence as his guiding principle. Recognizing the potential dangers and difficult work required of these ideals, he declared that all men "should have an equal chance," even if they are different. And he promised to do everything in his power as president to save the Union on these terms. Underlying Lincoln's prepared speech at Philadelphia, lacing the measured phrases, was John Hay's poetic verse—the iambic cadence, the alliteration, and the life-death polarities. Unveiling his powerful principles, Lincoln actively employed the talented writer at his side. He followed these two hundred words, eloquently composed, with an ad-libbed personal appeal, another two hundred words delivered in his plain, conversational style. He claimed the second half was "wholly an unprepared speech," a disclaimer of sorts.

Lincoln had cause to admire Hay's dexterity under the pressure of the last days of the train journey. He needed a heroic turnaround from his own self-styled country oratory. And he hoped to make a stand in Philadelphia, to preview his forthcoming First Inaugural address as commander in chief. "I would rather be assassinated on this spot then to surrender to it."[314]

That night, February 22, 1861, steaming south from Philadelphia, Hay wrote, "tomorrow we enter slave territory," meaning Maryland. Lincoln had separated from his suite. He had boarded another special train to Washington that evening at nine o'clock, an hour when he was assumed to be asleep, wearing a Scottish plaid cap and long military coat and accompanied by a bodyguard and friend.[315] He arrived in the nation's capital at dawn on Saturday, February 23. The special train passed through Baltimore without him.

As the light dipped below the horizon in downtown Washington on the late afternoon of February 23, horse-drawn carriages, laden with trunks and supplies, transported Mary Lincoln and the Lincoln boys, with Hay and Nicolay, through the half-frozen muddy streets. Two blocks from the White House, the Lincolns and the secretaries stepped into the Willard Hotel. This was to be their makeshift home for the next ten days. They had abandoned the idea of occupying the private house originally rented for the Lincoln party, due to the heightened security risks. Overbooked, the Willard hotel graciously welcomed the Lincoln family into a private suite, though the public house had no room for Hay, Nicolay, and others during inaugural week.[316]

Celebrating Willard's fashionable stature, Nathaniel Hawthorne had christened it "the center of Washington and the Union," the grand public meeting place of the nation's capital. Its prominence rose above "the Capitol, the White House, or the State Department," he said.[317] It was the place to see and be seen. Characteristically, in the days before the inauguration, Lincoln kept to himself and talked little with senators, congressmen, and lobbyists filing through his suite, what Hay described as a "moist delegation of bores" in a *New York World* filing. "That he is not before this torn in pieces, like Actaeon"—the mythological Greek hunter transformed into a stag and then killed by his hunting dogs—"is due to the vigor of his constitution, and the imperturbability of his temperament."[318] Lincoln worked in his methodical fashion, paying no mind to the political excitement around him. Instead, he remained troubled by the dangers of Southern secession and its drain on the government treasury. The urgency of the circumstances pressed on Hay and Nicolay, who worked "early and late with a mass of correspondence of the extent of which I can convey no adequate idea," Hay said.[319]

Even as the packed Willard appeared like a frat party before college graduation, with "many ladies in the parlors as to make it seem like having a party every night," Nicolay said, Southern defection left a gaping hole in Washington society. "The old race of self-serving, swaggering politicians" hailing from south of the Mason-Dixon Line, Hay explained, "whose ruling principle was selfishness tempered by whisky, was losing its absolute control."[320] Unlike the Virginia estates of George Washington, Thomas Jefferson, and George Mason, there was no Abraham Lincoln fortune or elegant plantation. "The old social leaders," said William O. Stoddard, an occasional presidential secretary, "were bitterly disloyal" to the Union and Lincoln presidency. Southern secession sentiment, Stoddard observed, filtered through Washington's residential neighborhoods. "Go up any street, and from the open windows you could hear the unwearied piano," said Stoddard, "dinging away at "Maryland, My Maryland," "The Bonny Blue Flag," or "Dixie"—patriotic tunes of the rebel South.[321] Southerners pointed the accusatory finger at Lincoln. The Republican president-elect was responsible for secession. Lincoln was to blame. "If he does not avert this impending disruption of the border states in his inaugural address, his life will be forfeit," an anonymous letter threatened, dated March 2, 1861.[322]

Setting aside politics and racial beliefs, the plain truth about ending slavery promised to bankrupt the United States government. Freeing four million slaves and compensating their owners the fair market value of $800 would add up to the extraordinary sum of $3.2 billion. Great Britain had done this in 1833 when it freed 130,000 African slaves, most living in the West Indies. Doing it here flamed fears of financial disaster. [323] The economic calamity turned out to be true, yet not as expected. The South's economic dependence on enslaved labor would slowly unravel during four years of civil war, devastating the Confederate states' wealth and prosperity.[324]

An odd mix of anxiety about the consequences of secession and the excitement of new beginnings percolated through Washington during the days leading up to the inauguration. "The golden days have fallen upon the capital," Hay wrote in the *New York World* on March 1. Infusing the air was the "drifting incense" of honeysuckle. A "premature balminess and warmth" softened the early spring days. Drawn by the rhythmic knocking and tapping of carpenters' hammers on the canopied platform going up over the east entrance of the United States Capitol for the inauguration, Hay approached the imposing classical building. In these halls, he would spend hundreds of hours during Lincoln's presidency, delivering presidential messages and waiting for bills, briefs, and replies from senators and congressmen. "I reached for my hat, and, shaking the dust of the gallery from my sandals," he said, "ascended the dome, or rather the pillared tiers," where sculptor Thomas Crawford's masterpiece, *Freedom,* was to be mounted. Standing 234 inches and weighing fifteen thousand pounds, the bronze statue's completion was delayed by war, ultimately completed on December 2, 1863.[325]

Hay scaled the one-hundred-fifty steps to the "light, aerial gallery," reaching the highest point and opening to the magnificent panorama before him. Pierre Charles L'Enfant's majestic 1791 plan for the federal city had failed to inspire buildings of equal merit in the seventy years since. Instead, "the city unrolls its dusty magnificences," Hay said, a curious place of false pretense and pompous airs. Polite Southern society lived side-by-side with squalid neighborhoods populated by eastern Europeans and freed Blacks. Looking out to Pennsylvania Avenue atop The Capitol, he gazed at the "sprawling, chaotic town," he wrote as "our own correspondent in the *New York World.* The stupendous harmonies of its design reveal themselves in broad avenues, which converge upon the capitol as all the roads of the Roman empire converged upon that golden milestone by the Pincian gate." Yet as splendid as it appeared, "it would be difficult to conceive of a meaner street in architectural adornments than Pennsylvania Avenue," he said.[326]

Volunteer troops swarmed the streets to raise security and suppress violent outbreaks. The city streamed with inaugural activity, celebrants "crowding the bars, shuffling along the aisles, populating the corridors of the bear caravans of hotels," Hay reported. The nation's capital teemed with "generals, and colonels, and majors, and captains, governors, senators," men chewing tobacco, spitting, swearing, and littering hotel halls with dirt, paper, and cigar stumps.

Five blocks north of the Capitol building, near the neo-Greco limestone post office, construction workers put the finishing touches on the temporary hall hosting the inaugural ball of six-thousand guests. Organized by the Republican Party of Cleveland, a group of Western bankers and entrepreneurs, the ball was led by Amasa Stone, the entrepreneurial bridge builder and railroad developer. Stone would become President Lincoln's chief railroad advisor during the war, planning Union rail routes that transported soldiers, horses, and supplies, even through enemy territory.[327]

Lincoln's arrival in the nation's capital marked a new era for the city, no less the nation: a western log-splitter unfamiliar with cosmopolitan ways. He had never held executive office of any kind, not as senator or governor nor military chief. Shocking as the newfangled Republican president was to Washington's traditional ranks, Abraham Lincoln's country manner proved to be a groundswell. Since the nation's founding, there had never been a western president.[328] Southern belles took matters in their own hands during the inaugural festivities. "Some of the most distinguished ladies [declined] to attend the ball," Hay said.[329] As Lincoln began the task of guiding the Union through its unprecedented crisis, John Hay answered the president's call to work by his side as his editor, correspondent, journalist, and speechwriter.

Chapter 12

THE CONFIDANT

Scattered rain through the early morning hours of March 4, 1861, gave way to a north wind and the promise of a clear day for the large crowd gathering around The Capitol. They watched the weary senators drifting out of the classical chambers after an all-night session, officially ending the 36th Congress. The congressmen returned to their lodgings before hurrying back for the afternoon's presidential inauguration. Patriotic band music filled the air as fife and drum marchers serenaded. Colorful flags and Republican banners fluttered in the stiff breeze. An infectious anticipation uplifted the assembled observers, rubbing off on even the dry-witted Montgomery Meigs, the fiercely loyal general and civil engineer who admired the "brilliant attendance" of the gathering masses.[330]

At noon, outgoing President James Buchanan arrived at Willard's in his fine open carriage to escort the president-elect to the ceremonies. Following them in separate carriages were Mary Lincoln and their sons, and private secretaries George Nicolay and John Hay. Twenty-five-hundred federal security personnel scoured the city. They marched along the two-mile processional along Pennsylvania Avenue between the White House (then called the Executive Mansion) and Capitol Hill, protecting the nation's capital and ensuring Abraham Lincoln's safety. Arriving at The Capitol, Hay walked with Lincoln to the President's Room, where the president-elect and Buchanan withdrew to speak privately before the ceremony began. Honoring the custom, the old and the new presidents appeared an odd pairing, "the petty past and the great future," said Hay. The seventy-year-old Buchanan, "gray and weather beaten," looked elderly and broken in contrast to Lincoln, fifty-two and visibly prepared to lead. Hay watched from the nearby corner. Expecting that "each word must have its value at such an instant," Hay admitted disappointment when he learned that the solitary old bachelor had advised Lincoln, "I think you will find the water of the right-hand well at the White House better than that at the left." Not a word about statecraft, Congress, or the impending crisis. Lincoln confided later to Hay that "he had 'not heard a word of" what Buchanan had said."[331] He was absorbed in his own thoughts, consumed "through every chamber of his heart and brain" with the ultimatum he intended to offer southern sympathizers in his inaugural speech.

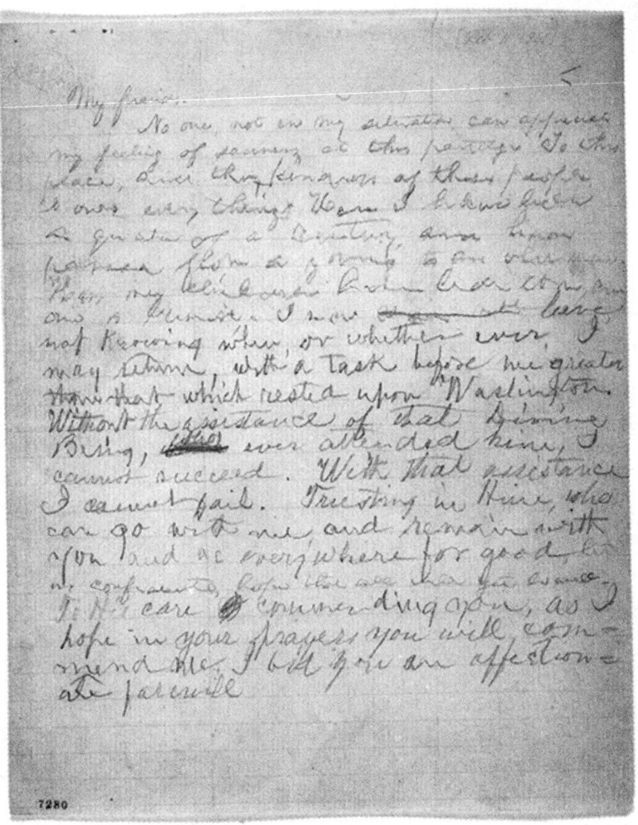
My friends
No one, not in my situation, can appreciate
my feeling of sadness at this parting. To this
place, and the kindness of these people
I owe every thing. Here I have lived
a quarter of a century, and have
passed from a young to an old man.
Here my children have been born, and
one is buried. I now leave,
not knowing when, or whether ever, I
may return, with a task before me greater
than that which rested upon Washington.
Without the assistance of that Divine
Being, who ever attended him, I
cannot succeed. With that assistance
I cannot fail. Trusting in Him, who
can go with me, and remain with
you and be everywhere for good, let
us confidently hope that all will yet be well.
To His care commending you, as I
hope in your prayers you will commend me, I bid you an affectionate farewell

7280

Abraham Lincoln's farewell speech, February 11, 1861, Springfield, Illinois; Lincoln's handwriting in first two lines; thereafter, John Hay's handwriting. Courtesy of Abraham Lincoln papers, Manuscript Division, Library of Congress.

At 1:15 pm, the military formed a double-ranked line as long as The Capitol was wide, forming a one-hundred-foot column in front of the semi-circular platform over the steps of the eastern portico. The robed justices of the Supreme Court entered, followed by Abraham Lincoln. Stepping forward onto the platform, his hat removed and held by his archrival Stephen Douglas, the ranking senator from Illinois, the president-elect delivered his First Inaugural speech. The address had been weeks in the making. It was originally printed in Springfield, then "Mr. Lincoln and Mr. Seward revised it in Washington," said Hay. Seward counseled Lincoln to temper his hostile tone. He also proposed language from a speech of his own delivered a year before on the Senate floor.[332] The final document reflected edits, additions, and the replacement of sixteen of the speech's thirty-seven paragraphs. Almost half of the original text was altered from its original form. It was an example of the making of a Lincoln speech, the product of multiple edits and voices. Nicolay penned the "good many changes," said Hay, the final of which was given to the press.[333]

Lincoln's intent was to establish the blueprint of his presidency and to define the ambiguous situation facing the nation. Seven states had seceded, forming the Confederate States of America and serving a devastating blow to the fabric and governance of the nation. It was a sneering protest to the Republican presidency, an act of treason against the Constitution. Lincoln remained silent on slavery as the reason for the crisis. Rather, he stressed the importance of preserving the Union and affirming the Declaration of Independence as the foundation of American government. He decried even one state's secession. The courtroom lawyer centered his argument in the law, the nation's constitution. As president, he stated he had no proper authority to negotiate with the seceded states. "'With you, not with me, rests the awful issue. Shall it be peace or the sword?'"

The rapt audience was at once captivated and also troubled. "Everywhere you could see among the crowds on the avenue and in the hotels," Hay said, "that spirit of hushed expectancy with which we watch the piling of the clouds for a summer storm." Only revolution and treason could lead to war. Only in self-defense would America take up arms, Lincoln said.[334] Shaping the speech to express the lasting bonds of friendship, appealing to a larger vision and a higher spirit, Lincoln concluded his address and the start of his presidency with allegorical and literary appeals.

We are not enemies, but friends.
We must not be enemies.

Though passion may have strained,
it must not break our bonds of affection.

The mystic chords of memory, stretching from every battlefield, and patriot grave,

To every living heart and hearthstone,

All over this broad land, will yet swell the chorus of the Union,
when again touched, as surely they will be,
By the better angels of our nature.

The president called on the South and the North to remember their shared past. He appealed to the South to honor "the mystic chords of memory," a metaphor for union and the United States of America.[335] The polarities of life and humanity—friends/enemies and passion/affection—intensified the emotional appeal of the closing sentence, which opened with "the mystic chords of memory" and closed with "the better angels of our nature." The writer beckoned to the past to inform the present sentiment, appealing to Southerners' love of heritage to remind them of their love for God and country.

The eloquent closing of the address—"By the better angels of our nature"—evoked Charles Dickens in an obscure yet beautiful passage from *Barnaby Rudge* (1841). It also recalled the reference to "better angel" in Shakespeare's *Othello,* a remark made by Gratiano, the Venetian nobleman, referring to restrained human impulses. "The keynote of the whole address will be found in this passage, which is so wise and excellent," Hay said. In his March 4, 1861, column in the *New York World,* John Hay revealed his personal insight into Lincoln's intent.[336] The speech's trained eloquence reflected Hay's contribution.

The literary allegory appeared as a new element in Lincoln's First Inaugural address, uniting with alliteration and giving a musical emphasis to the major themes. Key sections of the speech adopted the repetitive timbre of alliteration to heighten the listener's awareness of "property," "peace," and "personal security" in the third paragraph; "period," "precedent," and "peculiar" annotating time, tradition, and contemporary distress in the twelfth; and "principles," "proposition," "perpetual," "plighted," and "perfect" in the fifteenth paragraph. These words defined Lincoln's framework for his administration. He also appealed to the diverse views of his Cabinet members, paraphrasing the less-than-brilliant text suggested by Seward, who suggested Lincoln a "note of fraternal affection." Robert Schlesinger noted in *White House Ghosts* that the final address "polished the thought into poetry."[337] In a similar vein, Michael Burlingame said of the inaugural address's response to Seward's suggestion: "Like a rhetorical alchemist, Lincoln transformed those leaden words into a golden prose-poem."[338]

Upon closing the address, Lincoln turned to Chief Justice Roger B. Taney, who executed the Oath of Office, then the custom of the day. Taney, a southern Maryland Democrat and the author of the 1857 *Dred Scott* majority opinion opening slavery to the Western territories, was doing his duty rather than extending his honor to the Illinois Republican. Lincoln, his hand on the Bible, felt the same. Moments later, cheering broke out when the president vowed to "preserve, protect and defend the Constitution of the United States." The national press praised Lincoln's brilliant performance for its "intellectual and moral vigor," said the *New York Times*, its "conciliatory spirit," defended the Albany *Evening Journal*, and its affirmation that "the Federal Government is still in existence," reported the *New York Tribune*.

Lincoln's First Inaugural has been admired by historians for the "intellectual and studied" tone, said White, who viewed the newly minted orator as "a master of phrase and words."[339] Adam Goodheart regarded Lincoln's speech "as one of the greatest pieces of oratory in American history." Admiring its literary bones, he said, "it was inspired, tactful, perceptive, ageless in its eloquent final paragraph." Goodheart also admitted the president's address was "almost entirely ineffectual," it had no bearing on events.[340]

The divided political landscape gave voice to sharp biases splitting the nation apart along sectional and party lines. Southern politicians and newspapermen described the address as "incendiary," "a fiat of war," "a beastly thing." Answering the criticism, John Hay echoed Lincoln's outlook when he portrayed the speech to be "as conciliatory as it could possibly be in consistency with the obligation imposed by the official oath to preserve, protect, and defend the Constitution."[341]

Abraham Lincoln's literary acumen, a recent development, has been explained as a metaphor for his genius.[342] He is considered one of the country's most literary presidents. Despite these claims, Republican Party pillars were known to cringe at Lincoln's folksy storytelling and rambling invectives, as he displayed during the rail journey to Washington. It was a trait that belied his "defective" education, a fact Lincoln freely admitted. The president recognized his provincial oratory might well-nigh undermine the effectiveness of his office.[343] Having mastered political speech-making and legal court-room tactics, the Illinois politician was not known as poetic. In the past, Lincoln's public speaking was best described as interrogatory arguments in the courtroom and on the campaign trail.

His oratory aside, Lincoln's wise and inspiring ideals for the nation were without peer. He had cleverly drawn parallels between slavery and ignorance and between emancipation and enlightenment when he explained in an 1859 speech that writing and printing "emancipated the mind" from the "slavery of the mind."[344] Though untrained to write as well as he might like, Lincoln was naturally sensitive to speech and ear.[345]

Following the afternoon's ceremonies, the White House doorman of five presidents, Edward McManus of Ireland, a gray-haired man, welcomed President Lincoln and his family, with Nicolay and Hay, to their new home.[346] With his secretaries by his side, the long figure of the president shuffled up to the second floor's east side, taking in the Executive office, looking out the central window to the Potomac River running south. Here is where his upright desk stood. Next door in the adjacent space was the work room of Hay and Nicolay. The young men's sleeping room was across the hall. "We have very pleasant offices," Nicolay wrote his fiancée, "and a nice large bed room, though all of them sadly need new furniture and carpets."[347] Threadbare and dingy, Hay said the White House felt like "an epoch, if not of gloom, at least of a seriousness too intense to leave room for much mirth."[348] Mary Lincoln added to the gravity of the place. She was none too pleased that Hay and Nicolay had joined the presidential family. And when the first lady wasn't pleased, everyone paid the price.[349]

Judged by physical appearances alone, the tiny White House staff of 1861 seemed something of a motley crew for the chief executive of the United States government.[350] In addition to Hay and Nicolay, the Executive Mansion employed old Edward at the front door, assisted by Irish-American Thomas Burns. There was the president's messenger, a Louis Burgdorf of Germany; a cook, the president's butler, and the family's servants, the gardener of the grounds, and the first lady's seamstress, Elizabeth Keckley, a former slave.[351] These were joined on occasion by assistant secretaries to the president, and footmen and servers for official dinners and receptions.

US Capitol depicting Abraham Lincoln's first inaugural, March 4, 1861; Thomas Nast, illustrator, *New York Illustrated News.* Courtesy of John Hay collection, John Hay Library, Brown University.

It was the joyous play of the Lincoln boys, Willie, eleven, and Tad, eight, that sent a fresh breeze through the cheerless environment. The White House had never seen the likes of these two energetic youngsters, their imaginary patrols propelling them on expeditions to the rat-infested kitchen and servants' rooms in the basement, up the stairs to the grand East Room, and up another flight to their father's mahogany- and wainscot-trimmed office. Across the hall they clamored through the west side's private family rooms and up one more flight to the spider-webbed attic that housed a jumble of broken furniture.

Lincoln himself didn't exactly cut the image of a dignified chief executive, at least to the eyes of twenty-two-year-old Henry Adams, grandson and great-grandson of presidents. The western circuit court lawyer's gangly appearance, his long neck, rumpled suit, and large ears appeared anything but presidential.[352] Adams, like his father, Charles Francis Adams, who despaired Lincoln's public displays on the passage to Washington, saw a "plain [and] ploughed face; a mind, absent in part [and] features that expressed neither self-satisfaction nor any other familiar Americanism, but rather the same painful sense…of needing education."[353] Lincoln's easy and steady countenance undeniably gave the appearance of a life of prodigious manual labor. He exhibited a no-nonsense steadiness whether in conversation with one person or addressing a large crowd. And unlike Henry Adams, Lincoln had no airs of pretense, no attempt to stand straighter or look more handsome, to act more graceful.[354] Believing the president to be intelligent, confident, and sound, Hay, who became Henry Adams's closest friend after 1880, did not record speaking about Lincoln with Adams.

Faced with the grave prospects of his presidency, Lincoln chose Hay and Nicolay to fulfill what he believed to be the most important job of his office: communication. While the small personal team of amateurs looked nothing like the professional White House corps of contemporary strategists, economists, and foreign policy experts, "they steered through political waters," contemporary *New York Times* columnist David Brooks has explained, "relying on experience, instinct and conversations with friends."[355]

Nicolay, the political secretary and office manager, supervised the flow of visitors in the land of the outstretched hand. Called "Nico" by Hay, he was otherwise known as "the bulldog in the anteroom," the gatekeeper who filtered members of Congress, lobbyists, and office-seekers through the Executive offices. The latter-day chief of staff and front-of-house secretary, Nicolay controlled access to Lincoln and transmitted the president's messages to the Senate and House. He generally supervised the business of the Executive Mansion. His undivided devotion to Lincoln and his awkward manners earned him harsh critics.[356] Nicolay was soon a controversial figure. "The grim Cerberus of Teutonic descent who guards the last door which opens into the awful presence," said Noah Brooks, an occasional assistant secretary, describing Nicolay. He "has a very unhappy time of it answering the impatient demands of the gathering, growing crowd of applicants."[357] Nicolay cared nothing about the criticism and grumbled to his fiancée, Theresa Bates, "I become disgusted with all the glaring faults, the hollowness and heartlessness of the great crowd of people of both sexes whom I meet and see."[358]

Hay's admiration for Nicolay provided just the right duality to Lincoln's suite. The president secured Hay's official government appointment on March 20, 1861, as a clerk in the Interior Department detailed to the president's office. Hay was officially assigned to Lincoln's side, paid an annual salary of $1,500.[359] Nicolay was paid $2,500 a year as the official private secretary to the president.[360]

Hay, the literary secretary and the president's speechwriter, worked many days unseen by visitors. He was known, however, to give "exact expression to infinitely delicate shades and distinctions of meaning, dealt with situations that required the president's written word," said historian Charles W. Moores.[361] Hay later explained to William Herndon, with more than a hint of probity, that Lincoln "wrote very few letters...at last he gave the whole thing over to me, and signed without reading the letters I wrote in his name." The president also entrusted Hay or Nicolay to personally deliver messages of a "delicate matter" to individuals outside of Washington, rather than chance the written word and prying eyes.[362]

John Hay's blushed face and dashing attire struck seasoned Washington politicos as effete, arrogant. He appeared younger than his years. Precocious, handsome, and really a political nobody, Hay's confidence made little room for the humility to know that he still had a lot to learn. Obviously smart, Hay also needed to work on being smarter about being effective in Washington's partisan society. His innocence protected him.

Insiders were convinced that Lincoln had brought two novices to the epicenter of the nation's capital from Illinois. Perhaps, yet Hay and Nico were hard workers and capable companions. They "stood by the captain's side as the ship of state was steered through the tumbling seas, the heavens rent with fury and swept with passion, hatred, and death," Hay remembered.[363] Organizing Lincoln's schedule and cherry-picking newspaper articles for the president to read, the secretaries trafficked the immense volume of mail streaming into the Executive Mansion. They drafted responses when warranted. Hay and Nicolay also stood as the human barriers to the second-floor east offices, greeting visitors and filtering out undesirables. "The throng of office-seekers is something absolutely fearful," Hay said. "They come at daybreak and still are coming at midnight."[364] Men lingered in the mansion's East Room and outside on the portico and along the walks.

Hay and Nicolay also oversaw the assistant clerks assigned to the Executive offices, the temporary hires taking on the overflow of correspondence and copying Lincoln's speeches and messages. Every word and list were written by hand, often in fine script. The clerks drafted guest lists, menus, and seating charts for state dinners and receptions. Hay and Nicolay oversaw them, managing the socially delicate task for the president, instead of the petulant first lady.[365]

Their nicknames for the president, always out of earshot, ran the gamut from "The Chief" to "The Ancient," their favorite, "Old Abe" and the "Tycoon," an affectionate reference to the title that people in the Western Hemisphere used for *shōguns,* Japanese military commanders. "We were the daily and nightly witnesses of the incidents, the anxieties, the fears, and the hopes which pervaded the Executive Mansion and the national capital," said Nicolay and Hay in *Abraham Lincoln, A History.* "The President's correspondence, both official and private, passed through our hands; he gave us his daily official intercourse with Cabinet officers, members of Congress, governors, and military and naval officers."[366]

On the occasion of the first public reception of his presidency, Lincoln appeared robotic in his repetitious bows and nods, the shaking of one thousand hands that wearied even his "iron fingers." (Herman Melville once observed that Lincoln "shook hands like a good fellow—working hard at it like a man sawing wood at so much per cord."[367]) Socially awkward, the president's taciturn manner in mixed company failed to equal his decisive and principled nature. The long evening a success, Lincoln shuffled into the East Room with the first lady striding a few paces to his right, outfitted in an excessively expensive dress. Hay and Nicolay closed the suite.[368]

Working and living at the pleasure of the president, Hay and Nicolay "lived at the White House, worked next to the President's office, slept across the hall, accompanied him to the theater, and acted as his eyes and ears in Washington and beyond," said Nicolay.[369] Often viewed by observers as a team of two, a pair, Hay actually had a unique place in Lincoln's private world. The mercurial Nicolay did not. Except for Cabinet members Seward, Stanton, and Cameron, all others did not "equal [Hay] in real power," said Stoddard, the occasional assistant secretary.[370]

Within the first month, Nicolay felt sick from the intense pressure. He abhorred the endless stream of seemingly everyone "who wants to see the President *for only five minutes.*" At last, pleading, Nicolay persuaded Lincoln to limit the president's public reception to three hours a day, 10 a.m. to 1 p.m., ending before the midday meal.[371] Arguably unsuited for the constant day-to-day interface with people, Nicolay was notoriously "impassable." The sociable Hay had a gentler approach, calling on his clever wit, double-talking callers, leaving "fellows who went away, not [knowing] how much he told them."[372] He understood that "verbal needles" were sometimes the only defense against aggressive callers.

One bloke claimed he must see the chief executive at once.

"The President is engaged now," Hay replied. "What is your mission?"

"Do you know who I am?" the caller questioned.

"No, I must confess I do not," Hay replied.

"I am the son of God."

"The President will be delighted to see you when you come again," Hay said, "and perhaps you will bring along a letter of introduction from your father."[373]

Lincoln appreciated Hay's clever humor. So did John Russell Young, the Irish-born Philadelphia newspaperman, a contemporary of Hay's whose beat included the White House. He admired his "smooth, low-toned" speech and the fact that his social graces "did much to make the atmosphere of the war-environed White House grateful." He likened Hay to Alexander Hamilton of George Washington's presidency and his Revolutionary War command, a precedent so perfect it might have been scripted. "As Hamilton did in similar offices," Young explained, Hay showed "the tact and common sense which were to serve him as they served Hamilton."[374]

Ron Chernow revealed in *Alexander Hamilton* that "the relationship between Washington and Hamilton was so consequential in early American history—rivaled only by the intense comradeship between Jefferson and Madison—that it is difficult to conceive of their careers apart." With the pressing demands of war with England, President Washington claimed, "it is absolutely necessary…for me to have persons that can think for me, as well as execute orders." In Hamilton, he had a deputy who "was able to project himself into Washington's mind and intuit what the general wanted to say, writing it up with instinctive tact and deft diplomatic skills."[375] The Hamilton–Washington partnership bore close parallels to the Hay–Lincoln bond. Young's insight acknowledged a truth that few others understood: Hamilton was the first president's speechwriter and chief aide, just as Hay was for Lincoln. John Hay had reason to know of Alexander Hamilton's unique role with General Washington. In his own friendship with Colonel James A. Hamilton, Alexander Hamilton's son, Hay had received a lock of George Washington's hair. President Washington had given the gift to Mrs. Hamilton, and she to her son.[376] Col. Hamilton saw reason to give the lock to John Hay, whom he may have known had a similar role with President Lincoln that his father had had with President Washington.

Chapter 13

RECORDING THE CIVIL WAR PRESIDENCY

Within the first hundred days of his presidency, Abraham Lincoln had entrusted Hay with a personal, seamless, and unspoken alliance. It was an unusual bond. Hay loved to talk and "was so genuine and so obvious that it infected his listeners," said Joseph Bucklin Bishop, a Brown classmate. [377] He most of all cherished writing. The massive volume of written documentation Hay left in his personal and official papers—now residing in the archives of the Library of Congress, Brown University, and the National Archives—reflected the fact that he needed to write.[378] He had a natural tendency to commit words and phrases to paper, decades before the manual typewriter.

Hay chronicled the Lincoln presidency in his diaries, press columns, and correspondence.[379] The diaries, which Hay began at the start of the Civil War, filled several notebooks, some quite small, fitting into a breast pocket, others the size of a book. The diaries chronicled acts and conversations as they occurred in the Civil War White House. Recorded in real time, Hay's private journals were an analog of the modern-day Oval Office tape recorder or a transcript of a C-SPAN stream. They unveiled Lincoln up close, what he thought, what he said, and how and with whom he spent his time.[380] "He had a vast amount of other material, comprising much unwritten history," artist Frank G. Carpenter said.[381] Hay recorded private and confidential matters, with Lincoln's knowledge and permission. The president entrusted Hay, as well as Nicolay, with a generous latitude of discretion.

Planning a biography for future years, the two secretaries chronicled the Lincoln presidency.[382]

Hay's diary notes revealed verbatim conversations with the president. Similarly to Lincoln, Hay didn't rely on the recall of memory, a faulty mechanism, he believed. He wrote most of his diary entries within twenty-four hours (or less) of when they occurred. Hay distinguished himself within Lincoln's suite for "the literary flair of [his] journal," Burlingame said, the one historian who has read them all and transcribed many. "Sparkling as champagne" and "most attractive as literature," claimed *New York Evening Post* editor Horace White.[383] Sometimes with grace, other times with the course language of disgust, Hay committed four years of private confidences to paper.

The president's naturally passive temperament, his fatalism, also contributed to his traits of compassion and tolerance, his willingness to overlook mistakes. It was Lincoln's negative capability that contributed to his greatness. His gratitude for what he had in the absence of what he didn't have earlier in life gave him a fair-minded freedom to welcome able contributions from individuals of all kinds, young or old, ally or adversary.[384] In this, Lincoln tamed Hay's impatience, often triggered by a hungry office-seeker or contrary politician. Hay's impertinence, the president understood, reflected the young man's inexperience. Perhaps, too, it reflected his sensitive nature, a thin skin that cringed when annoyed.

From Lincoln, Hay came to learn about grace and forgiveness. Much later, Hay admitted his "rapid judgments, the hot prejudices, the pitiless condemnations, the lyric eulogies," were "born of an honest enthusiasm and unchecked by the reserve which comes of age and experience."[385] Years later, with the wisdom of age, fifty-five-year-old John Hay acknowledged the existence of his brash, young self. Inspired by Lincoln's goodwill, Hay began to soften his sarcastic observations, omitting the catty and off-color declarations in his diary.[386] He knew that the president "disliked anything that kept people from him who wanted to see him." The Executive Mansion, Lincoln explained, was the people's house. The president and the White House were open to the public.[387]

John Hay's days were prescribed by the president. At ease with this uncertainty, Hay's private journal revealed something of the unscripted nature of his job. His days were Lincoln's days. He was available any time to write, to ride, to walk over to the telegraph room, or the house of a general or a Cabinet member. He often accompanied the president into Washington society.

At Lincoln's urging, Hay continued to write for the press. He had ended his association with the *Missouri Democrat* after the election, now sending his journalism to the *Missouri Republican* of St. Louis and several New York City papers, including the *Times,* the *World,* the *Express,* and the *Tribune,* as well as the *Philadelphia Press*, the *Associated Press*, the *National Intelligencer,* the *Cleveland Leader,* the *Evening Post,* and *Harper's Weekly.*[388] Hay's hundreds of anonymous and pseudo-anonymous columns and editorials between spring 1861 and winter 1864 advocated Lincoln's beliefs and ideologies, often in the president's own words, recorded by Hay in his diary. His journalism advanced the president's plans, actions, and policies. "He had rare accomplishments, wrote with grace and precision, with the capacity for continuous silent industry," Nicolay said. "The touch of his pen can be felt in many of the letters that went from the Executive Mansion."[389] By contrast to Lincoln's self-taught Hebraic style born out of love of the Bible, Shakespeare, and Blackstone, which were stacked on the president's desk, Hay's style was that of a poet whose sense of literature lay deep in his soul.[390]

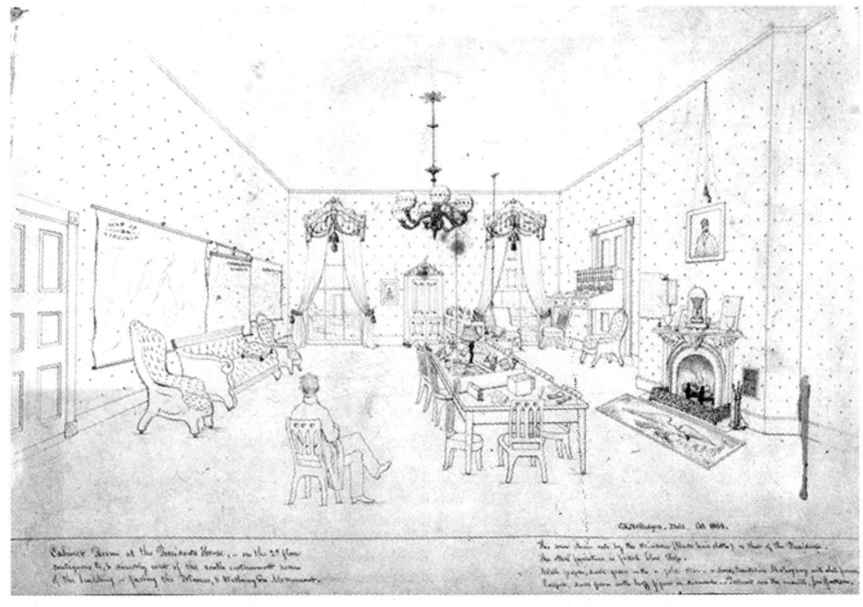

Sketch of President Abraham Lincoln's office, Executive Mansion, ca. 1861. Courtesy of Western Reserve Historical Society.

Hay compiled his Lincoln-era newspaper clips in four scrapbooks, now archived at the Library of Congress. Methodically assembled, the scrapbooks became the record of Hay's prose and journalism during his time with President Lincoln. He gathered just about every newspaper column he wrote during Lincoln's administration. Hay curated the diaries and scrapbooks with exacting accuracy, preserving by pasting into the scrapbooks the texts he wrote with and for Lincoln, the living record of his contribution to Lincoln's presidency. They also constituted a record in real time of the Lincoln presidency. Hay affixed on these pages presidential documents that Lincoln gave to him, messages and speeches in which Hay contributed material literary value—including the Gettysburg Address and the Second Inaugural. [391] Hay also affixed letters written by himself and signed by the president.[392]

John Hay, "Secretary to A. Lincoln," Washington, DC, 1861. Courtesy of John Hay collection, John Hay Library, Brown University.

In the days and weeks of March and early April 1861, before Confederate soldiers fired at Union troops on Fort Sumter in Charleston Harbor, anxiety hung over the White House grounds, filling the mansion's corridors. The president and his staff were on high alert. Lincoln spent hours planning for the eventuality of war. White House security, strung tight, led patrol guards to jump at a suspicious prompt. On the eve of Fort Sumter's fall, an on-duty sentinel assaulted Hay and Nicolay when they were returning to the Executive Mansion from a late-night jaunt, believing them to be enemy intruders. They escaped without harm.

Rising tensions took a toll on Lincoln, who remembered his determination during this uncertain time to "withhold from the public" his own dread about the impending prospect of war.[393] How could he reveal to the people who had voted him into office that he was mapping out top-secret military plans against American people and property in the seceding Southern states? He consulted the army's commanding three-star general, Winfield Scott, seventy-four, known as "Old Fuss and Feathers." The once-strapping soldier who had served with distinction in the War of 1812 and the Mexican-American War was now a rotund old man in poor health. General Scott, at over three hundred pounds, was incapable of mounting a horse or reviewing his troops during his brief, six-month command of the Civil War. Scott's previous field experience lent wisdom to his capabilities as a strategist, though his first-hand knowledge of modern equipment was nil.

The pre-dawn firing by the Confederate army on the Union-occupied Fort Sumter, April 12, 1861, handed Lincoln the act of aggression he needed to declare war against the seceding states. The president had waited until the South attacked American federal property, provoking the North to declare war. Within three days and in the Senate's absence, Lincoln issued a proclamation mustering state militias and seventy-five thousand volunteers. Enlisting each to a three-month term, the president expected the Union army to soon overpower Confederate troops, far shorter than the four-year war.

Lincoln stated the heart of his justification for taking up arms in the proclamation of April 15, 1861.

> I appeal to all loyal citizens to favor, facilitate, and aid this effort
>
> to maintain the honor, the integrity, and the existence of our National Union

> and the perpetuity of popular government,
>
> and to redress its wrongs already too long endured.
>
> I deem it proper to say that the first service assigned to the forces...
>
> will probably be to re-possess the forts, places, and property which have been seized from the Union;...
>
> the utmost care will be observed...to avoid any devastation,
>
> any destruction of...or any disturbance of peaceful citizens in any part of the country.

Entreating the wisdom of the people, the president called on Hay to infuse poetic weight to his statement. Hay added the musical emphasis of alliteration: favor/facilitate/effort; redress/already/endured; and, service/assigned/forces/seized.

A low cloud fell over the Executive Mansion the Sunday evening after "the president wrote his proclamation," Hay said. With Lincoln's "simple, firm, and dignified words that night," Hay wrote, the president reminded the American people that the war must come, and now it has. Historian Richard Hofstadter detected the cruel irony of Lincoln's presidency: The pinnacle of his political ambition was met on the doorstep of war. "To be confronted with the fruits of his victory only to find that it meant choosing between life and death for others was immensely sobering."[394]

Hay described Lincoln's response to the paradox of the moment, writing as Ecarte in the *Illinois Daily State Journal.* "There is something splendid, yet terrible, about this roused anger of the North. It is stern, quiet, implacable, irresistible." He echoed Lincoln's sentiments that war came by the sword of the South. "The necessity of war makes its very cruelty a source of hope and mercy to mankind," Hay concluded.[395] Hay's statement honored the dead, celebrated the living, and offered a sense of hope for some normalcy in their lives, intoning the verse of a Greek funeral ceremony.

Within the week of Sumter's fall, the White House was turned into barracks. A Kansas volunteer company made the East Room its armory. Turning up on the front portico of the White House one evening was English-born actress Jean Margaret Davenport, "the Medea, the Julia, the Mona Lisa of my stage-struck days," Hay said. Now the wife of General Frederick Lander, she came terrified by the alleged plot to assassinate President Lincoln. Doorkeeper Old Edward introduced her to Hay. "Lander has made her very womanly since he married her [in 1860]," Hay said, habitually drawn to beautiful women. He listened to Mrs. Lander's impassioned appeal, then went up to the second floor "to the bedside of the Chief *couché,*" where Lincoln retired in the family's private rooms. Explaining the actress's plea, Hay described the alarming plot against his life. Without speaking, the president grinned. Hay took the cue, returned to his bedroom and went to sleep.[396]

In the morning, still shaken by the night's caller and the specious threat, Hay set out to inspect house and grounds, to ensure that every precaution was in place to safeguard the president. Approaching David Hunter, the handsome cavalry major who was promoted within the month to the fourth-ranking brigadier general of volunteers, Hay instructed Hunter to be alert to the murder plot. Next, he went to Mrs. Lincoln, "to do some very dexterous lying to calm the awakened fears" about the rumored threat to her husband's life. This time, unlike many, her usual hysteria was well-founded. Hay also knew about the deadly riot that had erupted in Baltimore, forty-one miles northeast of Washington. An antiwar mob had clashed with Confederate sympathizers just as the Sixth Massachusetts Regiment marched through the city on its way to the District of Columbia. The mob killed members of the Northern troops and civilians in the crossfire. The dead were among the war's first casualties.[397]

The creeping danger affected Hay in ways he had not understood. Despite his frontier upbringing, he had never witnessed physical violence. For the first time since he had joined Lincoln's inner circle, he had misgivings about the Union's military leadership. "It would seem like a happy omen to have a General Washington living and fighting among us at this time," he confided in his diary on April 20, 1861. Ironically, Hay's encyclopedic memory failed him as he idolized Washington's military prowess: In fact, George Washington had lost the majority of the battles he commanded in the Revolution.[398] Fear may have fed Hay's longing for a strong military leader commanding the Union army, rather than Winfield Scott. "The town is full tonight of feverish rumors about the meditated assault upon this town," Hay journaled, suspecting that Fort McHenry in Baltimore Harbor was the bull's-eye of the enemy, not the capital. [399] Putting down his notebook and leaving his desk, he went up to Capitol Hill to visit the

Massachusetts troops after the assault in Baltimore. He admired the men of the regiment, admitting that they "made me envy the soldiers who should be quartered there." He admired their patriotism: "The Spirit of our institutions seemed visibly present to inspire and nerve the acolyte," envisioning President Lincoln, the commander in chief of the Union army and navy.[400]

On the clear spring evening of April 21, Lincoln and Hay "mounted the battlement of the Executive Mansion," to raise up the president to a level where he could take "a long look down the bay" of the Potomac River. Lincoln was anxious about the late arrival of naval reinforcements from the southern Chesapeake River region of Norfolk, Virginia, enemy territory. From the top of the White House, he hoped to see the Union troops coming into the Navy Yard. Regrettably, "it was a 'water-haul'"—a fruitless outcome, Hay said. Too bad. "'*Tant pis*,' we said, and slept."[401] During the night, the ships returned. "*Pocahontas* and the *Anacostia* came peacefully back from their cruise and folded their wings in the harbor." Writing in his journal, Hay felt relief for the president.[402]

Lincoln ordered a blockade of Southern ports, cutting off Southern trade and the transfer of supplies to Confederate forces, extending 3,500 miles along the Atlantic and Gulf coastlines. Designed as shrewd military strategy, it also depleted shops and pantries in the nation's capital. Common goods for households, hotels, and rooming houses were halted. Empty shelves lined the dry goods warehouses. Within twenty-four hours of the blockade, "great public anxiety" suspended business across the city. The next day, a Tuesday, the president called a meeting of his Cabinet for 3 p.m. in the afternoon rather than the customary 1 p.m. He needed time to assess the situation.[403]

Breaking news from the Navy Yard announced the arrival of two additional ships from Norfolk, the *Pawnee* and *Keystone,* bringing some relief with their stock of naval stores and marines. Secretary Seward, an arrogant man who believed himself superior to just about everyone, was anxious about a transport steamer that had left New York City harbor the day before. Slowed by Baltimore's destruction, Seward "cursed quietly because the *Baltic* had not come," Hay recorded.[404] Even worse, the depletion of basic cold-room supplies sent wholesale prices soaring. Flour spiked to eighteen dollars a bushel, and cornmeal rose to $2.50 a bushel. At Willard's, Hay was startled when he arrived for his midday meal to find the usual spread of complementary finger-food missing. "Preparing for war, furling all sails for the storm," he said, "the dinner-table is lorn of *cartes* and the tea table reduced to the severe simplicity of pound-cake."[405]

Gloom overhung the capital. Terror grew into panic. Only Lincoln seemed capable of good cheer. On the afternoon of April 24, a Wednesday, when soldiers from the Massachusetts Regiment wounded in Baltimore came to call on him, he greeted the men "kindly and cordially," Hay said. "They came in confused and flushed," defeated in a non-battle skirmish. "They went out easy, proud, and happy."[406] The soldiers were uplifted by the president's genuinely warm humor.

Logging White House conversations and meetings in his journal, Hay included his own experiences and feelings. In one passage, he vented a loathing for the Southern press's butchering of the English language, poor writing from the "seceding pen." Hay fumed, "nothing but the vilest folly and feculence, that might have simmered…in the narrow brain of a chimpanzee, flow from the pens of our…southern brethren." He drew parallels between biological inferiority and Southern birthright, an insight into the systemic foundations of ethnic typecasting. "I have seen rough company in the west," he said, but never in the "wild license of flat-boating on the Mississippi did I ever hear words that were…disgusting filtrations of the chivalric southern mind."[407] In the history of the world, rulers were known criminals and nations fell, Hay mused, "but it was reserved for the southern states to exhibit an infamy to which other crimes show white as mother's milk, and a madness to which an actor's frenzy is sane." Southern secession was more than criminal. It was dangerous. He crossed out this last sentence, feeling he had gone too far. In the solitude of his diary, he lay bare the peril of secession and war, a menace he felt every moment of every day. The plain worry on Lincoln's face and in his hands brought Hay to cry out with disdain on the pages of his private notebook.

He loved to bring the president good news, truly a joy that "straightaway gladdened the heart of the Ancient," Hay said.[408] Word of the safe passage of Union troops resting in port eased one vein of the commander-in-chief's pressures. Standing by this solemn man of few pleasures, Hay delighted in telling a tale to light up Lincoln's eyes. The president smiled with appreciation when Hay recited a passage from a classic poem, such as Homer's *Iliad,* or one of two Dickens's stories, such as *The Old Curiosity Shop.*

The mild evening of Thursday, April 25, a fresh air floating across the clipped South Lawn where gaily dressed women and men gathered and children played, the president stood on the White House portico with Mary Lincoln, sons Willie and Tad, War secretary Cameron, and Hay and Nicolay. The Seventh Regiment Band blared patriotic airs. Half-listening to the music and forever at work, Lincoln talked war with German American Carl Schurz, the new American minister to Spain, a man full of "vigor and animal arrogance," Hay said.[409] Turning to John, Lincoln confided, "'I intend to fill Fortress Monroe with men and stores; blockade the ports effectually; provide for the entire safety of the Capital; keep them quietly employed in this way, and then go down to Charleston and pay her the little debt we are owing her.'" That the president intended to stake out the largest fort on the southern peninsula of Virginia, the Union stronghold guarding all water transport approaching Washington and Baltimore from the south, signaled his intent to defend the safety of the North along the dangerous southern boundary. He also planned to fill it with food staples. "I felt like letting off an Illinois yell," Hay exclaimed. "I begged the privilege of scattering an intimation of the coming glory through the host." The president urged his private secretary to practice forbearance. "Not yet."[410]

Hay's natural poetry and literary knowledge enabled him to turn Lincoln's ideas and principles into eloquent communications. In one letter he wrote on the president's behalf, Hay answered Kentucky state senator John M. Johnson's "truculent letter." Johnson was protesting the occupation of Cairo, Illinois, by armed federal troops led by Ulysses S. Grant. The Illinois town sat across a narrow opening from Kentucky soil on the Mississippi and Ohio rivers. Hay responded to Johnson's rancor by telling him that President Lincoln "would certainly never have ordered the movement of troops…had he known that Cairo was in your senatorial district." Admiring his own droll wit, he confessed that "it will take the quiet satire of the note about half an hour to get through the thick skull of this Kentucky senator, and then he will think it a damned poor joke."[411] There was nothing funny about the matter of Union forces occupying the ground a stone's throw from a neutral border state. Surely respecting Kentucky's neutrality, Lincoln also believed that a defenseless border state was a damn-fool way to maintain peace.[412]

After months of working together, from early morning to late into the evening, patterns emerged in the Lincoln and Hay rapport. One force in both their lives was the majestic western river that coursed through Illinois. Lincoln had worked on flatboats on the Ohio and Mississippi Rivers, the early nineteenth-century channels of commerce and mobility in America.

Before the railroads took over, the rivers were the byways. Formative years on the river inevitably informed Lincoln and also Hay, independently, that one's vision was finite, limited by the horizon of the river, seeing to the next point and never beyond. The flatboat, too, was subject to the river currents, setting the vessel's route by the flow of the waterway. As far as the pilot could see, the picturesque velocity of the river was something magical. Growing up in Warsaw, Hay lived up the Mississippi River from Samuel Clemens in Hannibal, Missouri at around the same time. Captivated by the life and dialect of the riverfront, both writers portrayed Western scenes in their fiction, Hay in *Pike County Ballads* (1871) and Clemens in his travel journal through the so-called Wild West, *Roughing It* (1872). Clemens later implored Hay, when he was then on the editorial desk of the *New York Tribune* in the early 1870s, to review *Roughing It.* "You are the only one who understands this life."[413]

With Lincoln, Hay understood that the president's vision of events didn't advance beyond what he actually saw or knew. For now, Lincoln viewed Southern secession as the cause of the war. He was unable to name slavery as a source, even if the abolitionist in Hay did. Similar to the river's current, Lincoln didn't control events. Events controlled life. And, as with the flatboat pilot, the president's job was to steer the course that offered safe passage and the most comfortable journey. John Hay provided the most comfortable passage in his words and phrases, offering the American people eloquent assurance of Abraham Lincoln's vision, principles, and his dedication to a safe landing.[414] This, at a time when the nation was brought face-to-face with destruction.

Chapter 14

LINCOLN'S SPOKESPERSON

By the summer of 1861, America was facing ruin. Twice before, in 1773–1783 and in 1812, the land met devastating peril. President Lincoln sat at the head of a fractured nation and a disjointed Cabinet.[415] The Civil War was destroying federal property from Maryland and West Virginia, to South Carolina, Georgia, and Florida. It struck a deadly blow to Southern prosperity, the fertile farmland and charming towns. The collapse of the traditional order also broke the figurative shackles binding millions of slaves to their masters. They could almost taste freedom, what with many slaveholders absent. The first slaves who escaped begged to join the ranks of the Union army. In the absence of plantation masters, now engaged in the conflict, enslaved males fled in the early first months of Civil War, seeking refuge in Union forts. "What we could not have done in many lifetimes the madness and folly of the South has accomplished for us," Hay said. "Slavery offers itself more vulnerable to our attack than at any point in any century." Civil war was eroding slaveowners' hold on their chattels. Ironically, the act of secession to save slavery enabled its end.

In one case, slaves belonging to a Colonel Mallory of North Carolina escaped to the Union-held Fort Monroe on the Virginia coast. They fled to avoid building batteries on Confederate land. General Benjamin Butler, Fort Monroe's commander, denied the request to return the slaves. Being on foreign soil, which Virginia claimed to be when it seceded, annulled the Fugitive Slave Act of 1850.[416] Giving safe passage to contrabands of war, the Union army invoked their position in principles of international war. The seceding states had left the Union and were foreign enemies. The Union had every right to shelter runaway slaves. This one incident provoked a revolution in popular thought, said Adam Goodheart in *1861.*[417418]

On May 7, John Hay walked into the president's office with news from home. In passing, Lincoln mentioned a suggestion he had received from Colonel James A. Hamilton, seventy-three, the third son of Alexander Hamilton and a wealthy landowner on the Hudson River. Hamilton had put forth the idea of "enlisting the slaves in our army." Describing Hamilton as "a venerable and most respectable gentleman," Lincoln took note of the proposal. As Nicolay joined them, Hay responded by telling the president that Lincoln's daily mail from leading Northerners was "thickly interspersed" with advice about enlisting African-American slaves in the Union army.

Pondering the thought, Lincoln answered with characteristic deliberation, in his measured Kentucky drawl. "Some of our northerners seem bewildered and dazzled by the excitement of the hour," he said, noting their misplaced enthusiasm for freeing enslaved peoples.[419] The president could not bring himself to say the word slavery or speak of its role in Southern secession. "For my own part," Lincoln said and Hay recorded, "I consider the central idea pervading this struggle that popular government is not an absurdity. We must settle this question now, whether in a free government the minority have the right to break up the government whenever they choose. If we fail it will go far to prove the incapability of the people to govern themselves."[420] Lincoln could not accept democracy's failure in the hands of anarchy. "There exists in our case, an instance of a vast and far reaching disturbing element."[421]

Democracy was on the line, Lincoln argued, rather than slavery. Lincoln confided to Hay and Nicolay, "Admit the right of a minority to secede at will and the occasion for such secession would almost as likely be any other as the slavery question."[422] He continued, "If we fail, it will go far to prove the incapability of the people to govern themselves. Taking the government as we found it, we will see if the majority can preserve it," the president concluded.[423]

The onset of summer in Washington, with temperatures and humidity rising to 90 degrees before June, had Lincoln and his secretaries dreaming of the prairies of Illinois. The "thunder of hostile guns" within earshot, the Virginia and Maryland battlefields a short ten miles away, the occupants of the Executive Mansion were surrounded by the torrent of war.[424] Yet during this time, May and June 1861, the president was mostly occupied with his

Fourth of July message to the special war powers joint session of Congress. Lincoln's speech became the paramount focus of the Executive office. "It will be an exhaustive review of the questions of the hour and the future," Hay noted in his journal. Incorporating many suggestions by Secretary of State Seward, the president "revised his first draft extensively," Hay said. Lincoln also solicited comments and contributions from Cabinet members.

On July 4, 1861, Nicolay delivered the presidential message to Congress, the pages somewhat limp and stuck to Nicolay's cradled arm in Washington's humidity. He jumped on the rear platform of the Pennsylvania Avenue streetcar to the Capitol.[425] Despite the steady stream of senators and congressmen traveling the same road throughout the day, Lincoln trusted only Nicolay or Hay with the job of carrying his public messages to Congress. The president's private secretary climbed the steep steps up to the Capitol, his slender arm steady as it gripped the president's message. He opened the heavy mahogany door and entered the dimly lit House chamber, the galleries partly filled. On errand from Lincoln, he was entitled to "the privilege of the floor." (Only executive sessions of the Senate prevented this precedence.)

Nicolay's anticipated arrival produced the attention of House speaker Galusha Grow of Pennsylvania, bringing down his gavel with a percussive whack to announce the high moment in the early hours of the wartime Congress. "The President's Private Secretary!" Speaker Grow announced with his booming voice, resonating through the hall. "A message from the President of the United States!"[426]

Read to the joint session the following day, the custom then, Lincoln's July 4, 1861, message was regarded by Burlingame as "one of his most significant and eloquent state papers."[427] An "elaborate and carefully prepared paper," said Lincoln scholar James Garfield Randall, contained a clear chronicle of historical events, constitutional arguments, and the president's time-honored belief in democratic government.[428] Justifying war, for which he needed congressional support, Lincoln explained why he believed secession of the Southern states should be suppressed by force. His purpose was to unify and rally northern support for civil war. Defining the stakes of military engagement, Lincoln highlighted the heart of his message in clear and powerful language. The clarity of the words steadied the impact in three notable paragraphs.

In the eighth paragraph, Lincoln previewed themes he returned to two years later in the Gettysburg address, a speech even more poetic.

[Paragraph Eight]

This issue embraces more than the fate of [the] United States.

It presents to the whole family of man

the question whether a constitutional republic, or democracy

—a government of the people by the same people—

can or can not maintain its territorial integrity against its own domestic foes.

It presents the question whether discontented individuals,

...can always,...or arbitrarily without any pretense,

break up their government,

and...put an end to free government upon the earth.

It forces us to ask,

is there in all republics this inherent and fatal weakness?

Must a government of necessity be too strong for the liberties of its own people,

or too weak to maintain its own existence?

In paragraph twenty-eight, the most eloquent passage in the address, Lincoln defined the importance of the military conflict to the survival of democratic government.

[Paragraph Twenty Eight]

This is a People's contest.

On the side of the Union,

it is a struggle for maintaining in the world,

that form, and substance of government,

whose leading objects is to elevate the condition of men—

to lift artificial weights from all shoulders—
to clear the paths of laudable pursuit for all—
to afford all, an unfettered start,
and a fair chance, in the race of life
yielding to partial,
and temporary departures, (from necessity),
this is the leading object of the government
for whose existence we contend.

Paraphrasing Lincoln's statements and Hay's notes from their May 7 conversation, succinctly stated, the president presented the challenge of an electoral democracy in paragraph thirty-one.

[Paragraph Thirty One]

Our popular Government has often been called an experiment.

Two points in it our people have already settled

—the successful establishing and the successful administering of it.

One still remains—its successful maintenance against a formidable internal attempt to overthrow it.

It is now for them to demonstrate to the world

that those who can fairly carry an election

can also suppress a rebellion;

[that] ballots are the rightful and peaceful successors of bullets,

and [that] when ballots have fairly and constitutionally decided

there can be no successful appeal back to bullets;

[that] there can be no successful appeal

except to ballots themselves at succeeding elections.

Such will be a great lesson of peace,

teaching men that what they can not take by an election
neither can they take it by a war;
teaching all the folly of being the beginners of a war.

These three paragraphs formed the core of Lincoln's appeal and reasoning for war. The poetic tools demonstrated Hay's contribution to the speech. The ideological roots of the content were wholly President Lincoln's, as revealed in his May 7 remarks, which Hay had recorded in his diary. Recognized for its literary expression, the verses called on metaphors to life, polarities juxtaposed against parallel structure, and the Miltonic imitation of a Greek chorus. Intricately layered and nuanced phrases revealed the hand of Hay's literary craftsmanship.

"I do not believe it is a wild flight of fancy to attribute to John Hay some of the grace of expression which distinguishes Lincoln's literary style after he entered the White House from that of the earlier product of his pen," historian Charles W. Moores claimed years later. Recognizing "the same virility, the same simplicity, the same personality asserting itself in every word and phrase," he continued, "seems to have been added an indefinable smoothness and delicacy—at times distinctly poetic in its spirit."[429] "Some of us who doubted were wrong," claimed *Harper's Weekly* editor George William Curtis soon after, admiring Lincoln as "a people's President."[430]

President Lincoln's message produced results. The special war powers Congress, grappling with the mounting national debt, was roused to action by the president's resolve for the Union. The House and Senate moved quickly to transform measures into laws, Hay reported in the *New York World*.[431] The Senate voted to call up additional troops and raise funds to defend the Union. Both chambers sanctioned Lincoln's expansive war powers.

The steamy days of July in Washington slowed the pace of life. Yet all signs of languor ended on July 21, 1861, with the First Battle of Bull Run in nearby Manassas, Virginia. A stream of conflicting reports rolling into the nation's capital throughout the day progressed from victory to near defeat. By mid-afternoon, the president felt confident. General Scott's dispatches signaled promise. Lincoln left the executive office for a ride. Minutes later, Seward burst in, alarmed and anxious.

"Where is the President?" he asked.

"Gone to ride," the young men replied.

"Have you any late news?'"

Nicolay read him the last wire from the *New York World.*

"'Tell no one,'" Seward, instructed. "'The battle is lost. Find the President and tell him to come immediately to Gen. Scotts's.'" Within thirty minutes, Lincoln had returned. He left promptly to meet with the commanding general. Hay and Nicolay, sitting by the second-floor window, listened to the chilling echoes of "the heavy cannonading on the other side of the river," thirty-five miles south of the Executive Mansion. Their worst fears were confirmed the next morning. The victory, within grasp in late afternoon, rapidly turned "to an overwhelming defeat—a total and disgraceful rout of our men," Nicolay said.[432]

"There is nothing in this except the lives lost and the lives which must be lost to make it good," Lincoln said as Hay chronicled. Agitated by the ugliest fact of war—death—Lincoln paced around the Executive office that morning. The First Battle of Bull Run was the worst defeat of the three-month conflict. "No one regretted bloodshed and disaster more than he," Hay said, "and no one estimated the consequences of defeat more lightly."[433] With no experience in the field, the commander in chief had no way to fathom the magnitude of loss both the Union and Confederate armies were about to experience over the next forty-four months.

Into the city rolled a caravan of wagons filled with the dead and wounded, a sight so grotesque that people walking on the sidewalks and riding in the dirt streets stopped and stared. Soldiers without arms or legs or eyes—some with all three torn away—lay with the "bodies of the dead...piled on top of one another, the pallet faces and bloodstained garments telling a fearfully mute but sad story of the horrors of war," Hay reported in the *New York World* on July 22.[434] In the wake of the Union defeat, George B. McClellan, a vain, thirty-four-year-old Army general known as "Little Napoleon," for his modest height and big ego, took command of the Union forces around the Washington region. Lincoln had high hopes for McClellan, "daily proving himself to be what was expected of him," Hay wrote in the *World.* Lincoln's renewed trust in McClellan's army was enhanced by the West Point general's exacting command.[435]

Hay revealed confidential intelligence when he reported in the *New York World* on the Confederate army's "maturing plans for an attack on the city" of Washington, DC. He spoke of residents' dread, an arresting fear flamed by reliable reports from the war department. Ringing the nation's capital around each of its four corners, military camps occupied the once-peaceful fields. Blaring bugle calls at dawn, the rhythmic tramp of marching troops, the bark of commanding officers turned the city into a war camp. "Hundreds of white tents mushroomed in green fields around the city," said writer Jay Monaghan. Everywhere, cavalry clattered by as "hoop-skirted women waited for a gap in traffic, lifting farthingales with gloved fingers and darted before advancing columns." From his office, Lincoln looked across the Potomac to the movement of troops a few miles away, smoke rising from campfires. Up and down Pennsylvania Avenue, he witnessed the heartbeat of patriotism in the red-white-and-blue bunting draping brick commercial buildings.[436]

"Let them come, says our veteran chieftain; let them come, say our soldiers; let them come, say our loyal citizens," Hay wrote in the *New York World,* championing the Union army. "Such a fool-hardiness would end in the enemy's rout and ruin."[437] Thankfully, the Confederate attack on Washington came to nothing. It didn't happen.

President Lincoln had decided the public messaging for himself and his administration resided with John Hay alone. Hay took over Lincoln's communications through his journalism and also his ghostwriting for the president. Unlike the modern-day press secretary who conveys presidential policy and actions to a press corps, Hay was President Lincoln's singular pressman. He was the voice of the Lincoln White House, speaking directly to the people through the printed press.

Hay's acumen in his columns and his charm and common sense had earned him the president's regard and confidence. Goodwin attributed the evolution of the Lincoln–Hay relationship to their personal similarities, describing Hay in likeness to Lincoln: "the would-be lawyer, the writer, the native sarcasm and wit, the loyalty, the lover of literature and the theater, the hard worker and the natural diplomat."[438]

Lincoln's growing dependence during the early months of his presidency on Hay, who likely edited the Fourth of July message to the war powers Congress and also wrote his press reports, allowed Hay into all aspects of the president's life. The growing confidence opened Hay to Lincoln's rocky marriage and the first lady's violent emotions. He also came to understand the more complicated aspects of Lincoln's character, his wide mood swings staking claims to fatalism. The president was vastly complex. Little of this was foreign to Hay, the poet, the mystic, a sensitive soul.

The quiet of Washington in August left the town vacated, Congress having adjourned and departed and most foreign diplomats away at such toney watering holes as Newport, Rhode Island, or Bar Harbor, Maine, or to their native lands across the sea. The president, his days comparatively relaxed, offered Hay the chance to get away to a fashionable resort on the Jersey Shore. Not actually a vacation, Lincoln asked Hay to help him with a private matter. He sent him to Long Branch, New Jersey, to accompany Mary Lincoln on her five-day private retreat at the Mansion House Inn. Joined by Robert Lincoln, seventeen, who was home from Harvard, Hay left on August 14. The two young men enjoyed one another's company.

Scarcely two years before, Mary Lincoln had admired Hay in Springfield. For the Kentucky-bred society girl, John came from a good family and his college pedigree was a model for her own son. Yet White House life had changed the first lady's feelings for Hay, twenty-two. Her one-time admiration had turned to spite, even contempt. It was the Springfield to Washington train journey and the Baltimore assassination threat that had tarnished her good opinion, according to David Herbert Donald, when Hay "had to do some very dexterous lying to calm the awakened fear of Mrs. Lincoln." Since then, she mistrusted his easy rapport with the president and resented Nicolay's interference in White House affairs. They had taken the traditional social role of the first lady out of her spendthrift hands. "Hell-cat" and "the enemy," the private secretaries called her.[439]

At the Jersey Shore, Hay approached the fragile balance between his friendship with Robert Lincoln and his duty to the president. Robert, he knew, adored his mother and felt a cool distance from his father, a remote figure during his youth, often away on the circuit or stumping for the next elected office.[440] Hoping to keep a safe distance from Mary Lincoln as much as duty allowed, Hay looked to Robert to be his mother's personal chaperone. The special train carrying the first lady to Long Branch was met at the station by a buzzing swarm of girls dressed in crisp white frocks. They were excited to lay eyes on the first lady. Annoyed by the commotion, Mary Lincoln ignored them and went directly to her room in the crowded Mansion House Inn. Here, she remained secluded for five days, Hay wrote in the *New York World*.[441]

Under the Jersey shore's gray, cold sky, Hay felt relief from Washington's heat. He relished the cool ocean breezes. The salty sea air drenching his clothes and coating his skin with a crusty layer of salt, though, was not so wonderful.[442] Worse still were Long Branch's common hotels in high season, crowded to the rafters with people of "well-bred enthusiasm and pocket handkerchiefs." The bustle of packed rooms sent waves of claustrophobia over his skin. He was revolted by the "queer, half-baked New Jersey confectionary, with a tendency to stammer when spoken to."

After nightfall, John walked along the deserted beach. The powerful surf crashing in around, the dance band wailing in the background on a hotel porch, he sensed stormy weather pressing in from offshore. Stirring up "the stormy octaves of the ocean," whistling "mournfully through the lattice-work of the deserted pavilions," the heavy winds blew against the lean young man. On the edge of the world on this starless night, he rolled a cigarette to calm himself. "This solitary communion with the sea," he reported in the *World,* offered welcome isolation. He sat by the ocean and opened his thoughts to cadences of poetry and song, giving thanks to the beach and the water for saving the awkward dancer from the dance. He was happy to avoid the party. "There goes the final crash of the band," Hay said, walking back up to the darkened inn, safely removed from the retiring partygoers.[443]

In the light of day, wishing to avoid the crowds, Hay walked to the depot on the cool morning of August 19, a Monday, hopping a train to New York City. He expected to lunch with Colonel James Hamilton, who had telegraphed the day before. Without a firm plan, though, the two men just missed one another. Upon arriving, Hay went to his hotel and waited for Hamilton, then finally left. Taking the horsecar downtown, he lunched with Theodore Roosevelt Sr., the wealthy businessman who was an active supporter of the Union and Lincoln, and a charter member of the Union League Club, founded in 1861 to promote the Northern cause. He was also the father of the future president of the same name. Unfortunately, Hamilton had come to Hay's hotel soon after he left, waiting a bit then leaving for his home in Irvington-on-Hudson. Hay cursed the mix-up. "I concluded to take a royal revenge on myself by ordering myself back to Washington."[444]

Hay returned to the national capital in the late afternoon to find "the air like a damp oven." He also returned to his diary after a one-hundred-day hiatus. "The nights have been too busy for jottings," he explained in the privacy of his journal.[445] Consuming his waking hours were evenings out with Lincoln, penning correspondences, and aiding the president with writing messages. On the evening of August 22, a Thursday, he walked with Lincoln across Pennsylvania Avenue. The heavy-footed Lincoln and the sprightly Hay walked side by side without escort or security. They strolled along Lafayette Square's cast-iron fence and through its magnificent gate, illuminating their faces by the flickering gas lamps. The spacious urban park across from the White House attracted several of the city's leading families, who lived in elegant brick townhouses. Lincoln and Hay crossed the square to the Madison Place door of Secretary of State Seward's handsome townhouse. Entering, they found him, a slender figure with shaggy eyebrows and a big nose, "comfortably slippered."[446] Seward appeared "in a better humor" than recent days, Hay said.[447] After a time, the president and Hay walked on to General McClellan's home, where the president reviewed the general's comprehensive battle plans and the state of troops. "Discipline is perfecting" and "McClellan is growing jolly," Hay wrote in his journal.[448] Optimism for the general's success continued to swell.

President Lincoln's military leadership was also under the microscope. In New York City, Frederick Law Olmsted confessed to George Templeton Strong in late August, a partner of the nation's oldest law firm and a founder of the Union League Club of New York, his reservations about Lincoln's military acumen. "The government seems limp and nerveless and unequal to the crisis."[449] Thirty-nine years old, Olmsted, who formerly worked as a journalist and had traveled through England and then the American South for the *New York Times* documenting slavery, feared for the Northern troops in the face of Southern aggression. Now, in partnership with English-born landscape designer Calvert Vaux, the landscape architect was creating Manhattan's great Central Park.

The sluggish August in the nation's capital also allowed Hay the freedom to take some time to visit his family in Illinois. Departing on August 29, he boarded the train to New York City from the Baltimore & Ohio Railroad depot, just north of the Capitol building. He met briefly with Nicolay, who was returning from his three-week Newport vacation, then boarded the connecting rail line westward to Illinois.[450] The break restored his fragile constitution. "From present appearances, it will keep John and I both pretty busy to keep one well Secretary here all the time," Nicolay said.[451] The pressures of the White House, especially during wartime, bore down on their nerves.

Hay set his diary aside during the time with his family in Warsaw. The *Daily Illinois State Journal* of Springfield proudly announced that John Hay of Washington, DC, was "recruiting his health by a brief respite from his official labors."[452] Charles Hay, bursting with pride over his son's high-level work, bragged to his sister, "John has obtained a position in an axial and political point of view never before reached by a young man of his age in this government, as the son of the celebrated Alexander Hamilton lately said to him."

This statement confirmed that Colonel James Hamilton had indeed disclosed to Hay that Hay's role in Lincoln's administration was similar to Hamilton's own father's speechwriting role with George Washington. Hay had attained the position at twenty-two, actually the same age Hamilton was when he was General Washington's chief aide and speechwriter during the Revolutionary War. Hay, who was following in Hamilton's footsteps for the Civil War president, had earned the respect of the son of the first presidential speechwriter, James Hamilton. He also secured the esteem of his own father, who had reason for pride. Charles and Helen Hay's commitment to their son's education nurtured a young man with a key role in President Lincoln's administration. John was now "the guest of cabinet ministers, foreign ambassadors, and occupying a position in the public mind which causes a day's illness to be flashed across the continent as a matter in [public] interest," Dr. Hay said.[453] Charles Hay's pride marked a shift from his austere manner with John. His son's letters to his father still revealed a tone of caution, even stiffness. Young Hay took care not to misspeak or express himself in a way that appeared impertinent or too carefree to his father. By contrast to Lincoln's compassion, Charles Hay had been strict, bearing down on his gifted son, prone to laziness.

Hay returned to Washington and the White House in early October 1861.[454] The president was delighted to have him back in the White House. John Hay felt so uplifted upon his return to Lincoln and the White House that he burst forth with a humorous tale for Stoddard, the assistant secretary who remained after Nicolay's vacation. Before he could finish the full story, Hay broke down in giggles. Overhearing the uproar, Nicolay emerged from his room, pen in hand, to hear the tale. The three young men exploded in laughter.

"Now, John, just tell that thing again," a voice rang out from the president's doorway. Silently, Lincoln had appeared from his office. As fresh and funny as the first time, he retold the story to the assembled quartet. "Down came the President's foot from across his knee with a heavy stamp on the floor and out through the hall went an uproarious peal of laughter," Stoddard said.[455]

Chapter 15

LINCOLN'S JOURNALIST

The cool autumn evenings of October 1861 heralded the advance of winter's start. With each passing day and no Union movement against Confederate troops, Lincoln harbored a growing unease about the war. Before long, a cold snap soon felled the vibrant foliage, brilliant purple skies gave way to gray clouds, freezing rains, blistering winds, and frostbitten troops. With Hay at his side, Lincoln walked across Lafayette Square on the evening of October 10, a Thursday. He approached General McClellan's house on a spontaneous visit. The president was concerned about the general's guarded command of the Army of the Potomac. Pressing him on his arrangements against the enemy, Hay wrote in his diary, Lincoln became the object of McClellan's insolence.

Turning to the president, the general said, "I intend to do as well as possible. Don't let them hurry me, is all I ask."

"You shall have your own way in the matter, I assure you," Lincoln answered.

The president walked home to the White House with Hay. McClellan, for his part, was enraged, ranting to his wife, "I can't tell you how disgusted I am becoming with these wretched politicians." He seethed, "The Pres[i]d[en]t is nothing more than a well-meaning baboon."[456] Yet Lincoln's visit prompted action. The very next day, McClellan and his troops galloped "through the chilly mist, over the steaming and soggy roads, looking along the lines," making "a strong reconnaissance," Hay wrote in the *Missouri Republican,* echoing his own journal and the president's statements.

Transcribing his notes from his private conversation with Lincoln, Hay continued in the fashion of his spokesperson. He acknowledged the war's "slow, steady progress," and the chances missed in the field.[457]

For his next column in the *Missouri Republican,* Hay took up the issue of journalists' abuses of privileged information, accusing them of intercepting official dispatches addressed to the War Department. Because of the limited number of telegraph wires laid in the country, press wires crossed with government wires. The Associated Press telegraph crossed with confidential government dispatches from the field, ostensibly off-limits to journalists. In reality, newspapermen read the official wires, anxious for the inside track.

As Lincoln's spokesperson, the equivalent of today's official White House press secretary, Hay announced in his October 14 filing to the *Missouri Republican* that the president disparaged rumors of his intentions, "his plans bruited over the country either before or while they are in process of fulfillment." He admonished his fourth estate peers, directing them to honor the policy and confidentiality of the executive branch.[458] Further acting on Lincoln's instructions, Hay represented Lincoln's command, closing off the Executive Office to other reporters and leaving Hay alone to broadcast from the second-floor White House and Cabinet Room. Lincoln probably didn't intend to topple the free press. Instead, he was anxious to end the leaking of confidential information sent to him and his Cabinet members. Leaked to the press, classified background information had been used carelessly to alarm the public.

Hay distinguished his journalism, which he described as discreet and legitimate, from the hundreds of reporters filling print space with political biases. The partisan press, he argued, intentionally raised the public's fears, already shaken. "Unguarded or indiscreet disclosures in reference to the movement contemplated," he said, threatened "our national honor."[459] Lincoln recognized that Hay was all he needed to air his thoughts and policies in the press. He entrusted his political platform, as well as the actions of his Cabinet, to John Hay alone.

The president broke from tradition, ending invitations to journalists from the country's leading papers to attend Cabinet meetings and to cover the Executive Office. Choosing his in-house journalist alone to speak on behalf of his administration, Lincoln shut the White House doors to correspondents of the national press corps. The president made John Hay the singular journalistic voice of the Lincoln White House.

"Provokingly reticent," claimed papers clamoring for admission to the Executive Office. "Troubled," said other reporters. The Civil War president was not the first nor the last president to shut out journalists from the inner sanctum. The president and his Cabinet members were unanimous on the "the course which seems proper to them," Hay reported in the *Missouri Republican.* At this dangerous time of war and disunion, the administration shut down the "myriad voices" using the mask of authority to advance false "facts." Most news published in the partisan media of 1861 was "not founded upon that basis of entire information necessary to a complete understanding of political movements," said Hay.[460] This sensitive time, Lincoln stated, demanded that inflammatory misrepresentations about government affairs and military strategy must stop. He chose to roll the story out in a different way. He couldn't risk misinformation. Controlling the flow of news from the White House as well as the message of its content, the president depended on the one journalist he knew had his fingers on the pulse of the party and the president.

Every day brought devastating news from the war front. "This has been a heavy day," Hay journaled on October 22, 1861. The skirmish of a Union regiment stationed across the Potomac River from Leesburg, Virginia, had turned to combat around dusk when the Northern troops crossed the river, mounting the bluff overlooking the town. Lincoln knew that his Springfield friend Edward D. Baker, the recent *Illinois State Journal* editor who had reported on Lincoln's February train departure eight months earlier, was in the battle. Lincoln and Hay walked to the war telegraph office for news. "The quick clicking of the instrument attracted the attention of the operator," Hay said. Taking up a sheet of paper, the operator wrote out a few lines, handing them to the president. "An expression of awe and grief solemnized the massive features of Lincoln as he read the dispatch, 'Colonel Baker is dead.'" News of Baker's death at Leesburg, shot while raising the Union flag on a roof in the Confederate town, sent Lincoln into a dark place. His head bowed, his face pale, tears rolling down his cheeks, his heart heaved with the truth of war: the immeasurable loss of life.[461] Baker was not only the president's friend. He was the namesake of Edward Baker "Eddie" Lincoln, who had died a month before his fourth birthday in 1850. Eddie had been baptized and buried in Springfield. Tormented, the president left the telegraph room and walked with Hay to General McClellan's house. Here, they were joined by Seward and Cameron.[462] Through the night, the wires brought news of the courage of Union troops in the face of heavy losses.

Lincoln was impatient to prevent further bloodshed. He asked McClellan about his plans for the army at Leesburg. "It became painfully evident that he had *no plan* nor the slightest idea of what [his command] was about," wrote Hay in his diary.[463] Days later, October 26, they arrived at McClellan's front door unannounced. Lincoln and the general talked about the need for "an immediate battle to clean out the enemy," Hay reported. Lincoln and Seward pressed the commanding general of the Potomac region, spending "several evenings of every week in McClellan's private study" to advance an aggressive and winning plan.

Hay quoted McClellan from his diary notes when he repeated to Lincoln: "'I think we will succeed entirely if our friends will be patient and not hurry us.'

'I promise you,' said the President, 'you shall have your own way.'"[464]

Urged by his Cabinet and the Radical Republicans, the Northern faction imploring him to abandon his deference to Union officers and end the bloodshed, Lincoln balanced competing demands to advance Union wins versus acceding to his army generals, allowing them a free hand to command as they saw best. The void in the Union command was really at the very top: the ailing General Winfield Scott, seventy-five, for all intents and purposes was absent. On Friday, November 1, President Lincoln ordered Scott to retire, a leave old Fuss 'n Feathers had long desired.

In his place, Lincoln had the unanimous support of his Cabinet members to promote George B. McClellan, now thirty-five, to chief command of the Union army. Short, dark, and handsome, with his signature handlebar mustache the capping stroke, the West Point officer, they knew, had the best-drilled troops. McClellan made disciplined soldiers out of farmers and city slickers alike. On the very eve of his promotion, "Little Mac," as he was known by officers and his troops, expressed bitter animus for Lincoln and the president's Cabinet, confessing to his wife, "it is terrible to stand by and see the cowardice of the President, the vileness of Seward, and the rascality of Cameron."[465] Yet in Lincoln's personal company, McClellan appeared gracious. "It is a great relief, sir," McClellan said the next day upon receiving his promotion. "I am now in contact with you, and the Secretary. I am not embarrassed by intervention," lying as he masked his frustration with Lincoln and Seward's interference in battle plans.

"'Well,' said the Tycoon," Hay recorded in his diary, "'Draw on me for all the sense I have, and all the information, the supreme command of the army will entail a vast labor upon you.'

"'I can do it all,' McClellan said quietly."

Lincoln was anxious for McClellan's success, Hay journaled.

During early November 1861, mounting a public relations drive designed to strengthen the people's opinion of Lincoln's war strategy and the president's charge of the Union army, Hay dispatched a steady stream of "Washington correspondence" columns to the *Missouri Republican* paper. On November 2, he magnified McClellan's promotion, writing "the nation is fortunate in its new commander." He also reinforced Lincoln's image as a man in the saddle day and night.[466] Flowing from Hay's pen, the press crusade continued on November 4, addressing the uncomfortable truth that America was at war with itself. Hay characterized the government's relations with foreign allies as being "in sympathy with us," reflecting Britain's refusal during September and October to recognize Southern Confederates. The North's blockade of Southern ports, choking off the foreign export of cotton and crippling England's textile mills, failed to weaken the British allegiance to the Union. America's ambassador in London, Charles Francis Adams, confirmed the loyalty of Britain and France to the US government. "All which we knew a good while ago," recognizing Napolean, Hay wrote on November 7, 1861, in the *Missouri Republican*.[467]

A week later, Hay declared "poetic justice" when Union naval and army troops reclaimed "the still proud city of Beaufort" in South Carolina. "Sitting in the quiet reverie of wealth and ease upon the idle shores of the tidal river, cinctured by its net-work of guarding island," he eulogized the serenity of "sluggish lagoons," "clear sunlight," and "endless summer skies." He recalled the president's reason for closing off the Southern cotton economy: to weaken the demand for enslaved labor and break the bonds of slavery. Lincoln's lasting hope was to save the Union. "It was well that this crusade against the usurping divinity of cotton should first assert its invincible prowess upon the very throne and center of his power."[468] Stepping beyond Lincoln's own rationale for war—to save the Union and democratic government—Hay stated that slavery was a root cause of the war. It was a brutal system founded in an economy that worked to death generations of chattel slaves and purchased new ones. Only by cutting off the demand for slavery could the institution die, Hay concluded.

Lincoln allowed Hay to express his own views in the press, even if the president didn't entirely agree with him. In the Executive offices, Lincoln also welcomed plain dialogue, healthy debate among his inner circle and his Cabinet members. He was confident of his ability to snuff out acrimony.

"I talked tonight with the President about the opening of the cotton trade" between South, North, and Europe, Hay journaled on November 7. The triangular strangulation of Northern industry, Southern ports, and British commerce, Hay believed, was not productive. He "went in strong for the opening of the ports." Lincoln countered that his object was equality for all, "to show the world we were fair in this matter, favoring outsiders as much as ourselves."

Despite such claims, slavery was *not yet* a mandate in the president's mind. Hay, a lifelong advocate of free trade, argued for opening the ports. Lincoln listened to Hay's proposals, accepting some and dismissing others. "I don't know why, using all the arguments I could think of, and rather gained the idea that he also slanted in that direction."[469] All in all, John Hay advocated for abolition and also for open trade, ideas that gradually made their way into Abraham Lincoln's psyche.

The president was a private man who coveted the company of a few. John Hay was one. Lincoln's days were shaped by rituals of discipline and hard work. On evenings when Lincoln and Hay were not visiting Seward, McClellan, or others, the president worked alone in his second-floor room, across the hall from the family's private quarters and adjacent to Hay and Nicolay's workroom. Here, he depended on the quiet of his sanctuary to think through the issues transforming the nation.[470] "Evening after evening," Lincoln worked, said Stoddard, who claimed that Hay, Nicolay, and he remained "on guard" to "the footstep in the hall" when the towering figure padded from his desk and approached their work room. Hay, too, cherished his own uninterrupted hours of reading, writing, and poetic musing—absolute concentration.

With Robert Lincoln at Harvard and Mary Lincoln away in New Jersey and upstate New York, and Nicolay convalescing at home in Illinois for thirty-three days during October and November 1861, Lincoln and Hay had extended periods of solitary time together. Their rapport deepened. The president's growing trust in his twenty-three-year-old deputy extended beyond practical interactions of principal and scribe. Lincoln found fellowship in Hay's company, as he embraced his own role as the mentor to this young man. Hay, always an eager student, liked to accomplish and to be complimented, especially from President Lincoln.[471]

On the evening of November 13, 1861, a Wednesday, Lincoln with Seward and Hay arrived uninvited at McClellan's Lafayette Square townhouse. The general was not at home. He was attending an officer's wedding.

Lincoln waited. About an hour later, he heard McClellan's porter in the front hall, telling the arriving general about his visitors. Walking past the parlor's open door where Lincoln sat waiting, McClellan climbed the stairs to his second-floor bedroom. After thirty minutes, Lincoln sent a message to the servant. "The general has gone to bed," he answered.

Hay was furious. McClellan's impertinence, the "unparalleled insolence of epaulettes," he said, was "a portent of evil to come." Hay presaged Lincoln's difficulties with the commanding general. He could remain silent no more. He went to the president, who wasn't especially bothered by McClellan's behavior. He steadied Hay, offering counsel about self-control with irascible officials. Lincoln said, it is "'better at this time not to be making points of etiquette and personal dignity,'" rather than giving air to McClellan's snub after an evening of drinking.[472] Holding to the high ground, the president explained, "I will hold McClellan's horse if he will only bring us success."[473] He valued the general's contribution to the war effort. Lincoln explained that fairness sprang from discretion, a willful choice that demanded tact and caution. The president's moderation with his young secretary sprang from the same impulse that inspired him to tell a good yarn at tense moments.

Similar to many wars, the Civil War proved to be an engine of tremendous innovation, becoming the most modern of nineteenth-century wars. Technology, transportation, and health breakthroughs—submarines, ambulances, hot air balloons, long-range guns, ironclad ships, and torpedoes—spilled over into advances in literature, poetry, photography, and painting. Artists' (from literature to the visual arts, such as painting, photography, and illustration) involvement in the war were few—including Walt Whitman, Nathaniel Hawthorne, Thomas Nast, and Mathew Brady are the most notable. Most visual artists and those geared in the humanities "approached the Civil War in a more elliptical manner," rather than *plein air* depictions of Union and Confederate soldiers in the field, explained Eleanor Jones Harvey, author and curator of *The Civil War and American Art*. Landscape painting became a lens to portray the battlefield.[474] Photography, instead, produced vivid images of the carnage and suffering, led by Brady and Alexander Gardner. The literature of the time, too, from the divergent perspectives of North and South, narrated the war in the works of Herman Melville, Emily Dickinson, Ralph Waldo Emerson, Mark Twain, Walt Whiman, and Nathaniel Hawthorne. The poems and short stories published in the day's literary periodicals, especially the *Atlantic Monthly* and *Harper's Weekly,* portrayed the views and sentiments that consumed the minds of Americans.[475]

In November 1861, Hay hosted German-born, American landscape painters Alfred Bierstadt and Emanuel Leutze at the Executive Mansion, as they started out with their five-day army passes to the field, permitting them to view Union troops and camps around the Potomac River bluffs of Maryland and Virginia. Touring the White House, Hay opened the painters' eyes to the gorgeous panoramas of Washington, views only seen from the president's balcony. "I remember with pleasure your kindness to me," Bierstadt later wrote to Hay, "showing me that splendid view looking down the Potomac. I have a very strong desire to paint it." Though, he never did. For Bierstadt, with little battlefield experience, his one Civil War painting, *Guerilla Warfare,* was composed from a stereo photograph by his brother, Alfred. In his letter to Hay, Bierstadt enclosed photographs he had taken of Hay and also Lincoln. The artist invited Hay into his personal art world in New York City, an offer which Hay apparently didn't accept.[476]

John Hay, Washington, DC, Bierstadt Brothers, photographer, April 1861.
Courtesy of John Hay collection, John Hay Library, Brown University.

Bierstadt's 1861 photographic portrait of John Hay pictured a youthful man clad in natty attire—felt bowler hat, bow tie, stiff-collared button down, and cashmere lapel jacket with velvet trim. The swag of a fob chain draped from his belt to his watch pocket, his hands casually tucked into his jacket pockets, one shoulder tipped against louvred shutters, the opposite hip upturned to one side. Compensating for his apparent youth, Hay wore smart attire for a mature impression. Lincoln, by contrast, was indifferent to his own appearance. He "seldom knew or cared whether or not he was well dressed," said Stoddard. Hay, an impeccable dresser, soon began ordering his tailored suits from London's Saville Row.[477]

The return of congressmen to Washington in late autumn signaled the new season for the city's hostelries and theaters, new fashions in dress. "There are sounds of revelry by night in the stately mansions of the West End," Hay wrote in the *Missouri Republican* on November 24, 1861. Pennsylvania Avenue, *the* Avenue of the nation's capital, "is giving way to the increasing incursion of Northern beauty," thankfully displacing the depressing streams of ambulances and dark uniforms. Theaters shuttered since the outbreak of war seven months before now hung their marquees and reopened with patriotic gags, statuesque females imitating "Drake's Address to the Flag." Taking the stage was the beautiful Southern actress Josephine Chestney, "a full and splendid" belle, Hay said, "with sweet dark eyes and bonny brown hair." Playbills at every corner offered nightly entertainment. A carnival of eccentric acts played out in the blackened faces of White actors, what Hay called "the burnt-cork fraternity," all the rage in these discordant times. One transvestite equestrian male, elegantly styled as "the Cleopatra of the Ring," seduced audiences with lights, music, and his bisexual graces. By his very choices, Hay revealed his personal taste for exotic entertainment.[478]

The opening of the second session of the Thirty-Seventh Congress on December 3 found federal legislators grappling with the federal government's insolvency and an imperiled Supreme Court, what with three vacant seats and two ailing justices. It was impossible to maintain a quorum of five. The biggest news was President Lincoln's first annual message to Congress in December 1861. "One of the most truly admirable State papers that have ever issued from the Executive mansion," Hay reported in the *Missouri Republican*.

The work of several voices in his Cabinet, only the date and signature were in Lincoln's script. No trace of an original manuscript has been found.[479] The president chose to remain silent about slavery relating to the war, a decision that drew ire from the right-wing abolitionists in Boston. Avoiding a "fierce howl over the barbarism of slavery," the president instead held to the mantle of "the integrity of the Union…as the primary object of the contest," Hay said.

The lengthy message droned on about administrative concerns, the Southern conflict, Indian matters, agricultural progress, and reconstituting the national judiciary. Much of the text portrayed serpentine sentences, bureaucratic language, and Lincoln's traditional style:

> The war continues.
>
> In considering the policy to be adopted for suppressing the insurrection I have been anxious and careful that the inevitable conflict for this purpose shall not degenerate into a violent and remorseless revolutionary struggle.

The president went on in two long and winding sentences that framed military and legislative responsibilities and the Southern blockade. Then, a sharp shift occurred in the final and sixth paragraph, displaying a poetic tone and poignant attitude. The iambic rhythm and two-part cadence reflected Hay's poetic contribution to the culmination of Lincoln's first annual message.

> Obeying the dictates of prudence,
> as well as the obligations of law,
> I have adhered to the act of Congress
> to confiscate property used for insurrectionary purposes.
>
> If a new law upon the same subject shall be proposed,
> its propriety will be duly considered.
> The Union must be preserved,
> and all indispensable means must be employed.
>
> The inaugural address at the beginning of the
> Administration
> and the message to Congress at the late special session

were [devoted] to the domestic controversy
out of which the insurrection and consequent war
have sprung.

Nothing now occurs
to add or subtract
to or from the principles or general purposes stated
and expressed in those documents.

The last ray of hope
for preserving the Union
peaceably expired at the assault
upon Fort Sumter.

What was painfully uncertain then
is much better defined and more distinct now,
and the progress of events
is plainly in the right direction.[480]

In conclusion, the President restated that the conflict was "a war upon the first principle of popular government—the right of the people." John Hay's voice appears to have brought clarity to Abraham Lincoln's public voice. Yet, in this message, Hay's eloquence failed to elevate the praise of the press. The *New York Evening Post* claimed, "nothing in it seems up to the spirit of the times." Charles Eliot Norton, a scholar of Western civilization, found it to be "very poor in style, manner and thought."[481]

Tackling the debt, Congress debated the rising cost of arms, food, clothing, and transport for the Union's 700,000 troops. The senators and congressmen, all temporary visitors to Washington when the legislature was in session, filled the city's hotels with double and triple occupancies to each bed. "The publicans and shopkeepers are having a glorious time and reaping a golden harvest," Hay reported in the *Missouri Republican* on December 16.[482]

Accompanying Lincoln on the evening of December 18, a Wednesday, Hay walked with the president across Lafayette Square to Seward's house. The three walked on to General McClellan's. Until midnight, they talked openly about the political disruption with Britain. Tonight, the usually patronizing Seward spoke cheerfully while predicting that the Union government could soon "steer clear of war with [her] old mother." By the third week of December, weathering the simmering debate among American politicians and diplomats about the wisdom of the Trent capture, the president released the two Southern prisoners. "I fear the traitors will prove to be white elephants," said Hay. "We must stick to American principles concerning the rights of neutral."[483]

Seward and Lincoln's greater concern was McClellan. He was failing to advance the Union army.[484] As 1861 came to a close, and the hope of an early end to the human carnage of battle faded, President Lincoln's governance fell into question. Congress, Union generals, the press, and the abolitionist Radical Republicans challenged the president's management of the war and the country. For himself, Lincoln found his inner truth in God.

For his political ideals and principles, he relied on John Hay to record his thoughts and conversations in the young man's private journal, also giving public expression to his policies in the press. "Hay's humor, intelligence, love of wordplay, fondness for literature, and devotion to his boss made him a source of comfort to the beleaguered president in the loneliness of the White House," Burlingame explained.[485] He was indispensable to the president.

Chapter 16

THE MYSTERY OF LINCOLN'S ELOQUENCE

Historians have probed the extraordinary ascent of Abraham Lincoln's presidential eloquence for more than a century and a half since his death.[486] "It is a constant puzzle to many men of letters how a person growing up without the advantages of schools and books, could have acquired the art which enabled him to write the Gettysburg Address and the Second Inaugural," John "George" Nicolay wrote in an 1894 *Century* magazine article. In this, he aroused the riddle of the actual writer, whom he knew to be John Hay. "They naturally wonder how a laboring frontiersman could have gained it." It was Lincoln's "certain plainness of manner, of thought, and of speech," Nicolay continued. The president "was never in a college or academy as a student," he explained, yet drew his education in philosophy, literature, and law from "the Bible, Blackstone, and Shakespeare."[487]

In his article Nicolay was teasing out the mystery of Lincoln's literary surge. Having been witness to Hay's contribution to the president's oratory, Nicolay never answered the questions he posed. Historian Douglas L. Wilson, too, expressed astonishment about Lincoln's apparent literary output. It was "all the more remarkable," Wilson wrote, amid the daily barrage of the nation's deadliest war. The conflict's horrific adversities levied an enormous burden on Lincoln. With stresses so great, President Lincoln's poetic and philosophical creativity was baffling to reconcile.

Most of Lincoln's writing before his presidential election was prosaic—orders, directives, stump speeches, and courtroom derogatories. "In the search for words," remembered Stephen T. Logan, his law partner from

1841–1843, "Lincoln was often at a loss."[488] His early lectures in the 1840s and '50s portrayed a commonplace way of speaking, meeting with indifferent success. In 1859, for example, Lincoln said, "I am not a professional lecturer. Have never got up but one lecture; and that I think, a rather poor one."[489] Lincoln historian Harold Holzer reminded, in his introduction to a compiled work, *Abraham Lincoln the Writer,* that "few masters of the written word ever enjoyed so little training or education."[490] Lincoln had a year or so of formal schooling, scattered in a month here and a couple of months there.

In the wake of his abrupt ascendance from courthouse lawyer to president-elect, from folksy story-teller to eloquent orator, it is no surprise that Lincoln's literary revolution has captured the attention and inquiry of historians. It certainly was an exceptional shift. A mystery, really.

"The Lincoln of folklore," said David Herbert Donald, "is more significant than the Lincoln of actuality."[491] "We will never know for sure how young Abe Lincoln mastered the skill of self-expression," said John Channing Briggs, in *Lincoln's Speeches Reconsidered.* "What we do know is that few masters of the written word ever enjoyed so little training or education."[492] Indeed, said Wilson, "Writing, especially the drafting of consequential text, usually requires time, quiet, and an absence of interruptions, the very things that Lincoln most often lacked." He posed the very question. "How did he manage this?"[493]

Wilson described the astonishing ascent of Lincoln's eloquence in the context of his meager education. "In the four years that Abraham Lincoln would be president, the American public would gradually discover, much to its collective astonishment, that this unprepossessing Illinois politician had remarkable abilities as a writer. In that brief period and the relentless siege of crises, he would produce not one or two examples of provocative writing (which would itself be more than most presidents could manage) but a whole series of unmistakably impressive documents."[494]

Even Lincoln's ceremonial speeches, his messages to Congress, his proclamations and public letters printed in newspapers—most of these were engaging, compelling, and invested with inspiring language, language that was memorable, language that has been etched into the public's living memory.

"All of this came to the American public…as a revelation," concluded Wilson.[495]

"This new Lincoln was a protomodern stylist who sprang from nowhere as if by virgin birth," claimed Andrew Delbanco in "Lincoln's Sacramental Language," "a self-bred genius without foreground or precedent." Quoting Jacques Barzun's "Lincoln the Writer," Delbanco went on to portray Lincoln's detachment, and noted that his "'morbid regard for truth and abnormal suppression of aggressive impulses suggest that he hugged a secret wound.' Out of these secret torments he fashioned 'a style...unique in English prose and doubly astonishing in the history of American literature, for nothing led up to it.'"[496]

Ronald C. White has added to the conversation in *The Eloquent President.* In his own personal journey to understand the development of Lincoln's eloquence during his presidency, White discovered more questions than answers. "I found myself confronting a puzzle with many pieces," White said. "How did Lincoln, a person with so little formal education, become our most eloquent president?"

Without the foundation of a classical education, some historians have explained that it was Lincoln's towering genius. Yet White pressed further. "Why did he often stumble when attempting to speak extemporaneously?" He did, and badly—notably the train passage to Washington in early 1861. "In an era of presidential speechwriters," White concluded, "we need to ask, were these Lincoln speeches, or did others contribute?"[497]

Lincoln worked on frontier farms throughout his youth. He split rails. He rafted down the Mississippi River on a flatboat. He surveyed land and he worked in a store where he met and talked with farmers and citizens of the rural community. He grew up in nature, around wild beasts and farm animals. He listened to the forest and the running water of streams and rivers. He lived by the seasons and the cycle of crops, and with the people who earned a modest living from the land.[498] Yet this frontier boy was most of all a natural-born politician. He was making political speeches on tree stumps and fences at age fifteen.[499] By sixteen, he was "writing rather poor poetry."[500] Lincoln was known for his love of the King James Bible, William Shakespeare, Blackstone, and *Aesop's Fables*. Yet most of what he read, "he read specially for a special object," explained law partner William H. Herndon. He "thought things useless unless they could be of utility, use, and practice," very much the opposite of what poetry is about.[501]

During his twenties and thirties, the politician Lincoln was "missing... any indication of the depth of insight and of empathy that was to mark his greatest writing of the 1860s," David D. Anderson claimed in *The Literary Works of Abraham Lincoln.*[502] In fact, his early speeches played on his humble origins, himself the wood chopper, speeches full of conventional platform bombast.[503] Anderson has suggested that Lincoln's emotional awakening triggered his literary transformation. His soul opened to an inner life after the death in 1850 of his three-year-old son, Eddie, and the threat of his own political demise, when he returned full-time to the law with Herndon.[504]

Lincoln's success in the courtroom, and also in bringing the Illinois capital to Springfield in 1839, when he was leader of the Whig Party in the State House of Representatives, was propelled by his impeccable logic and his talent for winning the primary element of an argument. He had a special talent for backing away from the vulnerable points of debate. He conceded these to the opposition. A slow and methodical thinker, even calculating, some of his detractors considered him crafty, secretive.[505] He often kept his own counsel, shared little of his private views, and was strategic in his speeches. The Lyceum Address of 1838 has been noted as a nod toward his rising oratorical distinction. Certainly, the themes began to strike a higher chord of self-government. Yet the intricate layers and serpentine sentences were nothing like his addresses in 1860 and after, demonstrated here; Lincoln said the ambition of the Founding Fathers

> aspired to display before an admiring world, a practical demonstration of the truth of a proposition, which had hitherto been considered, at best no other, than problematical; namely, the capability of a people to govern themselves.[506]

Wilson argued in *Lincoln's Sword* that "the clue to much that is vital in Lincoln's thought and character lies in the fact that he was thoroughly and completely the politician, by preference and training."[507] Except for his law practice, which he was forced to return to full-time during 1848–1854 and again 1858–1860, his life was centered around caucuses and conventions, party speeches, campaign strategies, and political ambitions. It was Lincoln's fierce desire for national office that led him to understand John Hay's value to his political prospects, and ultimately, his presidency.

When Lincoln returned to politics after 1857, the political landscape had shifted dramatically after the *Dred Scott* ruling and the repeal of the Missouri Compromise. The opening of the Western territories led to the dissolution of the Whig Party and the creation of the Republican Party. Lincoln's hopes rose amid this fluid environment.[508] His soul was on fire; he was contributing to newspapers on a regular basis. He entered debates and made speeches.

The closest Lincoln came to eloquence was in the opening sentences of the House Divided speech of June 16, 1858:

> A house divided against itself, cannot stand.... I do not expect the Union to be dissolved—I do not expect the House to fall—but I do expect it to cease to be divided. It will become all one thing or all the other.

The speech then continued with Lincoln's characteristically long, winding sentences:

> Either the opponents of slavery will arrest the further spread of it, and place it where the public mind shall rest in the belief that it is in the course of ultimately extinction; or its advocates will push it forward, till it shall become alike lawful in all the States, old as well as new, North as well as South.[509]

The greatest gamble of his career, Lincoln's House Divided speech set forth a startling statement of his ideals and vision.

A speech against slavery on September 17, 1859, a few months before it is believed that Hay began working with Lincoln in early 1860, demonstrates the Republican politician's oratorical acuity, use of polarities—equality/inequality; hope/no hope; hope/rod—yet also the absence of precision that Hay soon brings to Lincoln's verse:

> *Equality*, in society, alike beats inequality, whether the... latter be of the British aristocratic sort, or of the domestic slavery sort...free labor has the inspiration of hope; pure slavery has no hope. The slave-master himself has a conception of it; and hence the system of tasks among slaves.... You have substituted hope, for the *rod*."[510]

Lincoln's first big, national political moment came on February 27, 1860, and his speech at Cooper Union in New York City. He had fully prepared and carefully written down every word on blue foolscap.[511] A short selection demonstrates the power of Lincoln's argument and also the stark difference between this prepared speech and those that came before. The selections below exhibit in Lincoln's first long-winded sentence of fifty-eight words, largely unedited, contrasting against verse edited by John Hay in the second and third selections.

The first:

> Wrong as we think slavery is, we can yet afford to let it alone where it is, because that much is due to the necessity arising from its actual presence in the nation; but can we, while our votes will prevent it, allow it to spread into the national Territories, and to overrun us here in the free States.[512]

The second, in which Abraham Lincoln is addressing the Southern states:

> You will break up the Union…
> You will destroy the Government…
> You will rule or ruin…
> you will destroy the Union; and then, you say, the great crime of having destroyed it will be upon us!

The third, addressing the Northern Republicans:

> Neither let us be slandered from our duty…
> nor frightened from it by menaces…
> Let us have faith that right makes might, and in that faith,
> let us, to the end, dare to do our duty as we understand it.[513]

Believing that this was the first time Lincoln tapped Hay to edit a speech, the literary uplifts are few and scattered, appearing as if Hay treaded lightly on Lincoln's manuscript, his maiden voyage ghosting Lincoln's oratory.

From relative obscurity, Abraham Lincoln achieved wide acclaim with the Cooper Union speech, boosting his prospects at the Republican nominating convention in Chicago, June 1860. "The speech that he delivered," said Donald, "quickly erased the impression of a crude politician. It was a masterful exploration of the political paths open to the nation."[514]

Lincoln's political ascent was startling. Equally remarkable was his parallel oratorical ascent. What was the new factor that changed during 1860, from Cooper Union in February to his election in November, and Lincoln's Farewell Address at the Springfield depot in February 1861? What influenced the poetic lyricism in Lincoln's First Inaugural Address in March 1861 and the message to the special joint session of Congress on July 4, 1861? What explained the pronounced shift in Lincoln's prepared speeches, resonating with the appearance of poetic formation, the masterful choice of words, perfectly chosen and placed?

The answer appeared in John Hay's arrival in Abraham Lincoln's inner world in May 1859. Working side-by-side in adjacent spaces in the law offices of Abraham Lincoln and Milton Hay, the politician and the writer *cum* poet created a literary flame among the law associates. Within the year Hay uplifted Lincoln's oratory to poetic lyricism. The timing was perfect. The results were transcendent.

Abraham Lincoln's prepared speech at the Springfield depot on February 11, 1861, as well as his written address at Philadelphia's Independence Hall on February 22, then his First Inaugural speech on March 4, and the closing paragraph of his first annual message to Congress in December 1861, are orations alive with poetic conventions. They alighted through rhythmic cadence and classic rhetorical devices such as alliteration, repetition, and parallel structure. Lincoln's First Inaugural, especially, became a legend. It "would be handed down to future generations as one of the greatest pieces of oratory in American history," Goodheart claimed in *1861*.[515] "The address very soon became—and remains—one of the most selectively quoted speeches ever given." Indeed, "to approach Lincoln's presidency from the aspect of his writing," claimed Wilson in *Lincoln's Sword,* "is to come to grips with the degree to which his pen, to alter the proverb, became his sword, arguably his most powerful presidential weapon."[516]

David D. Anderson and Harold Holzer have explained that Lincoln's literary craftsmanship sprang from the spiritual revolution he experienced during the Civil War.[517] Yet the explanations do not address the source of Lincoln's literary knowledge.

"The Lincoln cult is almost an American religion. It has its high priests in the form of Lincoln 'authorities' and its worshippers in the thousands of 'fans' who think, talk, and read Lincoln every day," said Donald, in *Lincoln*

Reconsidered.[518] "The Lincoln of folklore is more significant than the Lincoln of actuality."[519]

Lincoln's oratory shaped public opinion and his presidency. It also influenced the transformation of American literature generally, according to Barzun.[520] The austerity and brevity of the prose, especially in the Gettysburg Address, the Second Inaugural, and the Meditation on Divine Will, purged the English language of nineteenth-century pomp.[521] In fact, Lincoln has been most often compared with Mark Twain. The powerful influence of Lincoln and Twain, Barzun contended, slowly shifted literary taste in the decades approaching the twentieth century. Victorian flourishes and formality gave way to plain speech and an economy of words.[522] Gary Wills credited Lincoln with having "created a political prose for America, to rank with the vernacular excellence of Twain."[523]

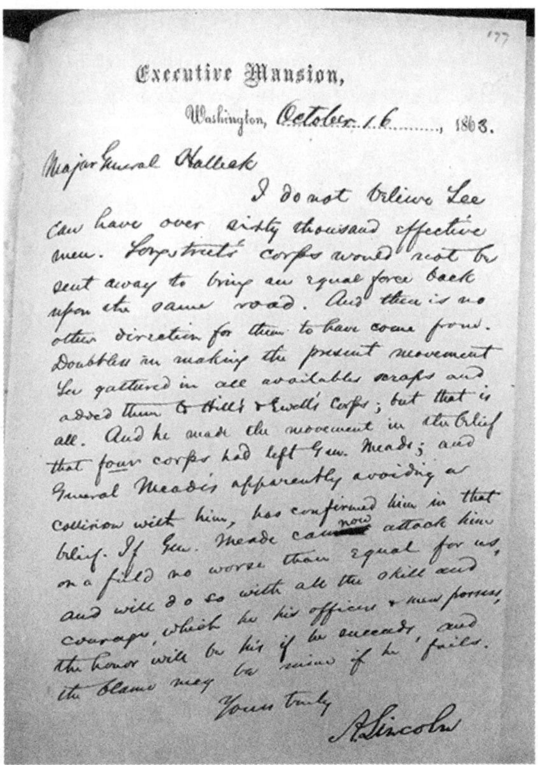

177

Executive Mansion,

Washington, October 16, 1863.

Major General Halleck

I do not believe Lee can have over sixty thousand effective men. Longstreet's corps would not be sent away to bring an equal force back upon the same road. And there is no other direction for them to have come from. Doubtless in making the present movement Lee gathered in all available scraps and added them to Hill's & Ewell's corps; but that is all. And he made the movement in the belief that four corps had left Gen. Meade; and General Meade's apparently avoiding a collision with him, has confirmed him in that belief. If Gen. Meade can now attack him on a field no worse than equal for us, and will do so with all the skill and courage, which he his officers & men possess, the honor will be his if he succeeds, and the blame may be mine if he fails.

Yours truly

A. Lincoln

Abraham Lincoln to Major General Henry Halleck, Executive Mansion, Washington, DC, October 10, 1863. Hand-written by John Hay. Courtesy of Abraham Lincoln papers, Manuscript Division, Library of Congress.

The question of why Hay's contribution remained unrecognized, except for Lincoln's Bixby letter that Burlingame reconstructed and attributed to Hay, stemmed from the absence of extensive research on Hay's original verse written before his time with Lincoln, archived at Brown University and the Library of Congress.[524] Another reason was the very fact that John Hay concealed his role in Lincoln's public messages and speeches. He rarely spoke of his contributions.

Reading what Hay wrote during his college days and after—letters, prose, poetry, blue books, and speeches—presented the evidence to detect the origins of Lincoln's poetic voice. Hay's own words, his timbre, rhythm, and cadence resonated in Lincoln's new oratory. His knowledge of and facility with Greek and Latin are undeniable evidence, a fact that Greek scholars maintain is impossible to replicate without learned intelligence and repetition.

Hay's scrapbooks were important clues in this discovery. Here he pasted his anonymous and pseudo-anonymous contributions to the press. He also attached documents President Lincoln gave to him in gratitude for Hay's material contribution.

One rare instance occurred soon after President Lincoln's death, when Hay admitted to Herndon that "he wrote most of Lincoln's letters."[525] He could forge the president's signature better than anyone but the man himself.

Hay's personal and official papers contained two copies of the Emancipation Proclamation of January 1863, which Hay had filed in a scrapbook of his own writings.[526] One copy of the Proclamation, his family gave to Harvard University in 1916. The second copy, his heirs included in the large collection of Hay's papers that they gave to the Library of Congress.

Historians have wondered why and how Hay came to possess two copies of this valued document, and also others of comparable value, such as the Gettysburg and the Second Inaugural addresses. Some have accused Hay of stealing precious documents from Abraham Lincoln's estate. Not true. Hay became a steward of original copies of the Emancipation Proclamation, the Gettysburg Address, and Lincoln's then-untitled Meditation on Divine Will out of the president's gratitude, his essential character. Kind and appreciative, Lincoln gave Hay the one gift he could give to the individual who contributed to his communication: the documents themselves.

Historian James McPherson, on the occasion of the two hundredth anniversary of Lincoln's birth on February 12, 2009, speaking on the "Jim Lehrer News Hour," said that the differences were so great between Lincoln's

First Inaugural Address and his Second Inaugural that it was as if the two orations were written by different people. Not entirely so, but largely: Hay wrote the last paragraph of the First Inaugural and drafted all of the Second Inaugural.

For Lincoln, John Hay was a rare talent who helped him broaden his reception and communicate his messages. Yet, different from modern presidential speechwriters, who master and reproduce the writing and speaking style of their principals, Hay mirrored Lincoln's tendencies toward reflection, idealism, and rhetoric. He created a new voice, a new writing and speaking style, for Lincoln that was infused with his own rhythm and cadence, succinct and with inspirational metric poetry. It is this verse that rose to define and distinguish the eloquence of Abraham Lincoln's presidency.

Lincoln's visionary direction for the nation and government filled John Hay's private journals. It gave breadth to the poetry and prose he composed for Lincoln. The long periods they spent together created a fruitful practice that became routine to the two men. Across thousands of hours each year, for four years, they talked. They spoke with one another spontaneously, from the president's office in the early morning and late afternoon, to Hay's bedroom in the middle of the night or early morning, during their walks and rides around the city, through Lafayette Square and out to The Old Soldiers' Home. The camaraderie grew to become a rare companionship that no one, not even Mary Lincoln, could breach.

Appearing younger than his years, Hay's self-confident demeanor and his exceptional proximity to Lincoln led some Washington insiders to view the president's private secretary as arrogant. Yet within the Executive offices, Lincoln's daily interactions with Hay required little time to realize that Hay was in complete harmony with the president. He had access to everything and everyone. With Lincoln's confidence, Hay was transformed into a political force in the nation's capital, a bit of an amateur luminary.

"He had great affection for him and every possible confidence in him," Robert Lincoln explained to William Roscoe Thayer, an early biographer of John Hay. Confirming that Lincoln welcomed and depended on Hay, Robert Lincoln willingly confirmed that "my father found especial pleasure in Hay's remarkable literary taste and poetic feeling."[527] Thomas Coke Evans, the *New York World* reporter who accompanied the presidential train journey to Washington and then became photographer Mathew Brady's agent for celebrity subjects in Civil War Washington, acknowledged that "Hay justified the President's discernment. The young man loved his master, serving him with fine loyalty, their relations recalling those between Hamilton and Washington"—Hamilton the speechwriter to President Washington.[528]

Remembering that the sixteenth president was not the revered national hero during his lifetime that he is today, Lincoln's presidency was scarred by a sickening civil war, the soaring national debt, and widespread public disapproval. That he was reelected to a second term was remarkable. Only posthumously did his esteem rise as he was revived as the Great Emancipator of Black slaves and the savior of the Union. "Initially," Ralph Waldo Emerson recalled in 1865, "there had been no shock of recognition" that Lincoln's speeches were great literature, compared to the lightening effects of Walt Whitman's works at the very same time. "Hidden now by the very closeness of their application to the moment," Emerson explained, Lincoln's letters, messages, and speeches were "destined hereafter to wide fame."[529]

Within his first year in the Executive Mansion, Lincoln soon became reluctant to improvise words and speeches in public. His impromptu speech-making betrayed sharp differences with his prepared oratory. He held his tongue rather than present two dissimilar voices to an already distressed nation. Receptions at the White House were the one place that left little room for the president to blunder. He stood for hours, speaking minor pleasantries, wearily shaking hundreds of hands.

The 1862 New Year's Grand Reception at the White House turned out a great jam—Cabinet members and Supreme Court justices, their families, officers of the army and navy, and the curious public. Illustrator Thomas Nast captured the drama of the guests "in all their stars and crosses and gold lace" for *Harper's Weekly.*[530] Private dinners were also a time for Lincoln to have some fun. "His keen appreciation of Shakespeare, and unrivalled faculty of story-telling" stamped the fondest memories of friends and family.[531] The president's fabled ascetic taste for food, beverage, and tobacco limited himself rather than others. British journalist Edward Dicey recalled one White House dinner when, the meal consumed, a few guests began smoking. Secretary of State Seward, who enjoyed his cigars and never missed a chance to chide Lincoln, laughed as he remarked,

"I have always wondered how any man could ever get to be President of the United States with so few vices."

"That, is a doubtful compliment," Lincoln answered.[532]

New Year's White House reception, A. Waud, illustrator, January 1862. John Hay, far left; George Nicolay, third from left; President Lincoln, sixth from left. Courtesy of John Hay collection, John Hay Library, Brown University.

Lincoln and Hay's shared regard for the spoken word mixed with a profound love for Shakespeare and biblical anthology, as well as their respective experiences with rhetoric—Lincoln on the stump and in the courtroom and John under the mantel of his Brown professors, the Phils, and his fraternity debates—elevating the content and cadence of their united product.

Yet Hay's writing was an innate gift, unlike Lincoln. "His mastery of English is as great as that of any man living. In his hands the language is a musical instrument," the *New York Times* reported years later, speaking of Secretary of State Hay's campaign speech for President Theodore Roosevelt in 1904, at the very place in Jackson, Michigan, where the Republican Party was founded fifty years before. "He chooses his words that, as with Lincoln's Gettysburg address, it seems that to alter even one of them would be to introduce a discord into perfect harmony."[533]

The literary artist also perfected the art of discretion to the point of anonymity in his time with Lincoln, a trait he also fine-tuned for his future novels, published anonymously. Hay's distinction for discretion also distinguished the United States in international affairs when he was secretary of state at the turn of the twentieth century.

He acquired the most ephemeral knowledge with ease, a readiness that nurtured his encyclopedic memory. A master of self-deprecation, Hay came to regard the disappearance of self as an asset. He shrouded his identity while he produced magnificent works of literature and diplomacy for President Lincoln during the 1860s, the *New York Tribune* in the early 1870s, as the bestselling and anonymous novelist of *The Breadwinners* during the 1880s, and as a statesman during the 1890s and early 1900s. To his dearest friends, from Abraham Lincoln to Henry and Clover Adams, Clarence King, William McKinley, and Teddy Roosevelt, he was a trusted confidant. Hay was loyal to the core, suppressing personal facts others wished to remain secret. A peculiar trait perhaps in contemporary life, yet in nineteenth-century America it was the mark of an individual of his word, a protector of honored confidence. "The keynote of Mr. Hay's character was loyalty," reported the *Washington Post,* many years after Lincoln.[534]

John Hay, who knew Lincoln as well as the president permitted himself to be known, found paid work applying his poetic craft.

Richard Watson Gilder said of John Hay, "his accomplishment in verse was considerable. Some of his lyrics have the authentic ring, while his ballads have a truth to character and a daring dramatic intensity that make them memorable." In the parts of *Abraham Lincoln* "which were from his pen he rose to the mastery of vivid, terse, and forcible expression. In his public addresses," Gilder concluded, "he showed a unique sense of form."[535]

Chapter 17

SILENT RESPECT

As the second year of war approached in 1862, the drone of human loss and missed chances on the field left Lincoln feeling depressed. For this sensitive man the wartime presidency was grim, casting a hopeless sense of isolation. He was the chief of a divided nation, exercising unimaginable influence in a time of crisis. Listening to "the angry notes of battle, the deep roar of cannon, and the fearful musketry, where new graves were being made every day," Lincoln felt unsettled, wrote former slave Elizabeth Keckley, Mary Lincoln's seamstress, having a view of the first lady's bedroom and the private Lincoln.[536] His "intense anxiety" spiked in the wake of the Union army's failure to make "an early and effective movement" against the enemy in Kentucky, said Hay. Union reverses persisted. In stark contrast, Stonewall Jackson advanced his Confederate troops in Virginia and West Virginia, creating defensible lines. "The war has reached a point now where compromise is not dreamed of on either side, and somebody must be whipped before a permanent peace can follow," Hay wrote. The only real expansion was the "monstrous public debt" and the conscription of a half-million troops.

An impatient Congress began to nurture "grumblers," malcontents who *New York Tribune* publisher Horace Greeley stoked. Wearing his characteristic white overcoat and broad-brimmed Quaker hat perched upon his bald head, Greeley came down to Washington to stir up lawmakers' anxieties.[537] He understood that his paper had influence. He intended to agitate for Union progress. Hay vilified Congress for its "cowardice" and "childish vanity," calling them "spouting wretches at the Capitol still wrangling over little things." What were they doing to raise taxes and restore the government's coffers, he asked. No doubt airing the president's frustrations with Congress, Hay admonished the legislators elected in peacetime to "come up on the level" in wartime. "There is no man more eager for a fight than the president," Hay reported in the St. Louis-based *Missouri Republican,* "and the men who are to do the fighting are equally so."[538]

At the highest levels of military command, apathy rose to a new level. Lincoln demanded the resignation of War Secretary Simon Cameron, the untrustworthy Pennsylvania politician who was pocketing kickbacks from the railroads and the armories producing thousands of cannons and small arms. Lincoln sent Cameron to St. Petersburg as the American minister to Russia, about as far from Washington as he could manage.[539] In his place, he appointed Edwin M. Stanton as secretary of war, an Ohio native and Episcopalian who abhorred slavery. Opinionated, domineering, stout, and bespectacled, his hair and eyes as black as night, Stanton lived off his wealth, enjoying a handsome life in his fashionable townhouse on Franklin Square.[540] Stanton informed Lincoln that the ten commanding Union generals were afraid to fight. He was desperate for fighting men at the highest ranks of the army. He also needed aggressive men to lead the navy's hundreds of war vessels and the tens of thousands of sailors and mariners.[541]

Lincoln decided to take executive control of the army and navy. He didn't consult his Cabinet. On January 27, 1862, he issued General War Order no. 1, instructing that on "the 22nd day of February, 1862, be the day for a general movement of the Land and Naval forces of the United States against the insurgent forces."[542] He also stopped catering to McClellan. He ordered the irascible general to come to him at the White House, no longer walking over to the general's house on many a night. Invigorated by the results of Lincoln's order, the *New York Tribune* shifted to a friendlier tone, reporting that the president "felt more confidence now than ever in the power of the Government to suppress the rebellion."[543] Hay's voice resonated with the conviction of Lincoln's power. "The welfare of the nation is in safe hands, when the Chief Magistrate has at once a genius in conception and a talent in execution that renders him at once independent of Generals and of politicians," he wrote in the *Missouri Republican* on February 21, 1862.[544]

Simultaneously, a dreadful omen fell over the White House: Willie and Tad Lincoln were seriously ill. Tad, age eight, held steady while eleven-year-old Willie grew weaker with fever and delirium, infected with the lethal bacteria of typhoid. The president nursed his boys, caring for them through the nights, "nearly worn out with grief and watching," said White House doorman Edward Bates. During this grave period, John Hay recorded not one word in his journal: not about Lincoln, his boys, nor the Union victories to retake Fort Henry, Roanoke Island, and Fort Donelson near the strategic Tennessee–Kentucky border. Hay's discretion appeared a profound silence. He put down his pen and left pages blank in his diary between January 28 and early March 1862. He wrote no letters or press columns. Hay's journaling was a talisman for the subject and the living image he memorialized in his writing, Abraham Lincoln. His silence spoke volumes. Typically writing on and on about Lincoln's fortitude, his bravery, his principled mien, recording confidential conversations with him, bringing to light the private thoughts of this solitary man, Hay's pen fell silent during Willie's illness.

The anguish surrounding the boy's frailty created a low place within the walls of the Executive Mansion. A bleak difference to the cherubic mirth of two little boys running about the house, Willie dressed in drag and Tad clad as a Black-faced minstrel showman, the infectious bacteria spreading through Willie's small body dulled his sparkling dark eyes and finally stopped his heart. The boy lay in his father's huge rosewood bed, growing wan and fragile by the day, a "shadow," in Burlingame's words.[545] William Wallace Lincoln died at 5 p.m. on February 20, 1862, a Thursday. Willie's death closed a chamber of Lincoln's heart. That afternoon, he shuffled from the family's quarters with an unsteady gait, stepping across the hallway to the Executive offices. He came first to Nicolay's room. The private secretary lay half asleep on his office sofa. "'Well, Nicolay,' said [Lincoln] choking with emotion, 'my boy is gone—he is actually gone!'" Bursting into tears, Lincoln retreated behind the door of the presidential office.[546]

Willie's funeral two days later was a private service, closed to family and intimate friends and officiated by Rev. Dr. Phineas D. Gurley of the New York Avenue Presbyterian Church, where the Lincolns worshipped. The president collapsed, his anguish unbearable, sobbing "This is the hardest trial of my life. Why is it? Oh, why is it?" Lincoln was said to have repeated. During his mourning, unable to tolerate large groups, he shut himself away from the week's White House receptions. He could see no one, artist F. B. Carpenter remembered.[547] In the months that followed, Lincoln found solace in his sweet little Tad, who frequently visited his father's office. The boy was also bereft, his older brother, his companion, gone, and his mother hiding in her bedroom, shrouded in a vast black veil and billowing mourning dress.

Hay honored Lincoln's mourning with absolute silence. His pen lay idle while Nicolay, Stoddard, Keckley, and others chronicled Lincoln's inner tragedy. Still, the closest person to him remained silent. Three decades passed before Hay spoke about the president's suffering, his bitter loss with Willie's death. In his 1890 *Century* essay, "Life in the White House in the Time of Lincoln," Hay explained that Willie's "father was profoundly moved by his death, though he gave no outward sign of his trouble, but kept about his work the same as ever." Even then, Hay shielded President Lincoln, denying public access during his heartache. Hay's loyalty tethered him to the people's image of the president, a portrait Hay had helped to create, the strong and stable commander in chief of the Union. He shrouded the fragile, emotionally broken man.

Abraham Lincoln's unstoppable political ambitions had landed him in the White House, with war and death surrounding him every day. Acrimony and criticism were his daily diet. By late March 1862, spring bloomed in the nation's capital, but balmy days and fresh breezes also brought impassable muddy streets after weeks of rain and melting snow. The president, with Hay's collaboration, was about to embark on another life-changing breakthrough, an advance that forever changed the lives of Americans, Black and White.

Chapter 18

INTRODUCING EMANCIPATION

A full five months before President Lincoln announced his plan to emancipate American slaves in rebel territory in September 1862, he enlisted Hay to begin previewing the pillars of his inner political and spiritual transformation in Hay's press columns. The president broadened his focus from saving the Union to encompass a policy of abolition. Month by month, Hay incrementally unveiled the president's astonishing shift, writing in the *Missouri Republican* as "Washington correspondence." With his journalism, a vivid portrait of Lincoln's awakening emerged. Watching the president come to grips with the emancipation of American slaves, Hay was among a few who were privy to Lincoln's personal revolution, a startling reversal from the president's long-held policy centered on preserving the Union and silent on slavery as the reason for disunion.

Beginning in spring 1862, Hay's press writing revealed the early stages of Lincoln's nascent antislavery policy. As the president approached his decision, Lincoln struggled to envision a nation with freed Black people.[548] Within the Executive Mansion, Hay, an abolitionist, was in step with William Seward, an influential voice within Lincoln's inner circle. Seward advocated an antislavery policy for the administration. As early as 1846, Seward understood that slavery was dragging down Southern culture. Referring to this broken society, he made use of the metaphor of broken fences, describing the South as "the land [that] was sterile, the fences mean."[549]

John Hay launched the press campaign on March 24, 1862, unveiling Lincoln's shifting moral stance on emancipation. He opened with vague statements about the historical evolution of beliefs and the loose causal relationship between slavery and the Civil War. "The progress of ideas in a revolution is more rapid than in any of the chartered colleges or universities," Hay wrote. Threatening that a prolonged conflict might well "degenerate into a pure antislavery war, and end in the utter devastation of the whole South," Hay explained that Lincoln's bedrock and the "noble stand he has taken upon this subject" remained the Constitution.[550] (This piece directly countered his own *Missouri Republican* column of November 16, 1861.) Democratic government, rather than slavery, was President Lincoln's bellwether of success or failure in the war with the Confederate rebels.

Hay then disclosed that Lincoln was offering "to the deluded people of the South, that if they will desert their leaders, lay down their arms and return to their allegiance, they shall receive friendly protection for the future, instead of punishment for the past." In this passage, Hay introduced the president's idea for the proclamation.[551]

The next month, Hay's press campaign championed Lincoln's April 16, 1862, message to Congress, advancing legislation to abolish slavery in the District of Columbia. Congress passed the bill that very day and the president signed it into law, marking a critical step forward.[552] Lincoln had begun his gradual emancipation policy in the nation's capital, where most Blacks lived free. "The time has come when the president can exercise *the full measure* of the powers which the Constitution confers," said Hay. This *Missouri Republican* column of April 21 was Hay's first use of the phrase, "the full measure," which later reappeared in the Gettysburg Address as "the last full measure of devotion," referring then as now to the metaphor of honor and a life worth saving. In April 1862, the lives worth saving were the Constitution and the United States of America, both under mortal siege in the civil war. "When Lincoln had approved the act for the release of the slaves in the District of Columbia," Hay explained, this settled the "doubts in the mind of nervous people," notably Northern abolitionist Republicans.

Hay concluded his portrait of Lincoln's antislavery advances by quoting seventeenth-century English poet John Dryden's tragic verse from *Annus Mirabilis*:

> Like a painted Jove
> With idle thunder in his lifted hand

Dryden's poem commemorated London's so-called "year of miracles" of 1667, in reality a year of catastrophe. It offered a parallel to 1862 America in the midst of war, death, and debt. Hay believed that the nation's vitality might rise anew from "a government strong enough to defend itself against the secret machinations of scheming traitors and the open assaults of armed rebels."[553]

Hay followed two days later, April 23, with a summary of the national discussion about "the question of slavery." He described the conversation as matter of fact, a picture that belied the sharp sectional debates and partisan arguments. "The mass of the people are beginning to talk and think of slavery as an ugly question," he said. Even the people in the largely non-slave border states, those unaccustomed to living side by side with Black neighbors, were beginning to talk of it "in a tone of resolute calmness," he said.[554]

Similar to other sweeping changes in American history, such as the right of women to vote, the freeing of American slaves was an idea that evolved over decades, voter by voter, state by state, one politician at a time, including Abraham Lincoln. John Hay's journalism eased the president's public path, opening incrementally to the ultimate acceptance of freed American Blacks. The president arrived gradually to his antislavery ideology. Vigorously opposing the recruitment of Black soldiers at the outset of the war, by mid-1862, Lincoln embraced the idea as a shrewd means to shore up Northern troops while crippling the Southern economy. In the words of McPherson, "The idea of putting arms in the hands of black men provoked even greater hostility among Northern Democrats and border state Unionists than did emancipation itself."[555]

The early morning of June 20, 1862, a clear summer day in Washington, Lincoln and Hay left the White House to join a presidential party steaming quietly down the Pamunkey River to Yorktown, south of the Potomac and Rappahannock Rivers. The administration planned the pleasant outing as a reconnaissance of war damage to coastal lands. Hay looked out upon Pamunkey's shores and saw what Lincoln already knew: Free Black people could not now achieve the equality of White men and women. Emancipation didn't resolve the realities of living in a society that considered Black people second class.[556] Hay witnessed "the inferiority of man to his circumstances" on the leisurely inspection of the Virginia peninsula.

Sending in his press report of the day's outing to the *Missouri Republican*, Hay portrayed the "scenes of natural loveliness" along the river, the fresh and bracing air, pink clusters of mountain laurel, and fertile soil that "laughs with fatness—rivulets plash and dance in the valleys—and vast water-courses roll their gigantic volumes of power idly to the sea." He asked, "what good reason is there" that this region, the very place where George Washington crossed the river's swollen current to first meet the widowed Martha Dandridge Custis, his future wife, "should not be as rich, inch for inch, as Rhode Island's" Seekonk and Blackstone rivers? Redundantly, Hay answered, because "the front door of the negro quarters with no shoes on its feet—its white tow breeches held up by one suspender—its black face agrin with childish delight—its shock head bare, while it waves its old wool hat as a banner in welcome to what it considers the abolition invasion." Hay spoke plainly, unvarnished words, racially offensive to twenty-first-century ears, portraying the pervasive views about Black people among Whites at the time. "It is the oppressed type," he said, "the image of God cut in ebony, as Fuller phrased it—the 'what-will-we-do-with-it?' as the earnest spirit of American patriotism must regard it."[557]

Bird's eye view of Sixth Street wharf, Washington, DC, hand-colored lithograph, Charles Magnus, publisher, ca. 1863. Courtesy of the Prints and Drawings Division, Library of Congress.

Lincoln believed—and so may have Hay—that colonization of freed slaves was a viable alternative to widespread racial discrimination in America. It was a belief the president had held for over a decade. He had long been in sympathy with the American Colonization Society's plan to settle freed Blacks in Liberia.

A few weeks after, on July 13, Hay's *Missouri Republican* column reflected Lincoln's views about emancipated Blacks in the District of Columbia, reporting that the president thought that freed blacks were better off in a new, distant land, rather than a "home for these unhappy people" in Washington. Echoing the racially prejudiced beliefs of many Americans, Hay said, "We cannot keep this ignorant and unenterprising population among us. The place for the great experiment," Hay concluded as he mirrored Lincoln's thoughts, is "where they may find the whole future open to them to work out their destiny under God, untrammeled by caste or ethnological hatred." Talk of colonization—Africa was most often named—grew in volume as arguments favoring emancipation of Blacks, especially by White Northern political leaders, advanced during the summer of 1862.[558] Thinking Blacks might be more secure in a distant place where they organized their own society, some abolitionists feared the evil treatment by White people against Blacks on American soil, an eerie foresight of the vile reality.

By July 1862, President Lincoln viewed Union army service as a practical blessing for both freed Blacks and the Union army, a means to overwhelm Confederate rebels and win the war. "Out of pure devotion to what he considers the best interests of humanity," Hay said, writing about Lincoln's outlook, the president "has been the bulwark of the institution he abhors. But he will not conserve slavery much longer."[559] This was four months after Hay began previewing the president's antislavery policy. Abraham Lincoln had experienced a remarkable life-changing shift in his moral and political philosophy.

John Hay watched his mentor negotiate with Congress. "The sad history of this sad war," Hay wrote in the *Missouri Republican* on July 21, calling on the rhetoric of repetition and parallel verse to lay emphasis on the grief of bloodshed. "If we have reclaimed territory, we have failed to conquer the rebellious heart."

On the last day of Congress's summer session, July 17, 1862, Hay accompanied President Lincoln to Capitol Hill. Knowing that the president was going to need firm political support from senators and congressmen on January 1, 1863, strategically thinking about his plans to sign the

Emancipation Proclamation on New Year's Day, Lincoln, freely signing end-of-session bills, appeared to curry favor with the politicians.

In the days after Congress adjourned, Hay joined a party of congressmen touring recaptured Virginia seaport villages along the Potomac River. Looking out, he witnessed the desperate loss and hard-fought glory, Southern towns torn asunder by battle and death. He was steadied by his privileged position on the richly provisioned government steamer, grappling with the dichotomies of death and life, destruction and victory. The boat glided snuggly between tugs, ships, schooners, sloops, and skiffs, seasick congressmen retching their downed whisky overboard into white-capped waves. At day's end, the party steamed back up the Potomac to the Navy Yard, just three-and-a-half miles from the White House. Hay looked out from the ship's deck to the sight of the "half-finished obelisk gleaming in the moonlight," the incomplete Washington Monument rising upon the horizon.

"The hour is gloomy; but never despair," Hay wrote in the *Missouri Republican*, "this last resting place of freedom—shall never perish!"

> This last resting place of freedom—
> Shall never perish!

These are the very words Hay wrote and published in the *Missouri Republican* on July 21, 1862, words that Lincoln would speak sixteen months later in the Gettysburg Address, both eulogizing the life of the nation.

The very next day, before Abraham Lincoln unveiled the draft Emancipation Proclamation to his Cabinet, the president called together his secretaries for their regular Tuesday afternoon Cabinet meeting on July 22, 1862.[560] "I have resolved upon this step. I have not called you together to ask your advice, but to lay the subject-matter of a proclamation before" you, he stated and Hay recorded. He announced his plan. "My mind has been much occupied with this subject," Salmon P. Chase wrote of Lincoln's conviction in his diary.[561] Not one among his Cabinet members had been consulted about the original draft of the Proclamation, only Hay.

He asked his Cabinet for suggestions.[562]

Secretary of State Seward spoke up. "Now sir," he said, adopting his chronic tendency to deprecate Lincoln while soliciting his esteem, "while I approve the measure, I suggest, sir, that you postpone its issue until you can give it to the country supported by military success." Seward thought the

Proclamation had a better chance of popular approval if Union people were buoyed by victory on the battlefield rather than low from the army's recent string of losses. Lincoln accepted Seward's suggestion. "I wish it were a better time. I wish it were a better time," the president muttered.[563] He agreed to introduce the Proclamation when the Union military wasn't overpowered by defeat and appearing as "our last shriek, on the retreat," said Hay.[564]

Casting a wide net to campaign his case for emancipation, Lincoln consulted friend and foe alike. One was political ally Reverdy Johnson, the Lincoln-appointed legal counsel to New Orleans, installed after the city's capture on May 1, 1862. Johnson, a conservative Democrat who opposed slavery and represented the defense in *Dred Scott*, entreated Lincoln for an explanation. Johnson was struggling to restore "Union feeling" in the South's leading port city. With the anticipated emancipation policy, Johnson feared it left him negotiating on thin ice.

The president turned to Hay to write the response to Johnson. Hay crafted a letter infusing literary references and polarities: friends/enemies; wisdom/sincerity; forgive/give; save/surrender. "The people of Louisiana know full well that I never had a wish to touch the foundations of their society," Hay wrote on Lincoln's behalf. "They very well know the way to avert all this is simply to take their place in the Union upon the old terms." If Louisiana and its Southern neighbors rejoined the Union, the Emancipation Proclamation was unnecessary. Hay, written in his own hand and over Lincoln's signature, continued:

> You are ready to say I apply to friends what is due only to enemies. I distrust the wisdom if not the sincerity of friends, who would hold my hands while my enemies stab me.... I am a patient man—always willing to forgive on the Christian terms of repentance; and also to give ample time for repentance. Still I must save this government if possible...it may as well be understood, once for all, that I shall not surrender this game leaving any available card unplayed.[565]

Lincoln's powerful ideas resounded through Hay's polemic. The president was committed to adopting a strategy that he now understood was the missing piece in the puzzle to save the Union. If that meant freeing slaves on rebel land, so be it. The commander in chief reached deep into his bag of wartime executive powers to lead the war, the draft, foreign relations, and reconstruction of the Union.

Lincoln recognized that dismantling slavery was also a promise to dismantle the Southern economy.

"The Tycoon is in fine whack," Hay told Nicolay on August 7. "I have rarely seen him more serene and busy." Hay's loyalty to Lincoln had grown more profound in the crossfire of recent months. Portraying a rare faith in deism, Hay averred his conviction in Lincoln's leadership. "There is no man in the country so wise, so gentle, so firm. I believe the hand of God placed him where he is."[566]

Lincoln's resolve was tested on August 20, 1862, when *New York Tribune* publisher Horace Greeley printed an open letter chastising the president for being "strangely and disastrously remiss," Lincoln failing to proclaim emancipation at once. Greeley trusted that his pitch at President Lincoln in the country's most influential daily had a good chance of influencing public opinion.[567]

Not to be outwitted by the bulldog Greeley, Lincoln asked Hay to draft a response to the *Tribune* publisher. Playing against Greeley's bait, the president played out the game of checkmate, capturing the king's offender. Published two days later in the Washington *National Intelligencer,* August 22, a Friday, perfect timing for the weekend editions to replicate the letter across the nation's press wires, the response resonated with the eloquence of the Hay–Lincoln collaboration:

> I would save the Union.
> I would save it the shortest way under the Constitution.
>
> The sooner the national authority can be restored,
> The nearer the Union will be 'the Union as it was.'
>
> If there be those who would not save the Union, unless
> they could at the same time <u>save</u> slavery,
> I do not agree with them.
>
> If there be those who would not save the Union unless
> they could at the same time <u>destroy</u> slavery,
> I do not agree with them.

> If I could save the Union without freeing any slaves,
> I would do it,
>
> And if I could save it by freeing all the slaves,
> I would do it;
>
> And if I could save it by freeing some and leaving others alone,
> I would also do that.[568]

The lyrical simplicity of verse was complete. John Hay's contribution to the poetic cadence and elegant structure resounded in each line. The strike against Greeley was a success.

In late August, on a fine Saturday, Hay mounted his horse and rode out to the President's summer house in northwest Washington, DC, his horse trotting at a leisurely pace, the one-hour ride filling his lungs with the crisp aroma of dry grass. He may have planned to spend the day working with Lincoln at the Old Soldiers' Home. Turning into the shaded landscape, he found the president's horse saddled up and standing by the door. Lincoln was ready to return to town. Momentarily, the president walked out and mounted. The tall and untidy figure who appeared ungainly on foot was the sight of grace in the saddle.[569]

Lincoln talked freely as they started for town. He was preoccupied with General McClellan's "dreadful panic…in the matter of Chain Bridge" in Virginia. Hay crossed out the word "cowardice" in his diary. McClellan had originally ordered blowing up the main bridge across the Potomac River, connecting Confederate Virginia with the capital city. The general's ploy was intended to prevent enemy troops from approaching Washington. At the last moment, though, the general retreated. "The President seemed to think him a little crazy." His fury rising, Lincoln seethed over McClellan's sham of a command. Hay, for his part, viewed the general's behavior to be driven by "envy, jealousy, and spite" against Lincoln.[570] Returning to the Executive office, Lincoln found on his desk a lengthy indictment of McClellan from Stanton, countersigned by three members of the Cabinet.

The very next day, McClellan again punted his lead, holding back troop advances led by five generals. Lincoln paused. Frustrated yet patient, he stood firm, not yet prepared to relieve the general from his command.[571]

A week later, on September 1, 1862, drenching rains saturating the earth, the Battle of Ox Hill at Chantilly, Virginia, broke out with rain-soaked ammunition. Weapons were useless and battle lines blurred in zero visibility. Two thousand Union soldiers fell in ninety minutes.

"The President came to my room as I was dressing," Hay wrote of that morning in his journal. He described the private encounter with Lincoln as informal, a commonplace private moment between the president and himself. After all, Lincoln often came into Hay and Nicolay's bedroom to talk about matters on his mind. "'We are whipped again, I am afraid.'" Lincoln's anger soured over McClellan's reckless command and the war's uneven strides. It didn't help that the season's downpours and swollen rivers halted the Union's advance on Richmond. Yet as quickly as his ire spiked, Lincoln rebounded.

"The President was in a singularly defiant tone of mind. 'We must hurt this enemy before it gets away,'" he said and Hay scribed, both rebellious in their attitudes.[572] "'We must whip these people now,'" he repeated. He demanded success. "It is due in great measure to his indomitable will, that army movements have been characterized by such energy and celerity for the last few days."[573]

The first week of September 1862, though, was a "terrible week" at "terrible cost" to the Union army, Hay said. Rumors of cowardice in the highest ranks filled The Willard's bars and dining rooms, while the sight of a large group of guests in frilled shirts, swilling bourbon, gin cocktails, and pure old rye by the horn, left the contemplative New England novelist Nathaniel Hawthorne disgusted. He abhorred the rowdy scene. Tall and trim, Hawthorne strolled out of Willard's, his identity lost in the crowds along Pennsylvania Avenue. John Hay, though, followed the magnificent vision of white hair and dark blue eyes.[574] The younger poet stood in awe of the dark Romantic.

In the privacy of the White House, the president shared with Hay that McClellan was "too useful just now to sacrifice." Lincoln's thinking departed from his Cabinet's united animosity towards McClellan—rare for this competitive group to agree about anything—and the public's generally poor feeling about Lincoln and the costly war. The president was committed to the

Union commander. He also recognized the need to assert his authority as commander in chief. With Hay, Lincoln walked over to the next-door telegraph room in the War Department, which Secretary Stanton had moved to the second floor adjoining his own office shortly after his arrival, a room of rare books and Audubon's birds of America.

Acting in defiance of the Union army's lack of progress, Lincoln took hold of army operations. As commander in chief, he spent hours sending instructions to the battlefield. Notwithstanding his active military involvement, Lincoln said to Hay about McClellan, "There is no man in the army [who] excels in making others ready to fight.'" Hay and Nicolay remembered this time as flawed for Lincoln, who actually bungled his command of the Army and failed to replace McClellan. With the clarity of hindsight, they wrote in their 1890 *Abraham Lincoln* biography, "there is no other official act of his life for which he has been more severely criticized."[575]

Meanwhile, Confederate advances into nearby Maryland paralyzed life in the nation's capital. The threat of a rebel attack traumatized the city's residents. "As I do not believe the death-bell of the nation has struck as yet," Hay penned in the *Missouri Republican* on September 7, "I do not believe that Washington is to be taken." He relied on high-level intelligence, hoping to relieve fears. Hay told his readers, "If we are not gloriously victorious before the frosts of October redden the leaves, with their falling will fall our hopes and the hopes of liberty in the world."[576] Hay drew on parallel uses of "fall" and "hope" to emphasize the approaching winter's chill carried with it the ominous promise of defeat.

Secretary of State Seward also confided his own gloom to Hay, he too failing to fully recognize the bitter spite and jealousies among Union generals that turned the Northern army against itself. Seward admitted it had prevented him and the president from acting in the country's best interest.[577] The army was desperate for a unifying commander to lead the generals and their troops.

Just as Northern enlistments plummeted, thousands of slaves fled their plantations, crossing into Union lines and bolstering Union troops. If they wielded firearms, it was not recorded, though they probably did. The Union army won its first major battle on native soil on September 17, at Antietam, Maryland, seventy miles northwest of Washington. The victory appeared a miracle. The win was bittersweet, the bloodiest single-day battle in all American history: 22,717 men dead, wounded, or missing.

The dazzling victory was just the win President Lincoln needed to issue the preliminary Emancipation Proclamation. Within five days of Antietam, September 22, 1862, a Monday, Lincoln called together his Cabinet at noon. He was anxious to move forward. He read to them the document that ultimately freed all slaves living on rebel land. He ordered the Confederacy to put down arms by the first day of 1863. If the rebels did not, he promised to set free the slaves in Confederate states.[578]

With Hay at his side at the Old Soldiers' Home the day before, Lincoln formulated the final draft. "The President wrote the Proclamation on Sunday morning, carefully," Hay said.[579] Hay alone was in the room with Lincoln as the president finalized the document.

Preparing to read the final draft Proclamation to his Cabinet members, President Lincoln thought he might relieve the tension around the table by reading a humorous passage by Artemus Ward. The interlude annoyed War secretary Stanton. Lincoln moved on. "I do not wish your advice about the main matter," he said, "for that I have determined for myself."[580] The opening paragraph, a legalistic preamble, was written in Hay's hand. Following that was a discursive recitation of the order:

> That on the first day of January, in the year of our Lord one thousand eight hundred and sixty three, all persons held as slaves within any State or designated part of a State…then be in rebellion against the United States, shall be then, thenceforward, and forever free.[581]

Eighteen months before in his inaugural address, President Lincoln had maintained that the institution of slavery was irrevocable and binding. Neither could it be, nor would it be reversed. He remained silent about slavery as a cause of Southern secession, a long-held position. Now, the Proclamation was a magnificent turn.

Abraham Lincoln's personal revolution forever opened the way for the promise of a diversified American society, a promise that has faltered for over one-hundred-sixty years in his wake. The president's astonishing shift in his thinking reflected what Nicolay and Hay defined as "a quick intuition of human nature." Lincoln had come to understand "the alarming portent of the slavery struggle" and the moral need to abolish the horrid institution. He needed to change and he did. John Hay was in awe of the president, his mentor. Lincoln had liberated himself from his own resolute beliefs, a freedom that allowed him to liberate American slaves in rebel territory. Hay learned something from this moment, informing his own actions as a mature statesman in future years.

Abraham Lincoln's lifetime of traveling the circuit and stumping the state of Illinois had fine-tuned his sensibilities to the "details and rivalries of local partisanship." Having observed the human intricacies of revolution from the ground up, Lincoln possessed a "comprehensive grasp of great causes and results in national politics."[582] The Proclamation was an extraordinary act of executive power. Humanitarian principles aside, Lincoln freed the slaves to win the war.

The writing of the Emancipation Proclamation curiously lacked any measure of poetry. It "had all the moral grandeur of a bill of lading," historian Richard Hofstadter professed.[583] Protection of the innocent was its legal linchpin. Well-read lawyers Lincoln and Hay, having mastered Blackstone's eighteenth-century *Commentaries,* chose the language of legal briefs to define the primary tenets that Hay had previewed in the press during the previous five months. During this time, Abraham Lincoln had remained silent about his plan, guarding it from Northern extremists who continued to urge complete abolition on both rebel and Union lands. Freeing slaves in the Confederate states, the president had decided, was the way to expedite the war's end. The president's regard for slaves by freeing them was an acquired respect, perhaps one influenced by Hay and Steward.

The day the president previewed his message, Hay said, "an attitude of dignified reticence" prevailed. Journalists from the leading papers wrote of Lincoln's beliefs, many hopelessly misquoted. Only Hay's press writings mirrored the president's thoughts.

"His highest hope has been the restoration of the Old Union," Hay wrote, echoing the president. "He has stood between slavery and those who would destroy it." Amid the blood of the nation and the burden of its debt, Hay claimed, Lincoln came to recognize that "the keenest and brightest and deadliest weapon in the whole arsenal of justice still hangs suspended over the weakest joint in the armor of red-handed and defiant treason." The weakest joint was slavery. President Lincoln's dismantling was his weapon. "He has withheld it as long as seemed to him just or expedient," said Hay, yet the commander in chief of the army and navy could suppress slavery's annihilation no longer.[584]

Just about this time, the early autumn of 1862, John Hay gained a deeper eloquence in his own voice, prosaic and philosophical.

Lincoln's design for freeing slaves delivered a crippling blow to the South. It was a strike intended to weaken the seditious Confederate army, also cutting off oxygen to the heart of the Southern economy. Since the war's outbreak, male slaves had been escaping plantations to join the Union ranks. By the time of the signing of the Emancipation Proclamation on January 1, 1863, thousands of free and formerly enslaved Black men were soldiers and sailors in the Union ranks.[585] The Civil War, after all, had become an economic war that threatened the very foundation of slave labor and its extension in Western territories.

Later in the evening of September 22, Lincoln and Hay stepped into the president's open carriage, waiting at the side door of the White House. They drove off unnoticed into the mild evening, traveling to the Old Soldiers' Home for the night.[586] Two days later, September 24, they returned to the city. The next evening, Hay accompanied Lincoln to a wine reception at the home of Treasury secretary Salmon P. Chase, a graceful if rigid man who toasted emancipation. "If the slaveholders had stayed in the Union," Chase said, "they might have kept the life in their institution for many years to come." Instead, "a great work had been done," Chase and his high-ranking guests seemed to think. "The President's Proclamation," Hay resolved, "had freed them as well as the slaves." Exhilarated, they called themselves abolitionists, Hay wrote in the *Missouri Republican,* "that horrible name."[587]

Chapter 19

KINDRED SPIRITS

President Lincoln depended on Hay to give voice to what he wanted to say and how he wanted to say it, better than he had the time to do himself. Their nighttime walks across Pennsylvania Avenue to elegant Lafayette Square residences, or their evening and morning rides on horseback to the Old Soldiers Home, offered relaxed intervals for informal conservation, interludes when the president felt a calmness of mind to confide to Hay something about a troubling situation or an unresolved idea. Day or night, Hay assimilated with ease the multiple roles the president required of him, communicating to Congress, the press, and the people messages of such diverse content as policy, strategy, legislation, state of the union, even concepts and emotions. Routine letters to public editorials, congressional messages, political speeches, and private communiqués encompassed the array of messages Lincoln asked Hay to draft.

Lincoln and Hay knew of the Washington–Hamilton partnership. "I find he is so much pestered with matters which cannot be avoided," Alexander Hamilton once said of President George Washington, "that I am obliged to refrain from troubling him on the occasion, especially as I conceive the only answer he would give may be given by myself."[588] It was Lincoln who brought Hay into a similar role, in light of his urgent need for a perfected public voice. During the first eighteen months of his presidency, Lincoln and Hay molded and refined the wordsmith's role of presidential journalist, counselor, and speechwriter. By Lincoln's time, while not a formal or institutionalized White House position, the presidential speechwriter was something of a familiar role.

British historian David Wootton, in his book *The Invention of Science*, has offered interesting insights into the reflexes of individuals who invent new cultural norms. Similar to scientific inventors, Lincoln and Hay had no idea "what the future would hold," in Wootton's words, "but they did have a clear sense of what they were trying to achieve. They were confident that they were making progress, and we cannot leave that progress out of our history, any more than we can leave out the influence they had on those who came after them."[589]

The president and his private secretary fulfilled corresponding needs in their respective work with one another. The poet Hay was fulfilling his aspirations as a writer and communicator, as his literary friends in Providence had hoped for him. Lincoln offered him the golden ring to realize his dream, an invitation that also secured for Lincoln a place in history as one of America's most eloquent presidents. With Lincoln as his mentor, guide, and collaborator, John Hay enjoyed extraordinary luck as he, along with his predecessors and successors, established the precedents for future presidential speechwriters.

"The instinct of Lincoln's genius divined a kindred spirit in his young secretary," Elihu Root remembered of Hay, his fellow statesman in President William McKinley's Cabinet—Root as secretary of war and Hay as secretary of state. Hay spoke "of the dark and dreadful time when Lincoln was… feeling his way among innumerable obstacles to his great conclusion of the emancipation of the slave." Root continued, "He told how the great President often in the dead of night gained relief from sleeplessness and restlessness by rising and seeking the chamber of…Mr. Hay, and sitting on the edge of the boy's bed, reading to him aloud from some favorite book." Root recalled Hay's portrayal of Lincoln pacing the White House halls in the middle of the night, the gaslit vision of the "tall, gaunt form in white, walking down the corridor in which he stood, and the rugged careworn face, seeking sympathy in the thoughts which might lift up his soul above the turmoil of the days of doubts and distress."[590]

John Hay had witnessed Lincoln's "momentous spiritual contest which he fought out alone with his own questioning soul," originally known as the Reflection on Providence and later renamed by Hay as the Meditation on Divine Will. Hay watched the president struggle as Lincoln came to grips with disbanding slavery in the rebel states, his soul at odds with his mind.

In September 1862, Lincoln created a soliloquy that expressed his struggle, poetic verse of his long and "deeply-solemn musings," said Hay, the one person who knew of the verse. Written at "a time of profound national gloom," Hay explained, Lincoln composed the dramatic monologue "with religious soul-searching, never intending it to be published nor to be seen by eyes other than his own."[591] The devastation of war, the infighting among his Cabinet, the partisan wrangling by Congress, and the sectional chasms between North and South left the president emotionally paralyzed, "beyond the power of human help," Hay said. "He shut out the world one day, and tried to put into form his double sense of responsibility to human duty and Divine Power."

Lincoln never spoke of the written meditation. That the original document came to rest in Hay's hands was a curiosity. How this came about remains unclear. Nicolay and Hay stated in their *Lincoln* biography that Hay found the meditation in a drawer in Lincoln's office while packing up the slain president's papers.[592] Perhaps, though unlikely. In retrospect and with the knowledge that President Lincoln characteristically gave Hay original documents in which he made a material contribution, the truth may lay in the fact that Lincoln entrusted the original document to Hay. A remarkable piece of literature, Hay called it, an "unflinching facing of absolute truth—this cold cross-examination of omnipotence."[593] "Burdened with the weightiest question of his life," said Nicolay and Hay, Lincoln struggled to discern God's purpose in the war, according to White, in *Lincoln in Private*.[594]

The lined piece of paper the president apparently gave to his young friend, his kindred spirit, the one person who above all others he entrusted with expressions of his private thoughts, his internal battles. Similar to other documents Lincoln gave Hay, usually at the time they were written or made public, the president likely handed Hay the original document, the evidence for him alone of his poetic contribution.

The meditation's two-part cadence, the measured metric train in each stanza's opening verse, as well as mortal themes of life/death/God, and dramatic polarities of may/must; for/against; saved/destroyed; and vivid/skin-deep revealed Hay's educated poetic contribution.[595] The verse, annotated below, highlighted Hay's poetic influences in the concise, six- to nine-syllable opening line of each couplet (in parentheses), and Hay's favored couplet itself. Abraham Lincoln's spiritual revelations and his wrestling "in secret with his God," said White, were entirely his own, uniting with Hay's literary capacity to create searching, reverential verse.

The will of God prevails. (6 syllables)
In great contests each party claims to act in accordance with the will of God.

Both *may be*, and one *must be*, wrong. (8 syllables)
God cannot be *for* and *against* the same thing at the same time.

In the present civil war (7 syllables)
It is quite possible that God's purpose is something different from the purpose of either party

[And yet] the human instrumentalities (9 syllables)
Working just as they do, are of the best adaptation to effect His purpose.

[I am almost ready to say that] this is probably true—(6 syllables)
that God wills this contest, and wills that it shall not end yet.

By his mere great power, (6 syllables)
On the minds of the now contestants,

He could have either *saved* or *destroyed* (9 syllables)
the Union without a human contest.

Yet the contest began. (6 syllables)
And, having begun, He could give the final victory to either side any day.

Yet the contest proceeds. (6 syllables)[596]

Hay's literary acumen and sympathetic rapport with Lincoln would have helped the president of the United States resolve his inner struggle. Once decided, the president had the conviction to dismantle slavery. Hay had offered the president a safe haven for spiritual abandon and literary repartee, enabling him to express his soul to create this meditation. It is possible that Hay's own abolitionist upbringing entered into their conversations, though the record is silent. Their like-minded souls in conversation generated a seamless dialogue of literary collaboration, an output of wisdom and poetry, surpassing anything Lincoln or Hay created without the other. Muting differences in age, status, education, and experience, each carried the other forward into higher forms of reverie. Lincoln expounded his ideas and principles while Hay took notes, arranging words and infusing literary elements to carry the point. The vision was all Lincoln, made into verse by Hay, infusing poetic intelligence to emphasize the president's ideals. Brilliant minds and dazzling recall of verse and phrase inspired mutual inspiration and confidential trust.

John Hay protected the written meditation on divine will, concealing it for nearly a decade and disclosing it for the first time in his 1871 lecture, "The Heroic Age in Washington," a narrative celebrating Abraham Lincoln's presidency. Taking it on the road, Hay booked his "Heroic Age" talk in several towns and cities from east to west. He hoped to revive the fallen leader's image in the public mind, having faded over the years. Then, Hay called the untitled poem "Reflections on Providence." He later renamed it "Meditation on Divine Will."[597]

During the summer months of 1862, the Lincoln family often escaped the Executive Mansion for the presidential retreat at the Old Soldiers' Home on the city's northeastern reaches, a pastoral environment of cooler air and retreat from the public eye. The president's family occupied the central building of nine structures standing upon 300 acres of tree-lined land, originally a military asylum for disabled army veterans. Hay often accompanied Lincoln on the four-mile trot. The relaxing ride and panoramic views offered some relief for the president to be more at ease, a hiatus from the war, Congress, and his Cabinet.[598] On mornings before breakfast in the country, Lincoln rose before six, moving into the wood-floored room with a small fireplace and his desk, reading the Bible or studying military operations. After a leisurely ride into town, he returned to the White House by 10 a.m.

On these occasions, John Hay joined the president not for reasons of security, but because Lincoln required Hay to make notes and talk freely while the president weighed national policy, military strategy, or personal trials. More than anyone else around him, according to William Dean Howells, a literary friend of Hay's who served in the US consulship in Venice during the Civil War, Hay shared Lincoln's peculiar sense of humor and parrying wit, a natural sentiment and style that the melancholy Lincoln depended on.[599] "Perhaps in all American public life, nothing is more charming than the story of the relations which existed between these two men," Brooks Adams recalled of the Lincoln–Hay friendship, "In public matters the older man reposed in the younger unlimited confidence."[600]

On September 25, 1862, three days after announcing the preliminary Emancipation Proclamation, enjoying one of their many evening rides to the Old Soldiers' Home, Lincoln was feeling especially good. He had been treated earlier in the day by Washington podiatrist Issachar Zacharie, who saw him regularly for his chronic feet discomfort.[601] Relieved from pain, the president shared with Hay some of his concerns about McClellan's military leadership. Lincoln recognized that McClellan fiercely protected his soldiers against disastrous enemy fire, usually at the cost of Union advances. Despite their private conversation, the president was unable to confide fully the true source of his unease about McClellan. Two years passed before Lincoln finally confessed to Hay what he could not admit that day: he believed he had botched the Union cause when he failed to instruct General McClellan to move against Confederate General Lee after the Union victory at Antietam on September 17, 1862.[602] Swayed by the general's reticence, Lincoln had been reluctant to press his own command.

In October 1862, autumn days bringing color to Washington's foliage, John Hay traveled west to his family in Warsaw. He stayed about six weeks, through much of November. He needed rest, his spirit longed for the nourishment of his family, and his boney constitution craved his mother's home cooking. Truthfully, he loved to celebrate his birthday on October 8, perhaps a day also remembered for the death of his older brother on the morning of his second birthday.

"I sit by the wood-fire all day and talk with my mother and at night I do a little unobtrusive sparring," Hay wrote Nicolay in Washington. "I am perfectly idle." Laziness melted away into hours with his father and mother, sister Helen and brother Leonard, who continued to restore his health. Walking along the dirt streets of Warsaw, neighbors shared their distrust of Lincoln and the dismal war. Many believed the president had ignited the conflict with the South. Hay also heard much the same traveling to Republican bases in Springfield and Cincinnati, where he wrote, "I have not heard one single man defend" McClellan.[603]

"Little Mac" had met partial defeat against Robert E. Lee during the Seven Days Battle on the Virginia peninsula, June 25 to July 1, 1862, sending ominous signs of Union weakness. Hay told Nicolay that McClellan's precarious "command in the East begins to shake the confidence of some of our best friends in the Government." In Illinois, the most loyal of Republican strongholds, "things look badly around here politically. The inaction of the Army and the ill success of our arms have a bad effect," he explained. Worse still was the fact that many of the most energetic Republican operatives had enlisted in the Army. "The captains of tens & captains of hundreds who, you know, do our best work, are all in the field," Hay said, echoing the frustration of people in southern Ohio and western Illinois. He forecast grim prospects for the Republican Party in Illinois in the upcoming midterm elections.[604]

Hay's observations foreshadowed the poor results of the 1862 Congressional elections: Republicans were defeated by a wide margin, losing twenty-five seats to the Democrats' gain of twenty-seven. A full fifty-nine of the 184 House seats, including Independents and Unionists, changed to another party. Volatile returns signaled popular unrest among voters, who were White and male.

The partisan press, Democrat and Republican papers alike, pinned the rout on the president's lapel, especially his failure to trim military defeats and advance war gains. Rising inflation, rising taxes, rising corruption, and the fear of a rising tide of freed slaves venturing north appearing to claim jobs from White laborers led to broad Democrat victories in Pennsylvania, Ohio, Indiana, and New York. Remarkably, the Republican Party maintained its control of the US House of Representatives, though with a bare 46 percent to take the lead.[605]

The November 1, 1862, midterm election results delivered the push that Lincoln needed to order General McClellan to stand down from his army command.[606] Within the week, the president turned the Army of the Potomac over to General Ambrose E. Burnside, a West Point officer and a close friend of McClellan. Burnside didn't want and had twice before turned down the command, believing McClellan better suited to the job.[607] Burnside's apprehensions were regrettably born out in the disastrously deadly battle at Fredericksburg, Virginia, December 11–14, 1862, killing 1,892 soldiers, wounding over 13,000, with 2,400 missing or captured. "The mind shrinks and sickens at the task of describing the carnage of the day," Hay and Nicolay later wrote of the needlessly blood-stained battle in their *Lincoln* biography, an unusually impassioned sentence in the massive ten-volume work.[608]

Returning to the White House the third week of November, Hay, now twenty-four, had barely unpacked his trunk in his second-floor bedroom when the president called him to his side. Lincoln was putting the final touches on his annual address to Congress. The Cabinet members had written their department reports, consuming significant portions of the lengthy State of the Union message. The president now turned to Hay for poetic punctuation in the culminating last paragraph.

At noon on December 1, 1862, calling together the last session of the present Congress, Speaker Galusha A. Grow, the one-term speaker whose handsome features were enhanced by his thick wavy beard and mustache, brought immediate order to the chamber with the sharp clap of his gavel. Soon, Nicolay appeared at the door of the hall and piped out in his shrill, high-pitched voice, "a message from his Excellency, the President of the United States." One highlight of the long message, which Sebastian Page of the *New York Times* called a perplexing show of "rhetorical fireworks," was Lincoln's proposed Constitutional amendment for the colonization of freed slaves and also a systematic plan for compensating slaveholders for their lost property. Neither program had much support in Congress, nor did the federal treasury have the funds to compensate slaveholders, as England had done in 1833. Lincoln abandoned both ideas.[609]

It was the closing paragraph, a succinct and precise statement of the president's views on citizenship and emancipation, in its way a spiritual reading on duty, honor, and patriotism that resounded with the drumbeat of iambic pentameter in each line. Themes of history, salvation, light and darkness, honor and dishonor, and life and death belied the educated voice of John Hay's literary mind. In addition to his signature couplets—emphasized below—the poet's rhetorical tools of repetition, polarities, and parallel structure resounded, highlighted in italics. Written in Hay's signature hand, which is neither proof nor evidence of his authorship in a day when most documents were written and copied by hand, the treasured original that resides in the National Archives in Washington, DC, displayed Hay's certain contribution. Lincoln's spiritual thinking joined with Hay's literature to create powerful poetic verse:

Fellow citizens
We cannot escape history

We of this Congress and this Administration
will be remembered in spite of ourselves.

No personal *significance* or <u>insignificance</u>
can spare one or another of us.

The fiery trial through which we pass
will light us down in *honor* or *dishonor* to the latest generation.

We say we are for the Union.
The world will not forget that we say this.

We *know* how to *save* the Union.
The world knows we do *know* how to *save* it.

We, even we here,
hold the power and bear the responsibility.

In giving *freedom* to the slave we assure *freedom* to the free,
honorable alike in what we *give* and what we *preserve*.

We shall nobly *save* or meanly *lose*
the last best hope of earth.

Other means may *succeed*;

this could not *fail.*

The way is plain, peaceful, generous, just

—a way which if followed the world will forever applaud and God must forever bless.

The Senate burst into applause and the muffled stamping of feet in the galleries signaled the public's approbation.[610] David Zarefsky, a scholar of speech and rhetoric, has called the president's second annual message the best embodiment of his "rhetorical leadership." Zarefsky argues that a commander in chief's effective communication grew "from his personal powers of persuasion." With this message, President Lincoln hoped to "mobilize public opinion," drawing on the past and appealing to the future.[611]

Yet the afterglow of the president's commanding annual message faded fast in the nation's capital. A demoralized Washington, overrun by 150,000 idle, displaced, and wounded soldiers, three times the town's 50,000 residents, wandered about the cold and cloudy December streets. More than 10,000 wounded soldiers occupied the twenty or so makeshift hospitals, bedding down without the heat of fire on the bare stone floors of churches, public halls, and the Patent Office.[612] Darkness falling over the gaslit city by late afternoon, the city's residents lived with a sense of fear every hour of every day: thunderous cannon fire echoed from the Maryland and Virginia battlefields, some less than ten miles away.

Adding to the unease was Burnside's Union defeat at Fredericksburg, Virginia, on December 13, fifty-three miles south, one more unsettling setback for President Lincoln. Carrying out ambiguous and ill-conceived orders, Burnside set off a wretched performance that appeared a "butchery" to his troops, according to one witness.[613]

The strain of war took a physical toll on Lincoln. His stooped gait, sallow countenance, and large, cavernous eyes revealed the president's inner turmoil.[614] He turned to Hay in confidence, and perhaps counsel. By mid-December, the president understood that Americans' nerves were raw and their confidence disheartened. At a time of year when twenty-first-century lives turn to holiday jingles, neither Christmas cheer nor Santa Claus existed in 1862. "The old Puritan feeling prevents it from being a cheerful, hearty holiday," said Henry Wadsworth Longfellow.[615] Just a few Boston families were sending out the first color New Year's cards before the war in 1860, picturing scenes of winter tales and plump celebrants. The now-familiar scene of St. Nicholas and his miniature sleigh on Christmas Eve, described in Clement Clarke Moore's whimsical 1823 poem, "A visit from St. Nicholas," popularized as "The Night before Christmas," was largely unknown. First published in 1847, the poem had limited distribution, emerging decades later as part of the Christmas tradition in American homes, well after the war.

In December 1862, President Lincoln had an idea to uplift the spirits of people at home and on the field. He wished to do something special for Christmas, a way to bring some joy to the depressed troops and their families. He turned to Hay, his literary conscience, who in turn developed the idea with German artist Thomas Nast, *Harper's Weekly's* political cartoonist. Nast's legendary caricatures had influenced the rise of modern editorial illustration in America, largely through his work for *Harper's*.

Hay had befriended the barrel-chested, German-born Nast during the Lincoln train journey in early 1861. It was on Nast's original February 1861 letter of introduction to Lincoln's special train that Hay fixed on Nast's editorial style.[616] Now, Hay invited the brilliant illustrator, who had also illustrated the President's inauguration and his first White House receptions, to create Christmastide scenes filled with a spirit of joy and generosity, scenes designed to boost the spirits of the troops, their families, also a nation of disheartened Americans. Hay may have envisioned Nast's German heritage from his Illinois boyhood, channeling some version of German-American parlors displaying a tree glittering with candles and decorations. Paying homage to the German holiday since the early nineteenth century, Christmas celebrations had filtered from the wealthy aristocracy to blue-collar working families, from city to country.[617] Even in the privileged surroundings of the Executive Mansion, Hay and Nicolay were home alone on Christmas day 1861; no tree, no gifts, no special meal.[618]

In Nast, Hay found distinct artistic creativity, the something special Lincoln had in mind. Nast's magnificent display in *Harper's Weekly*, January 3, 1863, the national Republican magazine with a circulation of 200,000, portrayed the gladness and solitude of Christmas Eve 1862. Premiering the now-traditional image of Father Christmas, he introduced the plump and jolly grandfatherly old man. Nast's caricature was the first known image in America of the bespectacled, white-bearded gent, drawn from his native German traditions of Saint Nicholas, the big-hearted fourth-century bishop. Nast's St. Nick with a long white beard donned a red suit, furry hat, and wide leather belt. The artist balanced the joy with a sensitive hand, portraying family sacrifice during the dark days of civil war, the wretched separation of soldiers from their families: a husband alone on the battlefield, resting on his rifle in front of the campfire, holding a photograph album of his family, while his wife, far away at home, kneeling in prayer on Christmas Eve, looked out the window up to the night sky, her children asleep in their small bed.

Thomas Nast, illustrator, Christmas scene, *Harper's Weekly,* cover, January 2, 1863.
Courtesy of John Hay collection, John Hay Library, Brown University.

Nast also created cheerful images of cherubic elves, Santa crawling into the chimney, and reindeer pulling Santa's sleigh, posed opposite heartbreaking images of soldiers marching in the snow and ships tossing aloft in a stormy winter sea. In one illustration, Nast depicted Santa visiting an army camp, handing out gifts to soldiers and waiflike children. In another, Santa held a dancing puppet with a string tied around his neck, a doll looking unmistakably like Jefferson Davis, in an apparent effigy lynching of the Confederate president.

It was classic Nast. None of this occurred in the American household on December 25, 1862, a day when factories, markets, and offices remained open and the cold, damp war camps ran routine drills and artillery repairs.[619] "The Union's best recruiting sergeant," Lincoln claimed of Nast and his inspiring cartoons that aroused the patriotic soul.[620] Widely popularizing the legendary Santa Claus to the American Christmas, Nast's *Harper's* cover appeared every bit the familiar icon of today. Thomas Nast introduced jolly 'ole Santa Claus to American life.

"Christmas is a great institution, especially in time of trouble and disaster and impending ruin," New York diarist George Templeton Strong confided on Christmas Eve 1862. "*Gloria in Excelsis Deo et in Terra Pax* are words of permanent meaning," he said with sadness. "Glory to God in the highest, and on earth peace to people of good will," a sentiment "most distinctly felt when war and revolution are shaking the foundations of society and threatening respectable citizens like myself with speedy insolvency."[621]

Sectional bitterness between North and South reached a high mark at year's end. No one, regardless of age, status, wealth, ethnicity, or education was untouched. In Washington, Christmas Day 1862 was one of extremes. Damp and gray, typical of a winter day in the city on the Potomac River, churches donned evergreens and held evening services. Street bonfires burned, firecrackers were sent shooting into the night sky.

"Free! Free! Free!' shouted one aged Negro," celebrating the imminent Emancipation Proclamation a week away. Freed Blacks in the nation's capital exalted for their Southern brethren, "out in all their glory," said Noah Brooks. They teemed "with an exultant and joyful burst of passion."[622]

As the year of 1862 drew to a close, President Lincoln's Emancipation Proclamation on New Year's day 1863 soon set free more than 3.5 million slaves in Confederate territory. As he had conceived the Union war against Confederates, the president again chose a dramatic and unconventional act to counter an immoral institution and cripple the Southern economy. He said just this in his annual message to Congress of December 1, 1862, a stirring statement reflecting John Hay's literary contribution:

> The dogmas of the quiet past, are inadequate to the stormy present. The occasion is piled high with difficulty, and we must rise—with the occasion. As our case is new, so we must think anew, and act anew. We must disenthrall ourselves, and then we shall save our country.

Repetition and parallel structure combined with poetic polarities of quiet/stormy; past/present; high/rise; new/anew. This was Hay's voice. The Lincoln–Hay collaboration depicted a precise language of morality and principle, a poetic verse that remains inspirational and memorable to this day.

Chapter 20

A CHANGING TIDE

On January 1, 1863, the United States entered a whole new world: the Emancipation Proclamation became law on this day in the nation's capital. The president set free all slaves in the Confederate states, from Virginia, Kentucky, North Carolina, South Carolina, and Georgia, to Tennessee, Mississippi, Alabama, Louisiana, Florida, Arkansas, and Texas. Lincoln's extraordinary war powers liberated 3.5 million slaves. Their emancipation allowed freed Black men, less than half of whom supported the Confederate rebellion, to officially join the Union army. John Hay commemorated the moment by writing under his pen name in the *Washington Chronicle*. "Although our military position is not all we could wish on this first day of the New Year, we have much to congratulate ourselves upon, if we compare our situation to-day with that of a year ago."[623]

Describing Lincoln the patriarch and God's active purpose in this war, Hay posed the redundant question: "With a President combining the zeal of a crusader with the common sense of an American; with a cause in which at last the feet of Liberty and Union, wedded forever, keep time to the measured tread of our soldiers, can we doubt that the smile of the God of Hosts will rest upon our banners, and conduct us through the dark and troublous days that are remaining, into the unfading sunshine of a righteous peace?"[624] He extolled Abraham Lincoln's ideal of liberty for all and union for the nation. Yet decades passed before "liberty" came to include women and Native Americans, in 1920 and 1924.

The population of slaves in the United States had grown by over fifty-one thousand individuals every decade since 1800. Treated as common property to be bought, sold, or given away like any other personal possession, a slave's life was entirely subject to the owner. Thankfully, this sad state was no longer. The civil fabric of the country was shaken to its core. Instead of growing and reproducing, "slavery is this day practically annihilated," Nicolay wrote in the *Washington Daily Morning Chronicle.*[625] Lincoln, he said, was "entitled to the everlasting gratitude of a despised race enfranchised."[626]

The Executive Mansion's New Year's afternoon reception was a dazzling display of silk, taffeta, and the finest wools and linens. Lincoln shook hands with hundreds of will-wishers, while John Hay casually courted Fanny Seward, the shy daughter of William Seward, who stood forlornly apart from the mix. Hay went to her side. He politely pointed out anyone worth knowing. "It was so pleasant to tell [her] who people were," John wrote in his diary.[627] Fanny was equally charmed, writing in her diary that he was "very witty—boyish in his manner, yet deep enough—bubbling over with some brilliant speech."[628] The night's mutual attraction came to nothing.

Later on in the afternoon, President Lincoln left the New Year's reception, walking upstairs to sign the Emancipation Proclamation. Pen in hand, shaking from exhaustion, he paused. "I do not want it to appear as if I hesitated." Lincoln's signature was firm and steady. He gave Hay two copies of the Proclamation, probably for his contribution to the document. One of these resides in the Library of Congress. The other is in Houghton Library at Harvard University, where Clarence Leonard Hay, the youngest of John Hay's four children, gave the document to his own alma mater in 1916.[629]

Historically, the Emancipation Proclamation has been somewhat misunderstood. It did not free all slaves in the country. It left at least 750,000 in bondage, those owned in the four non-Confederate southern border states, such as Missouri and eastern Tennessee, and those in Confederate territory occupied by the Union. The Proclamation declared that 3.5 million slaves "are, and henceforward shall be free." This order by President Lincoln marked "a dramatic transformation in the nature of the Civil War," said historian Eric Foner.[630] It proclaimed an unconditional liberty and freedom to slaves on Confederate land, even though the Union government could not enforce the directive in enemy territory.

Despite Lincoln's monumental initiative, the war went on. In January alone, Confederate troops were flush with the January 14 victory over the Union army on the road from Tappahannock to Richmond. "Fair fields had been stained with blood, thousands of brave men had fallen, and thousands of eyes were weeping for the fallen at home," wrote Mary Lincoln's seamstress, Elizabeth Keckley.[631] Twelve days later, commander of the Army of the Potomac, General Burnside, resigned. In his place, General Joseph Hooker took command of Union troops in northeastern Virginia, Maryland, and Washington, DC. Popular with tactical fighting men, Hooker was a dynamic man with a magnetic character. Tall, shapely, and imposing, "fighting Joe," as he was affectionately known among his troops, captivated Lincoln's hope for the war effort in the region surrounding the nation's capital.

February's harsh winter certainly didn't help to lift anyone's spirits. Rain, snow, and freezing cold swiftly turned to warm and steamy rain. Terrific seas of mud alternately froze to ice, then melted again. Twice in three weeks, Washington was paralyzed with huge snow falls. On February 21, for one, a blizzard suspended horsecars and produced erratic mails, in spite of the bright, clear, and cold air that followed. Sleighs, sleds, and cutters were pressed into service along Pennsylvania Avenue. "The early milk wagons and butcher carts labored painfully, their wheels miring down to the substratum," said one witness. It was "a motley panorama of vehicular contrivances laden with rosy, gay and laughing people," the joyous music of tinging bells. Then, followed by warm temperatures, snow melted to mud. On the last day of February 1863, the nation's capital turned into "the dirtiest and most ill-kept borough in the U.S.," said Noah Brooks, an occasional secretary to the president. The streets became "seas of canals of liquid mud." Trash and garbage fumed, putrid odors unbecoming a nation's capital.[632]

Hay's daily arrivals at Willard's for breakfast, lunch, and dinner cast him into the company of the city's Republican hobnobs. They saw much more of Hay than they did President Lincoln himself. Hay knew everyone worth knowing in the city's Republican field. And by nature, his social and literary mien embraced the Washington press corps, including John Russell Young, Whitelaw Reid, John W. Forney, and others. On the town after hours, Hay often drank to excess, rather enjoying his whiskey. He slept it off during the night, starting fresh the next day.

Daily wires from the battlefield carried differing news of either dramatic victory or perilous defeat. The circumstances were dire. Thrilling for twenty-four-year-old John Hay, who sat at his desk table in the Executive Mansion, feeling an impatience for action. He was desperate to enter battle. His admiration for General Hooker, forty-nine, an aggressive fighter and West Point graduate, inspired him. "Hooker is a fine fellow," Hay quoted the president in his diary. "Whenever trouble arises, I can always rely upon

Hooker's magnanimity," Lincoln said. Hay confessed in his journal, "I wish (to God) I was able to go with him."[633]

Early in March 1863, the president acquiesced, assigning Hay to serve in the field. Lincoln put particular emphasis on intelligence and he was willing to invest in it. He entrusted the young man to act on his behalf, giving Hay a special assignment, a reconnaissance of Union territory around Hilton Head, South Carolina and also the Union port towns of Florida. The president assigned Hay to serve as the aide-de-camp to adjutant General David Hunter, a soldier with political connections to the administration and an advocate for arming black men in the Union army. Hay was to accompany Hunter, commander of the Department of the South, overseeing the army corps occupying parts of Georgia, Florida, and South Carolina, on reconnaissance missions around Hilton Head and Beaufort.[634] Hay also had special orders from Secretary of the Navy Gideon Welles to deliver his personal dispatches by hand to Admiral Samuel Francis Du Point.

"Lincoln wished him to make advance negotiations in the South," explained Walt Whitman, a friend of Hay's. An admirer of handsome men, Whitman thought Hay attractive, especially mentioning his good body, open face, and easy manner.[635] Having a strong fancy for women, Hay did not return Whitman's attentions. The South Carolina assignment also offered John the chance to spend time with his brother Charles, an Army lieutenant and acting aide-de-camp to General Hunter.

Hay set off on his two-month assignment in April 1863, embracing the field service he coveted. Forney's *Washington Chronicle* newspaper stepped forward as Lincoln's journalist, having "the favorable side of the War Office," one observer noted, "mainly reliable news.[636] Still kept at bay from the Executive office were the *Washington Intelligencer*, the *Baltimore Sun, Philadelphia Inquirer*, *New York Herald*, *New York Tribune*, and others.

He departed New York harbor on April 4, sailing to Hilton Head on the *SS Arago,* a sidewheel steamer. For weeks before, Hay readied with packing and ordering up supplies of ink, pens, paper, notebooks, and journals for his daily recording.[637] *Arago's* 295-foot wooden hull, reinforced with wire bulwarks against the ocean's force, drove through high seas at a fast and maneuverable pace. Its heavy displacement of 2,240-gross-tons proved a worthy opponent against Confederate naval ships.[638] Steaming down the Hudson River at midday, the ship's crew set sail on the two square-rigged masts and out into the Atlantic Ocean, fixing a rum line southeastward along the coast. Before long, the steamer entered rough weather offshore. By evening, Hay was seasick, a nasty business. He suffered hapless fatigue and cursed the sea's motion. Thankfully, he slept.[639]

Determined to climb up on deck in the morning, Hay failed, his intestines churning with the sea.[640] The second day out, he ate some breakfast, all troops mustering on board. Watching porpoises and turtles swimming with the ship, the raging vultures above, Hay was calmed by the metronomic turn of *Arago's* engine. "The fresh breeze in the evening sunset and moonrise," he wrote in his diary, portended darkening skies and the "red & [waning] gibbous moon, starting like a bloody portent of the tumbling waves." More bad weather was on the horizon.

The third day out, sailing abreast of the forts in Charleston harbor at one p.m. on April 7, *Arago's* passengers witnessed Admiral DuPont's attack on the Confederate-held Fort Sumter. Enemy forces mounted a heavy defense against the slow-moving Union monitors. After forty minutes and severe damage to five of the nine ironclads, DuPont retreated and called off the offense. He intended to prevent further loss. The rally was an unmitigated disaster for the Union navy. The morning after, anchored thirty miles south of Charleston in Edisto Harbor, Hay journaled that he saw smoke rising from Charleston Harbor, unhappy evidence of the smoldering monitors.[641]

Arago moved on to Hilton Head, where Hay admired the quaint white cottages nestling along the coast, the "picturesque scenery of the circling shores." The crew dropped anchor and Hay promptly disembarked, happy to be free from the steamer. He was greeted by commanding officer General David Hunter and his aide, Charles G. Halpine. The three men walked directly to headquarters. Halpine and Hay, both journalists and press liaisons to their bosses, became fast friends.[642] Hay fell dreamily into South Carolina's soft and warm climate. "The air is like June at noon and like May at morning and evening," he wrote Nicolay. "The scenery is tropical. The sunsets…singularly quiet and solemn. The sun goes down over the pines through a sky like ashes-of-roses and hangs for an instant on the horizon like a bubble of blood." The magnificent display of fire just as the sun dropped below the horizon shimmered like smoldering crimson. Hay had never seen anything so brilliant.

General Hunter promoted Hay to volunteer aide-de-camp with the rank of colonel. Confessing his embarrassment for the title and the Army's press release, Hay confided to Nicolay, "they have made a d[amne]d burlesque of the thing by giving me so much rank." Hay paused, remembering back in March 1861: "I objected to being called Private Secretary."[643] In spite of his protest, he joked to Nicolay, "I am a Colonel *s'il vous plait.* Col. John Hay, Vol. A. D C."[644] Despite his personal amusement, some in the press criticized the presidential aide's speedy promotion. One newspaper sniped, "Why was Hay made a major and then an assistant adjutant-general over the heads of brave officers who were periling their lives upon the battlefield for honorable promotion?" Clearly the answer lay in the source of the promotion: the president of the United States.[645]

When Hay was not on duty with Hunter, he treasured his time with his younger brother, Charlie, who was sick with pneumonia.[646] John took him to the chief medical officers in the Department of the South, who diagnosed pneumonia. On the doctor's advice, Hay brought Charlie with him on a sea voyage to Florida, a mission Lincoln designed as a reconnaissance of the Union-held port cities. They sailed on April 24, a Friday, the one day of the week considered unlucky for sailors to set out to sea, an ancient superstition in many cultures.

Arago's captain sailed at 5 a.m. from Fort Pulaski, just south of Hilton Head. Skirting along within sight of land, Hay stood on the guardrail, captivated, watching the spirited porpoises and pelicans playing in the water around the ship. They arrived mid-afternoon in Fernandina, Union territory on Florida's northern border with Georgia. Disembarking, John and Charlie Hay walked about the town of white frame houses with attractive verandahs and tidy gardens. John witnessed a confused political scene, the product of the Union army's recapture from Confederate hands in March 1862. "I found there a good many sound Union people, though the majority are of course bitter rebels," he said.[647]

The following day, *Arago* moved around the peninsula to Fort Clinch, a beach exposed to the Atlantic sea. "The sea was too high to land," Hay said. The captain sailed the boat onto a sand bar. In their bare arms, freed black men carried the crew ashore Hay called it "the Mazeppa ride." Envisioning himself the hero strapped to his chaperone, he called up the romance of Lord Byron's *Mazeppa* of 1819. Hay's diary offered a glimpse of the songs sung by these Black boatmen.

> The bully boats a coming.
> Oh ho, Oh ho.
> Don't you hear the oars a humming?
> Hang boys hang.

Wall all hang together,
We will hang [with] one another

The beauty of the harmony was not lost on the young poet. They sang in perfect time to the click of the oars and the falsetto of the voices.[648]

The *Arago* pushed on the next day to St. Augustine, arriving soon after noon on April 28. The nation's oldest occupied settlement, founded in 1565 by Spanish explorers, St. Augustine's symbolic importance was matched by its stature as a strategic port. Hay's first sight of the town centered squarely on the Spanish Colonial citadel. He and Charlie walked through the narrow streets. John observed the character in the Black peoples' faces and the pretty Florida girls. Spending the evening in town, he drank heavily and ate abundantly. Yet John was sober enough to walk back to the boat, appreciating the narrow streets, confessing the "advantages to a tight man. [He] couldn't fall down." On board, the roar of the breakers against the sand bar rocked him to sleep.[649]

John Hay's official army inspections at St. Augustine were really something of a joy ride, a privileged experience and also safe duty in wartime. He and Charlie rode on horseback along the beach, through the woods, over the sand flats, and through the soldiers' burial grounds. "Everything [seemed] of a past age," he said. It was paradise. The bounty of blackberries, bananas, pomegranates, roses, palm, and cacti, he wrote to Nicolay, "is the only thing that smells of the Original Eden on the Continent." The Florida soil, he wrote his grandfather, was "almost as rich as our prairie land" in Illinois. He felt the allure of this utopia. "I wish I could buy the State for taxes & keep it for a castle of indolence," Hay said, sounding something of a giddy investor.

Returning to Hilton Head on May 1, Hay went directly to headquarters where he set out with General Hunter on a reconnaissance around the island, surveying the war's toll on the formerly affluent estates.[650] Riding from one plantation to another, Hay learned something about freed Black people. For their part, having largely known a life of slavery, they didn't feel quite so free. There is a "secret understanding among the Negroes," he recorded. "They are afraid of being caught and sent back, and not until lately were they sure in reception."[651]

Hay felt flattered when General Rufus Saxton, a brigadier general and West Point officer, joined him on his inspections of Beaufort and the Sea Islands. Hay knew something of the influential early-nineteenth-century writings by Saxton's father, Jonathan Ashley Saxton, a Unitarian and

Transcendentalist who championed such liberal ideologies as abolition and feminism. Now, Saxton's charge was to recruit freed Black men into the Union army. For reasons apart from Saxton, this day was memorable for John Hay. On May 19, 1863, he dressed for the first time in the blue and gold Brooks Brothers uniform of the Union army.[652] Pride was an understatement. He was an active member of the cause.

Saxton and Hay visited the groundbreaking of the school founded by Laura M. Towne and Ellen Murray of Pennsylvania. They were joined by Charlotte Forten, a well-educated Black woman from a prominent abolitionist family in Philadelphia. The three women were among the first Northern teachers to arrive in South Carolina, which had long forbade teaching slaves to read and write. Towne, Murray, and Forten called themselves the Port Royal Experiment, having among their pupils the First South Carolina Volunteers, a Black troop under the command of Col. Thomas W. Higginson, an enterprising mulatto of wealth, educated in Paris.[653]

Saxton and Hay were also the special guests of English-born actress Jean Davenport Lander, the widow of General Frederick W. Lander, who had died the year before of pneumonia. She hosted a festive picnic in honor of President Lincoln's aide. They had met previously on the evening of April 18, 1861, when Mrs. Lander arrived on the doorstep of the Executive Mansion in a panic, fearing an assassination plot against the president. Today, on the pastoral grounds of the old Gage plantation, she staged an impressive spread. Once magnificent, the tumbled-down house on the Broad River captured Hay's romantic imagination. He was awed by the "brute beauty," the superb "avenue of live oaks and pines." An aura of danger enhanced the adventure. "We were inside of the rebel pickets, which added zest to the dancing," he said. Mrs. Lander presided in dramatic fashion. The First South Carolina infantry stood by on guard, its commander Higginson portraying Hay as "unfortunately look[ing] about 17 and is impressed with the necessity of behaving like 70…not to appear newmown."[654] Conscious that he looked younger than his years, Hay epitomized his college-day's moniker: hay that is green can never be dry.[655]

He took pleasure joining General Saxton's party again the next day of May 23, crossing the Broad River to inspect Parris Island, north of Hilton Head. They met Frances Dana Parker Gage, an abolitionist working with the national Freedman's Relief Association. She introduced the party to several of the five hundred freed Blacks living on the island, offering the White Unionists a private view of the former slaves' new lives. Hay affectionately called them "darkies" and "pickaninnies," in the racist and profane language common in the day.

The Black people flocked in from the adjoining plantation, dressed in their gayest colors, reported the *New York Tribune*. "Mr. Hay, in eloquent yet to the Blacks comprehensible language, as one who in official positions stood near the person of their good friend [Abraham Lincoln], told them that the president took the greatest interest in their welfare." The president was gratified, he said, "to hear that they were learning to read and write, to work for themselves, to accumulate."[656] Saying good-bye, "the Blacks all came forward to shake hands with their distinguished visitors." Three cheers for General Saxton and three cheers for Hay, the Blacks then broke into song, "[swaying] to and fro as they sang with great feeling," Hay said:

> Death he is a little man
> He goes from do' to do'
> Oh Lord remember me.
> Oh Lord remember me.
> Remember me when the years go round.
> Oh Lord remember me.

Grateful to be unshackled, the freed souls closed their revelry with three rounds of "Roll Jordan Roll." The party returned home, contented with the splendid picnic and the "joyous" sight of the Black people on Parris Island, filling the Broad River with twilight music.[657]

Arriving in New York Harbor on June, 1, John Hay had been away from Washington, DC, for two months, a long time. Soon learning that Secretary Welles had accepted Admiral DuPont's request to be relieved of his command, Hay also discovered that the president and Secretary Stanton admired General Hunter's course of action in South Carolina and Florida. Hunter had made peace with the Southerners who stayed in their homes during the war and also aided the freed slaves.[658]

Around the capital region, the news of the Army of the Potomac was less promising. General Hooker's poor military command had left the Union line unguarded, opening the way for Confederate troops under General Lee's command to escape across the Potomac River and into Pennsylvania. Hooker asked to be relieved, a request War Secretary Stanton readily granted, replacing him with General George G. Meade.

Meade, a tall man, straight and wiry, with spectacles and a pale face appearing ashen against his gray hair, was an easygoing officer without airs.[659] Pitting Meade's Union forces against Lee's Confederate troops in Pennsylvania, a Union state, the famed Gettysburg campaign began to take formation in late June. The Gettysburg battlefield lay eighty-five miles north of the nation's capital. Fortifications encircled the city for miles around. The war crowded in, guns sweeping "every road leading to Washington," reported one observer.[660]

As the national press prepared for the historic standoff at Gettysburg, John Hay met on June 30 with Thomas Nast, his friend and the illustrator for *Harper's Weekly.* Desiring to sketch the battlefields in Maryland and Pennsylvania, Nast carried with him a letter from his editor, John Bonner, requesting freedom of movement around the Gettysburg arena. "All military and civil authorities are respectfully requested to give him such facilities for the discharge of his functions," Hay confirmed.[661]

The eighty-seventh anniversary of the signing of the Declaration at Philadelphia on July 4, 1863, was a pivotal day in the history of the United States. It marked the day the Union army achieved two dramatic victories: over-powering Confederate forces in the Battle of Gettysburg and also the Siege of Vicksburg in Mississippi. Suffering the largest number of casualties of the war, Gettysburg was also the most important battle for the Union army in the Civil War, with General Meade leading Northern forces to an unmitigated, if deadly, victory. Lee's losses amounted to more than one-third of his army. At Vicksburg, General Grant captured the last major Confederate stronghold on the Mississippi River, silencing almost one-half of Lee's rebel forces. This victory succeeded in placing the Mississippi firmly in the hands of the Union army.

Grant, age forty-one in 1863, had risen swiftly through Union ranks since the start of the war. A West Point graduate and expert horseman, Grant joined the war effort as military aide to Illinois governor Richard Yates, mustering ten regiments for the state's ranks. Promoted by Governor Yates to colonel and charged with the command of the Twenty-First Illinois Volunteer Infantry Regiment, Grant and his troops transferred to Missouri. In August 1861, he was promoted to commander of southeastern Missouri.

By November 1861, Grant had demonstrated to Lincoln his willingness to fight, in contrast to the more reticent commanders, orchestrating movements to open up the Cumberland and Tennessee rivers, clearing Union access to the south. Known to favor Kentucky bourbon whiskey—Old Crow was his label—as well as to slight the orders of commanding officers when drunk, Grant was glorified by the Northern papers for his valiant military advances against all odds. His heroism, though, soon turned controversial, drawing outrage from the press for his willingness to tolerate inhumanely high battle casualties among his troops. All the while, President Lincoln and Stanton supported him. When Grant's commanding officer, General Henry Halleck, relieved him of his field command in spring 1862, Lincoln stepped forward. "I can't spare this man; he fights."[662] Grant was reinstated as commander of the Tennessee army in July 1862, and accepted overall command of the state's troops in January 1863. He was also an early proponent of recruiting former slaves into the Union army. The Vicksburg win on July 4, 1863, became an important stepping stone for Grant's rise in the Union army.

President Lincoln's popularity also soared in the wake of the Gettysburg and Vicksburg successes. He promised serenaders outside the Executive Mansion that "the war was midwifing 'a new birth of freedom'" by liberating slaves and moving the country closer to realizing the Founders' " vision of equality."[663] Yet Confederate troops were still within striking distance of the capital region. A week later on July 11, the President "had pretty good evidence that the enemy was still on the north side of the Potomac," stationed in Falling Water, Pennsylvania, too close to the nation's capital for comfort. He contended that the Confederates must be pressed into Southern territory. During the week since the Gettysburg battle, Lincoln was impatient with General Meade's slow movements and failure to push the enemy out of Northern territory.[664] "There was nothing to prevent the enemy from getting away," Hay mentioned to him, "if they were not vigorously attacked." He said to Lincoln, "nothing can save them if Meade does his duty." He also expressed doubt about Meade, an engineer who thought logically rather than strategically. Hay thought Meade was unlikely to attack. The general didn't move. Confederate troops remained on Union land, eventually and slowly moving south.[665]

Lincoln's frustration with Meade rose with each day. Complaining to Navy Secretary Welles, the president said, "it is the same old story of this Army of the Potomac. Imbecility, inefficiency—don't want to *do*." He groaned, "oh, it is terrible, terrible, this weakness, this indifference of our Potomac generals."[666] When Lee and his Confederate troops escaped, Lincoln confided to his son Robert, "if I had gone up there I could have whipped them myself."[667] Hay's diary echoed the president's grieved frustration. "Every day he has watched the progress of the Army with agonizing patience, hopes struggling with fear."[668]

Robert Lincoln was on summer recess from Harvard. Joining Hay on the town, the two young men hit concerts and saloons, enthusiastically indulging in "some very queer dancing and singing at one place and some very colorful singing at a great Hall where *mann sauft and treiukt and raucht"*—where men drink and smoke.[669] Hay, five years older than Robert, led the president's son into the seamier corners of life in the nation's capital.

Within days, President Lincoln rallied from the torment of the lost chance of a rout against the Confederates. Looking out from the White House balcony on a clear night, he viewed the beautiful sight of "the thousands of camp fires gleaming in the darkness from the rolling hills across Antietam." It was a splendid show. The "president was in very good humor," Hay said. "Battles are won and campaigns frequently decided by the accomplishment of what seems impossible or absurd," Hay wrote in his journal. He captured Lincoln's spiritual outlook in his own words, his own voice, echoing the president's deistic outlook. Hay continued in his diary, "It seemed as if the Lord was managing this thing so that no vast or overshadowing success of any soldier or sailor should occur, to endanger the new liberty of the people." [670] Lincoln's fatalism channeled his judgment. No stranger to despair, Hay recognized the isolation the president felt during low moments. He wished he could buck him up, helping Lincoln to feel better about his world. Instead, Lincoln scribbled a doggerel for Hay titled "Gen. Lee's Invasion of the North."

In eighteen sixty three, with
    Pomp and might swell,
Me and Jeff's Confederacy,
    Went forth to sack Phil-del,
The Yankees they got arter us,
    And gin us partic-lar h-ll,
And now we skedaddled back
    Again, and didn't sack Phil-del.

The president asked Hay to attest the rhyme by signing "morning, July 19, 1863." The contrast between this ditty and the president's eloquent messages and speeches, even his private "meditation on divine will," were evidence of the origins of the president's otherwise powerful, moving prose.[671]

Tolerant of his own shortcomings, Abraham Lincoln also possessed a forbearance to forgive individuals of transgressions of a criminal nature, respecting as he did others' redeeming virtues.

Chapter 21

FORGIVENESS, TOLERANCE, TRUST

Abraham Lincoln's liberal empathy was on display when judging whether a court-martialed soldier was to live or die for his actions.[672] Plowing through a pile of court martials during the third week of July 1863, Lincoln settled dozens of cases with Advocate General Joseph Holt of Kentucky, the president's chief arbiter. Hay assisted. "A steady sitting of six hours" and one hundred cases, Hay said, the president impressing him with decisions based more on nuances of fairness and forgiveness rather than the bare facts of wrongdoing. "I was amused at the eagerness with which the president caught at any fact which would justify him in saving the life of a condemned soldier," Hay wrote in his diary.[673]

One crime alone prompted Lincoln to be merciless: cruelty to another human being, especially a woman. "There was only one crime I always found him prompt to punch," Judge Holt remembered, "outrages upon women."[674] Almost 10 percent of Union soldiers executed during the Civil War, 22 of 276, were guilty of rape. John Hay readily embraced Lincoln's exceptionalism regarding women, as he honored his mother, and later his wife, daughters, and his lifelong female friends.

For his part, Hay treated Lincoln to a "talk on philology." Alone in the Executive Mansion in late July, with Mary and Robert Lincoln vacationing in Philadelphia and the White Mountains of New Hampshire, and Nicolay in Colorado, Hay rode with the president out to the Soldiers Home on the early evening of July 25, a Friday. The "Tycoon has a little indulged inclination" for the study of language in ancient texts, Hay recorded. What a pleasure for Lincoln to talk with Hay about a subject the college-educated scholar knew so well from his classical training in ancient Greek and Latin. The president continued to learn about the ancient texts from John Hay at his side.[675]

Abraham Lincoln, age fifty-four in 1863, also possessed an unusual ability to shift his beliefs or behavior when he recognized the circumstances as dire. The freeing of slaves in Confederate territory was probably his biggest and most obvious transformation. Witnessing the power of Lincoln's influence to shape events, Hay crystallized what he saw as Lincoln's aptitude to grasp and give life to seismic changes. "He is a man accustomed through a long lifetime to watch with eager interest the intentions of power and the course of events, till he has acquired an instinct of expediency which answer to him the place of sagacity and principle," Hay journaled. "He is a straw which shows whither the wind is blowing."[676]

By August 1863, eight months after issuing the Emancipation Proclamation and almost a year since Lincoln publicized the draft, the president was now passionate about advancing the education and employment of freed slaves. He even offered to back any politician or senator who supported emancipation and its blanket enactment in any state, expanding beyond Confederate states alone. "I consider it the greatest question ever presented to practical statesmanship," Lincoln told Hay.

"The old man is working with the strength of a giant and the purity of an angel to do this great work," Hay observed.[677] Lincoln appealed to General Grant to employ more freed Blacks in his Union ranks. "I believe it is a resource which, if vigorously applied now, will soon close the contest. It works double, weakening the enemy and strengthening us."[678]

President Lincoln also invited former slave Frederick Douglass, the abolitionist, educator, and activist, to meet with him in the White House. A landmark event in the American presidency, Lincoln hoped that Douglass might "go south and help the recruiting among his people," Hay recorded.[679] Meeting in the Executive Mansion on August 10, 1863, Douglass recalled the encounter with the president: "I entered it with a moderate estimate of my own consequence, and yet there I was to talk with, and even to advise, the head man of a great nation." Seated in a low armchair, his feet extended on the floor, Lincoln surrounded himself with piles of documents as well as his secretaries. Lincoln explained his dilemma to Douglass: He was finding it "not easy to induce colored men to enter service as the government didn't deal fairly with them." Douglass reminded the president about the inequities in pay, protection, and promotion for Black soldiers, arguing that fair treatment was essential for recruiting a large number of former slaves. Only with the same wages as White soldiers, and the same protections when taken prisoner, Douglass emphasized to Lincoln, they should also "be rewarded by distinction and promotion precisely as white soldiers are rewarded for like services." Lincoln in turn explained that he was plainly unable to promise equal pay, protection, or advancement.

Disagreeing with some of what Lincoln said, Frederick Douglass was impressed by the president's "solid gravity of...character, by his silent listening not less than by his earnest reply to my words." Douglass concluded, "in all this, I saw the tender heart of a man rather than the stern warrior and commander in chief of the American army and navy." Douglass respected the president's "humane spirit." He agreed to do the best he could, under less-than-ideal circumstances.[680]

In late August, John Hay departed for a summer break, a few days on the Jersey Shore, a day in New York City with friends, then a few days in Providence at Brown University. Attending Brown's commencement ceremonies, the annual ritual he treasured, and also the evening's dinner on September 2, 1863, Hay rose to speak at John Larkin Lincoln's invitation. The honor from his Greek and Latin professor, Hay unveiled his poem that was to be a centerpiece of Brown's one hundredth anniversary celebration in 1864, reciting to the students and assembled faculty members "The Hundred Bells of Brown." "Verses of great beauty and grace, which showed that the lyre, which in former days charmed the hearers, had not lost its charms, even in the prosaic atmosphere of Washington," the *Providence Journal* praised Brown's poet laureate of 1858. References to Greek mythology, the Civil War, and the ritual of scholars passing through Brown's gates of life, Hay infused the verses with his characteristic alliteration and chiastic rhyme pattern.[681] "Surprised to find with what affectionate and hearty confidence" the Civil War president was regarded at the evening's dinner, Hay said, "I heard nothing but the most emphatic expression of advanced and liberal Republicanism."[682]

Hay felt renewed by his alma mater. He was also eager to return to Lincoln and Washington, the city he had come to enjoy. In the languorous days before Congress returned in November, Hay had some time to relax with buddies. On a few nights, he pulled together "some quiet little orgies of whiskey and cheese in [his] room" as well as all-male dinners with West Point officer General Joseph Hooker and a few Army chaps. On others, he went out on the town, yet only when Lincoln didn't need him. Hay's rumored taste for the city's brothels apparently matched his fondness for seedy music halls. The Canterbury was his favorite, reputed to attract soldiers and ruffians who spat, smoked, and shouted. Hay was drawn to the Bowery-flavored low theater of plumped-up female anatomy and eccentric masks coating performers' faces.[683] He indulged the rawness of his Mississippi riverboat days. As much as he could, Hay also joined the president on his evenings at Ford's New Theater, fine dramatic performances of Shakespeare and popular comedy and tragedy. On one night, Hay swooned over the curvaceous Maggie Mitchell of New York, playing to stifling crowds of standing room-only audiences.

As the autumn evenings of 1863 grew cooler, Hay sat down to his writing table in the second-floor Executive offices. He wrote Nicolay about Lincoln's virtually deistic reach. "The old man sits here and wields like a backwoods Jupiter," Hay wrote. "The bolts of war and the machinery of government with a hand equally steady and equally firm."[684] Hay was especially struck by Lincoln's majestic acumen. With finesse and stability, the president oversaw the massively complex war as well as managing his quarrelsome Cabinet members. The war's drain on the nation wore heavily on Lincoln. The thirty-month engagement, which the president had expected to be a three-month affair, strained his nerves. It especially showed in his face. The pronounced physical toll on the president troubled Hay, who hated to see the weight of war exhaust Lincoln.

"Hay was flung suddenly into the dark vortex of the greatest modern struggle. The friend, the intimate of the President," William Dean Howells remembered, "living with him in the White House, sustaining, day after day, relations of the closest confidant, he saw the whole complex progress of events, and from the very force of position gained an accurate knowledge of the truth of that swiftly made history, free from the mixture of falsehood and distortion." Howells concluded of Hay, "he knew from the lips of his chief the motives, estimates, and intentions of the man…which rested with crushing weight on the shoulders of Lincoln."[685] It was true, Hay especially enjoyed raising the "Ancient" out of his burden, bringing him to a place of humor and laughter. Conveying news to the president of Union advances gladdened Hay, joyful when Lincoln's face lightened. Yet, in the crushing Union defeat at Chickamauga on September 20, 1863, a Sunday, sorrow shadowed the president's brow as gains turned to defeat and heavy loss of life.

"The next morning," Hay wrote in his journal, Lincoln "came into my bedroom before I was up, and sitting on my bed said, 'Well, Rosecrans has been whipped, as I feared.'" He confessed his premonitions to Hay. "I believe I feel trouble in the air before it comes." Lincoln's spiritual intuition offered rare insight, yet the depth of his foreshadowing carried a heavy responsibility. Later that morning, the President and Hay rode north to the Old Soldiers' Home. Throughout the day, they worked in the refreshing country air. Riding back into town around 10 p.m., they returned to the Executive Mansion to sleep close by the telegraph room. Lincoln was restless for news from the front.[686]

The president returned to the Old Soldiers' Home two nights later. Before midnight, War Secretary Stanton, a stout and opinionated man, urged Hay to rally Lincoln to return to the White House. He needed him to attend a council of war meeting. The Chattanooga campaign demanded his command. Hay immediately left, riding in a splendid moonlight. He found the weary president asleep in bed. Gently, he woke him.

Lincoln dressed while Hay explained the secretary of war's unusual request for an executive meeting on this grave matter. "It was the first time Stanton had ever sent for him," he penned in his diary. Rosecrans and his Union forces stationed in Chattanooga were under siege from the Confederate army. The Union men cowered. "Rosey" seemed to have lost his nerve. Lincoln had lost his confidence in the general. The president told Hay that Rosecrans seemed "confused and stunned like a duck hit on the head.[687]

At midnight, the president arrived at the telegraph office. Stanton handed Lincoln the wire from Rosecrans, who said he could hold Chattanooga. Hay looked on while Lincoln convened Cabinet members Stanton, Seward, and Chase with General Halleck, who offered field counsel. This night, as other times, Lincoln invited differing opinions among his Cabinet members. The dynamic helped him to resolve his own thinking. They decided to reinforce Rosecrans with additional troops. This September evening, ending late after a supper at Stanton's elegant townhouse near Franklin Square, Lincoln and Hay returned the four blocks to the White House, after one o'clock in the morning.[688] Later in October, unable to break the Confederate siege, Rosecrans was relieved of his command.

Lincoln also valued Hay's fresh perspective. On the rare occasions when they disagreed, Lincoln welcomed a good argument. In late September 1863, for example, Hay pleaded with the president to join with abolitionist

Radical Republicans of Missouri and call for immediate emancipation. "I have spoken to the president several times and have urged others to speak to him," he wrote in his diary. He was disheartened when Lincoln rebuffed the Missouri men.[689] The president explained that he had decided not to use his democratically elected national office to meddle in local affairs. He had promised gradual emancipation in the Proclamation of January 1, 1863. He was committed to the democratic process. "I think I understand this matter perfectly and I cannot do anything contrary to my convictions to please these men," Lincoln told Hay.[690] In this, the young man learned a crucial lesson about civil government: principles of democracy and government by the people took precedence over politics and personal crusades, win or lose.

Their hours together—working, talking, and riding, as mentor and apprentice, as collaborators, and with every day as genuine friends—grew into a unique rapport. Lincoln's spiritual wisdom informed Hay, and Hay's brilliant mind and eloquence inspired the president to shape his thoughts to a higher, wider, and even deeper level. The words, phrases, and messages they produced could not have been created by one without the other, or with anyone else. Hay's work as Lincoln's journalist, scribe, poet, and speechwriter evolved from Lincoln's direction. Gary Wills explained in *Lincoln at Gettysburg* that "Lincoln's desire for honest literary discussion" drew him to "[become] ever more intimated with Hay." Reflecting upon their creative process, the word "poetry" stood foremost. It derived from the ancient Greek word *poiesis,* signaling the act of making. In the classical tradition in which Hay was taught, poetry didn't refer to the writing of verse. Instead, it was the act of making, of bringing something into being that didn't before exist. This is exactly what Lincoln and Hay accomplished together. [691] Warren Zimmerman explained in *The First Great Triumph:* "compassion, dignity, reserve, charity, serenity, tenderness, wisdom, gentleness: These qualities, which Hay respected and described in Lincoln, became lodestones for Hay himself."[692]

By late fall 1863, Washington, DC, was simmering with electoral talk in advance of the presidential campaign and the 1864 election. Republicans turned squarely to Lincoln. "He does not seek the nomination, but really desires it," said Noah Brooks, the occasional assistant secretary who was known to exaggerate his familiarity with the president.[693] On November 2, a conference of Republican Party leaders met in Washington, DC, unanimously backing Abraham Lincoln for the 1864 ticket. "The feeling of the country on this matter demands it," one participant confided to Hay, who swore him to secrecy. "He laid his finger mysteriously on his lips and flitted [away] like an elderly owl," Hay recorded in his journal.

Just weeks before, Hay, too, had heard similar sentiments from Republicans in Illinois. During his October visit to Warsaw to attend the wedding of his older sister, Mary, stopping over in Springfield, he discovered that Lincoln had recovered the support of the party's state leaders.[694] They were "friendly as ever to the President in spite of what they call his fault." Chiefly, they opposed local presidential appointments.[695]

Still, Lincoln was not without his adversaries. Secretary of the Treasury Chase, for one, was making a play to undercut the president while advancing his own ambitions to occupy the White House. Upon Hay's return from Illinois, Lincoln lost no time confiding the nature of Chase's scheming, freely admitting the treasury secretary "was in very bad taste." In spite of Chase's intemperate behavior, Lincoln, invariably fair, was "determined to shut his eyes to all these performances." He vowed to keep Chase in the Cabinet. Seward, too, uncharacteristically sided with the president and opposed Chase.[696] Lincoln described Chase's fleeting presidential aspirations as "a horsefly on the neck of a plowhorse."[697] He was amused by Chase's mad hunt for the presidency.

Lincoln's forbearance surprised Hay. Laughing, the president claimed that Chase's vindictive manner of hitting a wounded man when he was down—referring to himself with the torrent of Union defeats—was nothing better than "the bluebottle fly, [who will] lay his eggs in every rotten spot he can find." Lincoln said to Hay, "If he becomes President, all right. I hope we may never have a worse man."[698]

Moving off the subject of Chase, Lincoln and Hay continued their stream of consciousness conversation throughout the day, touching on many subjects. They had a lot to talk about after two weeks apart. The president spoke of one individual, then read Hay a letter he had written to another. Hay was excited to tell Lincoln about the generally favorable mood of Republicans in the West. In the evening, Hay returned to the second-floor Executive offices after a dinner at Willard's with a few of his Army buddies. Lincoln was at work in his room. Hay settled in to write in the adjacent room, their doors ajar until day's end.

Beyond his own pleasant moments with Lincoln, Hay treasured the sight of the president relaxing with political friends. Two East Tennessee patriots visited him the morning of October 21. Lincoln appeared "more at ease" than usual, Hay observed. The Southern Unionists of East Tennessee, comprising twenty-six counties, had fought hard in their push to secede from their own state, after Tennessee joined Confederate ranks in June 1861. Many East Tennesseans were Union sympathizers enlisting in the Union army. The climax came in 1862, when Lincoln had asked Ohio patron Amasa Stone to oversee the construction of a Union-held railroad line between Louisville, Kentucky and Chattanooga, Tennessee—Confederate territory.[699] In fact, it was the East Tennessee vanguard that supplied guerrilla warriors to burn bridges, cut telegraph wires, and spy for the North to protect the road building. The iron road literally transported the Union army to victory in the 1863 drive to recapture Nashville, Memphis, and Chattanooga. "They were full of admiration for the president's way of doing things," Hay reflected, "and especially for that farsighted military instinct." The East Tennessee patriots successfully built a Union railroad on rebel land.[700]

In the sober flow of the commonplace in Washington, DC, three hundred days after the Emancipation Proclamation became law, the Washington Horse Railroad Company at long last acceded to public pressure to permit "colored persons to ride in this car." The day was October 29, 1863. The private omnibus integrated, offering Blacks a seat, a real luxury. Yet the economic divide between Blacks and Whites was far from equal. Blacks had neither the same job opportunities nor equal compensation. They paid market prices for food, housing, and transportation. "Their regular five cents is just as freely taken by the fare-taker as a white man's," Noah Brooks recalled.[701] Just over a dollar today, the five-cent fare was a burden to Black families, who would continue to suffer for a full century and more.

A sense of fairness, a willingness to debate, and an ability to change were the defining characteristics of Abraham Lincoln in 1863. He led a fractured nation during one of the most treacherous periods in its history. Rallying around emancipation and advocating the hiring of Black soldiers into the Union army, Lincoln had made huge strides in his own views about social justice. Yet he endured the human consequences that prevailed due to the sharp inequalities between Black soldiers and White, a chasm that festered for decades to come.

Chapter 22

"THIS LAST RESTING PLACE OF FREEDOM"[702]

Just as the Republican Party and Lincoln's presidential nomination were gaining ground, the Executive office received an invitation from David Wills of Gettysburg, Pennsylvania, dated November 2, 1863. Wills, a thirty-two-year-old attorney, was organizing the dedication of the national burial ground in the pastoral town in the Blue Ridge Mountains. The July 4th Union victory on the Gettysburg battlefield, one of the most important engagements of the Civil War, killed approximately 3,500 Union men and 5,000 Confederate troops. Over 33,000 soldiers in both armies were injured and over 10,000 were reported missing. More died of mortal wounds in the days following, the bodies left "steaming in the sun" as Lee and his Confederate troops retreated.[703]

Wills was writing to invite President Lincoln to make "a few appropriate remarks" at the dedication, following the principal speaker, Edward Everett of Massachusetts. A brilliant orator and Republican loyalist, Everett had served as the Massachusetts governor, a US congressman and senator, the American minister to Great Britain, and as US secretary of state.[704] By all measures, he had a long and distinguished career. The president was indifferent about shining the light on a notable Northern ally. Though, he was uncertain if he could attend the dedication, what with the war and election demanding his attention.

Engaging the president throughout the day and into the next were General Grant's advances in Tennessee as well as the state elections in New York and Maryland.[705] In the days following, he reflected little if at all about the minor speech Wills invited him to deliver at Gettysburg. The evening of November 3, he was stationed with Hay, Stanton, and Seward in the telegraph office, monitoring election returns. The vote in New York appeared mixed. Lincoln thought the outcome was still undecided. Seward, a native New Yorker, remained confident. His predictions were correct. "No party can survive opposition to a war," Secretary of State Seward explained to Lincoln that night. "We are hereafter a nation of soldiers. These people will be trying to forget years hence that they ever opposed the war." [706] His prophetic foresight about the correlation between America's engagement in war and the outcome of national political campaigns proved eerily accurate. Across the course of two world wars, as well as the Korean and Vietnam wars, only once was the sitting presidential party ousted during wartime. It was Richard M. Nixon, the (almost) two-term president, 1969–1974, who, during the twenty-year Vietnam War, bucked the trend. The Republican Nixon served between Democrats Lyndon Baynes Johnson, 1963–1969, and Jimmy Carter, 1977–1981.

Washington's mild autumn turned icy cold the second week of November. Cutting winds whipped up clouds of dust while snowy flakes danced from the wintry sky. For the hundreds of homeless in the slums and alleys of the nation's capital, ominous signs of winter promised to hasten gnawing hunger and freezing distress, especially for freed Blacks. "Free at last" came at the cost of no place for many former slaves to lay their heads and fill their bellies. Inflationary prices pinched even the most bountiful pockets.[707] Only the city's privileged, John Hay among them, attended the theater, dined at Willard's and Wormley's, and feasted at the famed Harvey's Oyster Saloon on Pennsylvania Avenue at 11th Street, NW. Harvey's legendary steamed oysters consumed five thousand weekly wagonloads of sweet mollusks from the Chesapeake Bay.

In the days leading up to the Gettysburg dedication, the president remained focused on operational strategies of the Union forces, also spending a good deal of time preparing his annual message to Congress. Every year at this time, the annual December ordeal also presented the president with an opportunity to campaign his vision. In the face of grave official business, he cared less about what he planned to say at Gettysburg, or if he would go at all. During interludes in his scheduled appointments, Lincoln pulled from his large coat pocket a copy of Edward Everett's Gettysburg speech, published in the *Boston Journal* on November 8, 1863. The president read the lengthy narrative in preparation for his own speech, if he was able to go.[708] He was a minor part, an afterward to Everett's main event. As late as the day before their departure, "no definite arrangements for the journey had been made," Nicolay said.[709]

President Lincoln discussed the Gettysburg dedication with his Cabinet at their regular Tuesday afternoon meeting on November 17, the day before the portended departure. With his Cabinet members' counsel, he agreed to go. Lincoln decided the presidential party would depart at noon the day before the ceremony, spending the evening in Gettysburg. They planned to return to Washington immediately after the dedication.

The presidential train pulled out of the Capitol Hill train depot at noon on Wednesday, November 18, 1863. A winter chill freshened the air and hurried people's strides. Sitting glumly in his horse-drawn carriage as the driver made his way through the city's streets, Lincoln's face appeared a sullen mask. His head hung down toward his breast. He was bleak about ten-year-old Tad, who was sick and feverish. The boy's illness appeared untreatable, a dreadful echo of Willie's fatal illness. The doctor's regret and Mary Lincoln's hysteria unsettled him. At the rail station, the president was solemn greeting his guests. He stepped into the last car of the special four-car B&O (Baltimore and Ohio) train, the oldest railroad in the United States, the private parlor for Abraham Lincoln and his suite.

The distinguished party included Seward; the genial Secretary of the Interior John Palmer Usher; and the principled conservative Postmaster General Montgomery Blair, as well as Nicolay, Hay, and John W. Forney, the *Washington Chronicle* editor, plus a dozen Union army and navy officers, and the French and Italian ministers. Lincoln returned to high form once the train was underway, recovering his genial public face. The train's wheels screamed across the miles, black smoke billowing out of the engine. Revived, the president led a pleasant journey with amusing tales and jokes that lightened the mood. The rail car, rocking and jolting along the road, was smartly fitted out with an open bar for the five-hour journey.[710]

The train pulled into the Gettysburg station at 5 p.m., on schedule. Greeting the president were David Wills and Edward Everett. Unceremoniously, the rail clerk interrupted them with an urgent telegram for the president from War Secretary Stanton back in Washington. "Mrs. Lincoln informed me that your son is better this evening," he wrote.[711] Relief washed over the president's face. Tad was OK. Hay, who was "in attendance upon the president, and much to be troubled by the correspondents," the observer noted, was strikingly "handsome as a peach, the countenance of extreme youth." And so he remained for another decade.

The party, "a straggled, hungry set," according to one observer, quickly disbanded to their separate lodgings.[712] Wills and Everett escorted Lincoln to the Wills residence, where the president talked with Northern politicians invited to the dedication. Among them was Pennsylvania governor Andrew Curtin, who had thought up the idea for the memorial cemetery. Governor Curtin needed a place to bury five thousand bodies, including some Confederates, and eight thousand horses in the heat of July. His intent was to give meaning to the bloody tragedy. Curtin was also an important ally of Lincoln and his re-election, as the chief executive of the nation's second largest electoral state. Seeking a national platform for the Gettysburg victory, Curtin was no doubt pleased by President Lincoln's appearance at the dedication.

John Hay walked from the train and into town with Eddie Stanton, twenty-one, the war secretary's son. Strolling around Gettysburg, they discovered a town of brick houses and large fenced yards enclosing domestic gardens, pecking chickens, and ambling cows. The residents of Gettysburg had been struck hard by the devastating battle just four months before, July 1–4, only now beginning to put some normalcy back in their lives. Few citizens had evacuated during the battle, surviving by crawling down into their dark cellars, crouching in the smokey hot air thick with poisonous gunpowder.[713] Even now, the stench of death and rotting manure tinged the air.

Hay and Stanton headed straight for a meal in town. Devouring a chafing dish of oysters, they followed with some supper. Satisfied, they headed over to Forney's room for a round of whiskey. Forney and Wayne McVeigh, the thirty-year-old infantry captain and a rising Republican star in Pennsylvania, were pitchy after an afternoon at the train's open bar and an evening of more liquor and no food.

"'Hay,' a drunk McVeigh said, 'you are a fortunate man. You have kept yourself aloof from your office.... You have laughed through your term.'" Hay ignored him. He knew his own place better than anyone and certainly more than McVeigh, a man he never came to like. Pulling the lugubrious duo away from the bottle, Hay, Stanton, McVeigh, and Forney left to join the crowds jamming the town's narrow streets. They walked to the Wills's home, where a band serenaded the gathering mass. Hay noticed President Lincoln stepping out of the front door. He might have held his breath that his boss might hold his tongue. Thankfully, the president didn't blunder, offering a brief non-speech:

> I appear before you, fellow-citizens, merely to thank you for this compliment...I do not appear before you for the purpose of making a speech,...I have no speech to make. [Laughter] In my position it is somewhat important that I should not say any foolish things... [and] the only way to help it is to say nothing at all. [Laughter]"[714]

Admitting the reason for his prepared speeches—ostensibly drafted by John Hay—the president stated that without one, he said "nothing at all."

He stepped back inside. Lincoln met with a few guests before soon retiring to his room "to work on his speech," according to Burlingame.[715] The statement "to work on his speech," might refer to any number of acts—writing, editing, practicing, or memorizing. He was not writing, for the speech had been drafted in Washington. Lincoln consulted with Seward that night, yet it is unknown what they discussed.[716] Lincoln may well have been rehearsing and memorizing the speech, perfecting the aural impact of each word. This was Abraham Lincoln's characteristic practice, engaging physical and mental faculties, committing each word and line to memory, making it his own. The "few appropriate remarks" that Wills had requested required unusual care. Lincoln used "great deliberation in arranging his thoughts, and molding his phrases mentally," Nicolay recalled in his 1894 essay, "Lincoln and the Gettysburg Address," in *Century Magazine.*[717]

When Lincoln went inside, Hay walked back to Forney's room, collecting Nicolay on the way. Unusually gregarious, Nicolay jumped into revelry and sang the "Three Thieves." Reaching the others, Hay, Nicolay, Forney, and McVeigh all fell into song, crooning "John Brown." Street cheers for "speech! speech! speech!" brought the drunken Forney down from his garret. The secretary of the US Senate and a major presence in Washington's press corps, Forney's tailored three-piece suit gave the impression of a life of good living. He was a storyteller par excellence.

"My friends, these are the first hearty cheers I have heard tonight. You gave no such cheers to your President."

"Do you know what you owe to that great man?' You owe your country—you owe your name as American citizens."[718]

John Russell Young, Forney's managing editor at the *Chronicle* and also the *Philadelphia Press*, saw Hay taking notes. He tried to stop him.

"That speech must not be written out yet. He will see further about it when he gets sober," Young pleaded. Clearheaded or not, Hay wrote down every word of Forney's speech in his diary. It was his record of the evening.[719]

The day of the Gettysburg dedication, November 19, 1863, dawned with gray, gentle light. Hay and Nicolay ate a proper breakfast at their lodgings before leaving for the president in his second-floor room at the Wills home. He was at work on his speech. They stayed with him for about an hour, "while he finished writing the Gettysburg address," Nicolay recalled in the *Century* article. A lead pencil in his hand, his private secretaries at his side, Lincoln apparently copied the original draft written in Washington. Writing each letter, each word, each phrase, he committed the speech to memory. He fixed the oratory in his mind.[720] He crossed out the last three words of the phrase, "It is rather for us the living to stand here," and replaced them with "we here be dedicated." This was just one example of Lincoln rewording a draft while he practiced his delivery of the speech. The president liked to read aloud. He once told Herndon, "I catch the idea by two senses, for when I read aloud I *hear* what is read and I *see* it...and remember it better."[721]

Historian Garry Wills confirmed in *Lincoln at Gettysburg* that "the secret of Lincoln's eloquence" was that "he not only read aloud, to think his way into sounds, but wrote as a way of ordering his thought." He memorized his words and phrases, listening to and visualizing them as he spoke.[722] "Lincoln's genius grew not from spontaneity but from hard, painstaking work with words," said Ronald C. White, describing Lincoln's deliberate approach in the making of the address at Gettysburg.[723] The president's process was meticulous. It was also collaborative.

By the time of the Gettysburg ceremony, Lincoln understood that he was the presumptive Republican candidate for the 1864 presidential campaign. He also recognized the power of the press to leverage his position and the national platform at the cemetery dedication. Once he had agreed to speak at Gettysburg, the president decided to christen his experiment of liberty.

Mounted on horseback, Lincoln rode with Hay, Nicolay, and his suite to the national burial ground. Departing the Wills residence about ten o'clock in the morning, they trotted slowly and stopped frequently to greet crowds of sympathizers packing in around the president. The Marine Band played patriotic tunes to the firing of minute guns. The slow-moving parade, "[forming] itself in an orphanly sort of way," said Hay, arrived an hour later.[724] At noon, the ceremony got under way. Edward Everett's retelling of the three-day battle, a graphic portrait drawn out across two hours, offered a dramatic narrative of the horrible clash between Union and Confederate troops. The audience sat enraptured, many moved to tears by the speaker's emotional display. Everett ended. The band played a hymn by Benjamin B. French, a reflective interlude for the nine thousand or more onlookers gathering in a semicircle around the podium.

President Lincoln rose. He had removed his top hat, leaving his head of sparse hair bare to the clearing breeze. The crowd fell silent the moment the president stood. His footfalls, one observer remembered, awoke echoes "with the creaking of the boards, it was as if someone were walking through the hallways of an empty house."[725] Taking out his wire-rimmed glasses from his topcoat, he drew a paper from his pocket. He began to speak "in a very deliberate manner, with strong emphasis, and with a most businesslike air," the *New York Times* reported. Forney's *Washington Chronicle* described Lincoln's address as one that "glittered with gems, evincing the gentleness and goodness of heart peculiar to him."[726] The audience, including six Northern governors, was "totally unprepared for what they heard," recalled Nicolay. John Hay was reassured by Lincoln's "firm, free way, with more grace than is his wont said his half-dozen lines of consecration."[727]

John Hay, 1863. Courtesy of John Hay collection, John Hay Library, Brown University.

The Associated Press correspondent, writing in shorthand, recorded every word Lincoln spoke. At its end, he dashed off to the train depot's telegraph office, wiring the address to the nation. This is the version of Lincoln's Gettysburg speech that reached more Americans than any other. [The stanzas are the author's.]

Four score and seven years ago
our fathers brought forth on this continent
a new Nation,
conceived in Liberty,
and dedicated to the proposition
that all men are created equal. *[Applause]*

Now we are engaged in a great civil war,
Testing whether that Nation,
or any Nation
so conceived
and so dedicated
can long endure.

We are met on a great battlefield of that war.
We have come to dedicate a portion of that field,
as the final resting-place
of those who here
gave their lives
that that nation might live.

It is altogether fitting and proper
that we should do this.
But, in a larger sense
we cannot dedicate—
we cannot consecrate—
we cannot hallow—this ground.

The brave men,
living and dead,
who struggled here,
have consecrated it,

far above our poor power
to add or detract. *[Applause]*

The world will little note,
nor long remember
what we say here,
but it can never forget
what they did here. *[Applause]*

It is for us
the living,
rather, we here be dedicated
to the unfinished work
which they who fought here
have thus far so nobly advanced. *[Applause]*

It is rather for us
to be here dedicated
to the great task
remaining before us—

that from these honored dead
we take increased devotion
to that cause
for which they gave
the last full measure of devotion—

that we here highly resolve
that these dead
shall not have died in vain—*[Applause]*
that this nation,
under God,
shall have a new birth of freedom.

and that Government
of the people,
by the people,
for the people,

> shall not perish
> from the earth.
> *[Long applause]*[728]

The Gettysburg oratory projected a voice different from Lincoln's unscripted, down-to-earth manner for which he was commonly known. On this day, the soul of the president's ideals, the significance of the events, and the American experiment in liberty and democracy appeared in poetic verse. President Lincoln captured the political moment of the hour. Strategically, he understood that the Gettysburg ceremony was a partisan affair. As President of the United States, he held the undivided attention of leading Northern Republicans as well as the press. That day, Abraham Lincoln launched the themes of his 1864 presidential campaign.

Gary Wills offered a brilliant analysis of the address in *Lincoln at Gettysburg*, demonstrating the relationship between the speech's structural formation and Greek funereal oration. Wills's scholarship established the crucial clue to John Hay's contribution to the address. The disciplined curriculum in the ancient Greek and Latin languages, which Hay mastered at Brown, was the foundation of the speech and Hay's facility. Themes of life and death, the Miltonic style, alliteration, the parallel structure, the suppression of self, and the brilliant interweaving of the 272 words reflected the critical rhetoric that defined the speech's literary power.

Life and death themes were apparent:

> Now we are engaged in a great civil war
> Testing whether that nation...can long endure.
> The brave men, living and dead
> Government of the people...shall not perish from the earth.

The Miltonic style triumphed.

> We are met on a great battlefield of that war.
>
> We have come to dedicate a portion of that field, as the final resting-place...
>
> It is rather for us to be here dedicated to the great task remaining before us—

Polarities and parallel construction emphasized the notes of conflict, challenge, and victory.

> Nation conceived in Liberty…all men created equal.
> Those who here gave their lives that that nation
> might live
> long remember…never forget
> died in vain…have a new birth

And, the music of alliteration lent a lyrical chord.

> continent…conceived…created
> Nation…Nation…dedicated…endure
> Cannot…cannot…cannot
> Poor power
> will…what…what…work
> It is…It is…It is…
> dead…devotion…devotion…dead…died
> people…people…people

Structured around classic Greek funeral homilies, in the manner of Greek funereal orations, the Gettysburg address comprised two major sections: praise for the fallen (*epainesis*) and advice for the living (*parainesis*). "What is astonishing about Lincoln's speech," Wills said, "is that he arrived at so similar a vision" as the Greek authors.[729] Wills also highlighted the Latin Mass incarnated in Lincoln's oratory when he said, "It is altogether fitting and proper that we should do this," highlighting the themes of "right" and "just." *Dignum et justum est.*

The elegant classical formation was created by the one person within Lincoln's inner circle possessing the knowledge of Greek and Latin literature: John Hay. Twenty-five years old in November 1863, Hay had been reading, memorizing, and investigating ancient Greek and Latin literature since the age of eight, beginning with his tutored classes in Warsaw, continuing at Pittsfield and Springfield, and culminating at Brown University. At Brown, under the classical tutelage of Professor John L. Lincoln (no relation), Hay's scholarship rose to a refined level of literary excellence. In his draft of President Lincoln's address, built into the Greek funereal oration and Latin themes, he added what James M. McPherson has called "structural metaphors," invisible yet essential. Hay intricately interwove three parallel sets of metaphorical images into the poetic narrative: past, present, and future; nation, continent, and battlefield; and birth, death, and rebirth.[730]

Eminent rhetorician Edwin Black also explained that Lincoln's rhetorical leadership lay in "his disappearance." "In place of his vanished ego, he proposed a set of principles of which he became the personification," Black said.[731] Adopting Lincoln's principles, Hay imprinted the president within the verse. White wrote in *Lincoln's Greatest Speech: The Second Inaugural,* that "Lincoln's rhetoric is Lincoln himself." [732] This is exactly what Hay had been doing since 1860, when he had begun ghostwriting for Lincoln. He reflected the Lincoln that Lincoln himself admired.

Lincoln habitually made notes on scrap paper, what was known as foolscap, jottings that clarified ideas, thoughts, and actions. Hay's own journal was often the essence of Lincoln talking or dictating as Hay recorded. For the address at Gettysburg, Lincoln defined the underpinning philosophies of liberty, equality, and democratic government. These he defined for Hay, who imparted poetic verse from the Greek oration to dramatize the "experiment" in liberty, the "unfinished work," and the "task remaining before us." Lincoln dictated while Hay recorded. By all accounts, the two inspired one another to bursts of literary references to carry a point. Their individual recall of Shakespeare and Burns must have been remarkable. Lincoln and Hay were brilliant collaborators of communication, believing in the power of words to inspire and lead.

They approached words from a multitude of angles. In each speech and message they created together, Lincoln and Hay methodically and precisely developed each phrase. Lincoln advanced the concept, the ideology, while Hay did most of the writing. The president edited the text, as he did for the Gettysburg Address and the Second Inaugural, practicing and memorizing for aural impact, completing the verse with his actual spoken oratory. Lincoln's acuity to the ear, the auditory sensation of speaking and hearing, appeared particularly important in the Gettysburg speech. Garry Wills, quoting Lane Cooper, gave emphasis to this: "The balance in thought and phrase is easily detected by both eye and ear."[733] The rhetorical completeness of Lincoln's delivery arose from an inner voice. An eloquent statement on the mutual dependence of equality and democracy, the Gettysburg Address defended Lincoln's administration and explained why the war must continue.

The poetic construction of meter and cadence, and the rhetorical conventions of polarity and parallelism reflected Hay's understanding of the ancient Greek literary patterns and iambic metrical foot. Classical scholars have confirmed with the author that without Hay's rigorous training in the Latin and Greek classics, the writer could not have replicated the Greek meter and structure. In the absence of actually speaking the ancient Greek texts, the underlying foundation of the Gettysburg Address was impossible to capture.

John Hay's education offered the context; Lincoln's self-education and occasional school study did not. This historical background is the foundation for reconstructing the bases of the address Lincoln spoke at Gettysburg. The eloquent verse ascended to capture Lincoln's powerful ideas. Hay borrowed from Senator Daniel Webster's 1830 letter in which he spoke of the "people's government, made for the people, made by the people, and answerable to the people." Hay had also referred to Webster's letter in his draft of Lincoln's first message to Congress in July 1861: "a government of the people by the same people."[734]

Hay also quoted from his own writing. One reference echoed his *Missouri Republican* column of April 21, 1862.

> The time has come when the President can exercise *the full measure* of the powers which the Constitution confers.

In the Gettysburg address, Hay developed "the full measure" phrase when writing about the men who gave "*the last full measure of their devotion*." In this, he referred to the metaphor of honor and a life worth saving.

He also quoted from another of his *Missouri Republican* columns, this one of July 21, 1862, in a eulogy to the ordeal of war and America's heritage:

> The hour is gloomy; but never despair, t*his last resting place of freedom—shall never perish!*[735]

This chilling parallel with Lincoln's speech at Gettysburg, in which he states "the final resting-place of those who here gave their lives that that nation might live," originally appeared in Hay's writing sixteen months before, echoing the actual author's own voice. Written and published by Hay well before Lincoln spoke these words at Gettysburg, the *Missouri Republican* columns attest to Hay's contribution to the address. Reflecting the thinking and ideals of Abraham Lincoln in both his journalism and his speechwriting for the president, Hay revealed the synchronicity of his remarkable collaboration with Lincoln.

It was not a strain for Lincoln to adjust to Hay, or for Hay to adjust to Lincoln. Classical tendencies appearing in Lincoln's speech patterns before 1860 signaled his aptitude for Hay's own classicism, the latest and most obvious being the House Divided speech of June 1858, opening with "a house divided against itself cannot stand."

Gary Wills professed that the Gettysburg Address marked a revolution in literary style. It "anticipated the shift to vernacular rhythms that Mark Twain would complete twenty years later," he said. "Hemingway claimed that all modern American novels are the offspring of *Huckleberry Finn*. It is no greater exaggeration to say that all modern political prose descended from the Gettysburg Address."[736] If true, and if true that Hay drafted the foundation of the address in the style of Greek and Latin classics, here stated, then it is remarkable that Hay and Twain, who were two boys growing up along the Mississippi River and friends and colleagues in later years, were also the original authors of American dialect.

From the moment Abraham Lincoln spoke the last word at the Gettysburg dedication, returning to his seat on the podium, the president's two-minute address became a living legend. As fast as press reporters telegraphed their shorthand transcriptions to editors, or mounted messengers carried the news by horseback, galloping at top speed to a nearby press office, the address burned the wires worldwide. Lincoln's Gettysburg Address headlined the next morning's early editions, even in the rebel South.[737]

Chapter 23

THE GETTYSBURG LEGACY

The president and his private party returned to Washington after a long and emotional day. The private train steamed into the depot around midnight. The next morning, in a self-effacing remark to his Illinois friend Ward Hill Lamon, Lincoln said that mixing a live metaphor with a dead simile "fell upon the audience like a wet blanket."[738] This self-deprecation reflected Lincoln's humility. Forney celebrated the speech by creating a hand-pressed pamphlet of the address, a prized keepsake for Republican friends. In Rhode Island, *Providence Journal* editor Angell praised the address as "beautiful," "touching," "inspiring," "thrilling."[739] *Harper's Weekly* stated simply that the superb speech was spoken "from the heart to the heart."[740] The poetic Miltonic verse transcended the moment. As great art, and doing what great art accomplished, Wills explained, the speech drew attention "to something *beyond* itself and the one who made it.[741] The cherished address marked more than the hallowed ground of the Gettysburg battlefield.

Except for the one reference by French ambassador Jusserand regarding Hay's contribution to Lincoln's Gettysburg Address, the record is silent about whether Hay ever explained or talked about his contribution to others. There was no extant correspondence between Hay and Nicolay that hinted at Hay's role. Long after the fact, Hay and Nicolay offered different explanations about the preparations for Gettysburg. Hay's private diary offered no details about the preparation of the address. He recorded not a word about his contribution, though years later he flattered President Theodore

Roosevelt when he showed him his handwritten copy, pasted in Hay's scrapbook. As Lincoln's personal speechwriter, it was his duty, his responsibility to the president, to remain silent. Paradoxically, Hay's role reflected his own disappearance of self. Hay respected the president's confidence. He did at the time of Willie's death. He did now with the Gettysburg speech. His literary contributions were solely in the line of duty to the president of the United States. His discretion contrasted with the hubris of Seward, Cameron, Chase, and Blair, Lincoln's Cabinet members. Hay suppressed his persona, his ego, remaining reverent to Abraham Lincoln throughout his life.

During the mid-1880s and 1890s, when Hay and Nicolay were editing the manuscript for their *Abraham Lincoln* biography, Hay argued that the Gettysburg oration didn't warrant a chapter, which Nicolay had suggested. Hay suggested "tacking it on to the end of the battle campaign" in July 1863. He apparently wished to underplay the Gettysburg Address, if not entirely mask any discussion of its creation.

In December 1890, Hay further explained to *Century* editor Richard Watson Gilder about the Gettysburg speech. In a veiled statement, he said, "Mr. Lincoln's Gettysburg speech cannot be considered in any sense an extemporaneous effort," he said. "It was not only carefully considered but was reduced to writing before delivered and very little changed in the subsequent issue." Uncharacteristically, Hay used the passive voice and impersonal references—"it was not only carefully considered" and "reduced to writing before delivered"—failing to mention who carried out these actions. Hay's typically direct manner when speaking or writing is absent in his explanation to Gilder. He was ambiguous about the making of the address, masking the person who did the writing.[742]

One can imagine a mature John Hay, years later, sitting in front of a blazing fire one evening with Henry Adams, his closest friend and confidant in later years, quietly talking in one of their adjacent houses on Lafayette Square, a glass of whiskey in hand, telling Adams about his confidential work with President Lincoln. The chink in this speculation is that Adams neither liked nor admired Lincoln, which Hay knew. He may never have said a word about his speechwriting for the president.

George Nicolay's 1894 *Century* article about Lincoln at Gettysburg gave the impression that "thou protest too much." It read as a forced declaration of Lincoln's supremacy, veiling the interludes of the making, the creation of poetry. The one decisive statement made by Nicolay in his carefully obfuscated prose had to do with the actual writing of the speech: "There is no decisive record of when Mr. Lincoln wrote the final sentences of his proposed address."[743] Lincoln biographer Burlingame also confirmed the inscrutable nature of the making of this speech: "It is not clear when and how Lincoln composed his Gettysburg address."[744] A full record of all that happened between the arrival of Lincoln's invitation to the Gettysburg dedication and the morning of November 19, 1863, remains incomplete.

In the days after Gettysburg, Hay and Nicolay compared the Associated Press reporter's copy with the original draft and Lincoln's recall of what he actually said. Settled into the Executive Mansion, they created new autograph copies for presentation purposes. Five authenticated copies of the Address were the result, all scripted in Abraham Lincoln's hand.

One copy, the "Nicolay copy," appeared to be a working draft based on the original manuscript. Lincoln gave this to Nicolay, which Nicolay printed in his 1894 *Century* article. Sometime later, before his death, Nicolay gave his copy to Hay.[745]

The second copy, written in ink on lined paper and known as the Hay Copy, was closest to Lincoln's delivery text that reporters took down and their newspapers published the next day, according to a number of Lincoln historians, including Ray P. Basler and Gabor Borritt.[746] Lincoln gave this copy of the address to Hay, likely in gratitude for his contribution. Hay bound the original in a red Morocco leather portfolio beside a printed version. The volume also contained a collection of other important Lincoln manuscripts written by Hay, such as the Second Inaugural.[747] So proud of the prized Gettysburg document, Hay exhibited it to the newly inaugurated President Theodore Roosevelt in 1901, who shared a love for Abraham Lincoln.

John Hay apparently never spoke with Robert Lincoln about the original Gettysburg copies, nor that he and Nicolay each possessed one. The keeper of his father's papers and steward of his legacy, Robert Lincoln sent a trunk filled with all of Lincoln's papers to Hay and Nicolay while they were writing the authorized ten-volume *Abraham Lincoln* biography during 1875–1889. They later returned the archives to Robert Lincoln then living in Chicago.

John Hay did mention to the younger Lincoln that he had in his possession personal copies of known presidential documents. This was in 1888: "I own a few of your father's manuscripts, which he gave me from time to time, and I take it for granted that you will not suspect me of boning them." Without identifying which manuscripts he possessed, Hay appeared confident that Robert Lincoln was not of a mind to think he had stolen the documents. "I have handed over to Nicolay, to be placed among your papers, some of these your father gave me. The rest, which are few in number," Hay said, "are very precious to me."[748] The "very precious" documents are thought to include the Gettysburg Address, the Emancipation Proclamation, the Meditation on Divine Will, and President Lincoln's Second Inaugural Address.

After Hay's death in July 1905, the Hay and Nicolay copies of the Gettysburg Address went missing.[749] Reclaiming Robert Lincoln's attention in late 1908, as he prepared for the centennial of his father's birth in 1909 and wishing to include the historic document, he pressed further on their whereabouts. Yet he was unable to locate any one of the original five presentation copies. Nor was there a copy in all of his father's papers. He inquired about them with Hay's widow, Clara Hay, and George Nicolay's daughter, Helen Nicolay, her father's executor. Neither knew anything of their whereabouts. "It is a mystery that has puzzled and distressed me for a long time," Helen Nicolay confided to Robert Lincoln.[750]

"Touch any aspect of the address and you touch a mystery," said David Mearns, who was chief of the manuscript division of the Library of Congress from 1951–1967. The mysteries, Mearns believed, centered around the Hay Copy, which he described as "the most inexplicable" document. Mearns also understood that President Lincoln gave John Hay the copy that reflected his actual remarks at the Gettysburg dedication.[751]

The nearing of the Lincoln centennial in February 1909 hastened a crisis about the missing Gettysburg originals. Only weeks away, *Century* publisher Gilder appealed to Clara Hay. At his urging, she went to Riggs Bank, where her late husband's papers were stored in a vault, only a block east of the Hay mansion in Lafayette Square. Clara Hay entered the safe deposit vault, opening the box that contained her husband's papers. Amid his scrapbooks and leather-bound albums, she found the original Hay Copy of Lincoln's Gettysburg Address. Her discovery, and the very fact that she and Helen Nicolay had vowed they knew nothing of the manuscript's whereabouts, shocked her. Her apparent dishonesty, which she had not intended, sickened her inner soul. A profoundly religious woman, she felt she had sinned.

"If you have ever made a mistake in your life you will sympathize with Miss Nicolay and me," she confessed to Gilder on December 7, 1908. "We both feel greatly humiliated and beg pardon for a sin which we have committed in ignorance. We have both denied any knowledge of the Gettysburg address and we have both been sincere in our denials. Now! I have found the precious manuscript and as it was found in the same way that the other Lincoln manuscripts were found—there is no question but that it was given to him by Mr. Lincoln."[752] She put down her pen, took up a fresh sheet of letterhead, and wrote a similar apologia to Robert Lincoln.[753]

For a half-century after the Gettysburg dedication, most Americans gave little notice to President Lincoln's address.

It was in the months leading up to America's entry into the Great War in 1918 that invigorated the nation's commitment to democratic government and revived the Gettysburg Address. During this incendiary time entering World War I, Americans came to revere the address and Abraham Lincoln as they venerated democracy, the free press, and human rights. The words and verse transcended time and place. And they remain as vital today as they were in November 1863.

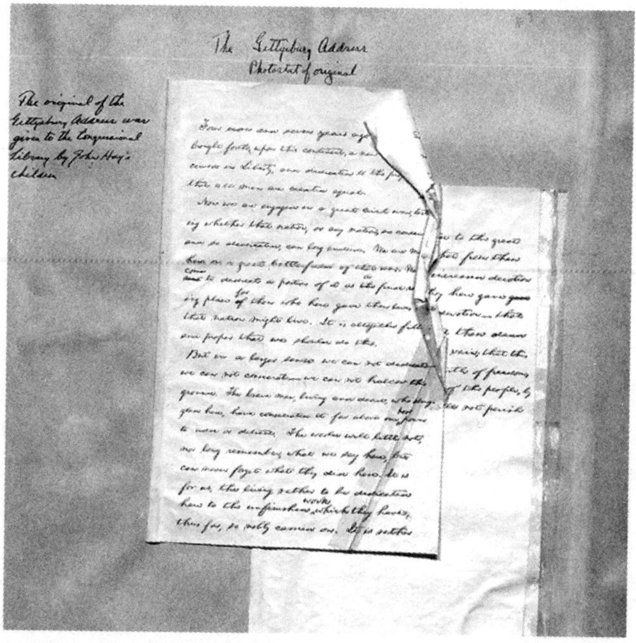

Abraham Lincoln, Gettysburg Address, given to John Hay by the president; in John Hay's hand and scrapbook. Courtesy of John Hay papers, OV 40, Manuscript Division, Library of Congress.

Chapter 24

LINCOLN'S ATTACHÉ

In the days after Gettysburg, Lincoln felt no particular joy. Rather than being uplifted in the spirit that history remembered the Gettysburg Address, he was thoroughly glum. Hay trailed him, hoping to boost his spirits and "setting all sorts of dexterous traps for a joke, telling good stories myself to draw him out." But alas, he said, "not a joke flashed from the Tycoonial thunder-cloud."[754]Under the pall of the lapsing war, Lincoln's step was slow and heavy, his face sad. "Like a tired child he threw himself upon a sofa," observed Elizabeth Keckley. The president "shaded his eyes with his hands. He was a complete picture of dejection."[755] Within days, however, Grant's victory in the Battle of Chattanooga boosted Lincoln's spirits. The November 26 triumph on Missionary Ridge in Chattanooga was a true blessing. Adding to the good news, General William Sherman and his Union troops were advancing toward Atlanta.[756]

Yet on the first national Thanksgiving holiday on November 26, 1863, President Lincoln was in bed with a mild case of smallpox. During his three-week convalescence, he appointed Hay as his deputy. The twenty-six-year-old took on principal duties in Lincoln's stead. He signed a reprieve of a soldier's death sentence. He wrote and signed the retraction of a reprimand to Naval Commodore James B. Rodgers, which the president countersigned. He signed one letter without Lincoln's countersignature, and wrote and signed a telegram in the same manner.[757] Even Seward brought Hay his contributions to the president's annual message for the December 8 reading to the joint session of Congress.

On the opening day of Congress, December 7, President Lincoln remained out of sight in the family's private quarters, slowly regaining his health. The joint session of senators and congressmen, in addition to their staff and lobbyists, filled the city to the gills. Hotels were overbooked and streetcars were "loaded to the gunwales," said one observer, all the while Willard's hotel, restaurant, and bars coined money. The very next day, Lincoln's annual message was read to the joint session, as was the president's Proclamation of Amnesty and Reconstruction, laying forth Lincoln's plan for restoring the Confederate states to the Union, and requiring each state to promise both allegiance and emancipation.

Each message was written in a workmanlike manner without any apparent literary contribution by John Hay. "Devilish good," said Greeley, a high compliment from the peace-loving radical. Senator Kellogg of Michigan claimed Lincoln to be "the great man of the century" for his proclamation. Ohio congressman James Garfield said in his quiet manner, "the president has struck a great blow for the country and himself." Surprisingly agreeable to Republican radicals and conservatives alike, Lincoln's reconstruction plan for the secessionist states resolved in a unified chord.[758]

Lincoln himself believed that the silent giant lurking in his 1863 annual message to Congress was the United States of America. "Who constitutes the state?," he asked Hay.[759] This was the question. The Civil War, now thirty-two months long without an end in sight, had thrown the whole concept of the US government and its three branches into question. The entire body of Lincoln's presidential oratory, from his First Inaugural speech in March 1861 through the most recent address at Gettysburg, had as its central theme sustaining and preserving the United States of America.

That very day from his bed, Lincoln talked with Hay about another matter that preoccupied him: his re-election in November. He desired to do everything humanly possible to bring in Republican votes. Describing his plan to recruit rebel prisoners who took the oath of loyalty to the Union, the president decided to test the idea. He planned to send Hay to a southern Maryland prison, Point Lookout, on the peninsula where the Potomac River entered the Chesapeake Bay. Hay was to execute the Oath of Citizenship to Confederate prisoners, with the idea that they might become Republican voters once freed.[760]

In this mission, commencing shortly after New Year's Day 1864, Lincoln depended on Hay to secure written documents and messages of a delicate nature. He relied on Hay's tact. He trusted the young man to go into the world on his behalf. Despite the president's confidence, Lincoln's critics were not entirely sure about entrusting important matters to a mere boy.[761] Lincoln knew better. A person's outer shell, which in Hay's case appeared youthful, did not reflect his true character. Hay's light beard and self-assured countenance didn't matter to Lincoln. He admired Hay, trusting him to fulfill the assigned job.

Following his three-week illness, the president treated Hay, Nicolay, and Stoddard to an evening at Ford's Theatre in the presidential box. Admiring Hackett's dramatic reading of Falstaff in Shakespeare's *Henry IV*, Hay disagreed with Lincoln's criticism of Hackett's interpretation of one line. The actor said, "Mainly *thrust* at me." The president thought it ought to be read, "Mainly thrust at *me*." Hay gently explained to his boss that in this one instance he was wrong. Relying on his trained literary intelligence, Hay illuminated for Lincoln that Shakespeare's use of "mainly" meant strongly or fiercely, placing the emphasis on the verb it modified, "thrust."[762]

On Christmas Day, though, John Hay's confidence ebbed. The Lincolns gathered privately *enfamil* and Nicolay was away in Philadelphia. The sociable young man felt lonely on this traditional day of big-hearted celebrations. "I breakfasted, dined, and supped alone," he wrote in his private journal. "Went to the theatre and saw *Macbeth* alone. Came home and slept alone."[763] By week's end, however, he was back in his element, reveling at Forney's New Year's Eve party. In tight with political people, Hay felt lively and loose, entertaining the guests with Lincoln's plans for the year ahead. "Above the clouds," he said. "The mists of prejudice…seemed at last beneath our feet and we might hope to finish the business in the higher sunshine."[764] Everyone shared the prayer for the war's end.[765]

Setting in motion his scheme to reinstate and release Confederate prisoners at Point Lookout, Maryland, the president commissioned Hay his aide-de-camp. A good many Union prisoners were actually Northern men and immigrants, soldiers who had been duped into conscription by the enemy. A full one-half of all Confederate prisoners asked not to be returned to rebel troops, eager to rejoin the Union by taking the Oath of Allegiance. Lincoln was readily capitalizing on prisoners' desires for citizenship, gaining Union loyalists and Republican votes.[766]

In his duty, Hay served briefly under Major General Benjamin Butler, a Massachusetts trial lawyer who served as a US congressman and state governor. Hay carried with him a letter from the president outlining his instructions as the president's attaché, as well as a blank book to record the names of new loyalists. On the bitterly cold day of January 3, a northerly wind blowing on the Potomac River, Hay boarded a little tug at the Washington Navy Yard, rattling through the ice south to Alexandria, Virginia. Here he boarded what he described as a palatial steam tug, the *Clyde.* Hay's pretty cabin with steam-heated berths felt "altogether sybaritic," he said. Sensually gratifying, he described the accommodations in the spirit of the ancient Greek port Sybarus, known for its opulent living, in what is now southern Italy. "I shut myself up in my gorgeous little cabin," Hay explained, "and scribbled and read and slept all day."

Coming into Point Lookout in the early morning, ashore, Hay shrugged against the blustery chill, going first to General Gilman Marston, the brigadier general of the prison. He found Marston, a New Hampshire native, crass and ungentlemanly. The general's crude joke, about a White man raping a Black soldier, whom he called a "contraband," slithered with racism, poor taste, and male violence against men.

Entering the prison, he found the prisoners "dirty, ragged, yet jolly." Hay walked on, to General Butler's quarters. At once, Butler called up five hundred men to take the Oath of Allegiance. The day "was as lively as Wall Street on days when Taurus climbs the Zenith," Hay wrote in his diary, invoking the bull scaling the pinnacle. His duty completed before sunset, Hay boarded Butler's flagship, *Hudson City,* arriving the next morning into the port of Baltimore, where Hay and Butler boarded a special train to Washington. Meeting with the president and Secretary of War Stanton, Hay had had enough time with General Butler to see that the man was hopeless. Known to have used his army position for financial gain, the general was also "perfectly useless and incapable for campaigning" his troops, Hay said.[767]

Even with this routine administrative mission, Hay cherished boots on the ground. He longed to defend the Union by his actions, not just his pen. Day to day, idleness felt like the enemy. He yearned to be active and in the field. His service to Lincoln and the gravity of its value were recognized by the president alone. At least at this time. For John Hay, he fulfilled his responsibility to the president, drafting messages, speeches, and letters. Not unlike many young men during the Civil War years, Hay felt a nagging desire to participate actively in the war on the field. "I can only fancy that he became tired of his work, and the dinners and receptions…as was my own case," Robert Lincoln explained decades later, "he wanted to be seen as an officer."[768] Young Lincoln himself, returning home to the White House from

Harvard every few months, pleaded with his parents to allow him to join the Union corps. His mother was firmly opposed. She had already lost one son during this war. Willie's death, she told her husband, was "as much as I can bear." He argued that "our son is not more dear to us than the sons of other people are to their mothers." Mary Lincoln refused to relent, until 1865.[769]

The president understood Hay's desire to serve. Lincoln may have even seen a bit of himself in the young man, as Goodwin explained in *Team of Rivals*. Hay's values certainly mirrored the president's. Hay and Lincoln, both highly principled, Goodwin said, respected one another's desires, whether they agreed or not.[770] Finally, on January 12, Lincoln commissioned Hay to serve in the Union army. He assigned him to Florida, an expedition designed to recruit Confederate soldiers, detained in Union prisons, to become US citizens and, ideally, Republican voters. At least that was the idea. Lincoln expected the new recruits to parlay their gratitude for their freedom into Republican allegiance. He appointed Hay the position of assistant adjutant general with the rank of Major, reporting to General Quincy Adams Gillmore stationed at Hilton Head, South Carolina.[771] Hay took the Oath of Allegiance in the presence of a notary, then walked into the president's room, announcing he was ready to start. "Great good luck and God's blessing go with you, John," said President Lincoln.[772]

Hay set sail out of New York Harbor for Hilton Head on January 16, a raw day with a stiff headwind. Landing in Hilton Head three days later, he presented his special orders to General Gillmore, the commanding general of the Department of the South, the army division managing Union troops in eastern Florida, Georgia, and South Carolina, largely rebel territory. Their first evening together, Gillmore spoke frankly to Hay. "I hope we will get enough voters out of the territory already in our hands in Florida," he said, "if not, we will occupy more territory." Gillmore was willing to engage military action to advance Union occupation of the state.

Before moving on to St. Augustine, Hay stopped in Fernandina on Amelia Island to swear in some new Union voters, trying desperately to fill up his record book. He also paid a visit to the real estate properties he had acquired during the December 1863 auction with the help of local tax commissioner William C. Morrill. Returning to the sweet land of orange and fruit trees, Hay walked first to the grove he owned in a joint venture with five other partners, including Morrill and Lyman Stickney. Among the several lots he had purchased, this orchard appeared to be his favorite. He was in love. "The magnificent show of bitter sweets and the promise of the fruited year," Hay said as he admired the bountiful crops of lemons, guava, plum peaches, figs, and pomegranates.[773] So enamored was he with Florida's beauty and prospects that he bought three more lots from Morrill during February 1864 and another in St. Augustine. Withal, he sunk his entire life savings of $4,000 in Florida real estate. Hay anticipated a return on his investment of "several hundred percent," a fanciful dream that never earned him a penny. The dismal return on investment was a painful lesson for Hay.[774]

He met with Stickney in Fernandino before shipping out to St. Augustine the next day. Hay told Stickney about the dismal voter registration numbers in Jacksonville. "The President's plan for the restoration of Florida will be a failure," Stickney wrote to Chase later that the day. "That is now the opinion of his secretary, Mr. Hay," who agreed the program was a bust.[775] Hay wrote privately "that to alter the suffrage law for a bare tithe would not give us the moral force we want."[776] He believed that the only path to more Union control was more military advances. "We must wait for further developments in military operations before we can hope for a reorganization of the state under a loyal government," Hay wrote from Key West to General Banks, the Gulf Coast commanding officer.

The coincidence of President Lincoln's personal attaché in Florida at the time of the horrific Union defeat at Olustee, Florida, fifty miles inland from Jacksonville, was a disaster slamming up against Hay's ill-fated mission. It gave the glaring impression that the Olustee battle and Hay's expedition were intertwined. The Union army appeared to advance to control more Florida territory, more citizens, and more Republican votes, which was not the case. In fact, the commanding general on the ground in Florida, Truman Seymour, had progressed westward against General Gillmore's orders. On February 20, the largest battle in Florida also became the Union army's biggest loss in the state. Of the 1,831 Union men killed, a full one-third (626 men) were from one regiment alone, the Eighth US Colored Infantry. Compounding defeat with injustice, wounded Black troops were abandoned by their comrades on the Olustee field. The Union army had no policy to protect Black soldiers and Black prisoners of war. Confederates clubbed some to death. Another was left with a bullet lodged in his scalp. While this could be somewhat easily removed, it was instead left to infect and kill the man.

Hay's Florida mission, otherwise minor news, exploded into scandalous headlines.[777] For days, Hay knew nothing of the firestorm in the nation's newspapers. He was virtually beyond civilization, sailing southward on the Atlantic Ocean to Key West. Thankfully, in this paradise breaking news was scarce. Only when he returned to Hilton Head a few days later, March 12, did he read the "blackguardly savage article about me."[778] Shocked, Hay felt betrayed. The press held him and the president responsible for the Olustee disaster. "Brigades of our brave armies are sent into rebellious states to water with their precious blood the soil that may produce presidential votes," the *New York Herald* protested.[779] "The President and his secretary are the only ones to blame in the business."[780] The searing criticism was widespread and passionate. The *New York World*, the paper of eastern Democrats, claimed that Hay's mission and Gillmore's military operations in Florida were part and parcel of a Republican strategy designed to carry the 1864 election by admitting states to the Union.[781] Hay felt stung and deeply injured.[782] It was no business of the press to explain his instructions. He believed in the fourth estate, the press—the advocate of reality. Yet this time it had stepped beyond its boundaries, beyond truth and right. Upon his return to the Executive Mansion, Hay fell into easy conversation with Lincoln, who assured John that he was not "the least annoyed by the newspaper falsehoods about the matter."[783] Instead, he remained fully confident of Hay's ability.

One evening in late spring, when Hay was still at work in the Executive office, Lincoln walked in after midnight. The president was dressed in his nightshirt. He laughed as he read a volume of Thomas Hood's works, utterly unconscious of his appearance. A funny sight, Lincoln certainly looked sillier than the book he was laughing at, Hay thought. "His short shirt hanging about his long legs" made Lincoln look "like the tail feathers of an enormous ostrich." On another evening, Hay complimented his boss "on the amount of underpinning he still has left." Apparently referring to his sturdy construction, Lincoln was pleased to report he weighed 180 pounds.

Awakening from bed on many nights, the restless president walked across the hall to the Executive offices from the private family quarters in little more than his underwear to read a passage to his literary friend. From Robert Burns to Daniel Defoe, Lincoln valued reading with Hay, especially William Shakespeare above all others. The president was particularly fascinated by the third act of *Richard the Second,* when Richard falls into gloom and misery, certainly sentiments felt by the president on many days during the war.[784]

Hay stayed with President Lincoln while the national Republican nominating convention convened in Baltimore. Nicolay, as in 1860, was on the ground with delegates. Describing their unanimous backing of the president, Hay read Nicolay's letter of June 5 to Lincoln, asking him for his choice of a vice president.[785] In a split second, Lincoln gave the nominating committee a free hand. He wished "not to interfere…even by a confidential suggestion," Hay wrote Nicolay. "He also declines suggesting anything in regard to platform."[786] In his mind, Lincoln believed the issues of the 1864 presidential election were clearly defined. The Union party stood firmly on a platform of union versus disunion, freedom versus slavery, peace versus war.

On the convention's official opening day of June 7, chairman Simon Cameron of Pennsylvania and Lincoln's first secretary of war moved to nominate Abraham Lincoln. He triumphed with 507 electoral votes to Grant's 22. Moving that the nomination be declared unanimous, Cameron's pronouncement met with thunderous applause and a flurry of hats and flags filling the air in an explosion of color. The president's acceptance speech emphasized the platform's themes of Union, liberty, and abolition. The prepared speech reflected John Hay's measured tempo, concise phrases, careful choice of words, and the lilt of alliteration—liberty, labor, and legal in the closing sentence.

> I approve the declaration in favor of so amending the Constitution as to prohibit slavery throughout the nation…as is now proposed a fitting and necessary conclusion to the final success of the Union cause.… In the joint names of Liberty and Union let us labor to give it legal form and practical effort.[787]

On the night of June 9, after the close of the Baltimore convention, Lincoln came into Hay's room before the young man had doused the candles lighting the room. The president told him of a secret plot to overthrow the government. General Rosecrans, stationed in St. Louis, Missouri, had unearthed details of the operation. Lincoln wanted Hay to investigate, acting in his stead, doing and saying for him what he himself might do in the same situation. Well before dawn the next morning and before Hay was out of bed, Lincoln handed him the note he wished Hay to present to Rosecrans, the president instructing the general to communicate directly with Hay.[788]

Lincoln also gave him his orders, titled AGO Special Order no. 213. "Major John Hay, Assistant Adjutant General, will repair at once to St. Louis, and, having executed my verbal instructions, will return to his station here."[789]

That morning, Hay boarded the 5:20 a.m. train at the Washington depot, June 10, passing a leisurely three days on the rails before arriving in St. Louis. "I sat and wrote rhymes in the same compartment with a brace of whiskey smugglers."[790] He dined the evening of his arrival with General Rosecrans, a heavy man unsteady on his feet. "Heavy-whiskered, blond, keen eyes, with light brows and lashes," Hay said of Rosecrans, he thought the general abrupt in manner and speech.

"There is a secret conspiracy on foot against the government, carried forward by a society called the Order of American Knights," Rosecrans told Hay, who agreed the plot was serious. Puffing away on a cigar, which Hay had declined, Rosecrans talked freely and loudly about the so-called knights, also known as the Sons of Liberty. Numbering up to two hundred thousand, the general claimed the secret society was plotting to poison public feeling against the Union, to even murder Northern men and target rebel invasions in Ohio, Illinois, Indiana, Kentucky, and Missouri. Hay left Rosecrans and spent the next evening with his brother Charlie in Springfield, returning to the White House on June 17. Unlike his passage west, the return journey was as bad as could be, missing connections and late trains. He arrived tired and dusty.[791]

Hay went directly to the president. He explained Rosecrans's request for "the greatest secrecy." Lincoln shrugged. "A secret which had already been confided" to at least five others, he said, "would scarcely be worth the keeping now." He was equally unphased by the threat, regarding it "a mere political organization." Lincoln decided to do nothing. The pragmatic chief executive winced at the thought of suppressing a threatening revolt that dampened free speech, in turn fanning much larger fires. Hay considered Lincoln's reaction. "In the stress of this war," he wrote in his diary, "politics have drifted out of the hands of politicians, and are now more than ever subject to genuine popular currents." Writing to Nicolay, Hay explained Lincoln's unvarnished response to the intelligence from Rosecrans. "The Tycoon thinks small beer of Rosey's mare's nest. Too small, I rather think."[792]

Upon Hay's return, Lincoln invited Hay to join him at Ford's Theatre on Sunday, June 19. Mary Lincoln was away at the Fifth Avenue Hotel in Manhattan, spending money neither she nor the president had. Hay shared the president's private box and the two men flirted with showgirls standing in the stage flies for the profane concert of sacred music. All good fun.[793] For a man living in a miserable marriage with no end in sight, Abraham Lincoln treasured the ease and reciprocity with John Hay.

Chapter 25

LINCOLN'S NEGOTIATOR

By late June, Washington's mercury rose above 90 degrees, the parched dirt streets roiling up dust clouds, flies swarming. Turmoil also brewed at the White House.

On the morning of June 30, the president told Hay that this day was going to be a hard one. He needed him to calm the panic that was certain to arise.

"When does the Senate meet this morning?" Lincoln asked.

"Eleven o'clock," said Hay.

"I wish you to be there when they meet," the president said. "Mr. Chase has resigned and I have accepted his resignation. I thought I could not stand it any longer."

Lincoln depended on Hay's ease with the unexpected, helping the president steady the rancor of Chase's testy rivalry. The night before, Lincoln had found the treasury secretary's resignation in a clutch of papers in his greatcoat pocket, Chase's third offer to leave the Cabinet. Struck by the irony of his timing, Lincoln interpreted the move as a clever ploy to hurt his prospects in the campaign. Lincoln told Hay that Chase was implying in his letter, "you have been acting very badly. Unless you say you are sorry and ask me to stay and agree that I shall be absolute and that you shall have nothing, no matter how you beg for it, I will go." One or the other must go, Lincoln decided. The power-hungry Chase offered. The president accepted.[794]

Hay arrived at the Senate door while the chaplain was in morning prayer. Once his Bible closed, Hay delivered the message and quickly left.

He despaired the looming clouds hovering over Lincoln. "In Congress and on the street there is a general feeling of depression and gloom," he wrote in his journal. "Chase's leaving at this time is little less than a crime." The absence of the Union's treasury minister endangered US finances, already weakened by the war. Lincoln, too, was nervous, feeling that Chase hadn't raised the funds needed to pay for the war.

The next morning when Hay went into the president' room, Lincoln handed him the nomination for treasury secretary: Maine Senator William Pitt Fessenden. Two days later, which felt more like two months, Fessenden accepted. Hay chafed to write a rebuttal to the *Tribune's* false account of Chase's departure. The president declined. "Let 'em wriggle," he said.[795] The president also mentioned that he might name Chase to the Supreme Court when the next vacancy turned up. Lincoln's casual afterthought resounded like a thunderclap to Hay. The very idea that the president might nominate his archrival to the highest judicial bench in the land struck the young man as incredible, an idea only the most forgiving individual could entertain. Lincoln waited until after the presidential election, a move intended to avoid adding a controversial issue into the campaign.[796] (President Lincoln nominated Chase to the Supreme Court in December 1864, after Chief Justice Taney died in mid-October.)

Instead, President Lincoln got himself and Hay into an unseemly mess in July 1864, in the name of what he thought was a diplomatic gesture toward peace. Both Lincoln and Hay were blindsided by the drama that unfolded, their desire for peace masking their judgment. On July 8, Hay brought the president a letter from Greeley, a known meddler and a pest. Hay was surprised by Greeley's claim that a reliable source had informed him about a three-man commission in Canada, sent to Niagara Falls by Jefferson Davis, the Confederate president. The commissioners were there to fix a peace plan with the Union. Greeley assured Lincoln his intelligence was trustworthy. He also reminded the president of "our bleeding, bankrupt, almost dying country [that] longs for peace." Pressing the jugular, Greeley urged Lincoln to at least listen to the Confederates.

Hay wrote the president's reply to Greeley, saying Lincoln was as anxious as anyone for peace. He explained that if Greeley knew anyone who had a written offer from the Confederate president, an offer that included restoration of the Union and abandonment of slavery, Lincoln promised the person a writ of safe conduct to meet with him in Washington.[797] In response, Greeley departed at once for Niagara Falls, inviting the commissioners to Washington. Though once in Canada, Greeley discovered the commissioners had no official credentials. They simply wanted to make a gesture to end the war, defiling the "bogus government at Richmond" and Davis's Confederates.

At the telegraph room when Lincoln received the *Tribune* publisher's reply, Hay walked with the president back to the Executive Mansion. Lincoln continued to say to Greeley that he was eager for peace with the South, yet he was impatient with his lack of progress.[798] He repeated to Greeley he was expecting him "to bring [him] a man, or men."[799] The president continued, "I am disappointed that you have not already reached here with those commissioners…I not only intend a sincere effort for peace, but I intend that you shall be a personal witness that it is made."[800] Carrying Lincoln's letter to Greeley, Hay started the next morning for upstate New York and Niagara Falls. The Canadian border, a remote and dangerous place, Hay knew, was unsafe for life and property. People who lived out in the wild were desperate. Hay used caution. Upon his arrival at Niagara Falls, he delivered Lincoln's letter to Greeley. "He didn't like it," said Hay. He was not surprised. Greeley opposed the president's conditions. He didn't think the commissioners would accept Lincoln's demands. Even so, Greeley started across the border with Lincoln's letter to the Confederates.[801]

Hay immediately turned back to Washington, reaching the White House the next morning. The president said that Greeley had wired that he saw an opening for negotiation. After conferring with Seward, Lincoln sent Hay back up to Niagara Falls, leaving the night of his morning return. The president continued communicating with Greeley, countering with specific terms for a creditable deal: peace, reunion, and the end of slavery.[802] Lincoln entrusted Hay to represent him and the Union position.

At the Falls, Hay faced a furious Greeley, enraged that Lincoln refused to enter into negotiations without restrictions. Hay reminded him that the president stood firmly on "the moral sentiment of the country." As had Lincoln, Hay refused to loosen the preconditions, insisting that Greeley join him when he met with the commissioners at Clifton House on the Canadian side. First up was George N. Sanders of Kentucky, "a seedy-looking rebel with grizzled whiskers and a flavor of old clo'," Hay observed. He then climbed the stairs to the room of James P. Holcombe, a former law professor at the University of Virginia, who was now active in the Confederate Congress and Confederate Secret Service. [803] At first sight, Hay was suspicious of Holcombe, a "false-looking man with false teeth, false eyes and false hair."[804] (The alliteration!) His instincts proved true. After Hay laid out the president's offer, Holcombe said he intended to give his answer by evening. Greeley continued to grumble about the strict position Lincoln had remained fixed on. Hay was in no mood to pacify Greeley's temper, feeling he was the nuisance he was known to be.[805]

When Hay returned to Clifton House in the morning, he discovered that Holcombe had no answer for President Lincoln. He also learned that the two Southerners had no authority from Jefferson Davis to negotiate a peace treaty on behalf of the Confederate government. They were acting in bad faith. It didn't take long for Hay to see that the whole matter was a sham. Insane. His willful ignorance from the start of the fiasco was founded in good intentions: Hay desired to help Lincoln bring peace to the country. Nothing less powerful could have brought Hay to lie to himself. Greeley had involved the president in a fruitless scheme. A poor politician and worse diplomat, Greeley had pulled Lincoln and Hay into an embarrassing situation, foolishly advocating the war's end. How far he was willing to go to choreograph a great moment. In the high-stakes folly, the *Tribune* publisher was coveting his "morbid appetite for notoriety," Navy Secretary Welles claimed.[806] Greeley cared nothing about dragging others into his crazed schemes.[807]

To be sure, Lincoln felt bedeviled by Greeley.[808] The otherwise savvy politician was misled by Greeley's delusional belief in his capacity to end the war. He had entrusted Hay to negotiate on his behalf. The "reliance he placed on [Hay's] judgment," Robert Lincoln remembered of his father, was apparent in sending Hay alone to open peace talks with the South.[809] The president, of course, had no evidence that Greeley's scheme was either legitimate or a bungled ploy, in a day before audio and video surveillance. When the truth unfolded, Lincoln retreated, folding his hopes in his prayer book.

Once the press got wind of the distorted triangle, the newspapers focused their gaze directly upon Hay and Lincoln. Just three months after the botched Florida mission, Hay's secret Niagara assignment became headline news. Critics claimed that John Hay's curt manner with the Confederate commissioners was the reason for the press's suspicions. In fact, candor defined Hay's diplomatic style. He refused to placate the opposition, upholding Lincoln's ideals. Direct and candid, he kept to Lincoln's principled position.

Defeated, John Hay left behind the Niagara affair and Washington's August of putrid swamps and overheated humans for a five-week leave with his family in Illinois. While he restored his spirits, Lincoln's reelection prospects began to appear surprisingly shaky. Thurlow Reed, the New York Republican boss, had advised Secretary of State Seward to tell the president about New York's uncertain loyalty.[810] (The state remained a weak Republican foothold well into the twentieth century.[811]) In addition, some party pillars in the North, such as the ranking senator from Massachusetts, Charles Sumner, joined with Radical Republicans to abandon Lincoln. They scorned his prosecution of the war, thinking it too lenient; his piecemeal dismantling of slavery, thinking it incomplete; and his failure to destroy the Confederacy, a travesty. "Weak-kneed d[amne]d fools...are in the movement for a new candidate to supplant the Tycoon," Nicolay wrote Hay. The two agreed that Lincoln's infectious "patience and pluck" was sure to save his skin.[812]

Lincoln prepared for the worst. Believing the legitimacy of the threat, he came to his Cabinet members on August 23, 1864, asking each minister to sign the back of a memorandum he had penned: "It seems exceedingly probable that this Administration will not be re-elected," he told them. "It will be my duty to so co-operate with the president-elect...to save the Union between the election and the inauguration, as he will have secured his election on such grounds that he cannot possibly save it afterwards."[813] Lincoln didn't ask them to read the document they were signing.

Returning to Washington on September 18, 1864, a Sunday, Hay was pleased to tell Lincoln about a letter he had received from the Black Republicans. Despite the "damnation policy of the democracy" toward Black soldiers, including inequalities in pay and the absence of a wartime government policy of humane treatment, the Blacks "declared their fixed purpose to vote for Abraham Lincoln."[814]

Beating back the doubts about the Republican Party, the September state elections instead turned out sound Republican wins in New York, New Jersey, and Kentucky. Added to this, Nathaniel Banks, the commanding general of the Gulf Coast states, came into Hay's office in early October to announce with some pride that New Orleans was entirely loyal to Lincoln. Banks was convinced that "the experiment of rebellion [had] failed, [and] the national cause will triumph."[815]

Lincoln still took no chances. Fixing himself with Hay in the telegraph room throughout the night of October 11, the president closely monitored the state election returns in Pennsylvania, Indiana, and Ohio—known as the "October states," crucial swing blocks—harbingers of the November vote. Lincoln had told Hay he "was anxious about Pennsylvania because of her enormous weight and influence." Now, he thought otherwise. Indiana's win also brought Lincoln relief, saying to Hay, "I believe it saves Illinois in November."[816]

That evening, an idea came to Hay to help bolster Lincoln's prospects. He set about arranging with Treasury Secretary William Fessenden the dispatch of revenue cutters—today's Coast Guard—up and down the East Coast to collect the votes of naval troops policing Atlantic waters and Southern ports. Offshore and unable to mail their votes home, most sailors had little chance to send in their ballots. (Union soldiers on land mailed ballots to family members to cast by proxy.) Hay's plan offered the forty thousand Union navy sailors the benefit of having their votes counted.[817]

That very day, October 12, 1864, sixty thousand Maryland voters elected to make their Confederate state free of slavery. The ayes crept to victory with just 375 votes above the nays, less than 1 percent.[818] The new state constitution, effective November 1, freed all enslaved Blacks in Maryland. Next door in the nation's capital, freed Blacks rejoiced for the former Maryland slaves. They gathered for an impromptu jubilation on November 2, marching under torchlight to the White House. The revelers' cheers brought President Lincoln outside. In his hands, he held a prepared speech written in two parts and in John Hay's hand, each page numbered. Reading from the first, a blue-lined coated writing paper and labeled "1," Lincoln said:

> It is no secret that I have wished, and still do wish, mankind everywhere to be free. *[Cheers, "God bless Abraham Lincoln"]*
>
> And in the state of Maryland...where human slavery has existed for ages...the soil is made forever free! *[Cheers, long]*
>
> The extirpation of slavery constitutes the chief merit of the new constitution.
>
> Most heartily do I congratulate you, and Maryland, and the nation, and the world, upon the event.
>
> I regret that it did not occur two years sooner, which I am sure would have saved to the nation more money

> than would have met all the private loss incident to the measure.

Reading from the next pages, written on plain stationery, Lincoln said:

> Some have said that "if I shall be beaten at the election, I will, between then and the end of my constitutional term, do what I may be able, to ruin the government....
>
> "2" I am struggling to maintain government, not to overthrow it. I am struggling especially to prevent others from overthrowing it....
>
> "3" Between the election and the inauguration on March 4...I shall do my utmost that whoever is to hold the helm for the next voyage shall start with the best possible chance to save the ship.
>
> This is due to the people both on principle and under the Constitution. Their will, constitutionally expressed, is the ultimate law for all....
>
> "4" I believe...they are still resolved to preserve their country and their liberty; and in this...I am resolved to stand by them. I may add that in this purpose to save the country and its liberties, no classes of people seem so nearly unanamous [sic] as the soldiers in the field and the seaman afloat. Do they not have the hardest of it? Who should quail while they do not? God bless the soldiers and seamen, with all their brave commanders.

John Hay's unmistakable authorship was revealed in the rhythm of the cadences and the polarities of life/death and win/lose. The metaphors, too, especially the nautical references, atypical of Lincoln, a stranger to ocean voyages, was distinctly Hay. The president, as was his custom on like occasions, gave Hay the original document as a keepsake.[819]

On Election Day, November, 8, 1864, rain and dark skies overhung Washington. The White House was deserted. Congressmen stayed out of sight, Hay believed, embarrassed to be in the city rather than at home voting. Lincoln was pensive, struck by the irony of the presidential candidacy on this Election Day. "It is a little singular that I who am not a vindictive man, should have always been before the people for election in canvasses marked by their bitterness." Speaking in confidence, Lincoln confessed to Hay, all the "contests in which I have been prominent have been marked with great rancor.'" After a quiet afternoon, Lincoln walked with Hay to the telegraph room. It was seven o'clock in the evening. The day's drenching rains had flooded the short path between the White House and War department. "We splashed through the grounds to the side door," Hay said. During the night, they were joined by secretaries Welles and Stanton. Even Chase came to see the president.[820] Lincoln remained anxious across the hours. "I am far from being certain," he wrote to an aide. "I wish I were certain."[821]

Solid results poured in from Pennsylvania, Maryland, Ohio, and the Midwestern and New England states, signaling to the army band to strike up patriotic tunes in Lincoln's honor. Blaring with gusto, the band awakened the night at two-thirty in the morning. Lincoln responded to the commotion with a short speech from the telegraph room window. "Rather unusual dignity," Hay remarked about Lincoln's spontaneous, unwritten speech. They walked back to the Executive Mansion.

At this late hour, Hay's work was not yet done. He drafted Lincoln's acceptance speech for publication in the *National Washington Republican*.[822] Once written, he crawled into bed. There was a tap on his door. It was Ward Hill Lamon, the president's self-appointed bodyguard and an official US Marshal for the District of Columbia. He was anxious to talk with Hay. Lamon, a tall, burly man, a friend of Lincoln's from Springfield, helped himself to a glass of whiskey on Hay's bureau. He refused Hay's offer of the second bed, unused with Nicolay away. Instead, Lamon wrapped himself in a blanket and lay down in front of Lincoln's closed door. Hay smiled at "Lamon's touching and dumb fidelity" to the president, lying there on the floor surrounded by an arsenal of pistols and bowie knives in case of attack.[823]

"The verdict of the American people has been given," said General Montgomery Meigs, the quartermaster general who later designed and built the sprawling red-brick Pension Building in Washington, DC, affirming news of Lincoln's re-election.[824] Lincoln made his first official appearance two days later, November 10, speaking at the White House to the Union Club of Washington, reading the speech written by Hay in the wee hours of Wednesday morning.

> It has been a grave question whether any government,
> not too strong for the liberties of its people,
> can be strong enough
> to maintain its own existence, in great emergencies.
>
> We can not have free government without elections,
> and if the rebellion could force us to forego, or postpone a national election,
> it might fairly claim to have already conquered and ruined us.
>
> It [the election] has demonstrated that a people's government can sustain a national election,
> in the midst of a great civil war.
> Until now it has not been known to the world that this was a possibility.
> It shows also how sound and how strong we still are.

Hay admitted that the speech was "not very graceful."[825] Even with his characteristic literary elements, Lincoln's speechwriter felt it was not his best work. He soon hit a higher mark with a letter to Lydia Bixby, the mother of five sons slain in the war.

Chapter 26

"WHEN THE BOYS COME HOME"

Colonel John Hay, Union Army, 1864. Courtesy of John Hay collection, John Hay Library, Brown University.

The grim news from the War Department during the autumn of 1864 reported death, death, and more death. The military engagement between North and South caused perilous devastation of life and property. By late September, fall winds blew across the balconies of the Executive Mansion and War Department next door. Stanton received word of one mother's personal strife. She seemed to have suffered the extraordinary loss of five sons who died in their service to the Union. Stanton had a letter from the governor of Massachusetts, John A. Andrew, who wrote to say that the state's adjutant general, William Schouler, was recently visited by the mother, Lydia Bixby of Boston.[826] She presented five letters from five company commanders, each informing her that one of her sons had perished. Schouler viewed Mrs. Bixby, a widow, as "a true-hearted Union woman." Now, Governor Andrew wrote to ask Stanton to appeal to President Lincoln for a letter of condolence to the anguished mother. The president's office agreed to look into the matter. John Hay took up the task.

Hay requested more details about the sons from Schouler. From the records at hand, he was able to confirm through the central Army office that the five Bixby boys had lost their lives in the war: Sergeant Charles N. Bixby had died at Fredericksburg, Virginia on May 3, 1863; Henry Bixby was killed in the Battle of Gettysburg in early July 1863; Private Edward Bixby died in a hospital on Folly Island across from Charleston, South Carolina; Private Oliver S. Bixby of the East 58th Massachusetts Volunteers was killed before the battle of Petersburg on July 30, 1864; and, Private George Way Bixby, company B of the 56th Massachusetts Volunteers, was also killed before the Petersburg battle.[827]

At the time, neither Schouler nor Hay realized that some of the War Department records were wrong. For one, Henry Bixby was captured at Gettysburg on July 1, 1863, not killed; he was then confined in a Confederate prison at Richmond, furloughed at College Green, Maryland, and honorably discharged on December 19, 1864. The name of Edward Bixby neither appeared on the 22nd Massachusetts rolls nor in any hospital records. He may have enlisted under an assumed name, or, more likely, he never enlisted at all. Oliver Bixby was killed, as Schouler's records showed. And George Way Bixby, who registered as George Way to conceal the enlistment from his wife, did not die at Petersburg, but rather was captured and imprisoned at Richmond, then later transferred to the Salisbury, Maryland, prison where he died.

On November 21, 1864, John Hay knew none of this. That day, he drafted the letter to Lydia Bixby for President Lincoln's signature. No one seemed to know the full truth about the Bixby sons. With clear intention and compassion for the desolate mother, Hay wrote this letter to the Widow Bixby.

> Executive Mansion
> Washington, Nov. 21, 1864
> To Mrs. Bixby, Boston, Mass.
>
> Dear Madam,
>
> I have been shown in the files of the War Department a statement of the Adjutant General of Massachusetts that you are the mother of five sons who have died gloriously on the field of battle. I feel how weak and fruitless must be any word of mine which should attempt to beguile you from the grief of a loss so overwhelming. But I cannot refrain from tendering you the consolation that may be found in the thanks of the Republic they died to save. I pray that our Heavenly Father may assuage the anguish of your bereavement, and leave you only the cherished memory of the loved and lost, and the solemn pride that must be yours to have laid so costly a sacrifice upon the alter of freedom.
>
> Yours, very sincerely and respectfully,
>
> [signed] A. Lincoln[828]

William Schouler delivered the letter on November 24, Thanksgiving day. The *Boston Transcript* published the letter the next day.

Hay's Bixby letter echoed an earlier letter of condolence he had written to the parents of Illinois friend Elmer E. Ellsworth, that one on June 9, 1861. Ellsworth, a law student studying with Lincoln before the war, was killed by a Confederate soldier in Alexandria, Virginia. The comparison between Hay's Ellsworth letter and the Bixby letter shows certain similarities of structure and expression.

> "I will not intrude upon your sorrow further [Ellsworth letter]
>
> *I feel how weak and fruitless must be any word of mine which should attempt to beguile you... [Bixby letter]*
>
> other than to express my deep sympathy for your great loss [Ellsworth letter]
>
> *I cannot refrain from tendering you the consolation that may be found in the thanks of the Republic they died to save. [Bixby letter]*
>
> And my prayer that a merciful God may give you that consolation...[Ellsworth letter]
>
> *I pray that our Heavenly Father may assuage the anguish of your bereavement...[Bixby letter]*
>
> which mortal love is too weak to offer. [Ellsworth letter]
>
> *leave you only the cherished memory of the loved and lost... [Bixby letter]*[829]

Historians have widely praised the Bixby letter as one of the sixteenth president's finest literary works, along with the Gettysburg Address in November 1863 and the Second Inaugural Address of March 1865. James G. Randall has described the Bixby letter as taking "a pre-eminent place as a Lincoln gem and a classic in the language"[830] David A. Anderson, the editor of *The Literary Works of Abraham Lincoln,* claimed that "Lincoln's three greatest writings"—the Gettysburg Address, the Bixby letter, and the Second Inaugural—were compositions "upon which assessment of literary achievement must ultimately be based"[831] Carl Sandburg christened it "a piece of the American bible." *Century* publisher Richard Watson Gilder favorably compared the Bixby letter "with the Gettysburg address," written just one year before. Gilder also praised the Bixby text for "its simplicity and fitness, [recalling] the Greek spirit" with ancient classical references.[832]

Historian Michael Burlingame revealed in 1995 that the Bixby letter was written by John Hay.[833] "Rather than diminishing Lincoln," Burlingame said, "this new discovery should enhance the status of John Hay among literary critics and historians."[834] Indeed, beyond the telltale clue of the letter appearing in Hay's scrapbook, side-by-side with his anonymous and pseudonymous journalism, as well as the Gettysburg Address and the Second Inaugural, Hay was also known to have admitted to a few people during his life that he was the author of the Bixby letter. Burlingame also emphasized Hay's frequent and personal use of the words "beguiled" and "Heavenly Father," "Republic" and "gloriously," words not reflected in Lincoln's own vocabulary. Even John Hay's youngest daughter, Alice Hay Wadsworth, confided to William Tyler Dennett, an early biographer of her father, that when someone mentioned that John Hay wrote the Bixby letter, she claimed, "he never denied it."[835]

After Schouler delivered the original to Lydia Bixby, she apparently "destroyed the letter shortly after receiving it."[836] In fact, rather than being a "true-hearted Union woman," Mrs. Bixby, a native of Richmond, Virginia, was an ardent Southern sympathizer. A plump woman with shifty eyes and arrogant manner, she was disliked by people who employed her and those from whom she sought work, such as Sarah Cabot Wheelwright. Mrs. Bixby was known to be evasive. The Boston police discovered that the widow ran a brothel. She trafficked in prostitution as well as fraud. She was "perfectly untrustworthy and as bad as she could be," said Wheelwright.[837]

Lincoln historians who doubt that John Hay wrote significant works for the president also doubt his contribution to this meritorious letter. For one, Roy P. Basler, the prolific Lincoln historian, stated "most Lincoln scholars resist the notion that Bixby was Hay's work."[838] Basler bolstered his argument with an anatomical comparison of Lincoln's finest oratory. "If the student will read aloud the best of Lincoln's lyrical passages in the Farewell Address (from Springfield), the Gettysburg Address, or the Second Inaugural Address, and then read aloud the 'Letter to Mrs. Bixby,' [s/he] will find it exceedingly difficult to believe that anyone other than Lincoln composed such sentences."[839]

Recognizing that the president depended on Hay's literary acumen to uplift the power of his ideas in each of the documents Basler mentioned, Lincoln entrusted the brilliant writer to heighten the relevance of his own presidency. Beyond the value of Hay's prose and poetry, he fulfilled the job that Lincoln lacked the time to do himself. One incident occurred the day after Thanksgiving 1864, November 25, a Friday. The Lincoln & Johnson Campaign Club of New York City had written to ask the president to write a toast for its next meeting. Lincoln insisted on composing the text himself, rather than relying on Hay this time. Yet the president's best-laid plans went awry. In the end, his every waking hour was consumed by the war, his annual message to Congress, and the national debt. He failed to deliver the toast. With a ring of irony, Lincoln turned to Hay to write the apology. Hay addressed Charles S. Spencer, the club's meeting organizer, explaining the president's commitments overtook his best intentions. "The crush here just now is beyond endurance," Hay said.[840]

President Lincoln's annual message to Congress in early December had been a distraction for weeks. On December 6, 1864, a Tuesday, George Nicolay delivered the text to the speaker of the House and president of the Senate. Generally reading like a standard government report on commerce and the elections, the text sounded more like a bill of lading than prose or poetry. The message also underscored Lincoln's urgent desire to enact the proposed amendment abolishing slavery throughout the nation. It had passed the Senate on April 8, 1864, yet failed to secure a two-thirds majority in the House. Lincoln appealed to every congressman to push the amendment through.

About midway through the message, the language changed. The shift was dramatic. A refined oratory emerged, a welcome clearing in the forest of government statistics. The new verse reflected Hay's certain narrative, born out of the well-known literary conventions of repetition and parallel construction. It was entirely appropriate that Lincoln asked Hay to edit the message, to ensure absolute clarity. The president also desired a forgiving poetic description of Jefferson Davis's terms for peace. Citing the Confederate aim for disunion between South and North, Lincoln's message stated:

> He does not attempt to deceive us.
> He affords us no excuse to deceive ourselves.
>
> He cannot voluntarily accept the Union;
> We cannot voluntarily yield it.
>
> Between him and us
> the issue is distinct, simple, and inflexible.
>
> It is an issue that can only be tried by war,
> And decided by victory.[841]

Nicolay also carried Lincoln's nomination for chief justice of the United States Supreme Court up to Capitol Hill. The seat was left vacant by Roger B. Taney, the sallow-looking Maryland native who had died during the night of October 12. The president proposed Salmon P. Chase, his former treasury secretary. Preferring to be "shut pan," or closed-mouthed, until after the election, Lincoln waited two months to fill the seat previously occupied by the Democrat Taney, the Southern sympathizer who had written the majority opinion in *Dred Scott*. Taney's decision was ultimately arbitrated in the Civil War. Now, nominating Ohio Republican Chase, Lincoln's archrival, the president admitted to his private secretaries that he regretted the appointment before, during, and after he sent Chase's name to the Senate. He claimed he would rather "have eaten flat irons" than have advanced Chase to this powerfully influential position.

"No other man than Lincoln," Nicolay said to Hay, could have had the generosity of spirit to "forgive and exalt a rival who had so deeply and so unjustifiability intrigued against him."[842] Chase took the oath of office of chief justice on December 13, 1864, an act promoting him to the highest position in the Judicial Branch of the US government. Lincoln's appointment ensured the Supreme Court's leadership under a staunch Republican, while it also draped the Chase family in honor, power, and position.[843]

The president explained his unorthodox approach to Hay. "It is much better not to be led from the region of reason," he said, "into that of hot blood." Governing from a position of principle rather than angry passion, Abraham Lincoln counseled John Hay about the value of measured judgment rather than impetuous irritation. The president steadied his young deputy, counseling him to keep his sights on the larger goal, the path leading to calmer waters.[844]

The fall of the Confederate stronghold of Savannah on December 26, 1864, signaled an important Union advance. In sight now was the Confederate capital of Richmond. This strategic victory brightened spirits in the nation's capital, dampened by the unusually wet days of December 1864. "It rains and rains, and will rain," Hay said. His outlook was also somewhat complicated by Mary Lincoln's plotting to replace him and Nicolay with Noah Brooks, the one presidential aide who was happy to collude with her.[845] The president, assuring Hay that his place was sound, had long ago washed his hands of her mean-spirited schemes, ignoring his wife.

Hay's spirits were uplifted with the return of Robert Lincoln in January 1865. The president's son had left Harvard Law School to join General

Grant's staff in February. (Mary Lincoln had acquiesced to Robert's army service once she was confident that he was safe from field combat under Grant's immediate command.) Taking pleasure in socializing together, Hay and Robert Lincoln hit the town, escorting young women to the opera, a dance, and a special viewing of Congress. In the House, the high-stakes debates over national emancipation attracted standing-room-only onlookers. Young Lincoln and Hay had prime seats. The debates navigated between trust, passion, and acrimony. The vote promised to be close.[846] Urging undecided congressmen, Abraham Lincoln's lobbyists pressed the president's argument privately. The president did not forbid strong-armed tactics to persuade senators and congressmen.

While Lincoln strategized in the Executive offices with Seward and a small team of lobbyists, Nicolay and occasionally Hay monitored the debates on the Hill. In the final round of voting on January 31, 1865, an unease strained the House of Representatives. A deafening silence fell across the chambers as every congressman stated his vote, *voce.* Awaiting Nicolay's wire from Capitol Hill, President Lincoln stayed with Hay in the War Department telegraph room. The House narrowly approved the constitutional amendment, 119 to 56, just two votes above the necessary two-thirds. It was one of the biggest legislative victories of Lincoln's presidency. "Long and long applause" greeted the outcome, Nicolay reported.[847] The victory for national emancipation and the Civil War's end virtually assured, President Lincoln's star soared.

Though no one, especially Lincoln or Hay, thought it might be ascending to heaven.

Within days, peace negotiations were underway between Jefferson Davis, his authorized commissioners, and Lincoln and Seward. Two weeks later, February 18, the Union naval fleet captured Charleston. This pivotal victory was very good news. Equally remarkable, the first Union soldiers marching in to claim Charleston, the city where the Civil War was launched, presented a stark contrast to life just four years before. Two regiments of Black soldiers led the march in, signaling the official capture of this major port.[848] By month's end, Robert E. Lee's prospects were narrowing.[849]

As the day of Lincoln's inauguration approached on March 4, 1865, Union advances left no doubt that Grant promised to overtake Lee's army. Union troops positioned themselves to capture the last of the Confederate outposts. American flags flying, Union towns and cities blazed at night with houses lighted with candles and fiery rockets to rejoice the war's close.[850]

On the morning of Lincoln's second inauguration, dark skies and chilly rain failed to dampen the spirits of swelling crowds lining the processional route along Pennsylvania Avenue. Masses assembled, possibly twice the number of four years before.[851] The one ominous sign was the presidential carriage departed the Executive Mansion for Capitol Hill without Lincoln's prominent figure and top hat. Mary Lincoln, alone, led the parade. What appeared an alarming sight was nothing of the sort. Lincoln and Hay had gone up to the Capitol earlier in the morning, a day's time for the president to sign last-minute legislative bills in his outgoing first term.

In the early afternoon, President Lincoln appeared on the east portico of the Capitol building.

by whom the offence came, shall we discern therein any departure from those divine attributes which the believers in a living God always ascribe to Him? Fondly do we hope—fervently do we pray—that this mighty scourge of war may speedily pass away. Yet, if God wills that it continue, until all the wealth piled by the bond-man's two hundred and fifty years of unrequited toil shall be sunk, and until every drop of blood drawn with the lash, shall be paid by another drawn with the sword, as was said three thousand years ago, so still it must be said "the judgments of the Lord, are true and righteous altogether"

With malice toward none; with charity for all; with firmness in the right, as God gives us to see the right, let us strive on to finish the work we are in; to bind up the nation's wounds; to care for him who shall have borne the battle, and for his widow, and his orphan—to do all which may achieve and cherish a just and a lasting peace, among ourselves, and with all nations.

President Abraham Lincoln, second inaugural speech, March 4, 1865, Washington, DC; written in Abraham Lincoln's hand, inscribed "to Major John Hay, April 10, 1865." Courtesy of John Hay papers, OV 40, Manuscript Division, Library of Congress.

At that very moment, the hovering clouds evaporated through a brilliant glimmering sun. As if by magic, sapphire-blue skies appeared as a metaphor for the presidential inauguration.[852] Abraham Lincoln stepped forward. The massive crowd erupted in thunderous applause, fading at the far reaches. Lincoln towered tall and gaunt over the crowd, slowly striding forward to read his inaugural address.[853] Printed in two broad columns on a half-sheet of foolscap, Lincoln's Second Inaugural, one of the shortest speeches of its kind in American history, sounded nothing like the speeches from Abraham Lincoln of the Lincoln–Douglas debates in 1858.

In 703 words and twenty-five sentences, the verse portrayed several rhetorical devices. Only the first paragraph conveyed an impersonal nature with its businesslike language. The balance of the speech infused refined passages, the most prevalent being the simplicity of the language and 505 one-syllable words. Another, a favorite of both Lincoln and Hay, was grammatical inversion, the subject and verb exchanging places.

> "Fondly do we hope, fervently do we pray"[854]

Different from his First Inaugural, Lincoln now identified slavery as "the fundamental cause" of the war, Eric Foner has reminded us.[855] He expressed themes of disunion through the language of inversion and polarities of life/death and survival/destruction.

> "devoted altogether to saving"/"seeking to destroy"
> "one of them would make war"/"the other would accept war"
> "rather than let the nation survive"/"rather than let it perish"-

Alliteration and parallel structure portrayed ordinary actions and emotions. As the speech progressed, the dramatic tension rose to an eloquent crescendo in the last paragraph. The "prose had the timbre and reverberation we associate with great poetry," White claimed in *Lincoln's Greatest Speech*, as the Second Inaugural drew to its close.[856] On the brilliant afternoon of March 4, 1865, Abraham Lincoln spoke these words:

> Fellow-Countrymen
>
> At this second appearing to take the oath of the Presidential office, there is less occasion for an extended

address than there was at the first.... **With high hope for the future, no prediction in regard to it is ventured.**

On the occasion corresponding to this four years ago all thoughts were anxiously directed to an impending civil war. **All dreaded it, all sought to avert it. While the inaugural address was being delivered from this place, devoted altogether to saving the Union without war, insurgent agents were in the city seeking to destroy it without war—seeking to dissolve the Union and divide effects by negotiation. Both parties deprecated war, but one of them would make war rather than let the nation survive, and the other would accept war rather than let it perish.** And the war came.

One-eighth of the whole population were colored slaves, not distributed generally over the Union, but localized in the southern part of it. These slaves constituted **a peculiar and powerful interest.... Neither party expected for the war the magnitude or the duration which it has already attained. Neither anticipated that the cause of the conflict might cease with or even before the conflict itself should cease. Each looked for an easier triumph, and a result less fundamental and astounding. Both read the same Bible and pray to the same God, and each invokes His aid against the other.** It may seem strange that any men should dare to ask a just God's assistance in wringing their bread from the sweat of other men's faces, but **let us judge not, that we be not judged. The prayers of both could not be answered. That of neither has been answered fully.** The Almighty has His own purposes.... **He now wills to remove, and that He gives to both North and South this terrible war as the woe due to those by whom the offense came**, shall we discern therein any departure from those divine attributes which the believers in a living God always ascribe to

Him? **Fondly do we hope, fervently do we pray, that this mighty scourge of war may speedily pass away....**

With malice toward none,
with charity for all,
with firmness in the right
as God gives us to see the right,
let us strive on to finish the work we are in,
to bind up the nation's wounds,
to care for him who shall have borne the battle
and for his widow and his orphan,
to do all which may achieve and cherish
a just and lasting peace
among ourselves and with all nations.[857]

As President Lincoln spoke the last word, the air reverberated with the resonance of his deep voice. The crowd burst forth with long and thundering applause. Turning to Chief Justice Chase, the president stood with Hay on his right and Nicolay to his left. He laid his right hand upon the open book and solemnly promised, "so help me God!" He bent down, kissed the Bible, and commenced four more years of his presidency.

That day, the start of his second term, his horizons appeared peaceful.

Lincoln's Second Inaugural Address is a landmark of literature and philosophy. The central message moralized that the war was the divine penalty for slavery's sin. This was the climatic crescendo. He faced his maker when he claimed that the catastrophic struggle strained the people's trust in their democratically elected leader. Sacrificing more than 750,000 human lives, the war tested the supremacy of democratic government against tyranny.[858] The "high moral significance" of a Lincoln speech, Hay explained in 1902, carried the weight "of far-reaching importance." "Patriotism," he said, informed Lincoln's speeches through "rhetorical expression." Fusing this passionate emotion with "instinct, logic, and feeling," Lincoln's oratory interwove words with poetic meter and aural tones.[859] Hay knew better than anyone.

Now, the war fading, Lincoln proposed "charity for all" and peace with all, especially the war widows and orphans. At the time, the Second Inaugural met with mixed reviews. While the American press was generally respectful, most were puzzled by its stark poetic expression. The *Washington*

National Intelligencer, always friendly to President Lincoln, praised the final words as worthy of being "printed in gold."[860] The *Chicago Times,* instead, a Democrat paper, admonished it as "slipshod," "loose-jointed," and "puerile." The *New York World,* also a Democrat broadsheet that opposed civil rights reforms for Blacks, called the president's emancipation policy "miserable balderdash." Lincoln withstood the press's criticism with the courage of a leader. British newspaper editors, however, praised the poetic sensibility, perhaps appealing to ears shaped by centuries of great English poets whom Hay had absorbed into his own verse. The *London Star,* for one, called it "very remarkable."[861]

The rhetoric, poetry, and eloquence, of course, flowed from John Hay's mind and pen. In gratitude, President Lincoln gave Hay the original handwritten copy and also the typescript, from which Lincoln read at his inauguration. This second version, cut up from the original and pasted onto the large sheets of foolscap to make the words more readable to Lincoln, the president gave to Hay for his contribution to the speech. The president wrote on the bottom:

> Original manuscript of second Inaugeral [sic] presented
> to Major John Hay, April 10, 1865.[862]

Decades later, John Hay's widow, Clara, said that Lincoln's dedication was a "precious inscription." For safekeeping, Hay bound the manuscript in a red leather volume, storing it in a fireproof safe when it was not on display for special guests.[863]

This was one of the two last speeches delivered by Abraham Lincoln. (The last was given April 12, 1865, and also written by John Hay.)

Months before, Hay had set plans in motion to depart the White House at the start of Lincoln's second term. He was on his way to a life of foreign service. Another speechwriter was to soon take his place. President Lincoln's administration in his second term augured major changes in its personnel and direction.

The fate of history silenced Lincoln's new voice with a new speechwriter.

Doris Kearns Goodwin sets the stage of this moment: John Hay observed, "he was in mind, body and nerves a very different man, from the one who had taken the oath in 1861. He continued always the same kindly, genial, and cordial spirit he had at first, but the boisterous laughter became less frequent year by year; the eye grew veiled by constant meditation on momentous subjects; the air of reserve and detachment from his surroundings increased."[864] Four years of war had repressed Lincoln's spirit. "A face full of life, of energy, of vivid aspiration," which Hay observed of the mask of Lincoln produced by Leonard Volk in 1860, now had "a look of one on whom sorrow and care have done their worst...the whole expression is of unspeakable sadness and all-suffering strength," wrote Hay.

During the second week of Lincoln's new administration, Seward appointed Nicolay to the American consulate in Paris. Ten days later, Lincoln, with Seward's blessing, officially named Hay secretary of the American Legation in France, today's embassy. Both assigned to Paris, Hay was to serve in the US government's chief diplomatic office in France, and Nicolay in the regional office of Paris. Hay was appointed second-in-command under ambassador John Bigelow, the wealthy New York investor and former publisher of the New York *Evening Post.*[865] In Bigelow's absences, Hay directed the legation as *charge d'affaires,* another position of grave responsibility.[866]

Chapter 27

THE RECKONING

Late in March 1865, after four years of battle and a cost of almost $3 billion and 750,000 Union and Confederate deaths, war was ebbing.[867] "The Confederate army saw the time had come," Hay said. On April 3, the Union army seized the Confederate capital of Richmond. As Union soldiers pursued the Army of Northern Virginia, Grant ultimately forced Lee to surrender in the early morning of April 9, a Monday.

Five hundred guns fired through the damp mist in the nation's capital, heralding the decisive Union victory. "A great boom startled the misty air of Washington, shaking the earth and breaking the windows of the houses about Lafayette Square," said Stanton. Residents and soldiers poured into the city's streets, cheering and singing, thousands of American flags waving. Lincoln's Cabinet members gave their government employees a holiday. "Everybody here is in a state of exaltation at the brilliant and complete success of the campaign," said General Meigs.[868] Peace and glory filled the air.

"When the army of the Union saw it was no longer needed," Hay said, the soldiers laid down their arms and melted back "into the mass of peaceful citizens." Remarkably, during the four horrifying years of civil war, democratic government survived. "There is no event, since the nation was born, which has proved its solid capacity," Hay concluded.[869]

Democracy confirmed, the sprawling war effort also fostered an economic wellspring in Northern industry. The buildup amounted to unprecedented productivity. Burgeoning enterprises of steel, iron, trains, machinery, vessels, and weapons during the 1860s were incubators of innovation and fortune in the Northern United States. By war's end, the per capita wealth of North and South, roughly equal when the Civil War broke out, was now three-and-a-half times greater in the North than in the South.[870] Industry produced jobs, which in turn stimulated emigration from the impoverished border and former Confederate states, as well as immigration from abroad.[871]

In the South, huge loses of wealth in slaves and political power depressed life, finances, and Southern governance in the nation's capital. After decades of presidential dynasties from Virginia, Tennessee, and North Carolina, the next, post-Civil War southern presidents were those who inherited the office from their assassinated chiefs: Vice President Andrew Johnson in 1865 and Vice President Lyndon Baines Johnson in 1963. LBJ of Texas and Jimmy Carter of Georgia were the first democratically elected presidents from Southern states in 1964 and 1976, respectively, more than a century after the close of the Civil War. With their inaugurations, the South returned to the White House.[872]

"A man who denies to other men equality of rights is hardly worthy of freedom," Abraham Lincoln said to John Hay in April 1865. "But I would give even to him all the rights which I claim myself."[873] Praising Lincoln's statement for possessing "all the law and the prophets," Hay overlooked one important fact. He didn't see that the truth was complicated by the cultural context of the time. Abraham Lincoln, the emancipation maverick, stood firmly with the norm of the country in its torment of Indigenous peoples. Three hundred years of the British worldview toward Native Americans in their colonization experience wholly informed mid-nineteenth-century White peoples' standards. For Abraham Lincoln, the experience was personal. His father, Thomas Lincoln, watched as his grandfather was slaughtered by Indigenous warriors as his father and his brothers planted a cornfield on their property in 1786.[874] Native Americans, an independent people, were hostile to the White newcomers who had stolen rather than purchased their land and resources. Their cultural traditions also appeared alien to White settlers. During Lincoln's presidency, most White Americans viewed Indigenous peoples as neither equal nor citizens. The president himself, who led the charge to end slavery and establish Black people as American citizens, regarded Native tribes as inferior and warranting containment. Sadly, this was the prevailing view for the next six decades.[875]

The waning days of the Civil War in early April 1865, extended a "joyous influence…a general and profound thanksgiving," Nicolay and Hay wrote in *Abraham Lincoln.* Awash in new hopes and prosperity, Oliver Wendell Holmes, future Supreme Court justice and son of the revered nineteenth-century poet, wrote to Hay, "My heart is filled with awe as I see such rapid fulfillment of our long deferred hopes." From the Atlantic Ocean to the Mississippi River, Holmes said, "our long-deferred hopes" have resurrected the nation.[876]

The war's final days were filled with a sense of new beginnings. "The fourteenth of April was a day of deep and tranquil happiness throughout the United States," said Hay. With his characteristic repetition and dualities, he described the crucial moment: "peace, so strenuously fought for, so long sought and prayed for, with prayers uttered and unutterable, was at last near at hand, its dawn visible on the reddening hills." Nicolay and Hay remembered this historic day for the hours filled with work and pleasure. "From morning until evening, the country was filled with a solemn joy."[877]

On this Good Friday, President Lincoln ordered General Robert Anderson to raise the American flag above Fort Sumter in Charleston. The Southern city's formerly deserted wartime streets burst to the seams with officers and citizens from South and North. At noon on this day, General Anderson, his hands on the halyards of the flagpole, hoisted the American flag that he had lowered in the hour before the first Confederate guns fired on Sumter four years before. A roar of jubilant cheers flooded the town and harbor, the music of hundreds of instruments trilled in harmony, the full-throated roar of great guns thundered to salute the American flag. *The Star Bangled Banner* resounded in the ocean air.[878]

In the early morning, Robert Lincoln had returned to the Executive Mansion after three months of army service. His arrival enlightened his father's spirits. Lincoln was relieved that his eldest son was home and safe.[879] Robert traveled with Grant, having just witnessed Lee's surrender on the steps of the courthouse in Appomattox, Virginia. The sight was a rare occasion of triumph for Grant and the Union. Coming to Washington for the morning's special Cabinet meeting, Grant was just in time for breakfast with the president. Afterward, Lincoln invited Grant and Hay for a short drive in the presidential carriage, open to the day's fresh air. In this intimate setting, Grant confided his anxiety about the task currently before Sherman, the controversial yet acclaimed Union general currently negotiating the Confederate surrender, meeting on the boundary line between North and

South Carolina.[880] Successfully having swept his troops from Georgia's northern border through Confederate territory, claiming success in his wake, Sherman had driven his army clear down to the Atlantic seaboard. "The President answered him in that singular vein of poetic mysticism," Hay said, "which, though constantly held in check by his strong common sense, formed a remarkable element in his character."[881] Familiar as he was with Lincoln's private expressions, Hay revealed in this statement the power of Lincoln's spiritual thought.

The president assured Grant that he had confidence in Sherman and the Union's success. He had witnessed the massive territorial loss of secession four years before, followed by the pain of protracted, uneven, and incremental gains. The president was fully informed about the Confederacy's weakness in the face of the Union's strength. Lincoln knew that the South was outwitted, outplayed, and crumbling in defeat. He didn't share Grant's concerns about the risk. He was confident. He had no doubt.

The president told Grant about the prophetic dream he had had the night before. It was a dream that had previously appeared in Lincoln's subconscious just before other great events in the war, such as the Union victories at Antietam, Gettysburg, and Vicksburg. Lincoln described the vision: He found himself in an indescribable vessel, "moving with great rapidity towards a dark and indefinite shore."[882] What was the meaning of such a dream? Lincoln realized that the Union was rushing toward victory. Yet, he could not have known that he was approaching a reckoning of his own, a dark reckoning.

Meeting with his Cabinet at 11 a.m., the president described his friendly feelings toward the South. He said he was uneasy about punishing the Confederate states.[883] Lincoln wished to avoid reparations. He longed for peace between North and South. "On this day of unprecedented triumph, his heart overflowed with sentiments of gratitude," said Nicolay and Hay. His mood happy and tender throughout the day, Lincoln joined the first lady for the evening performance at Ford's Theatre.[884]

Since the early days of his presidency, Lincoln had received threats from enemies and warnings from friends, notices of assassination plots and dangerous omens to his well-being. He was aware of the murder campaigns against him that festered throughout the South. In December 1864, for one, a Selma, Alabama, newspaper published a call to raise funds to assassinate the president before the inauguration, a fatal plot that included Seward and Vice

President Johnson.[885] Lincoln considered the dangers remote, opening his door to friends and strangers, day after day.

He felt equally at ease walking at midnight from the Executive Mansion to the War Department and back, with Hay or alone. Lincoln frequently rode in the evening from the White House to the Old Soldiers' Home, often with Hay. The commander in chief, who was born in a log cabin, was maddened when Stanton stationed a guard at the mansion and assigned cavalry to accompany him on his daily ride.[886] He didn't believe in jumping at shadows. Trained by the river, he steered his own course based on what he saw. He had endured four years of threats that had come to nothing.

At noon on April 14, 1865, John Wilkes Booth, twenty-six, a stage actor and the leader of a small group of fanatical secessionists, got word that the president and first lady were planning to attend Ford's Theatre that night.[887] Booth, handsome and with any easy grace of manner, hurried his preparations for the night's attacks with his three co-conspirators. Booth knew the theater well, having easy access to service corridors and back entrances, currying the favor of the staff by way of his good looks.[888] The Lincolns arrived at Ford's shortly before 8:30 p.m. A gusty, wet breeze had kicked up. Joining them in the state box were guests Clara Harris, a dark and mature girl, and her fiancé, Major Henry Rathbone, a tall and slender soldier.

Back at the White House, John Hay and Robert Lincoln relaxed in young Lincoln's second-floor room, content to spend an informal evening together. After two weeks living in a covered wagon, Robert had declined his parent's invitation to join them at the theater. He was more than happy to sit and gossip with Hay. By 10:30 p.m., fully relaxed and enjoying glasses of whiskey, Lincoln and Hay were startled by the clatter of horses coming up the drive. Suddenly, a terrifying call arose from the front entry hall. "The president has been shot!" The news sent the two men running for the carriage waiting outside.[889] By then, the coachman knew where to go and as fast as possible. He headed five blocks east to Tenth Street, and there to Petersen House, a three-story brick residence hotel for actors and government clerks. Here, President Lincoln lay unconscious. The dense street crowd created a human barrier. Lincoln and Hay jumped from the stalled carriage, pushing through the wall of people, calling on their own extraordinary human strength.

The Lincoln family's physician, Robert K. Stone, MD, of Springfield, met them at the front door of Petersen House. Gently, Dr. Stone explained the president's condition was grave. There was no hope. "After a natural outburst of grief," Hay said, "young Lincoln devoted himself the rest of the night to soothing and comforting his mother."[890] Together in Petersen House, Hay walked with Robert to the bedroom where the president lay. His breathing was slow, his pulse weak. Charles Leale, MD, assistant surgeon general of US Volunteers, who had been the first responder in Ford's Theatre, remained at the president's side, periodically checking that the gaping bullet hole on the left side of Lincoln's head did not clot.[891]

John Hay stayed close to President Lincoln throughout the night, holding the president's life in his soul. He stood just behind his head or sat at his right hand. By dawn, the president's moaning eased. An overwhelming peace washed over his worn and furrowed face, his right eye swollen and purple, his lips blue, his legs cold. Life was ebbing. At 7:22 a.m. on April 15, Abraham Lincoln's pulse ceased. Robert wept openly. John Hay felt a hopeless and profound sadness.[892]

John Hay, "When the Boys Come Home," poem, June 18, 1864, *Harper's Weekly;* set to music and republished during World War I. Courtesy of John Hay collection, John Hay Library, Brown University.

On this miserable morning, a heavy rain drenched the streets of the nation's capital, the peals of church bells filling the air. The devastating news fell "with peculiar severity upon the hearts which were glowing with the joy of a great victory," said Hay.[893] Alarming newspaper headlines augured more danger brewing. The drained nation was numbed by President Lincoln's sudden death. One headline read:

> GREAT NATIONAL CALAMITY!
>
> ASSASSINATION OF PRESIDENT LINCOLN!
>
> THE FIENDISH ACT COMMITTED AT FORD'S THEATRE!
>
> ESCAPE OF THE ASSASSIN!
>
> J. WILKES BOOTH BELIEVED TO BE THE ASSASSIN!
>
> SECRETARY SEWARD STABBED IN HIS BED!
>
> ATTEMPTED MURDER OF HIS SON AND OTHERS![894]

Shrouded in black, the nation's capital mourned. The headline was true: Seward was also attacked in his home the night before, part of a triple plot to assassinate him, the president, and the vice president, the last of whom went totally unscathed. Seward, protected by a jaw brace from a carriage fall the week before, eluded severe injury from the attacker's knife. His son, Frederick, lay comatose for weeks. Both survived.

Perhaps in death, Hay said, Lincoln, who "hated the arrogance of triumph," might have been satisfied that his own death subdued triumphant praise for the victory that cost so many lives, including his own.[895] Preachers interpreted his assassination as the deity's way of preventing idolatry.[896] Nicolay called the sainted commander in chief a martyr. President Lincoln's death on the cusp of triumph was celebrated all the more, an untimely loss on the threshold of victory.

The sight of President Lincoln's corpse lying in state in the Capitol Rotunda filled the soaring space with the friendly aura of his humble character. The hastily constructed platform, reused many times since, was President Lincoln's catafalque.[897] On Friday, April 21, after two days on view in the Capitol, Lincoln's coffin was taken to the funeral train to Illinois.

His remains departed the Washington depot, as he had in life done many times before since March 1861. This time, the special train, draped in black, retraced the former president-elect's passage to the nation's capital four years before. When Willie Lincoln had died in 1862, his body had been placed in a mausoleum. And now, at Lincoln's death, Willie's body was disinterred and placed within the same railroad car—and so by this fateful act, the train now carried the corpses of both father and son. Twelve days, six states and 1,700 miles made up their passage to Illinois.

Abraham Lincoln's death sent shockwaves through the nation's capital, the American people, and world capitals. The shocking paradox of Lincoln's informal and friendly manner against the gravity of assassination, a tragic and startling loss, left Lincoln's contemporaries virtually speechless. In their disbelief, senators, congressmen, and foreign statesmen ranked him second only to George Washington.[898] Others thought him greater than President Washington, the stoic chief executive who had freed three million souls from the British Crown. Lincoln, in the course of civil war, freed 3.5 million slaves. "He was one of very few white Americans," Frederick Douglass said, "who could converse with a Negro without anything like the condescension, and without in anywise reminding him of the unpopularity of his color.[899] Remarkably, the president's murder failed to shake the American government or derail finance and commerce.[900]

John Hay remained in Washington to pack the president's papers with Robert Lincoln, who also looked after his tormented mother.[901] Nicolay soon joined them, the three working together in the Executive offices. Arranging Lincoln's papers was a monumental job extending into late April. George Nicolay resigned his position as private secretary to the president of the United States on April 20. Hay tendered his resignation as assistant adjutant-general of Volunteers of the Union Army on June 25. President Johnson gave him the rank of colonel for "faithful and meritorious service during the war." That very day, Hay set sail from New York Harbor to London, then on to the American Legation in Paris, where he set out as the *charge d' affaires*.

"I think Abraham Lincoln is rather to be envied in his death, as in his life somewhat," Henry Adams said, "history repeats itself."[902] Lincoln, however, believed just the opposite. He entrusted a progressive evolution to history.[903] Lincoln's fatalism informed his actions. By extension, Hay infused Immanuel Kant's fundamental principles in Lincoln's speeches, the principles of morality and reason among all persons that he had read and adopted at Brown. He also absorbed Lincoln's conviction in evolution in his writing for the president.

Living and working at Lincoln's side while in his early- to mid-twenties, Hay lacked the perspective of time to measure his own place in history. How could he? He served Lincoln with respect, a confidence really. He served the president with a sense of duty and honor. As historian David Wootton explained about the verisimilitudes of history in *The Invention of Science*, "sometimes people really do not have any sense of the significance of what they are doing."[904] Hay envisioned his work with Lincoln as simply doing his job. In this, the cumulative record of history and an understanding of Hay's contribution to President Lincoln's eloquence confirmed the value of John Hay's literary voice.[905] It was his exceptional literary gifts that amplified Lincoln's presidency.

When Abraham Lincoln and John Hay first met in Springfield in the spring of 1859, the young Ivy League graduate offered the courthouse lawyer the tools the older man needed to boost his political prospects. In the Cooper Union speech of February 1860, Lincoln soon recognized the consequence of Hay's literary talents. From that moment forward, John Hay heightened Abraham Lincoln's effectiveness as a brilliant communicator. He augmented Lincoln's stature in the clarity and beauty of his oratory, spoken and written.

Hay's wit also brought lightness to the depressive tendencies of the older man, miserable in his marriage and burdened by civil war. Rather than opposites of light and dark, elder and youth, Lincoln and Hay synced intellectually, psychologically, and emotionally. As a trusted friend and confidant, Hay offered the beleaguered Lincoln, before and during his presidency, a singular friendship. Hay was someone with whom the president felt at ease confiding his doubts, fears, uncertainties, and even intimacies. "Hay's reverence for Lincoln was a beautiful characteristic," said Jean Jules Jusserand, the French ambassador, who befriended Hay much later, when he was secretary of state and before his death in 1905.[906] At the most difficult and dangerous time of the Civil War, a time that demanded the utmost care to express information, President Lincoln and John Hay formed the friendship that inspired American eloquence. Together, they embraced the ideal of exacting words and phrases to advance true and principled ideals, producing unforgettable verse flowing with classical poetry and literary finesse.

One episode from their time together is worth retelling: Hay's anonymous journalism during the five months between March and July 1862, when his newspaper columns gradually unveiled Lincoln's spiritual revelation, the president was coming to grips with emancipation. In each piece, Hay fused Lincoln's principles and moral realizations with his own powerful journalism. The president's awakening was aided by Hay's measured, even moving, public coverage of Lincoln's reckoning. Perhaps Hay's journalism also helped others imagine emancipation in Confederate territory. Hay brought a clear, thoughtful, and forceful voice to the president's progressive thoughts and deeds. In this, the two men shared a unified vision of humanity, a humane policy that struggled to explain and change conventional thinking about the rights of all Americans.

For the intimate relationship of two individuals who were twenty-eight years apart in age, something special had to happen. The Lincoln–Hay rapport was manifest in its tenderness and creative output.[907] Lincoln appreciated that Hay, socially confident and attractive, possessed a natural wit. The young man's gift for verbal rhyme and superb memory and recitation was matched by Lincoln's majestic ideals, large voice, and extraordinary ear for words. It was Hay who discerned Lincoln's profound moral authority. He transported the elder's vision into poetic, transcendent words and verse.[908]

Lincoln also taught Hay something about diplomacy, lessons that stayed with him throughout his life, guidance Hay brought to his service as the US ambassador to the Court of St. James's (1897–1898) and as secretary of state (1898–1905). Lincoln revealed two essential elements of effective diplomacy, lessons he had learned from his Illinois law practice: keep the conversation moving, and act with measured deliberation. Lincoln, the natural negotiator, tutored Hay in the manner of intervention, embracing time and repetition over expedience. These principles became a distinct hallmark of Hay's future diplomatic roles. Hay's tact in global affairs during the era when the United States rose to become an international power at the dawn of the twentieth century was grounded in gradual compromise, step by step, as he learned from Lincoln. Despite all doubts and challenges, even when under stress, he, as Lincoln, upheld America's interests and values. "His training with Lincoln [engendered] his high ideals, his breadth of knowledge and wide experience," said Jusserand.[909]

Lincoln also demonstrated to Hay that the element of humor disarmed human tensions with lighthearted surprise. It diffused the strain of disagreement between adversaries. During his later statesmanship, Hay drew on Lincoln's counsel, his moral authority, infused with his own innate wit.

Inevitably, he seized the moment. Perhaps Lincoln's greatest gift to Hay extended from his resolute belief in democratic government. Self-rule had been on trial during the war. As Lincoln himself asked as late as December 1863, what constituted the United States of America? This, after all, was the looming question that incited the Civil War, the issue answered by the outcome of the conflict.

In this, President Lincoln reinforced that the highest principle of leadership in a democracy was duty to country. The Civil War president never swerved "one hair's breadth from what he considered the strict line of duty," said Nicolay. For decades, as an American ambassador and as secretary of state, Hay remained true to the best democratic interests of the United States.[910] He had inherited the slain president's moral authority, his vision of democracy, his sense of duty, and his respect for humor.

As Lincoln's journalist and speechwriter, as his envoy and attaché, Hay's job required him to work unnoticed. When a deadline neared, Hay wrote until 2 a.m. or 3 a.m. A speech consumed him until he had worked twenty-hour days to get it done, forgetting perhaps to write in his journal or to his parents in Illinois. Gregarious as he was, Hay spent more of his waking hours with the President Lincoln than he did with friends of his own age. He internalized Abraham Lincoln's tendency toward reflection and idealism. It came easily, channeled through an inclination of his own. By the second year of Lincoln's first term, the two men had formed a harmonized synchronicity. Hay's own voice came through in his love of poetic couplet, offering the telltale trademark of Lincoln's own voice.

In their five years together, President Lincoln and John Hay perfected their writing process, creating a shared voice. Lincoln's handwritten notes and their long conversations, many recorded in Hay's private journal, developed the themes, principles, and exact script for either a newspaper column, a written message, or a speech. Co-creation, a difficult concept for modern-day culture to understand, defined the Lincoln–Hay relationship, one the powerful voice of principle, the other the literary wordsmith. Their creative formula produced President Lincoln's poetic oratory and American eloquence.

No doubt, there were moments of euphoria bordering on disbelief for Hay, finding himself riding alongside the President of the United States. For all his self-deprecation, John Hay appeared to be aware of his value to the nation's chief commander, even if he couldn't see it through the prism of historical hindsight. In all, John Hay stayed true to himself. Whether writing for Lincoln or projecting Abraham Lincoln's vision for America's future, he wrote in his own voice. John Hay's life after April 15, 1865, reflected the poignant experiences that were shaped by this powerful creativity with Abraham Lincoln.

Within weeks after President Lincoln's death, John Hay celebrated the president in an unpublished poem. Expressing his sadness, the young man memorialized his profound gratitude and the softened memories of their days together. In the spirit of Shakespeare's *Hamlet,* Hay penned a loving testimonial to his friend. It offered a personal and poignant tribute to Abraham Lincoln.

When you shall leave us—When the clasp

n.d., May or June 1865

"And there is pansies—that's for thoughts"

William Shakespeare, *Hamlet*[911]

When you shall leave us—when the clasp
Of melting hands is broken,
And when with sad and faltering lips
The last farewell is spoken.[912]

We shall not love you utterly
For memory shall restore
The goodness, grace and loveliness,
That in our eyes you wore.

I shall not call you lost, dear friend,
While in my spirit lingers
The melody that woke for me
Beneath your slender fingers,
And if another wakes the strain
Your form shall over me beam
Touched with the spirit of the Song—
And eyes that nurse and dream.

And when midnights the moon shall rain
Thou golden summer's showers
And cast afar on waking hearts
That spell of magic power
Can I forget our cherished hour
When 'neath the sleeping skies
The moonlight kissed your rippled hair
And trembled in yours eyes?

Fare well my friend! You go to greet
The dear familiar fans
And soon your welcome feet will press
The springing Western daisies!
And I, as soon, I sail to seek
A far and alien shore
Will pray God's blessing on your tread
Now and forevermore.[913]

Epilogue

JOHN HAY, POET IN THE CIVIL WAR WHITE HOUSE: A SELECTION

A selection of John Hay's poetry that he wrote during his time with Abraham Lincoln exhibits his personal tase in literature, as well as his exploration of poetic themes. Reaching from the most personal matters of friendship, love, and marriage and the power of the (Mississippi) River, he delves into the pervasive issues affecting daily life in the Executive Mansion and the nation's capital—the Civil War and the divisive politics between the Republican and Democratic parties, North and South; Lincoln's presidential campaigns against Douglas and McClellan; Southern secession and national unity; the bravery of battle and the honor of death; and the almighty principles of liberty, democracy, and union. Below are a few selections.

Prayer of the Romans[14]

n.d., circa 1862

Not done, but near its ending,
Is the work that our eyes desired;
Not yet fulfilled, but near the goal,
Is the hope that our worn hearts fired.
And on the Alban Mountains,
Where the blushes of dawn increase,
We see the flash of the beautiful feet
Of Freedom and of Peace!

How long were our fond dreams baffled!—
    Novara's sad mischance,
The Kaiser's sword and fetter-lock,
    And the traitor stab of France;
Till at last came glorious Venice,
    In storm and tempest home;
And now God maddens the greedy kings,
    And gives to her people Rome.

Lame Lion of Caprera!
    Red-shirts of the lost campaigns!
Not idly shed was the costly blood
    You poured from generous veins.
For the shame of Aspromonte,
    And the stain of Mentana's sod,
But forged the curse of kings that sprang
    From your breaking hearts to God!

We lift our souls to Thee, O Lord
    Of Liberty and of Light!
Let not earth's kings pollute the work
    That was done in their despite;
Let not Thy light be darkened
    In the shade of a sordid crown,
Nor pampered swine devour the fruit
    Thou shook'st with an earthquake down!

Let the People come to their birthright,
    And crosier and crown pass away
Like phantasms that flit o'er the marshes
    At the glance of the clean, white day.
And then from the lava of Aetna
    To the ice of the Alps let there be
One freedom, one faith without fetters,
    One republic in Italy free!

Emancipation[315]

n.d., circa 1863

Beautiful under the Western skies
    Our Queen Columbia stands,
With Freedom's light in her royal eyes,
    And Victory's crown in her hands.
        And solemn and grand
        From every land
    Comes the murmur of future fame,
        Crying out, 'Well done—
        The dawn's begun,
In a chorus of loud acclaim.

And Liberty leans on her conquering sword'
    In joy that the fight is ending,
That the nation's faith is again restored
    In her birthright's brave defending.
        And a fadeless crown
        Comes grandly down
    On her blazing brow forever—
        Whose splendor beams
        In eternal gleams
From the Gulfs to the Beautiful River.

J. H.

Two on the Terrace

n.d., circa late 1863 or 1864[916]

Warm waves of lavish moonlight
    The Capitol enfold,
As if a richer noon light
    Bathed its white walls with gold.
The great bronze Freedom shining—
—Her head in ether shrining—
Peers Eastward, as divining
    The new day from the old.

Mark the mild planet pouring
    Her splendor o'er the ground;
See the white obelisk soaring
    To pierce the blue profound.
Beneath the still heavens beaming,
The lighted town lies gleaming,
In guarded slumber dreaming—
    A world without a sound.

No laughter and no sobbing
    From those dim roofs arise,
The myriad pulses throbbing
    Are silent as the skies.
To us their peace is given,
The need of spirits shriven;
I see the wide, pure heaven
    Reflected in your eyes.

Ah love! A thousand aeons
    Shall range their trooping years;
The morning-stars their paeons
    Shall sing to countless ears.
These married States may sever
Strong Time this dome may shiver,
But love shall last forever
    And lovers' hopes and fears.

So let us send our greeting,
  A wish for trust and bliss,
To future lovers meeting
  On far-off nights like this—
Who in these walls' undoing
Perforce of Time's rough wooing—
Amid the crumbling ruin
  Shall meet, clasp hands, and kiss.

Northward

March 9, 1864[917]

1.
Under the high unclouded sun
That makes the ship & shadow one
I sail away as from the fort
Booms sullenly the noonday gun

2.
The odorous air blow thin and fine,
The sparking waves like emeralds shine
The luster of the coral reefs
Gleams whitely through the tepid brine.

3.
And glitters o'er the liquid miles
The jeweled ring of verdant isles
Where wanton[918] Nature holds her court
Of ripened bloom and sunny smiles.

4.
Encompassed[919] by the faithful seas—
Inviolate gardens hold the breeze
Where flaunt like giant wander's plumes
The pennants of the cocoa-trees.[920]

5.
Enthroned in light and bathed in blue
In lonely majesty, the Palm
Blesses the isles with waving hands—
High Priest of the Eternal calm

6.
Yet northward with an equal mind
I steer my course, and leave behind
The rapture of the Southern skies,
The worry of the Southern wind.

7.
For here o'er Nature's riotous bloom
Falls far and near the shade of gloom
Cast from the hovering vulture-wings
Of one dark thought of woe and doom

8.
[this stanza is crossed out in the original text]
And though the way be drear & far
I know that neath the Northern star
Dwells Freedom in the dawning light
Of her imperial Avatar.

9.
I know that in the snow-white pines
The brave Norse fir of freedom shines
And fain for this I leave the land
Where endless summer pranks the vines

10.
Oh strong free North so wise & brave!
Oh South, too lovely for a slave!
Why read ye not the changeless truth—
The free can conquer but to save!

11.
May God upon these shining sands
Send love and victory clasping hands;
And Freedom's banners wave in peace
Forever o'er the rescued lands!

12.
And here in that triumphant hour
Shall yielding Beauty wed with Power;
And blushing earth & smiling sea
In dalliance deck the bridal tower.

Lése–Amour

March 21, 1864[921]

How will my heart remember
    Beside these camp-fire embers.
With eyes that smiled so far away.
    The joy that was November's.
Her voice to laughter moony
    So merrily reproving…
He wandered through the autumn
    And neither thought of loving woods
The hills with light were glowing
    The waves in joy were flowing
It was not to the clouded sun
    That the day's delight was varna [?].
Thought through the brown leaves straying
    Our lives seemed gone a-Maying
We knew not love was with us there.
    No look nor tone betraying.
How unbelief still misses,
    The best of being's blisses!
Our parting saw the first & last
    Of love's imagined kisses.
Now mid these scenes dearest
    I dream of her—the dearest.

At Sunset

Ecarte, Washington, DC[922]

Into the grave of twilight
The red gleam fades away,
And the westering clouds grow somber
With love of the dying day.
In the eve's soft flush
The gloaming's hush
Comes down on the rippled bay.

The towering hills stand saintly,
Each grand head halo-crowned—
And the vagrants shadows wander
To the slope of the grassy ground.
The languid breeze
Stirs not the trees
In the tracing twilight bound.

Now climbs the vanishing glimmer
To the mountain's crest;
The sunset's molten glory
Glows gold on the water's breast;
From heaven's dim crown
Comes kindly down
The gracious spirit of Rest.

The cordial soul of the sunset
Steals warm to my heart, like wine.
My weary eyes look fondly
Far over the glowing brine;
And tenderly beams
In the mist of dreams
A joy that shall never be mine.

Sweet eyes, who proud dark splendor
Is melted in love's soft beams,

The still queen-features glorious
    In the dawn of love's first gleams,
        Imperial lips
        In the dear eclipse
Of passion's tropical dreams.

Dear Heaven! To hear the rose-lips
    Breathe falteringly my name;
To see the soft cheek flushing
    With joy of maiden shame!
        And feel the bliss
        Of her passionate kiss
Touch every vein of flame!

And my saddened love seems lovelier
    In the tender evening shine—
And a vague hope wakes that a love so true
    With an answering love must twin;
        That heaven will bend
        And the love descend
Forever and ever mine.

Fades the fair light from the waters—
    Cold shimmer the stars above—
The desolate night-wind shudders
    Through the dusk of the gloomy grove.
        The Vision is gone—
        I sit alone—
With darkness, and silence, and love.

Advance Guard

1862–1865, first published 1871[923]

In the dream of the Northern poets—
    The brave who in battle die
Fight on in shadowy phalanx
    In the field of the upper sky;
And as we read the sounding rhyme,
    The reverent fancy hears
The ghostly ring of the viewless swords
    And the clash of the spectral spears.

We think with imperious questions,
    Of the brothers we have lost,
And we strive to track in death's mystery,
    The flight of each valiant ghost.
The Northern myth comes back to us,
    And we feel through our sorrow's night
That those young souls are striving still
    Somewhere for the truth and light.

It was not their time for rest and sleep;
    Their hearts beat high and strong;
In their fresh veins the blood of youth
    Was singing its hot, sweet song.
The open heaven bent over them,
    'Mid flowers their lithe feet trod,
Their lives lay vivid in light, and blest
    By the smiles of women and God.

Again they come! Again I hear
    The tread of that goodly band.
I know the flash of Ellsworth's eye
    And the grasp of his hard, warm hand;
And Putman, and Shaw, of the lion heart,
    With an eye like a Boston girl's;
And I see the light of heaven which shone
    On Ulric Dalghren's curls.

There is no power in the gloom of hell
    To quench those spirits' fire;
There is no charm in the bliss of heaven
    To bid them not aspire.
But, somewhere in the eternal plan
    That strength, that life survive.
And like the files on Lookout's crest,
    Above death's clouds they strive.

A chosen corps—they are marching on
    In a wider field than ours;
Those bright battalions still fulfill
    The scheme of the heavenly powers.
And high, brave thought float down to us,
    The echoes of that far fight,
Like the flash of a distant picket's gun
    Through the shades of the severing night.

No fear for them! In our lower field
    Let us keep our arms unstained,
That at last we be worthy to stand with them
    On the shining hearts they've gained.
We shall meet and greet in closing ranks,
    In Time's declining sun;
When the bugles of God shall sound recall,
    And the battle of Life be won.

When the Boys Come Home[924]

June 18, 1864, *Harper's Weekly*

There's a happy time coming when the boys come home
There's a glorious day coming when the boys come home
We will end the dreadful story of the battle dark and gory
In a sunburst of glory, when the boys come home.

The day will seem brighter when the boys come home,
And our hearts will be lighter when the boys come home;
Wives and sweethearts will press them in their arms and caress them,
And pray God to bless them when the boys come

The thin ranks will be proudest when the boys come home,
And our cheer will ring the loudest when the boys come home;
The full ranks will be shattered, and the bright arms will be battered,
And the battle standards tattered, when the boys come home.

Their bayonets may be rusty when the boys come home,
And their uniforms be dusty when the boys come home;
But all shall see the traces of battle's royal graces
In the brown and bearded faces when the boys come home.

Our love shall go to meet them when the boys come home,
To bless them and to greet them when the boys come home,
And the fame of their endeavor time and change shall not dissever
From the nation's heart forever, from the nation's heart forever.

On the Bluff[925]

n.d., circa 1865–1870

O grandly flowing River!
O silver-gliding River!
Thy springing willows shiver
In the sunset as of old;
They shiver in the silence
Of the willow-whitened islands,
While the sun-bars and the sand-bars
Fill air and wave with gold.

O gay, oblivious River!
O sunset-kindled River!
Do you remember ever
The eyes and skies so blue
On a summer day that shone here,
When we were all alone here,
And the blue eyes were too wise
To speak the love they knew?

O stern impassive River!
O still unanswering River!
The shivering willows quiver
As the night-winds moan and rave.
From the past a voice is calling,
From heaven a star is falling,
And dew swells in the bluebells
Above her hillside grave.

ENDNOTES

Preface

1 Elizabeth Winkler, *Shakespeare Was a Woman and Other Heresies: How Doubting the Bard Became the Biggest Taboo in Literature* (Simon & Schuster, 2023), 1.
2 Winkler, 13, 18.
3 Winkler, 23.
4 Gabor Boritt, *The Gettysburg Gospel: The Lincoln Speech That Nobody Knows* (Simon & Schuster, 2008), 82.
5 David Wootton offered an informative discussion on natural and man-made history in *The Invention of Science: A New History of the Scientific Revolution* (HarperCollins, 2015), 545–61.
6 Myra Helmer Pritchard, ed. Jason Emerson, *The Dark Days of Abraham Lincoln's Widow* (Southern Illinois University Press, 2011), introduction. The book was originally published in 1927. Pritchard is the granddaughter of Mary Lincoln's correspondent, Myra Bradwell, whom she wrote to during his 1875 incarceration in an insane asylum.
7 Michael Burlingame, ed., *An Oral History of Abraham Lincoln: John G. Nicolay's Interviews and Essays.* (Southern Illinois University Press, 1996), xii.
8 J. J. Jusserand, *What Me Befell: The Reminiscences of J. J. Jusserand* (Houghton Mifflin, 1933), 240.
9 Ronald C. White, *Lincoln in Private: What His Most Personal Reflections Tell Us About Our Greatest President* (Random House, 2021), 281.
10 Professor White meticulously compiled and transcribed an unprecedented record of Lincoln's handwritten fragments and notes, published in the appendix of *Lincoln in Private*, 165–279.
11 John Hay to Charles Francis Adams, December 19, 1903, Washington, DC, JH MSS, JHBU.
12 Hay to Nicolay, July 25, 1891, Cleveland, OH, Nicolay MSS, LCW.

Introduction

13 The book *Lincoln's Journalist* offers an excellent summary of contemporary view of John Hay during Abraham Lincoln's administration. See Michael Burlingame, ed. *Lincoln's Journalist: John Hay's Anonymous Writings for the Press, 1860–1864* (Southern Illinois University Press, 1999. See also, Galusha Grow, quoted in James T. DuBois and Gertrude S. Mathews, *Galusha A. Grow: Father of the Homestead Law* (Houghton Mifflin, 1917), 266–67.
14 Burlingame, ed. *Lincoln's Journalist,* xxiv.
15 John Russell Young, "John Hay, Secretary of State," *Munsey's Magazine,* January 8, 1899, 247. See also, Young, *Philadelphia Evening Star,* 22 Aug. 1891, p. 4, cc 3–6; p. 4, c 1;

and Young, writing in 1898, quoted in T. C. Evans, "Personal Reminiscences of John Hay," *Chattanooga Sunday Times,* July 30, 1905.

16 *St. Louis Dispatch,* May 30 [no year identified], clipping in scrapbook, JH MSS, RPB.

17 Adam Goodheart, *1861: The Civil War Awakening* (Alfred A. Knopf, 2011), 207.

18 James Russell Young, "John Hay, Secretary of State," *Munsey's Magazine,* January 8, 1929, 247.

19 Michael Burlingame and John R. Turner Ettlinger, eds., *Inside the Lincoln White House: The Complete Civil War Diary of John Hay,* xiii–xiv. In 1860, Burlingame and Ettlinger discovered, Hay evidently composed a thanksgiving proclamation for the signature of the governor of Illinois. A copy of this document is in the Nicolay–Hay Papers at the Illinois State Historical Library in Springfield, containing a marginal note indicating that Hay wrote it.

20 Daniel Mark Epstein, *Lincoln's Men: The President and His Private Secretaries* (HarperCollins, 2009), 23.

21 Epstein, 3. See also, David Herbert Donald, *Lincoln* (Simon & Schuster, 1996), 258. See also, Patricia O'Toole, The Five of Hearts: An Intimate Portrait of Henry Adams and His Friends, 1880–1918 (Simon & Schuster, 2006), 38.

22 Ronald C. White Jr., *The Eloquent President: A Portrait of Lincoln Through His Words* (Random House, 2006), 35.

23 Ted Widmer, *Lincoln on the Verge: Thirteen Days to Washington* (Simon & Schuster, 2020) 462. See also, Joshua Zeitz, *Lincoln's Boyas: John Hay, John Nicolay and the War for Lincoln's Image* (Viking, 2014), 2.

24 Doris Kearns Goodwin, *Team of Rivals: The Political Genius of Abraham Lincoln* (Simon & Schuster, 2006) 495. See also, Donald, 258.

25 Goodwin, 355–58.

26 White, 35, 116; Donald, 258; and Jon Meacham, And There Was Light: Abraham Lincoln and the American Struggle (Random House, 2022), 241.

27 Douglas L. Wilson, *Lincoln's Sword: The Presidency and the Power of Words* (New York: Alfred A. Knopf, 2007), 198.

28 Nicholas Murray Butler to Roy P. Basler, n.p., April 23, 1942, Basler Papers, LC.

29 Warren Zimmerman, *The First Great Triumph: How Five Americans Made Their Country a World Power* (Farrar, Straus and Giroux, 2004), 43.

30 Robert Schlesinger, *White House Ghosts: Presidents and their Speechwriters* (Simon & Schuster, 2008), 1.

31 Conversation with Sara Martin, editor in chief of The Adams Papers, MHS December 2019.

32 Schlesinger, *White House Ghosts,* 2.

33 Schlesinger, *White House Ghosts,* 2–3.

34 Schlesinger , *White House Ghosts,* 1–4.

35 Schlesinger, *White House Ghosts,* 214.

36 Ted Sorensen, *Counselor: A Life at the Edge of History* (Harper Perennial, 2008): 130–131.

37 President Barnas Sears's 1858 commencement address urged the graduates to enter public service and participate in government. He said of the scholars: "Their eloquence would possess popular power.... Their eloquence would possess an enduring power." John Hay fulfilled this one dream of Sears. Quoted in "Brown University Class of 1858," Providence, Rhode Island, 1858.

Chapter 1: 1840 AMERICA

38 United States Census, 1840, Salem, Washington County, IN.

39 The cause of Edward's death was not recorded, though his father's letters to his parents and brothers in the years leading up to the boy's death tell of a child prone to periodic and severe illness. Healthy at birth and his first year of life, he was taken ill during the winter of 1833–1834, probably by a cholera epidemic. The illness may have weakened the boy's constitution and lead to his death on October 8, 1840. Another explanation might have been milk sickness, rampant along the Ohio River Valley in the early nineteenth century, when cows grazed on white snakeroot containing the poison tremetol, known for gruesome symptoms of fever, vomiting, and trembling, as Edward's appeared to be.

40 Augustus Leonard Hay, born November 9, 1832, died October 8, 1840; Mary Pierce Hay, born December 17, 1836, married Captain A. C. Woolfolk, October 8, 1863, John Hay's 25th birthday, died March 21, 1914; Charles Edward Hay, born March 23, 1841, married Mary Ridgely, May 10, 1865, died January 15, 1916; Helen Jemima Hay, born September 13, 1844, married Harwood O. Whitney, July 19, 1870, died June 19, 1873. These are noted in Charles E. Hay to William Roscoe Thayer, Cambridge, MA, April 17, 1914, in WRT MSS, HLH.

41 Marylou Kelly Streznewski, in her fascinating chronicle, *Gifted Grownups: The Mixed Blessing of Extraordinary Potential* (John Wiley & Sons, 1999), 36–51.

42 Streznewski, 61.

Chapter 2: "I Am Nothing but an American"

43 John Hay, *Addresses of John Hay* (Books for Libraries Press, 1970), 220. This is a reprint of the original, published in 1906.

44 Based on a letter signed by Adam Hay, George Washington MSS, LCW; *Letters of John Hay and Extracts from Diary,* I, privately printed, 1908.

45 Today, West Virginia.

46 According to Virginia marriage records.

47 Few reliable facts remain of Adam Hay's war service, though George Washington's papers in the Library of Congress refer to correspondence about an "Adam Hay" and his imprisonment by the British, who is not the Adam Hay related to our subject, John Hay (1838–1905).

48 *Letters of John Hay;* "Hay," unpublished manuscript, n.d., n.p.; genealogy of Hay-Leonard-Stone families, given to author by Corrin Wadsworth Strong, Geneseo, NY, 2011.

49 United States Census, 1810, Lexington, Fayette Co., KY.

50 "Hay."

51 George W. Ranck, *History of Lexington, Kentucky: Its Early Annals and Regent Progress* (Robert Clarke & Co., 1872), 269.

52 Clay's career of national public service covered terms as Speaker of the US House of Representatives; US Senator, and Secretary of State. Clay references include Maurice G. Baxter, *Henry Clay and the American System* (University Press of Kentucky, 1995); Clement Eaton, *Henry Clay and the Art of American Politics* (Scott Foresman, 1957); and Glyndon G. Van Deusen, *The Life of Henry Clay* (Little, Brown, 1937).

For background on Lexington, see Ranck, sourced from Wikipedia, Webpage of "Lexington, Kentucky," https://en.wikipedia.org/wiki/Lexington,_Kentucky; and

Wikipedia, Webpage of "John C. Breckinridge," https://en.wikipedia.org/wiki/John_C._Breckinridge.

53 By 1850, the city was home to the largest congregation of free Blacks, the First African Baptist Church. Sourced from Wikipedia, "Lexington, Kentucky."

54 Charles Hay to John Hay (his father), June 6, 1829, Salem, Indiana, JH MSS, JHBU.

55 Charles Hay to Elizabeth Hay, July 28, 1829, Salem, JHC, JHB; see Charles Hay to Elmry Hay, August 28, 1829, Salem, JH MSS, JHBU.

56 Ancestry.com is the source of the author's information about "Tilford," who died in Salem, IN, on September 15, 1829, age 29. He had married Anna Marie Mary "Polly" Devault (1803–1871) on March 8, 1827, and their son, William M. Tilford (1828–1871), was born in 1828; see http://person.ancestry.com/tree/22952776/person/12496680287/facts.

57 Charles Hay to Nathaniel Hay, Sept 17, 1829, Salem, IN, JH MSS, JHBU.

58 Charles Hay to Deniza Hay, August 7, 1829, Salem, JH MSS, JHBU.

59 John Hay Farnham was a native of Newburyport, MA; Evelyn Leonard Farnham was a native of Bristol, RI.

60 Charles Hay to Elizabeth Hay, October 17, 1831, Salem, JH MSS, JHBU.

61 Renamed Brown University in 1804 in recognition of a $5,000 gift from alumnus Nicholas Brown.

Chapter 3: Illinois Heartland

62 Kentucky.com, Webpage of "1833 Cholera Epidemic," October 27, 2014, http://www.kentucky.com/2014/10/27/3504042/lexingtons-1833-cholera-epidemic.html#storylink=cpy.

63 Charles Hay to Nathaniel Hay, July 15, 1833, MSS, ALPL.

64 Charles Hay to sisters, April 29, 1834, Salem, JH MSS, ALPL; Charles Hay to Nathanial Hay, May 21, 1834, Salem, JH MSS, JHBU.

65 Charles Hay to Addison Hay, January 7, 1837, Salem, JH MSS, JHBU.

66 Charles Hay to Milton Hay, January 11 or 14, 1841, MSS, ALPL.

67 Charles Hay to Joseph Hay, November 3, 1839, JH MSS, JHBU.

68 Charles Hay to Milton Hay, April 17, 1838, Salem, MSS, ALPL.

69 Charles Hay to Milton Hay, January 11 or 14, 1841, Lincoln Presidential Library. Charles Hay echoed similar views when he wrote to his brother Theodore Hay on March 5, 1848, Warsaw, regarding Theodore's settlement in a new town: "I would go if I had my youth to go over again into some flourishing commercial town whose prospect for permanent prosperity were good. Louisville, Cincinnati, and New Albany, Indiana, would have been better locations for me." JH MSS, JHBU.

70 See Jackson Lears, *Rebirth of a Nation: The Making of Modern America, 1877–1920* (HarperCollins, 2009), 1.

71 Samuel Mather to Flora Stone Mather, February 27, 1885, Mather Family Papers, Cleveland History Center.

72 Carol McCartney, *Our Pike County: The Soul of Western Illinois* (James Stevenson Publisher, May 2004).

73 History of Pike County, vol. 1.

74 Quoted in Charles C. Chapman, *History of Pike County Illinois,* vol. 1 (1880).

75 John Hay, "The Press and Modern Progress," address at opening of the Press Parliament of the World, Louisiana Purchase Exposition, St. Louis, May 19, 1904, in John Hay, *Addresses of John Hay* (Books of Libraries Press, 1970). This was originally printed in 1906.

Chapter 4: The Gifted Child

76 Charles Hay to Addison Hay, January 7, 1837, Salem, Indiana, JH MSS, JHBU.

77 Charles E. Hay to William Roscoe Thayer, Dec. 22, 1913, describing the newel post in John Hay's Euclid Avenue house in Cleveland, inscribed with the three words, "Lex, Lux, and Pax," which he related to his younger brother, Charles. WRT MSS, HLH.

78 "Washington Correspondence," January 14, 1862, and January 19, 1862 *Missouri Republican, quoted in Burlingame, Lincoln's Journalist,* 192–98.

79 Bertrand Rockwell of Kansas City, MO, to William Roscoe Thayer, March 25, 1918, San Francisco, WRT MSS, HLH.

80 Vulgar monosyllabic words hit like the blow of a pioneer's ax.

81 Clarence King, "John Hay," *Scribner's* (April 1874): 736–739.

82 Recited by Charles E. Hay to William Roscoe Thayer, Dec. 29, 1913, WRT MSS, HLH.

83 Wikipedia, Webpage of "The Compromise of 1850," https://www.archives.gov/milestone-documents/compromise-of-1850#:~:text=The%20acts%20called%20for%20 the,amended%20the%20Fugitive%20Slave%20Act

84 John Hay's attraction to nature would lead him as a young adult to experience some of the most remote and beautiful places in America, Europe, and North Africa. Art and architecture were particularly captivating for him.

85 Charles E. Hay to William Roscoe Thayer, Dec. 22, 1913, WRT MSS, HLH.

86 Charles E. Hay to William Roscoe Thayer, Dec. 22, 1913, WRT MSS, HLH.

87 John Hay, "The Press and Modern Progress."

88 The Christ child and crèche scene first appeared in Europe in the Paris premier of 1854 by composer Hector Berlioz in the brilliant Christmas oratorio, "The Infant Christ." Modern Christmas traditions first appeared in America in 1863, a poignant moment in which John Hay took part.

89 The Kansas-Nebraska Act of May 30, 1854, repealed the Missouri Compromise.

90 Lincoln represented the seventh District of Sangamon County, IL.

91 Charles Hay to Theodore Hay, May 9, 1848, Warsaw. JH MSS, JHBU.

92 Charles E. Hay to William Roscoe Thayer, Dec. 22, 1913, WRT MSS, HLH.

93 John Hay's reading of antislavery messages by politicians, the press, and poets are reflected in the tenor and perspective of his view in rhetorical debates at Brown University, 1855–1858; JH MSS, University Archives, JHBU.

94 Longfellow's poem, "Slave in the Dismal Swamp" in "Poems of Slavery" (1842):

"A poor old slave, infirm and lame; / Great scars deformed his face; / On his forehead he bore the brand of shame, / And the rags, that hid his mangled frame, Were the livery of disgrace.

All things above were bright and fair, / All things were glad and free; / Lithe squirrels darted here and there, / And wild birds filled the echoing air /With songs of Liberty!"

Chapter 5: A Classical Education

95 Hancock County in 1850 was dominated by a German foreign-born population that was at least three times larger than other immigrant groups. The 1850 census for Illinois recorded a foreign-born population of 13 percent, of which German constituted 36 percent; Irish 27 percent, and English 18 percent. The Mississippi Valley counties of Hancock, Adams and Calhoun were predominantly German enclaves. See more at www.lib.niu.edu/1998/ih+519815.html.

96 Augustus Leonard Hay to John Hay, grandfather, April 17, 1850, Warsaw, in JH MSS, JHBU.

97 Charles Hay to Milton and John Hay (brothers), circa 1836–1838, JH MSS, ALPL.

98 "Hay," n.a., anonymous, n.d., n.p.

99 See Charles E. Hay to William Roscoe Thayer, Dec., 22, 1913. According to the 1850 Federal Census, John Milton Hay, eleven years old, was living with his parents and siblings in Warsaw, Hancock County, IL, on October 15, 1850, when the census taker recorded the household. Milton Hay, lawyer, was living in the Dillingham Hotel in Pittsfield, Pike County, IL; his net worth is recorded as $1,800. Also living in the hotel are 22-year-old carpenters Thomas Gaffrey and Joseph Leonard, and 18-year-old printers John G. Nicolay of Germany and Monroe Benson of New York. 1850 Federal Census, Library of Congress.

100 Milton Hay married within a few months of the 1850 Federal census taker's record, when he was living in the Dillingham Hotel in Pittsfield.

101 The house where John Hay reportedly lived with Milton Hay stands at 322 Washington Street, Pittsfield, IL.

102 Tyler Dennett papers relating to John Hay, Dennett MSS, LCW, container 5.

103 Springfield's growth, 1840 to 1857, was recorded in the Daily Illinois State Journal, July 25, 1857. John Hay's residence was on the site of the Springfield first dry-goods store.

104 Stuart-Hay Families, "Hay." See also, Lowell H. Harrison, *Lincoln of Kentucky* (Lexington: University Press of Kentucky, 2000), 45. In 1838, John T. Stuart defeated Stephen A. Douglas and was elected to the US House of Representatives. Lincoln passed the bar in 1836. See Wikipedia, Webpage of "Abraham Lincoln," per https://en.wikipedia.org/wiki/Abraham_Lincoln.

105 John Hay and son Nathaniel (known as "Nat") did brick masonry work for Lincoln, and Lincoln lent money for one of Hay's property investments and defending him in incidental cases of ejectment. Abraham Lincoln loaned John Hay Sr. $500, on May 7, 1849, Springfield, IL, Document 200702, ALPL. Lincoln recorded the mortgage on May 17, 1849; Lincoln recorded satisfaction of the mortgage on Dec. 6, 1851. See the website "The Lincoln Log," www.thelincolnlog.org. Abraham Lincoln contracted with Nathaniel Hay, John Hay Sr.'s son and also a brick-maker with him, to build a fence 50 feet long on a brick foundation in front of his house. See Roy P. Basler, ed., *The Collected Works of Abraham Lincoln* (New Brunswick, NJ: Rutgers University Press, 1953), based on John G. Nicolay and John Hay, eds., *Complete Works of Abraham Lincoln* (New York: Francis D. Tandy Company, 1894),). See also, letter of Abraham Lincoln to Nathaniel Hay, June 11, 1850, Springfield, IL. See also, Lowell H. Harrison, *Lincoln of Kentucky* (Lexington: University Press of Kentucky, 2000). Lincoln and Stuart dissolved their law practice in May 1841. Lincoln joined with Stephen T. Logan until the fall of 1844, when Lincoln requested more than the one-third profits for an equal partnership. Lincoln then hand-picked William H. Herndon, who had been studying

law with Logan and Lincoln since 1842, a choice many in the legal community viewed as an assistant rather than an equal partner.

106 Harrison, 47–48.

107 Wikipedia, "Abraham Lincoln."

108 Michael Burlingame, ed., *An Oral History of Abraham Lincoln: John G. Nicolay's Interviews and Essays.* Carbondale, IL: Southern Illinois University Press, 1996, 25–28.

109 Established Illinois politicians of the time included Colonel Baker, Logan, and Hardin at Jacksonville, and Browning and Williams at Quincy. In Burlingame, I, page?

110 Wikipedia, "Abraham Lincoln."

111 Burlingame, ed., *An Oral History of Abraham Lincoln. : John G. Nicolay's Interviews and Essays.* Carbondale, IL: Southern Illinois University Press, 1996.

112 Milton Hay set up a partnership with Edward D. Baker, though both lawyers practiced as much on their own as together. See Logan Hay, "Notes on the History of the Logan and Hay Families," May 30, 1939, MSS, ALPL.

113 Carol McCartney, *Our Pike County: The Soul of Western Illinois.*

114 Only when Lincoln's political prospects dimmed after serving out his term in the US House of Representatives, 1847–1849, did he return to the law for income, playing the role of a general legal practitioner and handling a variety of cases, as did most circuit lawyers.

115 Goodwin, Team of Rivals, 131.

116 Goodwin, Team of Rivals, 131–132.

117 Milton Hay interview, c. 1883–1888, Herndon's Informants, 729.

118 The 1850 federal census records Milton Hay living with Thomas Worthington and family, in what appears to be rooming house where also lived two 22-year-old carpenters, one from Ireland and one from Virginia, and two 18-year-old printers, with whom John G. Nicolay of Germany and Monroe Benson of New York shared rooms.

119 John Hay on Shakespeare, "John Hay Writing," reel 15, n.d., JH MSS, JHBU.

120 Thirty-five acre parcel bounded by Washington Street, Adams Street, and Todd Street, owned by Maria Bullock, aunt of Mary Todd Lincoln, whose attorney and power of attorney, Abraham Lincoln, sold; Nathaniel Hay, brother of Charles and Milton Hay and son of John Hay senior, bought 27 acres for $907.14, on June 15, 1855, cited in Daniel W. Stowell, ed. *The Papers of Abraham Lincoln: Legal Documents and Cases, vol. 4* (University of Virginia Press, 2008), 114–119.

121 Jemima Hay, Charles Hay's mother, had died eleven years before on, April 22, 1843, in Springfield, apparently of heart disease that "had been progressing imperceptibly for years…which led to her melancholy and sudden death." See, Charles Hay to Theodore Hay, May 4, 1843, Warsaw, IL, JH MSS, JHBU.

122 *Daily Illinois State Journal,* February 6, 1854, JH MSS, ALPL.

123 Charles Hay to Elisabeth Hay, March 30, 1854, Warsaw, IL. JH MSS, JHBU.

124 John Hay to "My Dear Sister," March 5, 1854, Springfield, JH MSS, JHBU.

125 Students at Illinois State University were tested in arithmetic, algebra, geometry, geography, natural philosophy, history, Latin, Greek, German, and rhetoric.

126 William Ridgely to William. Roscoe Thayer, December 9, 1913, Springfield, IL, WRT MSS, HLH.

127 Just before graduation, Leonard Hay struck out to support himself, entering into merchant life in St. Louis until the Civil War, when he enlisted as a private and was soon promoted to second lieutenant in the Ninth Infantry of the regular army. Hay to Bernard Leonard, April 17, 1889, Washington, DC, in JH MSS, JHBU.

Chapter 6: Brown University

128 John Hay, September 5, 1864, Brown University Archives (BUA), JHBU.

129 John Milton Hay, September 6, 1855, BUA, JHBU.

130 John Milton Hay, September 6, 1855, BUA, JHBU.

131 Brown University, "A catalogue of the officers and students of Brown University, 1855–56" (Knowles, Anthony, 1855).

132 *Register of Students, Brown University,* 1850-1863, Admission Registers, JHBU.

133 Architect Joseph Brown drew inspiration for the 185-foot steeple and bell from English architect's James Gibbs *Book of Architecture* (1728), in Raymond Rhinehart and Walter Smalling, *Brown University: The Campus Guide* (Princeton Architectural Press, 2014), 51–54.

134 Corporation Papers, Records, vol. 3, 1844–1875, specifically August 21 to September 5, 1855, BUA, JHBU. See also, Albert Harkness on Barnas Sears, n.d., BUA, JHBU. Greek classics professor Albert Harkness was known for his charming demeanor and national reputation as a founder of the American Philological Society.

135 Rachel Gold, "The Education of John Hay," Brown University, Dec. 15, 2015, unpublished manuscript.

136 Quoted in Romeo Elton to Barnas Sears, Exeter, England, August 13, 1864, BUA, JHBU.

137 Under Wayland's direction, the curriculum had tended toward the liberal, offering students electives rather than mandatory requirements. Sears, on the other hand, was a conservative educator, and returned Brown to a protocol of compulsory classes and few electives.

138 James Bradley, *Imperial Cruise: A Secret History of Empire and War* (Little, Brown, 2009).

139 Rhinehart and Smalling, *Brown University,* 64, 66–68, 77–79.

140 Albert Green Utley, Class of 1854, *Student Diary,* BUA, JHBU, 91.

141 Brown University remained the leading Baptist institution of higher learning until 1892, when the University of Chicago reopened its doors.

142 James B. Angell, University of Michigan president at University of Chicago commencement, *Chicago Record,* July 11, 1899, on college life 50 years ago, based on J. Carter Brown's 1783 pamphlet.

143 Students (and their parents) retained a butler for $7 a term, as John Hay was able to do his third year.

144 Students (and their parents) retained a butler.

145 Hay, September 5, 1864, BUA, JHBU.

146 Martha Mitchell, *Encyclopedia Brunoniana* (Brown University Library, 1993).

147 Brown University, "A catalogue of the officers and students of Brown University, 1855–56," (Knowles, Anthony 1855). See also, "James Angell," BUA, JHBU.

148 Albert Greene Utley, *Student Diary,* p. 91, BUA, JHBU.

149 John Hay to Helen Leonard Hay, Nov. 28, 1855, Brown University, JH MSS, JHBU. Early biographies of John Hay by William Roscoe Thayer (1917) and Tyler Dennett (1936) state that Milton Hay paid for John Hay's Brown education, though I've found evidence that Dr. Charles Hay paid the Brown University treasurer for most of his son's student expenses for tuition, room, the library, registrar, a servant's hire, fuel, general and personal repairs, and private damages, totaling $33 for each term in 1855 and 1856 ($876 in 2025), rising to $33.50 in 1857 and 1858 (or, $889 in 2025). Hay's college tuition remained unchanged during his time at Brown—$18 then, or approximately $478 to $498 in current value. Brown charged students an additional $5 for graduation

and $15 for commencement expenses. Dr. Hay usually paid Brown's bills promptly, with the exception of 1857 when his payments arrived two and four months late, apparently lean years for the doctor during the 1857–1858 recession.

150 "Hay," n.a., n.p., unpublished manuscript (genealogy of Hay-Leonard-Stone family), n.d., given to author by Corrin Wadsworth Strong, Geneseo, NY, in 2011. See also, Henry MacFarland, "Secretary John Hay," *American Monthly Review of Reviews,* January 1900: 33–41. This is a laudatory portrait that misstates John Hay's middle name as Malcom rather than Milton, perhaps an error of the writer or printer.

151 William Easton Loutti '25, "John Hay in Theta Delta Chi," *Shield* of Theta Delta Chi, January 1939. Loutti's essay is dated November 6, 1938. The historian is cautious of the author's hyperbole, as he is writing more than fifty years after the fact and about Brown's revered alumnus. William L. Stone was writing in 1905, memorializing John Hay at the time of his death, when the US Secretary of State died in office on July 1, 1905.

152 *The Brown Paper,* Brown University, Providence, RI, November 1857, vol. 2, John Hay Library, BU.

153 Martha Mitchell, *Encyclopedia Brunoniana* (Brown University Library, 1993).

154 Mitchell, *Encyclopedia Brunoniana,* 190.

155 John Hay to family, "dear friends," November 28, 1855, JH MSS, JHBU.

156 The three-week winter vacation, January 25 through February 14, 1856, was the only vacation noted in the school register records for John Milton Hay, in BUA, JHBU.

157 Mitchell, *Brunoniana,* 89.

158 John Hay's grades for the spring 1856 term, February through July, recorded a 19.37 out of a perfect 20 in Latin, 19.21 in physics, 18.90 for Greek, and 18.79 for rhetoric. John Hay, student records, BUA, JHBU.

159 John Hay to Milton Hay, March 30, 1856, JH MSS, JHBU.

160 Mitchell, *Brunoniana,* 113.

161 John Hay, "Indian Traditions," May 3, 1856, Brown University. Signed, John M. Hay, Warsaw, Ill., May 3d 1856, ix," JH MSS, JHBU and ALPL.

162 Barnas Sears, Monthly Report to Executive Board of the Corporation, June 7, 1856, BUA, JHBU.

163 Richard Olney preceded John Hay as secretary of state by eighteen months.

164 Abraham Lincoln's speech at Peoria, IL, October 16, 1854, signified early opposition to slavery's spread into Western territories.

165 Brown University, "A Catalogue of the Officers and Students of Brown University, 1855–56," (Knowles, Anthony, 1855).

166 John Hay, "The interest connected with the History of Civilization," n.d., c. spring 1856, based on handwriting and date of similar essays.

167 Harry Lyman Koopman, "Literary Men of Brown: VI, John Hay," *Brown Alumni Monthly 9* no. 9 (April 1909): 207.

168 W. Easton Louttit Jr., "John Hay," n.d., n.p.

Chapter 7: Brown Poet Laureate

169 Mitchell, *Brunoniana,* 105.

170 Rhinehart and Smalling, *Brown University,* 64–65; Mitchell, *Brunoniana,* 133.

171 March 3, 1857 and March 4, 1857, meeting of the faculty, BUA, JHBU. Brown University Archives, Scrapbooks, vol. 1, in JH MSS, JHBU.

172 Hay earned a 19.10 average in French literature, and a 19.32 in German. Hay, BUA, JHBU.

173 Philermenian Society, BUA, JHBU.

174 Jan. 9, 1858, Philermenian Society, 1857–1858, JH MSS, JHBU. The Philermenian society elected John Hay as their vice president in June 1858.

175 Philermenian Society Records, 1855–1858, JHBU."Opium Eater in New York," reprinted in *Daily Illinois State Journal,* July 25, 1857. The writer claimed that "Opium eating is extensively practiced by all classes in New York," from "the belle and the dowager of fashionable life, [to] the employee of the Avenue, the journalists, the clergyman and the advocate." The growing pressures of modern life, the fast excitement of an industrializing economy and the feverish ambition it fostered, were eased by the relaxing, euphoric effects of marijuana and hashish. By the early 1880s, private hashish parlors in many cities in the United States were inciting controversy about the legality and morality of cannabis intoxication. Even at the Philadelphia Centennial Exposition of 1876, considered a refined showing of intelligentsia, fair-goers could purchase hashish in the hall. See also, *Illustrated Police News*, December 2, 1876.

176 *Histoire des croisades*, 9th ed., (Huillard-Bréholles, 1856).

177 Mitchell, Brunoniana, 90. At about the time that John Hay became friends with a few among Providence's literati, President Sears was reporting to the executive board of the corporation about the college's exposed condition during the nights as the boys, believed to be in their rooms though unsupervised, were venturing unchaperoned into the city's evil corners. See, Barnas Sears to Executive Board of Corporation, Jan. 2, 1858, BUA, JHBU.

178 Joseph LeRoy Harrison, "Providence Athenaeum, 1753–1911," *New England Magazine*, Sept-Oct 1911, reprinted in the *Seventy-Sixth Annual Report of the Board of Directors of The Providence Athenaeum* (The Providence Press, Sept. 25, 1911).

179 *Annual reports*, "List of Proprietors," Providence Athenaeum, 1856, 1857, 1858.

180 *Accession Book no. 4*, Sept. 1850–August 1857, Providence Athanaeum.

181 George H. Whitney published a collection of Sarah Helen Whitman's poems in 1860, in defense of Edgar Allen Poe and against his critics. See, *Edgar Allan Poe and His Critics* (George H. Whitney, 1860).

182 Thomas, Dwight and David K. Jackson,*The Poe Log: A Documentary Life of Edgar Allan Poe, 1809–1849* (G. K. Hall, 1987), 614. See also, Wikipedia, Webpage of "Sarah Helen Whitman," http://en.wikipedia.org/wiki/Sarah_Helen_Whitman.

183 Quoting S. Helen Whitman in Edgar Allen Poe to Helen Whitman, October 1, 1848, Fordham, NY, in James A. Harrison, ed., *The Last Letters of Edgar Allan Poe to Sarah Helen Whitman* (G.P. Putnam's Sons, 1909).

184 Harry L. Koopman to Clara Stone Hay, January 27, 1909. Brown University Library. In the letter, he is referring to an 1858 portrait of himself that John Hay gave to Sarah Helen Whitman. "I have the promise from the owner that I may have it copied." John Hay Papers, reel 8, John Hay Library, BU.

185 John M. Hay, BUA, JHBU.

186 Amy A. C. Montague, ed., *A College Friendship: A Series of Letters from John Hay to Hannah Angell* (Privately printed, 1938), v–x.

187 Caroline Ticknor, ed., *A Poet in Exile* (Andesite Press, 2018), 6.

188 William Roscoe Thayer, *The Life and Letters of John Hay,* vol. 1 (Houghton Mifflin, 1915), 66.

189 "John Hay," BUA, JHBU.

190 Wikipedia, "Pierre-Jean de Beranger," https://en.wikipedia.org/wiki/Pierre-Jean_de_Béranger.
191 John Hay to Hannah Angell, June 5, 1858, Providence, quoted in Montague, 4–6.
192 *Providence Journal,* June 10, 1858.
193 JH MSS, JHBU.
194 John Hay to Hannah Angell, circa July 6, 1858, Providence, in Montague, 12–15.

Chapter 8: Return to Illinois

195 John Hay to Hannah Angell, July 19, 1858, postmark; the letter appears to have been started when Hay was still at Brown, and completed and posted after he had arrived home in Warsaw, IL, quoted in Montague, 15–18.
196 John Hay to Hannah Angell, July 27, 1858, Springfield, JH MSS, JHBU.
197 United States Federal Census, 1860, Springfield, Sangamon County, IL.
198 John Hay to Hannah Angell, July 19, 1858, postmark; this is the last part of the letter that Hay started at Brown; he has now arrived home in Warsaw. Quoted in Montague, 17–18.
199 Interview with Marc Mytar, PhD, clinical psychologist, October 24, 2019 in Ellsworth, ME.
200 John Hay to Hannah Angell, postmarked October 20, 1858. Quoted in Montague, 32–33.
201 John Hay to Hannah Angell, September 1, 1858, Warsaw, Illinois. Quoted in Montague, 28–32.
202 Hay to Angell, September 1, 1858. Quoted in Montague, 28–32.
203 Charles Hay to Milton Hay, Sept 6, 1858, Warsaw, Illinois, JH MSS, JHBU.
204 John Hay to Nora Perry, May 15, 1859, Springfield. Quoted in Caroline Ticknor, ed., *Poet in Exile: Early Letters of John Hay* (Houghton Mifflin, 1919), 39–40.
205 Charles E. Hay to William Roscoe Thayer, Dec 22, 1913, WRT MSS, HLH.
206 n.a., n.d., "Hay," in genealogy of Hay-Leonard-Stone family. This was an unpublished manuscript given to the author by Corrin Wadsworth Strong, a great-grandson of John Hay, in Geneseo, NY, in 2011.
207 John Hay to Nora Perry, May 15, 1859, Springfield. Quoted in Ticknor, 42. "On arriving here yesterday I was no less surprised than delighted to find a letter from you." Milton Hay owned $20,000 in real and personal property, more than double Charles Hay's net worth of $9,650.
208 "Hay," n.d, n.p.
209 John Hay to William L. Stone, May 20, 1859, Springfield, IL, JH MSS, JHBU.
210 John Hay to William L. Stone, May 20, 1859, Springfield, JH MSS, JHBU.
211 David Zarefsky, The House Divided Speech, in *Abraham Lincoln: In His Own Words* (Great Courses, 1999).
212 Quoted in Joseph B. Bishop, "John Hay, Scholar, Statesman," an address delivered before the Alumni Association of Brown University, June 19, 1906 (Standard Printing, 1906), in JH MSS, JHBU.
213 http://www. mrlincolnandfriends.org/inside.asp?pageID=43
214 Charles C. Chapman, *History of Pike County Illinois* vol. 1 (1880). Hatch's Statehouse office became the center of Springfield political activity in those years, according to Nicolay.
215 John Hay to Hannah Angell Coggeshall, January 6, 1861, Springfield, Illinois. Quoted in Montague, 55, 58.

216 Mary Ridgely Hay, "Springfield, Illinois, in 1860, by a Native Springfielder," December 1913, unpublished typed manuscript, five pages, in JH MSS, JHBU, microfilm reel 7. Mary Ridgely Hay was the wife of Charles Edward Hay, John Hay's younger brother.

Chapter 9: At Lincoln's Side

217 *History of Pike County Illinois,* vol. 1, Charles C. Chapman, 1880, 12.
218 Shelby M. Cullom to William Roscoe Thayer, December 1, 1913, Washington, DC, WRT MSS, HLH.
219 In P. J. Staudenraus, ed., *Mr. Lincoln's Washington: Selections from the Writings of Noah Brooks, Civil War Correspondent* (Thomas Yoseloff, 1967), 9.
220 Jason Emerson, *Giant in the Shadows: The Life of Robert T. Lincoln* (Southern Illinois University Press, 2012).
221 Hay to Hannah Angell, January 1, 1860, Springfield, Illinois, JH MSS, JHBU.
222 Hay to Hannah Angell, January 1, 1860, Springfield, Illinois, JH MSS, JHBU
223 Milton Hay to John Hay, February 8, 1887, Springfield, JH MSS, JHBU.
224 Donald, *Lincoln,* 238.
225 Harold Holzer, "Still a Great Hall After All," *American Heritage Magazine* 55 no. 2 (April/May 2004).
226 Wilson, *Lincoln's Sword,* 4.
227 Thomas Jefferson to Edward Carrington, 16 Jan. 1787. Quoted in Julian P. Boyd, et al, eds. *The Papers of Thomas Jefferson.* vol. 11. (Princeton University Press, 1950),48–49.
228 Joseph B. Bishop, "John Hay, scholar, statesman." Bishop, a Brown classmate, was also a co-worker with Hay at the *New York Tribune* in the early 1870s.
229 Stephen Douglas was nominated at the Democratic National Convention on April 23, 1860, in Charleston, SC.
230 John Hay, scrapbook, JH MSS, JHBU.
231 Nicolay wrote the piece at the personal request of editor Daniel Bush.
232 "Ecarte," a.k.a. John Hay, *Providence Journal,* May 26, 1860; written and dispatched on May 21, 1860, scrapbook, vol. 54, JH MSS, LCW.
233 "Ecarte," *Providence Journal,* May 26, 1860.
234 "Ecarte," *Providence Journal,* May 26, 1860.
235 Carl Schurz had recently transferred his allegiance from Seward to Lincoln. Quoted in Goodwin, 271–72.
236 Roy P. Basler, ed., *The Collected Works of Abraham Lincoln* vol. 4 (Rutgers University Press, 1953), 51.
237 John George Nicolay and John Hay, *Abraham Lincoln: A Biography* vol. 6 (Francis D. Tandy). This volume quotes the material from May 19, 1860. See also, Brown University news release, October 30, 1938, Brown University Collection, JH MSS, JHBU.
238 Paraphrasing the last paragraph of "Ecarte," *Providence Journal,* May 26, 1860.
239 "Ecarte," *Providence Journal,* May 26, 1860.
240 Lowell H. Harrison, *Lincoln in Kentucky* (University Press of Kentucky, 2000), 50.
241 Burlingame, *Abraham Lincoln,* I.
242 Burlingame, *Abraham Lincoln,* vol. 1, 652. See also, John W. Bunn to Weik, Springfield, July 20, 1916, in Jesse W. Weik and Michael Burlingame, ed., *The Real Lincoln: A portrait* (Big Byte Books, 2019), 321. Weik's book was originally published in 1923, long before Burlingame edited the 2019 edition.
243 Nicolay to Therena Bates, Springfield, June 7, 1860, JGN MSS, LC.

244 Michael Burlingame, ed., *At Lincoln's Side: John Hay's Civil War Correspondence and Selected Writing* (Southern Illinois University Press, 2000), xviii.

245 Mary Ridgeley Hay, a close friend of John Hay's at the time and later his sister-in-law as Charlie Hay's wife, in "Springfield, Illinois 1860," n.d.

246 Thayer, 171–72.

247 Robert C. Williams, *Horace Greeley: Champion of American Freedom* (New York University Press, 2006).

248 Hay scrapbook, JH MSS, JHBU.

249 Nicolay to Therena Bates, Aug 9, 1860, Springfield, JGN MSS, LC.

250 Newberry Library, Chicago History Museum collection, photograph of August 8, 1860, political campaign demonstration, ICHi-22208.

251 John Hay, a.k.a. Ecarte, *Missouri Democrat,* August 9, 1860 in Scrapbook, JH MSS, JHBU; JGN to Therena Bates, Aug 9, 1860, Springfield, JGN MSS, LC. "We had an immense meeting here yesterday—too large to count."

Chapter 10: Finding His Muse

252 Zarefsky, *Abraham Lincoln: In His Own Words,* "Debate on the Debates."

253 "Ecarte," a.k.a. John Hay, *Providence Journal,* Aug 29, 1860, in Burlingame, *Lincoln's Journalist,* 6–9.

254 "Ecarte," a.k.a. John Hay, *Missouri Democrat, October 11, 1860, published October 15, 1860, JH MSS, LCW.*

255 "Ecarte," *Missouri Democrat,* October 11, 1860.

256 "Ecarte," a.k.a. John Hay, November 15, 1860, Springfield, *Providence Journal,* JH MSS, JHBU.

257 On May 19, 1860, the letter of acceptance that Abraham Lincoln submitted to the Republican National Committee used the terms "high honor" twice in two sentences, referring to the enormous responsibility for which he had been nominated. John Hay penned the archival manuscript of this letter, and he likely drafted the original letter. Hay's "Ecarte" dispatch to the *Providence Journal* of May 21, 1860, mentioned "honor" three times. Ecarte filed his last column with the *Missouri Democrat* on November 16, 1860, though he continued to write anonymously for the St. Louis-based paper.

258 According to Michael Burlingame, the *Illinois State Journal* was "widely regarded as his mouthpiece." See Burlingame, *Abraham Lincoln: A History* vol. 1 (Johns Hopkins University Press, 2008), 703.

259 Burlingame, *Abraham Lincoln: A History* vol. 2, 247. See also, Burlingame, *With Lincoln in the White House,* 21.

260 "Springfield correspondence," January 9, 1861, and January 11, 1861, in *Missouri Democrat,* 18.

261 David Herbert Donald, "*We are Lincoln Men": Abraham Lincoln and His Friends* (Simon & Schuster, 2003), 180.

262 Thayer, vol. 1, 87. Lincoln secured an administrative post in the Department of the Interior for Hay, with an assignment in the White House; he was originally paid $1,500 annually, later increased to $1,800. John George Nicolay to Therena Bates, March 10, 1861, Washington, DC, JGN MSS, LCW.

263 Don E. and Virginia E. Fehrenbacher, editors, *Recollected Words of Abraham Lincoln,* 1996, 341.

264 Charles Hay to sisters, December 17, 1856, Warsaw, IL, JH MSS, ALPL.

265 Charles Hay to Milton Hay, September 6, 1858, Warsaw, IL, JH MSS, JHBU.

Chapter 11: Dexterity Under Pressure

266 Burlingame, *Abraham Lincoln,* vol. 2, 257.

267 "From Washington," *New York Times,* December 13, 1860, JH scrapbook, newspaper clippings, miscellaneous, 1860–1865. From the collection of Robert Hoffman, in Rochester, NY.

268 Quoted in Burlingame, *Abraham Lincoln,* II: 259.

269 Michael Burlingame described Lincoln's confidence as "profound self-respect." See Burlingame, *Abraham Lincoln,* vol. 1, 685.

270 Special Dispatch to *Cincinnati Enquirer,* December 17, 1860, in JH scrapbook, newspaper clippings, miscellaneous, 1860–1865. From the collection of Robert Hoffman.

271 Robert C. Williams, *Horace Greeley: Champion of American Freedom* (New York University Press, 2006), 218.

272 Goodwin, *Team of Rivals.* See also, David Donald, ed., *Inside Lincoln's Cabinet: The Civil War Diaries of Salmon P. Chase* (Longmans, Green, 1954).

273 Springfield correspondence, Illinois *Daily State Journal,* January 22, 1861. The notion that the anonymous writings by Hay, Nicolay, and Stoddard may reflect Abraham Lincoln's thinking is discussed by Michael Burlingame in "Lincoln Spins the Press," in Charles M. Hubbard, *Lincoln Reshapes the Presidency* (Mercer University Press, 2003), 66–67.

274 In this letter, John Hay to Hannah Angell, Hay referred to the early Republican Roman farmer and dictator who became the model of Roman virtue, Lucius Quinctius Cincinnatus. See Montague, *A College Friendship,* 58.

275 Certificate of [Law] License, John Hay, Esq., February 4, 1861, in JH MSS, JHBU, microfilm reel 7.

276 https://www.abrahamlincolnonline.org/lincoln/speeches/house.htm. August 26, 2025.

277 February 1861 invitation, signed by N. J. Wood [Illinois Governor John Wood?], Hay letter, Lincoln-Herndon papers, "Originals sent to Mrs. Whitney, July 16, 1930," LCW; and, James Wadsworth Family Papers, manuscript division, LCW, "undated poems."

278 Walter B. Noyes [Brown classmate] to John Hay, Feb. 7, 1861, Providence, RI, in Wadsworth Family Papers, MS division, LCW, "undated poems."

279 Springfield correspondence, *Missouri Democrat,* January 28, 1861. Quoted in Burlingame, *Lincoln's Journalist,* 21.

280 Jason Emerson, *Giant in the Shadows: The Life of Robert T. Lincoln* (Southern Illinois University Press, 2012), 53.

281 February 10, 1861, Mary Ridgely Hay, "Springfield, Illinois, in 1860," December 1913, JH MSS, JHBU.

282 Henry Villard, *New York Herald,* February 11, 1861.

283 John Hay, as Ecarte, February 11, 1861, *New York World,* February 15, 1861. Quoted in Burlingame, *Lincoln's Journalist,* 23–27.

284 Wilson, *Lincoln's Sword,* 12–13.

285 Abraham Lincoln's address in Springfield on Feb. 11, 1861 is quoted in Nicolay and Hay, *Abraham Lincoln* vol. 3, 291. This address, according to note 1, was "correctly printed for the first time in the *Century Magazine* of December 1887, from original manuscript, having been written down immediately after the train started, partly by Mr.

Lincoln's own hand [the first 58 words] and partly [the latter 90] by that of his private secretary."

286 Zarefsky, *Abraham Lincoln: In His Own Words.*

287 Gabor Boritt, *The Gettysburg Gospel: The Lincoln Speech that Nobody Knows* (Simon & Schuster, 2006), 92.

288 Edward D. Baker, ed., *Illinois State Journal,* Springfield, Feb. 12, 1861.

289 Vernon Louis Parrington, *Main Currents in American Thought,* 3 volumes, (1927).

290 Ronald C. White, *The Eloquent President: A Portrait of Lincoln Through his Words* (Random House, 2005), 18, 22.

291 John Hay, "The Heroic Age in Washington" 1870, Hay presented the lecture in several cities, including Buffalo, Chicago, and Warsaw, in JH MSS, JHBU.

292 John Hay, "The Heroic Age in Washington."

293 Ward Hill Lamon, *Recollections of Abraham Lincoln* (Dorothy Lamon Teillard, 1911), 32.

294 John Hay, Indianapolis correspondence, February 11, *New York World,* Feb. 15, 1861. Quoted in Burlingame, *Lincoln's Journalist,* 25.

295 Nicolay and Hay, *Abraham Lincoln: A History* vol. 3 (The Century, 1914), 291, n. 1.

296 According to Burlingame in *Abraham Lincoln* vol. 2, p. 3, Lincoln's address at the Springfield depot was "correctly printed for the first time in the *Century Magazine* for December 1887, from original manuscript, having been written down immediately after the train started, partly by Mr. Lincoln's own hand and partly by that of his private secretary from his dictation." See also, Henry Villard, *Memoirs of Henry Villard, Journalist and Financier, 1835–1900* vol. 1 (Houghton Mifflin, 1904), 152. This volume quotes Villard's Herald article from February 11, 1861.

297 Lincoln's Springfield address remained out of sight for almost three decades, until it was printed in the *Century Magazine* in December 1887. See Burlingame and Jonathan P. White, ed., *Abraham Lincoln: A Life* (Johns Hopkins University Press, 2023), 298. This edition was also abridged by White.

298 T. C. Evans, "Personal Reminiscences of John Hay: By a Veteran Journalist," *New York Times,* July 8, 1905, 8.

299 Cincinnati correspondence, February 12, 1861, and February 15, 1861, *New York World.* Quoted in Burlingame, *Lincoln's Journalist,* 28.

300 Nicolay to Therena Bates, Feb 17, 1861, Buffalo. Quoted in Burlingame, *With Lincoln in the White House,* 28.

301 Quoted in Burlingame, *Abraham Lincoln* vol. 2, p. 10.

302 Quoted in Goodheart, *1861,* 102.

303 Henry Villard, *Memoirs* vol. 1, 152.

304 Charles Francis Adams Jr. to Richard Henry Dana, February 18, 1861, Washington, DC; Charles Francis Adams Jr., diary, February 16, 20, and 21, 1861. Adams Family Papers, MHS, Boston.

305 Bigelow, to serve as Lincoln's minister to France, would later join with Adams as the Civil War minister to the United Kingdom, to block France and England from intervening in the war on the side of the Confederacy. John Bigelow to William Hargreaves, February 21, 1861, New York, in the Bigelow Papers, New York Public Library. See also, Edward Everett, diary, February 15, 1861, Everett Papers, MHS, Boston.

306 Ninety percent of urban dailies were closely affiliated with one political party.

307 According to Matthew Gentzlow, Edward L. Glaeser and Claudia Goldin in "The Rise of the Fourth Estate: How Newspapers Became Informative and Why it Matters," in *Corruption and Reform: Lessons from America's Economic History* (University of Chicago

Press, 2006), 189; in 1850, 85 percent of urban dailies were affiliated with a political party and in 1870 the partisan press had increased to 89 percent of city papers. And, Ronald C. White, on page 43 of *The Eloquent President,* stated "Lincoln was aware of the problems that could develop when he allowed himself to speak spontaneously."

308 Walt Whitman, published in unnamed newspaper, Feburary 18 or 19, 1861, New York, ALPL.

309 John Hay, "The Heroic Age in Washington," lecture, in JH MSS, JHBU.

310 Burlingame, *Abraham Lincoln* vol 2, 32. Nicolay and Hay, *Abraham Lincoln* vol 3, 299.

311 John Hay to Annie Johnston, February 22, 1861, Harrisburg, PA, JH MSS, JHBU.

312 Emerson, *Giant in the Shadows.*

313 John Hay to Annie Johnston, February 22, 1861, Harrisburgh, PA, JH collection, JHL, BU.

314 Quoted in Burlingame, *Abraham Lincoln* vol 2, 35. See also, Basler, 4: 240.

315 "Movements of the President Elect," Harrisburg, PA, February 23, 1861, unnamed newspaper, JH scrapbook, newspaper clippings, miscellaneous, 1860–1865. From the collection of Robert Hoffman.

316 Nicolay to Therena Bates, February 24, 1861, Washington, DC, quoted in Burlingame, *Abraham Lincoln,* 28.

317 Quoted in Burlingame and Ettlinger, eds., *Inside Lincoln's White House,* 270, note 1.

318 "From our own correspondent," March 1, 1861, and March 4, 1861, *New York World* , p. 3, c. 2, quoted in Burlingame, *Lincoln's Journalist,* 50.

319 "From our own correspondent," *New York World* of February 26, 1861.

320 George Nicolay to Therena Bates, March 5, 1861, White House, Washington, DC. Quoted in Burlingame, *Lincoln's Journalist,* 29. See also, John Hay, "Heroic Age of Washington," in JH MSS, JHBU.

321 William O. Stoddard and Michael Burlingame, ed., *Inside the White House in War Times: Memoirs and Reports of Lincoln's Secretary* (University of Nebraska Press, 2000), 144.

322 Anonymous to Abe Lincoln, M[ar]ch 2d, no year, Washington, in John Hay letters, Lincoln-Herndon papers, "Originals sent to Mrs. Whitney, July 16, 1930," manuscript division, Library of Congress.

323 Kevin Phillips, *Wealth and Democracy: A Political History of the American Rich* (Broadway Books, 2002), 31.

324 Slavery was fueled by money and prosperity. Southern slaveowners had long ago discovered that it was more cost-effective to work a slave to death and buy a new slave than to care humanely for enslaved Americans.

325 Completion of the dome's top tier and the statue of freedom, her helmet crowned by a regal eagle's head symbolizing liberty and union, was delayed two years by the Civil War, ultimately completed December 2, 1863.

326 "From our own correspondent," March 1, 1861, and March 4, 1861, *New York World,* p. 3, c. 2, quoted in Burlingame, *Lincoln's Journalist,* 48–49.

327 Cleveland *Leader,* March 8, 1861.

328 Stoddard, *Inside the White House in War Times,* 27.

329 Stoddard, *Inside the White House in War Times,* 27. See also, John Hay, "From our own correspondent," February 26, 1861, *New York World,* February 28, 1861, 3, c. 1, in Burlingame, *Lincoln's Journalist,* 47.

Chapter 12: The Confidant

330 Montgomery Meigs, writing in his diary on March 8, 1861, of the March 4, inauguration, Montgomery Meigs papers, LCW.

331 John Hay, "The Heroic Age in Washington," lecture delivered in Buffalo, NY, and other cities, 1871–1872. This lecture is transcribed in Burlingame, *At Lincoln's Side,* 188–89, and quoted in Burlingame, *Abraham Lincoln,* 59–60.

332 Seward, the state senator of New York, delivered the speech he recommended Lincoln quote on February 29, 1860.

333 John Hay to Charles Eliot Norton, Washington, March 25, 1889, in Hay MSS, HLH.

334 Zarefsky, *Abraham Lincoln: In His Own Words.* Here, Zarefsky analyzes Lincoln's First Inaugural Speech.

335 James M. McPherson, *Abraham Lincoln and the Second American Revolution* (Oxford University Press, 1991).

336 "Correspondence of the World," March 4, 1861, and March 6, 1861, *New York World,* p. 3, c. 1, in Burlingame, *Lincoln's Journalist,* 53.

337 Robert Schlesinger, *White House Ghosts: Presidents and Their Speechwriters* (Simon & Schuster, 2008), 2.

338 Burlingame, *Abraham Lincoln,* 46.

339 White, *Lincoln's Greatest Speech,* 77.

340 Goodheart, 130.

341 "Correspondence of the World," March 4, 1861, and March 6, 1861, *New York World,* quoted in Burlingame, *Lincoln's Journalist,* 53.

342 The passage by Charles Dickens in *Barnaby Rudge* is worth quoting, as it provokes a thoughtful and spiritual understanding of human nature that would have captured John Hay's interest and memory: "The thoughts of worldly men are for ever regulated by a moral law of gravitation, which, like the physical one, holds them down to earth. The bright glory of day, and the silent wonders of a starlit night, appeal to their minds in vain. There are no signs in the sun, or in the moon, or in the stars, for their reading. They are like some wise men, who, learning to know each planet by its Latin name, have quite forgotten such small heavenly constellations as Charity, Forbearance, Universal Love, and Mercy, although they shine by night and day so brightly that the blind may see them; and who, looking upward at the spangled sky, see nothing there but the reflection of their own great wisdom and book-learning.... It is curious to imagine these people of the world, busy in thought, turning their eyes towards the countless spheres that shine above us, and making them reflect the only images their minds contain...So do the shadows of our own desires stand between us and *our better angels*, and thus their brightness is eclipsed."

343 Lincoln described his education as "defective" in an 1858 survey by Charles Lanman, who was preparing the *Dictionary of Congress.* Quoted in White, *Lincoln's Greatest Speech,* 67.

344 Lincoln, lecture on "Discoveries, Inventions, and Improvements," [Feb. 4, 1859], delivered in neighboring town in Illinois during winter 1859, and before the Springfield Library Association on February 21, 1860. Quoted in Nicolay and Hay, *Complete Works of Abraham Lincoln,* vol. 5, 105–112.

345 Two examples of Abraham Lincoln's personal poetry reveal his untrained style. The first he writes to Andrew Johnston, April 18, 1846, when he was thirty-seven years old. It is quoted in *Complete Works,* vol. 1, 378.

"My childhood's home I see again,
And sadden with the view;
And still, as memory crowds my brain,
There's pleasure in it too.

O Memory! Though midway world
'Twixt earth and paradise,
Where things decayed and loved ones lost
In dreamy shadows rise,

And, freed from all that's earthly vile,
Seem hallowed, pure, and bright,
Like scenes in some enchanted isle
All bathed in liquid light."

Another is his 1854 Peoria Address:
"If we do this, we shall not only have saved the Union, but we shall have so saved it as to make and to keep it forever worthy of the saving. We shall have so saved it that the succeeding millions of free happy people (the world over) shall rise up, and call us blessed to the latest generations."

346 Stoddard, Inside the White House in War, 3.
347 Nicolay to Therena Bates, March 5, 1861, White House, Washington, DC. Quoted in Burlingame, With Lincoln in the White House, 29.
348 John Hay, "Life in the White House in the Time of Lincoln," Century Magazine 41 (November 1890), 33–37.
349 J.G. Randall and Richard N. Current, Lincoln the President: The Last Full Measure (University of Illinois Press, 1999), 294.
350 Zimmerman's term, 43.
351 John Hay to Charles G. Halpine, Washington, DC, November 22, 1863, Charles Graham Halpine Papers, Huntington Library.
352 Burlingame presents a compelling portrait of Lincoln by English journalist William Howard Russell in Abraham Lincoln, vol. 2, 256.
353 Henry Adams, The Education of Henry Adams (The Modern Library, 1931), 107. An earlier printing includes 1918 in Boston.
354 Andrew Jackson Davis, "A Pyschometrical Examination of Abraham Lincoln," unnamed newspaper, November 2, 1861, in John Hay scrapbook, newspaper clippings, miscellaneous, 1860–1865. From the collection of Robert Hoffman, Rochester, NY.
355 David Brooks, "The Leadership Emotions," Opinion, New York Times, April 21, 2014.
356 John Hay to William Herndon, Paris, September 5, 1866, JH MSS, JHBU. See John R. Sellers, "Serving President Lincoln: The Public Career of John G. Nicolay," in Hubbard, Lincoln Reshapes the Presidency, 60, who wrote, "Although he was not a true political insider, he thought of himself as a 'high government official,' and he attempted to act the part." See also, David M. Potter, The Impending Crisis: 1848–1861, 555.
357 Noah Brooks, dispatch, November 7, 1863, Washington, DC. Quoted in Burlingame, Lincoln Observed: Civil War Dispatches of Noah Brooks, 11.
358 John G. Nicolay to Therena Bates, March 17, 1861, JGN MSS, LCW.

359 Daily Illinois State Journal, March 20, 1861. Quoted in Burlingame, With Lincoln in the White House, 31.
360 Stoddard, Inside the White House in War Times, 156.
361 Charles W. Moores, "John Hay: The Making of a Great Diplomat," Putnam's Magazine (June 1904): 300.
362 John Hay to William Herndon, September 5, 1866, Paris, JH MSS, JHBU.
363 John Hay with John George Nicolay, advance page proofs from The Century magazine, Abraham Lincoln: A History, 1886–1890, tear sheets, proof sheets, and other printed material relating to the serial edition, JH MSS, JHBU.
364 John Hay to William L. Stone Jr., March 16, 1861, JH MSS, LCW, container 3.
365 Zimmerman, 43. Assistant clerks included William O. Stoddard, the former editor of the Central Illinois Gazette; Edward D. Neill, who stood in during Stoddard's frequent illnesses or absences; Charles Henry Philbrick, who John viewed as a lazy and unreformed alcoholic.
366 Nicolay and Hay, Abraham Lincoln vol. 2, xii.
367 John Hay, "Life in the White House," quoted in Burlingame, At Lincoln's Side, 135.
368 Stoddard, 50-51.
369 Burlingame, With Lincoln in the White House, 30. Here, he quotes Nicolay to Bates, March 7, 1861.
370 Burlingame, Inside the White House in War Times, 157.
371 John George Nicolay to Therena Bates, Washington, March 24 and April 2, 1861, quoted in Burlingame, With Lincoln in the White House, 31–32.
372 Stoddard, Inside the White House in War Times, 109.
373 Quoted in John W. Starr, "Lincoln and the Office Seekers," typescript 1936, addenda, page 6, Lincoln files, "Patronage" folder, Lincoln Memorial University, Harrogate, TN.
374 John Russell Young, Philadelphia Evening Start, August 22, 1891, p. 4, col. 1 and 3–6. John Russell Young, "Secretary of State," Munsey's Magazine, Nov. 1898, a copy of which was pasted inside the front cover of John Hay's Castilian Days (Houghton, Mifflin, 1882), owned by Dewitt Miller, Esq. This material is quoted in Burlingame, Abraham Lincoln, vol. 2, 74.
375 John Russell Young, "John Hay," Nov. 1898, who had distinguished himself covering the First Battle of Bull Run and as managing editor of Horace Greeley's New York Tribune when Hay wrote the editorial page leaders after 1870. See Ron Chernow, Alexander Hamilton (Penguin Books, 2004), 89.
376 John Hay to Julia Stone, upon the occasion of sending his future mother-in-law locks of George Washington's hair, March 23, 1873, New York, NY. Found in Wadsworth Family Papers, MS Division, LCW.

Chapter 13: Recording the Civil War Presidency

377 Joseph Bucklin Bishop, "A Friendship with John Hay," *Century Magazine* 71 (March 1906), 778.
378 The John Hay collections archived in the John Hay Library at Brown University, the Library of Congress Manuscript Division, the National Archives & Records Service, the Massachusetts Historical Society, and others, contain a large number of manuscripts.
379 John Hay, scrapbooks. Two of Hay's four scrapbooks are archived in the John Hay Papers at the Library of Congress, and two are at the John Hay Library, Brown University. And two are archived at JHBU and five at LCW.

380 Hay journal diaries and scrapbooks, JH MSS, JHBU.

381 "John Hay," *Boston Evening Times,* July 1, 1905.

382 Hay diaries, letters, and anonymous writings for the press have been meticulously transcribed by Michael Burlingame, as he did for Nicolay's correspondence and memorandum, as well as by Stoddard, and by Banks.

383 Quoted in Burlingame, ed., *At Lincoln's Side,* xii.

384 Discussed in Donald, 15; and Goodwin, 104.

385 John Hay, *Castilian Days,* preface to revised ed., (Houghton Mifflin, 1890), iv.

386 Notes and names were crossed out in Hay's diary, perhaps by John Hay or by Clara Stone Hay, his widow and the keeper of his papers. Clara Hay disavowed her husband's profanity.

387 John Hay, "Life in the Lincoln White House," *Addresses of John Hay,* 321.

388 Journal Book, 1861–62, JH MSS, LCW.

389 Nicolay and Hay, *Abraham Lincoln,* published serially in *The Century* magazine, 1886–1890.

390 John Hay with John George Nicolay, advance page proofs from *The Century* magazine. See also, Nicolay and Hay, *Abraham Lincoln: A History,* 1886–1890. Tear sheets, proof sheets, and other printed material relating to the serial edition, JH MSS, JHBU. Also quoted in T. C. Evans, "Personal Reminiscences of John Hay: By a Veteran Journalist," *New York Times,* July 8, 1905, 8.

391 John Hay, scrapbooks. In addition to the two at LCW and two at JHBU, one is in the private collection of Robert Hoffman.

392 Scrapbook vol. 56, p. 71, 107–09, 82–106, John Hay Papers, LCW.

393 John Hay to George Plumer Smith, Washington, January 10, 1863. Quoted in Burlingame, *At Lincoln's Side,* 30.

394 Richard Hofstadter, *American Political Tradition,* 17.

395 "Ecarte," April 18, 1861, and April 23, 1861, *Illinois Daily State Journal.* Quoted in Burlingame, *Inside Lincoln's White House,* 56–57. E. L. Baker, editor of the *Illinois State Journal,* to John Hay, April 29, 1861, Springfield, acknowledged Hay's column and noted, "People here are rampant for war," Hay letter, Lincoln-Herndon Papers, MS Division, LCW.

396 John Hay, diary, April 18, 1861. Quoted in Burlingame, *Inside Lincoln's White House,* 1–2.

397 John Hay, diary, April 19, 1861. Quoted in Burlingame, *Inside Lincoln's White House,* 3.

398 Chernow, *Alexander Hamilton,* 89.

399 John Hay, diary, April 20, 1861. Quoted in Burlingame, *Inside Lincoln's White House,* 3.

400 John Hay, diary, April 20, 1861. Quoted in Burlingame, *Inside Lincoln's White House,* 4.

401 John Hay, diary, April 21, 1864. Quoted in Burlingame, *Inside Lincoln's White House,* 5–6.

402 John Hay, diary, April 21, 1861 and April 22, 1861. Quoted in Burlingame, *Inside Lincoln's White House,* 6, 7.

403 Nicolay to Therena Bates, April 23, 1861. Quoted in Burlingame, *With Lincoln in the White House.*

404 John Hay, diary, April 23, 1861. Quoted in Burlingame, *Inside Lincoln's White House,* 8

405 John Hay, diary, April 22, 1861. Quoted in Burlingame, *Inside Lincoln's White House,* 8.

406 John Hay, diary, April 24, 1861. Quoted in Burlingame, *Inside Lincoln's White House,* 10.

407 John Hay, diary, April 24, 1861. Quoted in Burlingame, *Inside Lincoln's White House,* 9–10.

408 John Hay, diary, April 25, 1861. Quoted in Burlingame, *Inside Lincoln's White House,* 11.
409 John Hay, diary, April 30, 1861. Quoted in Burlingame, *Inside Lincoln's White House,* 15.
410 John Hay, diary, April 25, 1861. Quoted in Burlingame, *Inside Lincoln's White House,* 11. For a description of the White House portico party, see Burlingame, *Inside Lincoln's White House,* 276, n. 48.
411 John Hay, diary, May 6, 1861. Quoted in Burlingame, *Inside Lincoln's White House,* 19.
412 Burlingame, *Abraham Lincoln,* vol. 2, 155.
413 Mark Twain to John Hay, March 17, 1862, New Haven, CT, JH MSS, JHBU.
414 Conversation with Marc Myter, PhD, October 24, 2019.

Chapter 14: Lincoln's Spokesperson

415 The Lincoln's disjointed marriage is discussed by Goodwin, 729.
416 Nicolay and Hay, vol. 4: 387.
417 Adam Goodheart, *1861,* 387–88.
418 Burlingame and Ettlinger, editors, *Inside Lincoln's White House: The Complete Civil War Diary of John Hay,* May 10, 1861, p. 22.
419 Hay, diary, May 7, 1861. Quoted in Burlingame, *Inside Lincoln's White House,* 19
420 John Hay, diary, May 7, 1861. Quoted in Burlingame, *Inside Lincoln's White House,* 19–20.
421 John Hay, diary, May 7, 1861. Quoted in Burlingame, *Inside Lincoln's White House,* 20.
422 Nicolay, Memorandum, May 7, 1861, Nicolay MSS, LCW.
423 Hay, diary, May 7, 1861, 20; Nicolay, "Memorandum," May 7, 1861. Quoted in Burlingame, *With Lincoln in the White House,* 41.
424 T. C. Evans, "Personal Reminiscences of John Hay: By a Veteran Journalist," *New York Times,* July 8, 1905, 8.
425 Nicolay, July 3, 1861 Memorandum. Quoted in Burlingame, *With Lincoln in the White House,* 46.
426 The reception of the president's private secretary at the Capitol is explained in Stoddard, quoted in Burlingame, 78–79.
427 Burlingame, *Abraham Lincoln,* vol. 2, 168.
428 James G. Randall, *Lincoln the President: Springfield to Gettysburg* vol. 1 (Dodd, Mead, 1945), 381.
429 Moores, 301.
430 George William Curtis, ed., *Harper's Weekly,* quoted in William E. Gienapp, *Abraham Lincoln and Civil War America* (Oxford University Press, 2001), 85.
431 "From our own correspondent," July 9, 1861, *New York World,* July 11, 1861. Quoted in Burlingame, *With Lincoln in the White House,* 71–72.
432 Nicolay to Therena Bates, July 21–22, 1861. Quoted in Burlingame, *With Lincoln in the White House,* 51–52.
433 Hay, "The Heroic Age of Washington," 1870–71. Quoted in Burlingame, *At Lincoln's Side,* 126.
434 "From our own correspondent," *New York World,* July 24, 1861. Quoted in Burlingame, *Lincoln's Journalist,* 78.
435 "From our own correspondent," July 30, 1861, and August 1, 1861, *New York World*. Quoted in Burlingame, *Lincoln's Journalist,* 82.
436 Jay Monaghan, *Diplomat in Carpet Slippers: Abraham Lincoln deals with Foreign Affairs* (Bobbs-Merrill, 1945), 122.

437 "From our own correspondent," July 28, 1861, and July 30, 1861, *New York World,* . Quoted in Burlingame, *Lincoln's Journalist,* 81–82; July 30, 1861, and August 1, 1861, *New York World,* . Quoted in Burlingame, *Lincoln's Journalist,* 82.
438 Goodwin, 545.
439 Donald, 195–196.
440 This view of John Hay's relationship with Robert Todd Lincoln, complicated by the different relations he had with Abraham Lincoln and with Mary Lincoln, was previously developed by Donald in Donald, *"We are Lincoln Men," 183.*
441 Donald, 183.
442 "From our own correspondent," Long Branch, New Jersey, August 16, 1861, and August 17, 1861, *New York World.* Quoted in Burlingame, *Lincoln's Journalist,* 93.
443 "From our own correspondent," Long Branch, New Jersey, August 17, 1861, and August 19, 1861, *New York World.* Quoted in Burlingame, *Lincoln's Journalist,* 96–98.
444 John Hay to James A. Hamilton, Executive Mansion, August 19, 1861, Abraham Lincoln Presidential Library, John Hay Papers; John Hay to Mrs. Eames, Executive Mansion, August 21, 1861, JH MSS, LCW, cont. 3.
445 Hay diary, August 22, 1861. Quoted in Burlingame, *Inside Lincoln's White House,* 24.
446 Description of Seward in Henry Adams, *Education of Henry Adams* (Modern Library, 1931). First published in 1918 by the Massachusetts Historical Society.
447
448 Hay to Nicolay, August 24, 1861, Washington, JH MSS, JHBU.
449 Allan Nevins and Milton H. Thomas, eds., *The Diary of George Templeton Strong, The Civil War, 1860–1865* (Macmillan, 1952), 175.
450 *Washington Star,* August 29, 1861, in JH, Civil War scrapbook, JH MSS, LCW.
451 Nicolay to Therena Bates, August 31, 1861, Washington. Quoted in Burlingame, *With Lincoln in the White House,* 54.
452 *Daily Illinois State Journal,* "The City," September 6, 1861, ALPL.
453 Charles Hay to sister, Oct 3, 1861, Warsaw, in JH MSS, JHBU.
454 His private journal remained silent another week until October 10, forty-three days in all.
455 W. O. Stoddard Jr., ed., *Lincoln's Third Secretary: The Memoirs of William O. Stoddard* (Exposition Press, 1955), 166–67.

Chapter 15: Lincoln's Journalist

456 Hay, diary, October 10, 1861. Quoted in Burlingame, *Inside the Lincoln White House,* 25; quoted in Burlingame, 282, n. 92 from October 11, 1861. See also, Stephen W. Sears, ed., *The Civil War Papers of George B. McClellan; Selected Correspondence, 1860–1865,* (Ticknor & Fields, 1989), 106–107.
457 October 11, 1861, dispatch, *Missouri Republican,* October 14, 1861, John Hay scrapbook, JH MSS, JHBU. Quoted in Burlingame, *Lincoln's Journalist,* 105–08.
458 "Washington correspondence," October 14, 1861, *Missouri Republican,* October 21, 1861. Quoted in Burlingame, *Lincoln's Journalist,* 113.
459 "Washington correspondence," October 14, 1861, *Missouri Republican,* October 19, 1861. Quoted in Burlingame, *Lincoln's Journalist,* 108–109.
460 "Washington correspondence," December 23, 1861, *Missouri Democrat,* December 28, 1861. Quoted in Burlingame, *Lincoln's Journalist,* 177.

461 Michael Burlingame, ed., *Lincoln Observed: Civil War Dispatches of Noah Brooks* (Johns Hopkins University Press, 2002), 215.

462 "Washington correspondence," October 22, 1861, *Missouri Republican,* October 27, 1865. Quoted in Burlingame, *Lincoln's Journalist,* 121–22.

463 Hay, diary, October 22, 1861. Quoted in Burlingame, *Inside the Lincoln White House,* 27–28. According to *Encyclopedia of American Civil War* (p. 1867–1868, n. 161), General McClellan had ordered Brigadier General Charles P. Stone to position his troops on the Maryland side of the Potomac River, opposite Leesburg. Stone claimed he had not ordered Baker to cross the river, which he did and deployed troops near the top of the Ball's Bluff, where the Union forces were attacked by superior Confederate forces; Baker was killed and his troops were slaughtered. General Stone was arrested without charge and imprisoned for 189 days for the Ball's Bluff debacle, for which he denied he had done anything wrong. For the balance of the war, Stone held no important command.

464 "Washington correspondence," October 26, 1861, *Missouri Republican,* October 31, 1861. Quoted in Burlingame, *Lincoln's Journalist,* 124–126.

465 McClellan to wife, October 31, 1861. Quoted in *The Civil War Papers of George B. McClellan: Selected Correspondence* (Ticknor & Fields, 1989), 114.

466 "Washington correspondence," November 2, 1861, *Missouri Republican,* Nov. 8, 1861. Quoted in Burlingame, *Lincoln's Journalist,* 128, 130–31.

467 "Washington correspondence," November 4 and 7, 1861, and November 8 and 12, 1861, *Missouri Republican.* Quoted in Burlingame, *Lincoln's Journalist,* 131, 136–137. See also, Original, JH scrapbook vol. 54, LCW. Henry Adams to Charles Francis Adams II, September 28,1861, London, HA MSS, MHS.

468 "Washington correspondence," November 11, 1861, and November 16, 1861, *Missouri Republican.* Quoted in Burlingame, *Lincoln's Journalist,* 137.

469 Hay, diary, November 7, 1861. Quoted in Burlingame, *Inside the Lincoln White House,* 30–31.

470 Myra Helmer Pritchard and Jason Emerson, ed., *The Dark Days of Abraham Lincoln's Widow, as Revealed by Her Own Letters* (Southern Illinois University Press, 2011). Reprint from 1927.

471 Burlingame discusses Lincoln's mentoring of aspiring lawyers who came to him for advice and guidance, in chapter 4 of *The Inner World of Abraham Lincoln* (University of Illinois Press, 1997).

472 Hay, diary, November 13, 1861. Quoted in Burlingame, *Inside the Lincoln White House,* 32, 289, n. 122.

473 Burlingame, *Inside Lincoln's White House,* 289, n. 123.

474 The center of the country's most vibrant art market was New York City, and there, the National Academy of Design, which stimulated working artists to reflect the Northern perspective of the conflict.

475 The author is grateful to Eleanor Jones Harvey and the Smithsonian America Art Museum, Washington, DC, for its publication and exhibition, *The Civil War and American Art* (Yale University Press, 2012), 1–15.

476 Harvey, *The Civil War and American Art* (Yale University Press, 2012), 146, 147. See also, Alfred Bierstadt to John Hay, November 22, 1861, Mather Family Papers, Hay letters, WRHS.

477 Stoddard, *Inside the White House in War Times.* Quoted in Burlingame, 149.

478 "Washington correspondence," November 24, 1861, *Missouri Republican,* November 29, 1861. Quoted in Burlingame, *Lincoln's Journalist,* 146–48.

479 Roy P. Basler, ed. *The Collected Works of Abraham Lincoln* (Rutgers University Press, 1953), based on John G. Nicolay and John Hay, eds., *Complete Works of Abraham* Lincoln (Francis D. Tandy, 1894).

480 The President's annual message to the 37th Congress, second session, is quoted in *The American Presidency Project. Retrieved March 11, 2024.*

481 Quoted in Burlingame, *Abraham Lincoln* vol. 2, 232.

482 "Washington correspondence," December 16, 1861, *Missouri Republican,* December 18, 1861. Quoted in Burlingame, *Lincoln's Journalist,* 167–71.

483 Wikipedia, Webpage of "Trent Affair," http://en.wikipedia.org/wiki/Trent_Affair. This material is quoted from this webpage.

484 Quartermaster General Montgomery Meigs wrote to his father on December 25, 1861, Washington, DC, "We seem to starve unstrung waiting for our leader." Meigs confided to his father on Christmas Day that year, feeling unusually vulnerable under McClellan.
Material quoted is found in MM MSS, LCW.

485 Nicolay and Hay, *Abraham Lincoln, A History* vol. 2, 74.

Chapter 16: The Mystery of Lincoln's Eloquence

486 Daniel K. Dodge, *Abraham Lincoln: Master of Words* (D. Appleton, 1924). See also, Don E. Fehrenbacher, "The Words of Lincoln," in *Lincoln in Text and Context: Collected Essays* (Stanford University Press, 1987), and Fred Kaplan, *Lincoln: The Biography of a Writer* (HarperCollins, 2000).

487 John George Nicolay, "Lincoln's Literary Experiments," *Century* magazine 47 no. 6 (April 1894): 823–825. Nicolay's apologia was published when he and Hay were completing the 10-volume *Abraham Lincoln: A Life.* Hay appealed to publisher Gilder to exclude a chapter about the Gettysburg Address.

488 Quoted in Harold Holzer, ed., comp. *Abraham Lincoln The Writer: A Treasury of His Greatest Speeches and Letters* (Calkins Creek, 2000), 13.

489 Abraham Lincoln, April 6, 1858, "First Lecture on Discoveries and Inventions," in Basler, CW 2: 437–442.

490 Holzer, *Abraham Lincoln The Writer,* 9.

491 Donald, *Lincoln Reconsidered,* 164.

492 John Channing Briggs, *Lincoln's Speeches Reconsidered* (Johns Hopkins University Press, 2005), 9.

493 Briggs, 6.

494 Wilson, *Lincoln's Sword,* 3.

495 Wilson, 3.

496 Andrew Delbanco, "Lincoln's Sacramental Language," in Eric Foner, ed., *Our Lincoln: New Perspectives on Lincoln and his World* (W. W. Norton, 2008), 199. See also, Jacques Barzun, "Lincoln the Writer," in David Foster Wallace and J. C. Hallman, eds., *The Story about the Story: Great Writers Explore Great Literature* vol. 2 (Tin House Books, 2013), 228.

497 White Jr., *The Eloquent President.*

498 James M. McPherson, *Abraham Lincoln and the Second American Revolution & the Men Who Made It* (Vintage Books, 1948), 95.

499 Donald, 122.

500 Briggs, 11.
501 Richard Hofstadter, *The American Political Tradition & the Men Who Made It* (Vintage Books, 1948), 122.
502 David D. Anderson, *The Literary Works of Abraham Lincoln* (Charles E. Merrill Publishing, 1970), x. The quoted portion is within the book's introduction.
503 Hofstadter, 119–120.
504 Edward Baker Lincoln, the second son of Abraham and Mary Lincoln, died February 1, 1850, a month before his fourth birthday on March 6.
505 Briggs, 7.
506 Briggs, 2.
507 Wilson, 122.
508 Hofstadter, 125.
509 Basler, CW 2, 462–469.
510 Quoted in White, *Lincoln in Private,* 225–265.
511 Donald, 238.
512 Nicolay and Hay, vol. 2, 223–224.
513 Basler, CW 3, 522–550.
514 Donald, *Lincoln,* 238.
515 Goodheart, 130.
516 Wilson, 8.
517 Anderson, xi; Holzer, 13.
518 Donald, 164.
519 Donald, 144.
520 Jacques Barzun, "Lincoln the Writer," in Barzun, *On Writing, Editing, and Publishing: Essays Explicative and Hortatory* (University of Chicago Press, 1971), 66, 81. The piece "Lincoln the Literary Genius" was first published in the *Saturday Evening Post,* February 14, 1959.
521 Andrew Delbanco, "Lincoln's Sacramental Language," in Eric Foner, ed., *Our Lincoln: New Perspectives on Lincoln and his World* (W. W. Norton, 2008), 199.
522 Delbanco, 200.
523 Delbanco, 201.
524 When Alice and Clarence Hay, two of John Hay's four children, gave the personal papers of John Hay to Brown University, the Lincoln manuscripts written in Lincoln's hand, which Lincoln had given to Hay and were part of his papers, were separated from the Hay manuscripts and filed with the university's Lincoln Collection. Regrettably, a manifest of these Lincoln items was not made at the time.
525 Hay and Nicolay penned many of his official letters, which are preserved in *The Collected Works of Abraham Lincoln,* originally compiled by them. See Roy P. Basler, ed., *The Collected Works of Abraham Lincoln* (Rutgers University Press, 1953), based on John G. Nicolay and John Hay, eds., *Complete Works of Abraham Lincoln* (Francis D. Tandy, 1894). See also, Randall and Current, *Lincoln the President* vol. 4 .Earlier printings of the four-volume work were 1955 and 1983.
526 John Hay's personal papers are archived in the John Hay Library at Brown University, and at the Massachusetts Historical Society and the Houghton Library at Harvard University. His personal and government diaries, scrapbooks, and correspondence—in the Lincoln White House, 1861–1865, in foreign service, 1865–1870, as assistant secretary of state, 1879–1881, as ambassador to Great Britain, 1897–1898, and as secretary of state, 1898–1905—are archived in the Library of Congress Manuscripts Division.

527 Robert Todd Lincoln to William Roscoe Thayer, August 6, 1914, Hildene, Manchester, VT. Found in the William Roscoe Thayer letters (MS Am 1081), HLH.

528 Thomas Coke Evans, "Personal Reminiscences of John Hay: By a Veteran Journalist," *New York Times,* July 8, 1905, 8. This was a memoriam to Hay seven days after his death.

529 Ralph Waldo Emerson, "Abraham Lincoln: Remarks at the Funeral Services Held in Concord, April 19, 1865," *Miscellanies,* vol. 11 of *The Complete Works of Ralph Waldo Emerson* (Houghton Mifflin, 1906), 333.

530 Nicolay to Therena Bates, January 19, 1862, Washington, DC. Quoted in Burlingame, *With Lincoln in the White House, 65.*

531 This is described in George Wills, *Lincoln at Gettysburg: The Words that Remade America* (Simon & Schuster, 1992), 29–34.

532 Edward Dicey, *Spectator of America,* 93.

533 "John Hay, the Man of International Crises," *New York Times,* May 16, 1904.

534 "Eulogies of John Hay," *Washington Post,* July 2, 1905, 3.

535 Richard Watson Gilder, "John Hay," *New York Times,* July 1905. Gilder was writing on the occasion of Hay's death at the age of sixty-six.

Chapter 17: Silent Respect

536 Elizabeth Keckley and Frances Smith Foster, ed., *Behind the Scenes: Thirty Years a Slave and Four Years in the White House.* (University of Illinois Press, 1998), 84.

537 "Washington correspondence," Jan. 6, 1862, *Missouri Republican,* January 10, 1862. Quoted in Burlingame, *Lincoln's Journalist,* 187–188.

538 "Washington correspondence," January 27, 1862, *Missouri Republican,* January 31, 1862. Quoted in Burlingame, *Inside Lincoln's White House,* 205.

539 Simon Cameron served as secretary of war from March 5, 1861 to January 14, 1862, and as the American minister to Russia from June 25, 1862 to September 18, 1862. He was the US senator from Pennsylvania from March 1857–March 1861, and from March 1867–March 1877.

540 Brooks, *Mr. Lincoln's Washington,* 176.

541 By the end of the war, the Union navy had 671 vessels and 84,415 personnel. "Washington correspondence," January 14, 1862, *Missouri Republican,* January 18, 1862. Quoted in Burlingame, *Lincoln's Journalist,* 193–194. Burlingame regarded Stanton as "a remarkably capable war secretary who worked well with the president." See Burlingame, *Abraham Lincoln,* vol. 2, 247.

542 Hay, diary, January 27, 1862. Quoted in Burlingame, *Inside Lincoln's White House,* 35.

543 "Washington correspondence," New York *Tribune,* February 7, 1862. The "Washington correspondence" published on February 7, 1862, had the trademark characteristics of Hay's intimate knowledge of Lincoln's thoughts, which signaled his anonymous reporting to the press, though it is uncertain that he penned the column as he rarely contributed news columns to the *Tribune* (until he joined the editorial staff of Greeley's daily rag in 1870).

544 "Washington correspondence," Feb. 21, 1862, *Missouri Republican,* Feb. 26, 1862. Quoted in Burlingame, *Lincoln's Journalist,* 219.

545 Burlingame, *Abraham Lincoln* vol 2, 298.

546 John George Nicolay, journal entries, February 11 and 20, 1862. Quoted in Burlingame, *With Lincoln in the White House,* 71. See also, Donald, *"We are Lincoln Men,"* 194, and Villard, *Memoirs,* vol. 1: 147–148.

547 Burlingame, *Abraham Lincoln,* vol. 2, 298.

Chapter 18: Introducing Emancipation

548 On March 6, 1862, Lincoln sent to Congress his recommendation for a program of gradual, compensated emancipation, Found in Basler, CWL, 5: 152–153.

549 Philip Kennicott, "Painful Lessons the Civil War Taught Us," the *Washington Post,* November 7, 2010, R3.

550 "Washington correspondence," March 24, 1862, *Missouri Republican,* March 27, 1862. Quoted in Burlingame, *Lincoln's Journalist,* 233, 234.

551 "Washington correspondence," March 24, 1862. Quoted in Burlingame, *Lincoln's Journalist,* 234–235.

552 The Senate passed the Emancipation bill for the District of Columbia by a vote of 29–14, and after long and exciting debate, the House passed the Senate bill by more than a two-fold margin, 92–38.

553 "Washington correspondence," April 21, 1862, *Missouri Republican,* April 26, 1862. Quoted in Burlingame, *Lincoln's Journalist,* 250, 251–252. For April, 11, 1862, see David Donald, ed., *Inside Lincoln's Cabinet: The Civil War Diaries of Salmon P. Chase* (Longmans, Green, 1954), 70–71.

554 "Washington correspondence," April 23, 1862, *Missouri Republican.* Quoted in Burlingame, *Lincoln's Journalist,* 253–257.

555 James D. McPherson, *Tried by War: Abraham Lincoln as Commander in Chief* (Penguin, 2009), 158.

556 Eric Foner, "The Emancipation of Abe Lincoln," *New York Times,* Op-Ed, January 1, 2013, A19. This column discusses the topic.

557 "Yorktown, VA." See also, Burlingame, ed., *Dispatches from Lincoln's White House: The Anonymous Civil War Journalism of Presidential Secretary William O. Stoddard,* (University of Nebraska Press, 2002), xix.

558 "Washington correspondence," July 1, 1862, and July 13, 1862, *Missouri Republican.* Quoted in Burlingame, *Lincoln's Journalist,* 278–281.

559 John Hay to Mary Jay, July 20, 1862, Washington, DC. Quoted in Burlingame, *At Lincoln's Side,* 23.

560 "Washington correspondence," *Missouri Republican,* July 21, 1862. Quoted in Burlingame, *Lincoln's Journalist,* 284–285. The date this was written is unknown.

561 Chase diary, September 22, 1862.

562 Burlingame, *Abraham Lincoln,* vol. 2, 362.

563 Chase diary, September 22, 1862.

564 F. B. Carpenter, *Six Months in the White House with Abraham Lincoln.*

565 Basler, CW 5: 145–46.

566 Hay to Nicolay, August 7, 1862, quoted in *Lebanon Daily News,* Lebanon, PA, November 18, 1954, in JH MSS, JHBU.

567 The *New York Weekly Tribune,* distributed through the East and West, had the largest circulation of any newspaper in the country from the 1850s to the 1870s.

568 White, *The Eloquent President,* 188; and Wilson, *Lincoln's Sword,* 160.

569 Cited by Nicolay, November 20, 1861, Memorandum. Quoted in Burlingame, *With Lincoln in the White House,* 62.

570 McClellan's own letters to his wife confirmed this. See also, Hay, diary, September 1, 1862, quoted in Burlingame, *Inside Lincoln's White House,* 293, n. 9.

571 Hay to Nicolay, August 11, 1862, Executive Mansion, Washington. Quoted in Burlingame, *At Lincoln's Side*. See also, Flower, *Stanton,* 176–179.

572 Hay, diary, September 1, 1862. Quoted in Burlingame, *Inside Lincoln's White House,* 38. See, "Washington correspondence," August 31, 1862, *Missouri Republican,* Sept. 5, 1862, quoted in Burlingame, *Lincoln's Journalist,* 300.

573 Hay, diary, September 1, 1862. Quoted in Burlingame, *Inside Lincoln's White House,* 38.

574 "Washington correspondence," September 3, 1862, *Missouri Republican,* September 7, 1862. Quoted in Burlingame, *Lincoln's Journalist,* 302–303.

575 Hay, diary, September 5, 1862. Quoted in Burlingame, *Inside Lincoln's White House,* 38–39.

576 "Washington correspondence," September 7, 1862, *Missouri Republican,* September 11, 1862. Quoted in Burlingame, *Lincoln's Journalist,* 306.

577 Hay, diary, mid-September 1862. Quoted in Burlingame, *Inside Lincoln's White House,* 40.

578 Foner, "The Emancipation of Abe Lincoln," A19.

579 Hay, diary, September 24, 1862, in Burlingame, *Inside Lincoln's White House,* 40.

580 Jay Monaghan, *Diplomat in Carpet Slippers: Abraham Lincoln deals with Foreign Affairs* (Bobbs-Merrill, 1945), 254. This contains Artemus Ward and Secretary Stanton references. Also quoted in David Donald, ed., *Inside Lincoln's Cabinet: The Civil War Diaries of Salmon P. Chase* (Longmans, Green, 1954), 149.

581 The Emancipation Proclamation copy in John Hay's possession was given to Harvard University by Clarence Leonard Hay, his son. See also, papers of John Hay and Abraham Lincoln (MS Am 1845.8–1845.9), Houghton Library, Harvard. The Proclamation applied only to the states and territories in active rebellion—Arkansas, Texas, Mississippi, Alabama, Florida, Georgia, South Carolina, North Carolina, and Virginia. This excluded the 48 counties comprising West Virginia, and one bordering West Virginia and six lying along the Potomac and Chesapeake Rivers, and a part of Louisiana (excepting thirteen parishes, including New Orleans). The Proclamation freed Union army officers from returning runaway slaves to their owners under the Fugitive Slave Act of 1850.

582 Nicolay and Hay, *Abraham Lincoln,* vol. 6, 373.

583 Wilson, *Lincoln's Sword,* 106, 142. Hofstadter, *The American Political Tradition*, 131.

584 "Washington correspondence," September 22, 1862, *Missouri Republican,* September 26, 1862. Quoted in Burlingame, *Lincoln's Journalist,* 307–308, 310–311.

585 The Union navy employed about 19,000 Black men, approximately 25 percent, and the Union army had approximately 179,000 Black soldiers, about 10 percent.

586 "Washington correspondence," September 25, 1862, *Missouri Republican,* September 29, 1862. Quoted in Burlingame, *Lincoln's Journalist,* 312–313.

587 Hay, diary, circa September 24, 1862, in Burlingame, *Inside Lincoln's White,* 40–41.

Chapter 19: Kindred Spirits

588 Chernow, 86.

589 David Wootton, *The Invention of Science: A New History of the Scientific Revolution* (Harper Perennial, 2016) 545–561.

590 Elihu Root spoke at Keneseth Israel Temple, Philadelphia, at the unveiling of the John Hay Memorial window. See, "Hay Memorial Window Unveiled," the *New York Times,* December 8, 1905, in JH MSS, JHBU.

591 Abraham Lincoln's "Reflections on Providence," which Hay later renamed "Meditation on Divine Will," is one of the Lincoln manuscripts John Hay kept for himself. Found in JH MSS, JHBU. Quoted in Hay, "Heroic Age of Washington," in Burlingame, *At Lincoln's Side,* 26–27.

592 Nicolay and Hay, *Abraham Lincoln,* vol. 1, 342.

593 John Hay, "Heroic Age in Washington." This lecture, which he gave in Buffalo, NY, and Chicago and Warsaw in 1871, is quoted in Burlingame, *At Lincoln's Side,* 26–27.

594 Nicolay and Hay, *Abraham Lincoln* vol. 6, 341–42. See also, White, 152; 153.

595 John Hay, "Remarks," New York Avenue Presbyterian Church one hundredth anniversary, Nov. 16, 1902. This is quoted in John Hay, *Addresses of John Hay* (Books for Libraries Press, 1970), and in Lincoln Centennial Commission, *Lincoln Centennial: Addresses* (Springfield: Illinois Centennial Commission, 1909), 157. *Addresses of John Hay* was first published in 1906.

596 Number of syllables in the first line of each "stanza" added by author to highlight the verse's regular poetic cadence.

597 "The Meditation on Divine Will" was among John Hay's personal papers given in 1939 by his family to the special collections of Brown University, John Hay Library, in JH MSS, JHBU.

598 Matthew Pinsker, *Lincoln's Sanctuary: Abraham Lincoln and the Soldiers' Home* (Oxford University Press, 2003), 2–5.

599 William Dean Howells, "John Hay," in Topics of the Times, *The Century Magazine,* September 1905 70 (5), 792–793.

600 Brooks Adams, c. 1900, reported in *Boston Evening Times,* July 1, 1905, p 1.

601 The *New York Herald* reported that President Lincoln's foot pain was caused by a sprain, which was unconfirmed.

602 Hay, diary, September 25, 1862. Quoted in Burlingame, 41, 295, n. 20–21. On November 5, 1862, Lincoln ordered Gen. George McClellan removed from command of the Army of the Potomac, and replaced by Gen. Ambrose Burnside on November 9, 1862.

603 Hay to Nicolay, October 28, 1862, Warsaw, Illinois, *At Lincoln's Side,* p. 27.

604 John Hay to John George Nicolay, October 28, 1862, Warsaw, IL. Quoted in Tyler Dennett, *Lincoln and the Civil War in the Diaries and Letters of John Hay* (Dodd, Mead, 1939), 51–52.

605 Wikipedia, Webpage of "1862-63 United States House of Representatives elections," https://en.wikipedia.org/wiki/United_States_House_of_Representatives_elections,_1862.

606 Lincoln wrote the order on November 5, 1862; it was delivered to Gen. McClellan in the field on November 7, 1862.

607 Nicolay and Hay, *Abraham Lincoln* vol. 6, 188–189.

608 Nicolay and Hay, *Abraham Lincoln* vol. 6, 205.

609 American Antiquarian Society Online Resource, "Abraham Lincoln, 'Second Annual Message,' December 1, 1862," https://www.americanantiquarian.org/Freedmen/Manuscripts/lincolnsecondannual.html.

610 P. J. Staudenraus, ed., *Mr. Lincoln's Washington: Selections from the Writings of Noah Brooks, Civil War Correspondent* (Thomas Yoseloff, 1967), 26–27. Noah Brooks, a correspondent for the Dixon, IL, *Telegraph* arrived in Washington in December 1862 as the special correspondent for the Sacramento *Daily Union.* Thirty-two years old; short, dark, powerfully-built, his penname was "Castine," having been born October 24, 1830, in Castine, ME.

611 White, *The Eloquent President,* 189. Zarefsky, "Lincoln's 1862 Annual Message: A Paradigm of Rhetorical Leadership," *Rhetoric and Public Affairs* 3 no. 1 (Spring 2000): 5–14.

612 Staudenraus, 23–25, 47.

613 William K. Goolrick, ed., et al, *Rebels Resurgent: Fredericksburg to Chancellorsville* (Time-Life Books, 1985), 92–93.

614 Staudenraus, 29.

615 The Week Staff, "When Americans Banned Christmas," *The Week* magazine, December 30, 2011, 11. https://theweek.com/articles/479184/when-americans-banned-christmas. Henry Wadsworth Longfellow was quoted here.

616 Thomas Nast was introduced to Lincoln's private secretary, who was not named, during the train journey from Springfield to Washington, DC, in February 1861. John Hay took up the introduction and on the back of this letter, he sketched three figurines in pencil, apparently indicating his interest in Nast's caricatures.

617 In Germany, early nineteenth-century Christmas celebrations filtered down from aristocratic elites to working families, from city to countryside, and from Germany's Protestant north to the Catholic south. See, Joe Perry, *Christmas in Germany: A Cultural History* (University of North Carolina Press, 2010), 1–34.

618 Perhaps the German-born Nicolay, who had emigrated to America with his parents at age six, might have retained some knowledge of German Christmas traditions, though desperately poor in his youth, the memory would have been of a tiny, bare pine tree with a single candle alongside.

619 Thomas Nast, artist, "Christmas Eve 1862," *Harper's Weekly,* January 3, 1862, cover, 8–9; Smithsonian magazine, February 2015, 66.

620 *Thomas Nast's Christmas Drawings, with an introduction by Thomas Nast* (Dover Fine Art, 1978), v. Nast's scrapbook is comprised of 234 pencil sketches; thirty-two wash drawings; ten woodcut proofs; and 638 photographs of Civil War officers, troops, and battlefield scenes, including a photograph of John Hay on p. 77, about three times larger than most of the postage-size photographic prints that are found in the scrapbook at the John Hay Library of Brown University.

621 Strong, *The Civil War, 1860–1865,* 282.

622 Staudenraus, 52.

Chapter 20: A Changing Tide

623 Jan. 1, 1863, *Washington Chronicle,* 2, column 2, scrapbook, vol. 54, JH MSS, LCW, 331.

624 White, in *Lincoln in Private,* highlighted Lincoln's wrestling with his God, who the president believed must be acting in this war, for better or worse (127, 152, 153). Hay, Jan. 1, 1863, *Washington Chronicle,* 2, column 2, scrapbook, vol. 54, JH MSS, LCW, 332. With Republican support waning in the West, John Hay ended his "Washington correspondence" column in the *Missouri Republican* and handed his anonymous press contributions to John W. Forney's *Washington Chronicle. Forney* had smartly positioned

himself as an insider of Washington politics, having served six years as clerk of the House then secretary of the Senate in 1861. With his thumb on the pulse of the legislative branch, Forney had become a powerful source of political intelligence, and his daily Chronicle served from its founding in November 1862 as Lincoln's effective press agent. "Hay is charged with occasional sparkling editorials in the Chronicle," war correspondent for Cincinnati Gazette, Whitelaw Reid, announced in his chatty "Literary Gossip at Washington" piece, found in "Correspondence of the Cincinnati Gazette, scrapbook vol. 54, LC. We lack information on the full date.

625 Nicolay's scrapbook, editorial, "The Proclamation," *Washington Daily Morning Chronicle,* 2. Quoted in Donald, 102.

626 Hay, diary, October 29, 1863. Quoted in Burlingame, *Inside the Lincoln White House,* 102. Northern Democrats disagreed. They opposed the Proclamation, organizing to counter the war, posing a troubling prospect for the White House. They represented the minority sentiment among Union sympathizers.

627 Donald, *"We are Lincoln Men,"* 183.

628 Patricia Carley Johnson, "Sensitivity and Civil War: The Selected Diaries and Papers, 1858–1866, of Frances Adeline [Fanny] Seward," PhD dissertation, University of Rochester, 1963, 617–618.

629 "Deposited in Harvard College Library, 1916," Papers of John Hay and Abraham Lincoln (MS Am 1845.9-1845.9), Houghton, Harvard.

630 Eric Foner, "Emancipation of Abe Lincoln."

631 Keckley and Foster, 8.

632 Staudenraus, February 6–February 28, 1863, 99-117.

633 Hay, diary, September 27, 1863. Quoted in Burlingame, *Inside Lincoln's White House,* 87. President Lincoln had appointed Hooker as commander of the Army of the Potomac in late January 1863, and sent him to reinforce Lt. Gen. Ulysses S. Grant in his decisive victory at Chattanooga.

634 Nicolay to Therena Bates, March 15, 1863. Quoted in Burlingame, *With Lincoln in the White House,* 105–106.

635 Horace Traubel, *With Walt Whitman in Camden* (Oxford University Press, 1953), 32.

636 Staudenraus, 188.

637 *New York Times,* April 3, 1863, 9. Before departing for South Carolina, Hay had a brief visit with his family in Illinois.

638 *Arago* was built by Westervelt & Son, New York City, and launched in June 1855. It was named for steamship pioneer Francois Arago (1786–1853). In December 1859, William Seward had returned from an eight-month European and Middle Eastern tour on *Arago* to launch his Republican presidential campaign. After the Civil War, it returned to service as a transatlantic passenger ship and freight service. *Arago's* high moment in the war arrived late, in April 1865, returning the American flag to Fort Sumter. See, Wikipedia, Webpage of "SS Arago," https://en.wikipedia.org/w/index.php?title=SS_Arago_(1855)&oldid=691758507."

639 Hay, diary, April 4, 1863. Quoted in Burlingame, *Inside the Lincoln White House,* 42.

640 Hay, diary, April 5, 1863. Quoted in Burlingame, *Inside the Lincoln White House,* 42.

641 Hay, diary, April 8, 1863. Quoted in Burlingame, *Inside the Lincoln White House,* 43.

642 The Irish-born New York journalist Charles G. Halpine was Gen. Hunter's liaison with the press. He wrote under the penname Miles O'Reilly, contributing popular columns to the *New York Herald.* See Burlingame, *Inside the Lincoln White House,* 296, n. 6. Some of Halpine's correspondence is archived in Huntington Library.

643 Hay to Nicolay, April 10, 1863. Quoted in Burlingame, *At Lincoln's Side;* JH Scrapbook, 1870 following, JHC, JHBU.
644 Hay to Nicolay, May 1, 1863. Quoted in Burlingame, *At Lincoln's Side,* 39.
645 Scrapbook, JH MSS, LCW.
646 Hay, diary, April 15, 1863. Quoted in Burlingame, *Inside the Lincoln White House,* 46.
647 Hay to John Hay, grandfather, May 2, 1863. Quoted in Burlingame, *At Lincoln's Side,* 40.
648 Hay, diary, April 25, 1863. Quoted in Burlingame, *Inside the Lincoln White House,* 49. Hay to Nicolay, May 1, 1863. Quoted in Burlingame, *At Lincoln's Side,* 39.
649 Hay diary, April 28, 1863. Quoted in Burlingame, *Inside the Lincoln White House,* 51.
650 Hay, diary, May 1, 1863. Quoted in Burlingame, *Inside the Lincoln White House,* 52.
651 Hay, diary, May 10, 1863. Quoted in Burlingame, *Inside the Lincoln White House,* 54.
652 Hay, diary, May 19, 1863. Quoted in Burlingame, *Inside the Lincoln White House,* 57.
653 Hay, diary, May 21, 1863. Quoted in Burlingame, *Inside the Lincoln White House,* 57. See also, The White House Office of the Press Secretary, "Presidential Proclamations: Establishment of the Reconstruction Era National Monument," January 12, 2017, https://obamawhitehouse.archives.gov/the-press-office/2017/01/12/presidential-proclamations-establishment-reconstruction-era-national. This webpage is part of archived White House material.
654 Hay, diary, May 22, 1863. Quoted in Burlingame, *Inside the Lincoln White House,* 58.
655 Mary Thatcher Higginson, ed., *Letter and Journals of Thomas Wentworth Higginson, 1846–1906* (Houghton Mifflin, 1921), 201–02. See, *New York Tribune,* May 26, 1863, clip in Hay scrapbook, vol. 54, JH MSS, LCW for an account of this event.
656 *New York Tribune,* May 29, 1863, clip in Hay scrapbook, vol. 54, Hay MSS, LC; Quoted in Burlingame, *Inside the Lincoln White House,* 301, n. 63.
657 Hay, diary, May 23, 1863. Quoted in Burlingame, *Inside the Lincoln White House,* 59.
658 Burlingame, *Abraham Lincoln* vol. 2, 491. See also, Hay to Gen. Hunter, June 9, 1863, quoted in Burlingame, *At Lincoln's Side,* 43–44.
659 Staudenraus, 196–97, 210. See also, Wikipedia, Webpage of "Gettysburg campaign," https://en.wikipedia.org/wiki/Gettysburg_Campaign.
660 Staudenraus, 197.
661 Hay, diary, JH MSS, JHBU.
662 Ronald C. White, *American Ulysses: A Life of Ulysses S. Grant* (Random House, 2016), 225–226.
663 Burlingame, *Abraham Lincoln,* vol. 2, 569.
664 Hay, diary, July 11, 1863. Quoted in Burlingame, *Inside the Lincoln White House,* 61.
665 Hay diary, July 13, 1863. Quoted in Burlingame, *Inside the Lincoln White House,* 62.
666 Diary of Gideon Wells, 1861 to 1869, 1: 439.
667 Hay, diary July 15, 1863. Quoted in Burlingame, *Inside the Lincoln White House,* 63.
668 Hay, diary, July 15, 1863, in Burlingame, *Inside the Lincoln White House,* 63.
669 Hay, diary, July 15, 1863, in Burlingame, *Inside the Lincoln White House,* 63.
670 This statement, Hay's own thought, is crossed out in his diary, September 20, 1863. See it quoted in Burlingame, *Inside the Lincoln White House,* 95.
671 Hay, diary, July 19, 1863. Quoted in Burlingame, *Inside the Lincoln White House,* 64–65.
672 Donald, *Lincoln,* 14–15.

Chapter 21: Forgiveness, Tolerance, Trust

673 Hay, diary, July 18, 1863. Quoted in Burlingame, *Inside Lincoln's White House,* 64.

674 Nicolay interview with Joseph Holt, Oct 29, 1879, Nicolay MSS, LC. Quoted in Burlingame, *Inside Lincoln's White House,* 305, n. 78.
675 Hay, diary, July 25, 1863, in Burlingame, *Inside Lincoln's White House,* 67–68.
676 Hay, diary, August 1 and August 13, 1863. Quoted in Burlingame, *Inside Lincoln's White House,* 69, 73. On August 13, Hay recorded this statement by Seward: "Slavery is dead; the only trouble is that the fools who support it from the outside do not recognize this, and will not till the thing is over.... So now, though slavery is dead, the Democratic party insists on devoting itself to guarding the corpse."
677 Hay, diary, July 31, 1863. Quoted in Burlingame, *Inside Lincoln's White House,* 69.
678 Lincoln to Grant, August 9, 1863. Quoted in Roy P. Basler, Marion D. Pratt, Lloyd A. Dunlap, eds., *Collected Works of Abraham Lincoln* vol. 6 (Rutgers University Press, 1955), 374–75.
679 Hay, Diary, Aug 11, 1863 Quoted in Burlingame, *Inside Lincoln's White House,* 72.
680 Frederick Douglass, *The Life and Times of Frederick Douglass* (Park Publishing, 1881), 422–424. See also, Internet Archive, archive.org/details/lifetimesoffrede1881doug. This webpage contains a scanned, digitized version of the book. Also, Secretary of Interior John Usher issued him a letter of protection: "Douglass is...a loyal, free man and is hence entitled to travel, unmolested. We trust he will be recognized everywhere as a free man, and a gentleman." See, Hay, diary, August 10, 1863, quoted in Burlingame, *Inside Lincoln's White House,* 72.
681 *Providence Journal,* September 3, 1863. Quoted in Burlingame, *Lincoln's Journalist,* 236–37, n. 115.
682 Hay, diary, September 2, 1863, Brown commencement. Quoted in Burlingame, *Inside Lincoln's White House,* 78, 312, n.148.
683 Hay to Nicolay, September 25, 1863. Quoted in Burlingame, *At Lincoln's Side,* 56.
684 Hay to Nicolay, September 11, 1863. Quoted in Burlingame, *At Lincoln's Side,* 53–54.
685 William Dean Howells, "John Hay," in Topics of the Times, *Century magazine* 70 no. 5 (September 1905), 792–793.
686 Hay, diary, September 20, 1863; Samuel P. Heintzelman, Journal, September 21, 1863, Samuel P Heintzelman Papers, MSS, LCW.
687 William M. Lamers, *The Edge of Glory: A Biography of General William S. Rosecrans,* (Louisiana State University Press, 1961), 361.
688 Hay, diary, September 27, 1863. Quoted in Burlingame, *Inside Lincoln's White House,* 85–87.
689 Hay, diary, September 28, 1863. Quoted in Burlingame, *Inside Lincoln's White House,* 87–88.
690 Hay, diary, September 29, 1863. Quoted in Burlingame, *Inside Lincoln's White House,* 88–89.
691 Wills, 151.
692 Zimmerman, 48.
693 Staudenrause, ed., *Noah Brooks,* October 2, 1863, 23.
694 Hay, diary, October 8, 1863. Quoted in in Burlingame, *Inside Lincoln's White House,* 91.
695 Hay, diary, October 13, 1863. Quoted in Burlingame, *Inside Lincoln's White House,* 91–92. Nicolay's diary was silent from October 12 to November 14, 1863, while he was sport hunting buffalo in Pawnee Fork, Kansas, according to Richard C. McCormick to John Hay, October 14, 1863, in JH collection, JHL, BU, reel 8.
696 Staudenraus, *Noah Brooks,* October 24, 1863, 243–45.
697 Hay, diary, July 18, 1863. Quoted in Burlingame, *Inside Lincoln's White House,* 54.

698 Hay, diary, October 18, 1863. Quoted in Burlingame, *Inside Lincoln's White House,* 93–94.
699 Amasa Stone became John Hay's father-in-law on February 4, 1874, when Hay married Stone's oldest daughter, Clara Louise Stone.
700 Hay, diary, October 21, 1863. Quoted in Burlingame, *Inside Lincoln's White House,* 97.
701 Staudenraus, *Noah Brooks,* October 29, 1863, 245–46.
702 "Washington correspondence," *Missouri Republican,* July 21, 1862, quoted in Burlingame, *Lincoln's Journalist,* 284–85.

Chapter 22: "This Last Resting Place of Freedom"

703 History.com editors, "The Battle of Gettysburg," https://www.history.com/topics/american-civil-war/battle-of-gettysburg.
704 David Wills to Abraham Lincoln, November 2, 1863, in Louis A. Warren, *Lincoln's Gettysburg Declaration:* "A New Birth of Freedom" (Lincoln National Life Foundation, 1964), 45–46.
705 Hay, diary, November 2, 1863. Quoted in Burlingame, *Inside Lincoln's White House,* 108.
706 Hay, diary, November 8, 1863. Quoted in Burlingame, *Inside Lincoln's White House,* 109–110. In World War I, Woodrow Wilson, Democrat; World War II, Franklin Delano Roosevelt, Democrat, who was re-elected; during the Korean War, Harry S. Truman; during the Vietnam War, Democrats Kennedy and Johnson, though Richard M. Nixon broke the streak.
707 Washington weather, finances, and the squalid living conditions of former slaves are noted in Staudenraus, ed., *Mr. Lincoln's Washington,* 260.
708 Noah Brooks, November 15, 1863. Quoted in Burlingame, ed. *Lincoln Observed: Civil War Dispatches of Noah Brooks* (Johns Hopkins University Press, 1998), 89.
709 John G. Nicolay, "Lincoln's Gettysburg Address," *Century Illustrated Magazine* 47 no. 4 (February 1894), 596–608, 597.
710 Jay Monaghan, *Diplomat in Carpet Slippers: Abraham Lincoln Deals With Foreign Affairs* (Bobs-Merrill, 1962), 340–341. See also, *Washington Chronicle,* Nov. 19, 1863. See also, Allen Thorndike Rice, ed., *Reminiscences of Abraham Lincoln* (North American Publisher, 1886), 509–513. In Nicolay's writing "Lincoln's Gettysburg Address," on p. 601, he wrote: "There is neither record, evidence, nor well-founded tradition that Mr. Lincoln did any writing, or made any notes on the journey between Washington and Gettysburg."
711 Donald, *Lincoln,* 461.
712 John Russell Young, *Men and Memories: Personal Reminiscences,* vol. 1 (F. Tennyson Neely, 1901), 59–61.
713 Borritt, *The Gettysburg Gospel,* 3–5.
714 CWL, 7: 17; quoted in Burlingame, *Lincoln,* vol 2: 571; Nicolay, "Lincoln's Gettysburg Address," 601.
715 Burlingame, *Abraham Lincoln* vol 2, 571.
716 Wills, *Lincoln at Gettysburg,* 31–32.
717 Nicolay, "Lincoln's Gettysburg Address," 597.
718 Hay, diary, November 19, 1863. Quoted in Burlingame, *Inside Lincoln's White House,* 113–114.
719 Hay, diary, November 19, 1863. Quoted in Burlingame, *Inside Lincoln's White House,* 113–114.

720 Nicolay stated in the *Century* piece "Lincoln's Gettysburg Address," that the private secretary sat a few feet from Lincoln when he delivered the Gettysburg Address, and that the president did not read from the written pages, nor did he deliver the address in the exact form in which the address had been written.
721 Hofstedter, *The American Political Tradition,* 122.
722 Wills, 162.
723 Ronald White, 234.
724 Hay, diary, November 19, 1863. Quoted in Burlingame, *Inside Lincoln's White House,* 113.
725 Goodwin, *Team of Rivals,* 585.
726 *New York Times,* November 19, 1863 and Washington *Chronicle,* November 21, 1863, quoted in Burlingame, *Abraham Lincoln* vol. 2, 573–574.
727 Hay, diary, November 19, 1863. Quoted in Burlingame, *Inside Lincoln's White House,* 113.
728 Quoted in Jared Peatman, "The Long Shadow of Lincoln's Gettysburg Address," *The Lincoln Forum Bulletin* (Fall 2013): 9; and in Borritt, *Gettysburg Gospel.*
729 Garry Wills, *Lincoln at Gettysburg,* 53–62, 191–200.
730 James McPherson, *Abraham Lincoln and the Second American Revolution* (Oxford University Press, 1992), 111. See also, Herbert J. Edwards and John E. Hankins, *Lincoln, the Writer: the Development of His Literary Style* (University of Maine Press, 1962), 89.
731 Edwin Black, "The Ultimate Voice of Lincoln," *Rhetoric and Public Affairs* 3 no. 1 (2000): 49–50. See also, Ronald C. White, *Lincoln's Greatest Speech: The Second Inaugural* (Simon & Schuster, 2002), xxi. White stated that it is "unlikely that Lincoln ever read Aristotle" and his *Treatise on Rhetoric.*
732 White, *Lincoln's Greatest Speech,* 201, 84.
733 Quoted in Wills, 58; Lane Cooper, *The Rhetoric of Aristotle* (D. Appleton-Century, 1932), xxxiii.
734 Burlingame, *Abraham Lincoln,* vol 2, 569–70. Lincoln would later tell James Speed and Noah Brooks that he had begun "composing" the address in Washington and finished it in Pennsylvania.
735 "Washington correspondence," *Missouri Republican,* July 21, 1862. Date written unknown. Quoted in Burlingame, *Lincoln's Journalist,* 284–85.
736 Wills, 148.
737 Monaghan, 342.

Chapter 23: The Gettysburg Legacy

738 McPherson.
739 James B. Angell, "Gettysburg Address," *Providence Journal,* Nov. 21, 1863, in JH papers, JHL, BU.
740 "Gettysburg," *Harper's Weekly,* December 5, 1863.
741 Wills, *Lincoln at Gettysburg,* 62.
742 John Hay to Richard Watson Gilder, December 1890. Quoted in Thayer, vol. 2, 214.
743 Nicolay, "Lincoln's Gettysburg Address," 596–608, 597.
744 Burlingame, *Lincoln,* vol. 2, 569.
745 John Hay's children donated this copy to the Library of Congress in April 1916, plus the manuscript draft of Lincoln's Second Inaugural Address, inscribed by John Hay;

at the same time Helen Hay Whitney donated to the Library of Congress the "Blind Memo" of August 23, 1864, which Clara Stone Hay, John Hay's wife, had given to Helen Nicolay, John George Nicolay's daughter. Noted in Jared Peatman, "The Long Shadow of Lincoln's Gettysburg Address," *The Lincoln Forum Bulletin* (Fall 2013), 9.

746 Borritt, 272.

747 *Lincoln Lore* 1438 no. 3; Helen Nicolay to Richard Watson Gilder, Nov. 8, 1908, Gilder papers, NYPL. Copies Three, Four, and Five of the Gettysburg Address, as they have since become known, Lincoln gave to auctions, to the New York Metropolitan Fair (Copy Three) and the Baltimore Sanitary Fair (copies Four and Five). He understood the Address's value and wished to raise funds for sanitation and veterans. The latter two copies ultimately ended up in the White House. The last presentation copy, requested by George Bancroft, is the verse carved into the wall of the Lincoln Memorial in Washington, DC. Designed by architect Francis Bacon and sculptor Daniel Chester French, the memorial was completed in 1922.

748 Hay to Robert Lincoln, April 12, 1888. Quoted in Thayer, 2, 44 and 2, 37. See, Martin P. Johnson, "Who Stole the Gettysburg Address?," *Journal of the Abraham Lincoln Association* 24 no. 2 (2003): 1–19. See also, William Harrison Lambert to John Page Nicholson, April 19, 1909, Philadelphia, in JH Papers, JHL, BU, reel 8.

749 Nicolay to Richard Watson Gilder, 1885, stated, "The original manuscript is lying before my eyes.... I have also the manuscript notes of the revision before me," quoted in Johnson. Nicolay was thought to have given Hay his Gettysburg manuscript some time after he had written the 1894 *Century* article and before his death in 1901.

750 Helen Nicolay to Robert T. Lincoln, November 9, 1908, in "Some Correspondence Regarding a Missing Copy of the Gettysburg Address, Part 1," *Lincoln Lore* no. 1437 (Nov. 1957): 3, cited in Johnson.

751 David Mearns, chief of the Manuscript Division, Library of Congress, "Unknown at this Address," in *Long Remembered: Facsimiles of the Five Versions of the Gettysburg Address* (DC: Library of Congress, 1963), not paginated.

752 Clara Hay to Richard Watson Gilder, December 7, 1908, 800 Sixteenth Street, Washington, in RW Gilder Papers, Manuscripts and Archives Division, New York Public Library.

753 In 1916, Clarence Hay, John Hay's youngest child, claimed that his family owned two copies of the Gettysburg Address, the original Hay and the Nicolay copies. That year, the family donated both copies to the Library of Congress. Copies Three, Four, and Five were given to the White House by their respective owners.

Chapter 24: Lincoln's Attaché

754 Hay to Charles G. Halpine, November 22, 1863, Charles Graham Halpine Papers, Huntington Library.

755 Keckley and Foster, 50.

756 Hay, diary, November 26, 1863. Quoted in Burlingame, *Inside Lincoln's White House,* 118–119.

757 Basler, CWL 7: 33–34.

758 Hay, December 8, 1863, diary. Quoted in Burlingame, *Inside Lincoln's White House,* 121–24.

759 Hay, December 10, 1863, diary. Quoted in Burlingame, *Inside Lincoln's White House, p. 330,* n. 321.

760 Lincoln to Benjamin F. Butler, January 2, 1864, Washington, DC. Quoted in Basler, *CWL* 7:103

761 Harry Tennyson Domer, "John Hay: A Memorial History," *The Shield* 21 no. 3 (September 1905): 275–331. Domer was a Theta Delta Chi brother of Hay's at Brown.

762 Hay, diary, December 19, 1863. Quoted in Burlingame, *Inside Lincoln's White House,* 128–129.

763 Hay, diary, December 25, 1863. Quoted in Burlingame, *Inside Lincoln's White House,* 133–134.

764 Hay, diary, December 31, 1863. Quoted in Burlingame, *Inside Lincoln's White House,* 135–136.

765 On January 1, 1864, John Hay had a hangover from the night before. So wretched was he that he walked over to live at "the club," not wishing to leave the evidence of his own vomit in the waste pitcher. He checked himself into what is believed to be the nearby Metropolitan Club, a block north of the White House, the club that he, Nicolay, and friends called "our headquarters." He missed the president's New Year's reception at the White House, a crowded affair where he was probably missed by only Lincoln. He also started off the new year with a new diary book, a leather folio featuring a sewn-in pencil holder and an inside front pocket. Hay, diary, December 31, 1863 and January 1, 1864, quoted in Burlingame, *Inside Lincoln's White House,* 135–137.

766 Hay, diary, December 28, 1863 and January 2, 1864. Quoted in Burlingame, *Inside Lincoln's White House,* 134–135, 137–140.

767 Hay, diary, May 22, 1864. Quoted in Burlingame, *Inside Lincoln's White House,* 197–98.

768 Robert Todd Lincoln to William Roscoe Thayer, August 6, 1914, Manchester, NH, WRT MSS, Houghton Library, Harvard.

769 Lincoln to Ulysses S. Grant, January 19, 1865, Executive Mansion, in Basler, *CWL* 8: 223.

770 Goodwin, 565.

771 Reported in the *New York Times,* March 7, 1864, 6.

772 Hay, diary January 13, 1864. Quoted in Burlingame, *Inside Lincoln's White House,* 142

773 Hay, diary, February 14, 1864. Quoted in Burlingame, *Inside Lincoln's White House,* 165.

774 The US Treasury Department appointed tax commissioners to conduct sales. Cited in Burlingame, *Inside the Lincoln White House*, 299, n. 31. Hay had William C. Morrill represent him at the tax sale, December 21–28, 1863. Hay to William Alsop, Paris, October 9 and December 12, 1865, quoted in Burlingame, *At Lincoln's Side*, 232, n. 46. Hay's notation on profits was written on the last pages of his 1866–1870 diary. The actual payout, Hay revealed to Whitelaw Reid, who regrettably to Hay published the statement in Whitelaw Reid, *After the War: A Tour of the Southern States, 1865–1866* (Harper Torchbooks, 1965), 171–72. (Reprint from 1866 original.) See Hay to William Alsop, Paris, October 9 and December 12 1865; to an unidentified recipient, Paris, September 26, 1866; to Lyman Stickney, Paris, June 4, 1866; Alsop to Hay, New York, August 29, 1866, JH MSS, JHBU.

775 Stickney to Chase, February 16, 1864, St. Augustine, Florida, Chase MSS, LC.

776 Hay, diary, March 3, 1864. Quoted in Burlingame, *Inside Lincoln's White House,* 173.

777 Burlingame, *Inside Lincoln's White House,* 336, n. 14. See also Coles, 65.

778 Hay, diary, March 12, 1864. Quoted in Burlingame, *Inside Lincoln's White House,* 179 and 341, n. 87.

779 Hay, diary, March 12, 1864. Quoted in Burlingame, *Inside Lincoln's White House,* 179.

780 *New York Herald,* March 1, 1864, 5.

781 William C. Harris, *With Charity for All, Lincoln and the Restoration of the Union* (The University Press of Kentucky, 1999) 132.

782 Hay, diary, March 12 to April 16, 1864. Quoted in Burlingame, *Inside Lincoln's White House,* 179–88.

783 A Congressional Joint Committee on the Conduct of War agreed. After interrogating Hay, the congressmen cleared him and "the President from any interference" in local and state affairs, the *New York Times* headlined on page one of March 25. Washington correspondence, March 25, 1864, *New York Times,* 1.

784 Hay, diary, April 30 and May 14, 1864. Quoted in Burlingame, *Inside Lincoln's White House,* 192–193, 196; and in Burlingame, *At Lincoln's Side,* 137.

785 The *New York Tribune* did not support Lincoln in advance of the Republican convention during May 1864. Horace Greeley stayed in close touch with the White House through Hay and Nicolay. See Robert C. Williams, *Horace Greeley: Champion of American Freedom* (New York University Press, 2006), 264.

786 Hay, diary, June 6, 1864. Quoted in Burlingame, *Inside Lincoln's White House,* 200–202.

787 Lincoln's acceptance speech, Lincoln, Reply to Committee Notifying Lincoln of His Renomination, June 9, 1864, in Basler, *CWL* 7: 380.

788 Hay, diary, June 17, 1864. Quoted in Burlingame, *Inside Lincoln's White House,* 203.

789 Lincoln to John Hay, June 10, 1864, Executive Mansion; and Lincoln to William S. Rosecrans, June 10, 1864, Executive Mansion, in Basler, *CWL* 7: 386.

790 Hay, diary, recorded on June 17, 1864. Quoted in Burlingame, *Inside Lincoln's White House,* 204–207.

791 Hay, diary, recorded on June 17, 1864. Quoted in Burlingame, *Inside Lincoln's White House,* 204–205.

792 Hay, diary, recorded on June 17, 1864. Quoted in Burlingame *Inside Lincoln's White House,* 208.

793 Thayer, *Life and Letters* vol. 1, 147. See also, Hay to Nicolay, June 20, 1864, *At Lincoln's Side,* 85. Tad Lincoln also returned to his father this day, having been in New York City with Mary Lincoln, in Basler *CWL* 7: 401.

Chapter 25: Lincoln's Negotiator

794 Hay, diary, June 30, 1864. Quoted in Burlingame, *Inside Lincoln's White House,* 212.

795 For an explanation of this favorite phrase of Lincoln's, see Burlingame, *Inside Lincoln's White House,* 356, n. 213.

796 Hay, diary, July 1, 1864, recording three days. Quoted in Burlingame, *Inside Lincoln's White House,* 215–217. On December 6, 1864, Lincoln nominated Simon Chase as Chief Justice of the United States, serving on the Supreme Court.

797 Hay, July 22 diary, note written on leaves folded and inserted into Hay's journal, recapping the events July 8–22, perhaps notes Hay intended for a newspaper article correcting the *New York Tribune's* own piece of July 22, 1864. Quoted in Burlingame, *Inside Lincoln's White House,* 224–227. See also, Lincoln to Greeley, July 9, 1864, Executive Mansion, Washington DC, JH MSS, JHBU.

798 Hay, diary, July 15, 1864. Quoted in Burlingame, *Inside Lincoln's White House,* 219–20.

799 Nicolay and Hay, *Collected Works* vol. 10, 158.

800 Nicolay and Hay, *Collected Works,* vol. 10, 159.

801 Hay to Lincoln, July 17, 1864. Quoted in Burlingame, *At Lincoln's Side,* 88.

802 Lincoln to Greeley, July 15, 1864, Executive Mansion, in Basler, *CWL* 7: 441–42.

803 Hay, diary, July 21–22, 1864. Quoted in Burlingame, *Inside Lincoln's White House,* 226. Sanders was a close correspondent with John Wilkes Booth.
804 Hay, diary, July 21, 1864. Quoted in Burlingame, *Inside Lincoln's White House,* 224–27.
805 Greeley was annoyed with Lincoln and Hay's strict position. After dinner with Greeley, Hay took the train down to Buffalo, a twenty-mile stretch, for an evening with William E. Dorsheimer, the lawyer-turned-major serving under Gen. John C. Frémont in Missouri. Hay had befriended Dorsheimer during his St. Louis visit, both lawyers and journalists. Dorsheimer (1832–1888) was an early devotee of a fellow Harvard classmate, architect Henry Hobson Richardson, who he hired to design his Delaware Avenue house in Buffalo, 1865. Hay later retained Richardson with Henry Adams, to design their attached houses on Lafayette Square in Washington, DC, 1885.
806 Gideon Welles, *Diary of Gideon Wells* vol. 2, August 19, 1864, 100.
807 See Welles, *Diary* vol. 2, August 13, 1864, 104. See also, Hay, diary, July 21, 1864, quoted in Burlingame, *Inside Lincoln's White House,* 227.
808 Lincoln to Henry Raymond, editor, August 15, 1864, Executive Mansion, Washington, DC, in Basler, CWL, VII: 494. President Lincoln mentioned to *New York Times* editor Raymond the false position in which Greeley placed him.
809 Robert T. Lincoln to William Roscoe Thayer, August 6, 1914, Hildene, Manchester, Vermont, WRT MSS, HLH.
810 Weed to Seward, August 22, 1864, RTL papers, AL MSS, LC.
811 Albert M. Palmer to Hay, September 11, 1864, New York, JH MSS, JHBU.
812 Nicolay to Hay, August 25, 1864. Quoted in Burlingame, *With Lincoln in the White House,* 152.
813 Hay, diary, Aug 23, 1864. Quoted in Burlingame, *Inside Lincoln's White House,* 247–248. See also, Randall and Current, *Lincoln, the President,* 215–216.
814 Black Republicans to Hay, September 22, 1864, Headquarters Out Posts, near New Berne, NC, JH MSS, JHBU. Black voters principally voted for the Republican Party during the late nineteenth century and the early twentieth century. On December 10, 1864, Thomas W. Higginson, commander of the First South Carolina Volunteers, wrote to Hay regarding the government's failure to fulfill its contractual promise to his regiment—the first organized Black soldiers, all volunteers, originally offered thirteen dollars per month, which they were paid for five months, then dropped to five dollars a month—and now notified each Black soldier to be seven dollars a month. Higginson asks Hay to say to Lincoln: "Is it not your duty, Sir, to make yourself responsible, so that your great gift of freedom shall not be sullied by this ignominious fraud?" in T.W. Higginson to Hay, December 10, 1863, Camp Sherman, South Carolina, First South Carolina Volunteers, JH MSS, JHLBU.
815 Hay, diary, October 9, 1864. Quoted in Burlingame, *Inside Lincoln's White House,* 226–237.
816 Hay, diary, October 11, 1864. Quoted in Burlingame, *Inside Lincoln's White House,* 238–241.
817 Hay, diary, October 12, 1864. Quoted in Burlingame, *Inside Lincoln's White House,* 241.
818 David H. Bates, *Lincoln in the Telegraph Office: Recollections of the United States Military Telegraph Corps During the Civil War* (University of Nebraska Press, 1995), 276. First published in 1906.
819 This speech, written by Hay and given to him by Lincoln, passed to John Hay's son Clarence Leonard Hay after his death. Clarence Hay bequeathed it to Houghton

Library, Harvard University, his alma mater, in JH MSS, HLH; the plain stationary paper, 4-1/2" by 9."

820 Hay, diary, November 8, 1864. Quoted in Burlingame, *Inside Lincoln's White House,* 243–246.

821 Lincoln to Noah Brooks, November 11, 1864, Sacramento *Daily Union,* December 10, 1864, quoted in Burlingame, *Abraham Lincoln* vol 2, 722.

822 Hay wrote Lincoln's acceptance speech, in diary, November 14, 1864. Quoted in Burlingame, *Inside Lincoln's White House,* 246.

823 Hay, diary, November 8, 1864. Quoted in Burlingame, *Inside Lincoln's White House,* 243–246.

824 Meigs to father, November 9, 1864, Washington, DC, MM MSS, LCW.

825 Hay, diary, November 16, 1864. Quoted in Burlingame, *Inside Lincoln's White House,* 250–251.

Chapter 26: "When the Boys Come Home"

826 John A. Andrew to Edwin Stanton, September 27, 1864, Boston, John A. Andrew Papers, MHS.

827 William Schouler to John Hay, October 12, 1865, JH MSS, HLH.

828 http://www.papersofabrahamlincoln.org/Bixby%20Letter.htm

829 John Hay to Elmer Ellsworth, June 9, 1861, Hay MSS, JHBU. Quoted in Burlingame, *At Lincoln's Side,* 22. Burlingame has identified many other examples of condolence letters written by Hay, cited in Burlingame, "New Light on the Bixby Letter," *Journal of the Abraham Lincoln Association* 16 (Winter 1995): 59–72.

830 Randall, *Lincoln, the President,* quoted in Burlingame, *Abraham Lincoln,* vol 2, 737.

831 David A. Anderson, ed., *The Literary Works of Abraham Lincoln* (Charles E. Merrill, 1970), xi.

832 Richard Watson Gilder, "Lincoln: Passages from his Speeches and Letters," *The Century* magazine, 1901, xlv, xlvii.

833 Burlingame, "New Light on the Bixby Letter," 59–72. Randall and Current regarded the Bixby Letter "as a masterpiece in the English language," standing "with the Gettysburg Address." See Randall and Current, 48–52.

834 Burlingame, *Journal of the Abraham Lincoln Association,* 71.

835 Scrapbook, JH MSS, LC; Alice H Wadsworth to Tyler Dennett, August 1, 1931, Washington, DC, Tyler Dennett papers related to JH, Manuscript Division, LC, container 2.

836 According to her great-grandson, Mrs. George M. Towser, *Providence Evening Bulletin,* August 12, 1925, quoted in Burlingame, *JALA.*

837 Sarah Cabot Wheelwright, "Reminiscences of Sarah Cabot Wheelwright," April 20, 1904, in George C. Shattuck, "Sarah Cabot Wheelwright's Account of the Widow Bixby," *Proceedings of the Massachusetts Historical Society* 75 (1963): 107–108.

838 Charles Basler, "Who Wrote the 'Letter to Mrs. Bixby'?" *Lincoln Herald,* February 1943, 3–8, quoted in Burlingame, *JALA,* 64.

839 Burlingame, *JALA,* 64.

840 John Hay to Charles S. Spencer, Washington, DC, November 25, 1864. Quoted in Burlingame, *At Lincoln's Side,* 101.

841 United States Congress, *Journal of the House of Representatives of the United States,* 38 no. 2 (1865): 21.

842 Nicolay to Hay, December 8, 1864. Quoted in Burlingame, *With Lincoln in the White House,* 255, n. 259.

843 Burlingame, *Abraham Lincoln* vol 2, 736.

844 Hay diary, December 18, 1864, the last entry in his diary; the entry before this one was November 17, 1864. Quoted in Burlingame, *Inside Lincoln's White House,* 252–254.

845 Nicolay to Therena Bates, December 16, 1864, Washington, DC. Quoted in Burlingame, *With Lincoln in the White House,* 167. See, Charles H. Philbrick to O. M. Hatch, December 30, 1864, quoted in Ronald D. Rietveld, "The Lincoln White House Community," *JALA* 20 no. 2 (1999), 68.

846 January 11, 1865, Mrs. Ann Eliza Harlan, wife of US Senator James Harlan (Iowa), invited Hay and Robert Lincoln to a parlor hop at National Hotel, hosted by daughter Mary Harlan and herself. Robert Lincoln was Mary Harlan's on-and-off main squeeze. See, Mrs. Ann Eliza Harlan to John Hay, January 11, 1865, JH MSS, JHBU. Hay escorted a Miss Neil to the Capitol. See, Miss Neil to John Hay, January 20, 1865, JH MSS, JHBU. Hay invited Mary Sherman to the opera on January 21, for the next evening, with Bob Lincoln and Mary Harlan, who shared a box; Sherman declined. See, John Hay to Mary Sherman, Janurary 21, 1865, JH MSS, JHBU.

847 Nicolay, who was in the House for the vote, telegraphed Lincoln in the War Department telegraph room. The government did not have funds of $4 million or more to compensate the owners or the four million freed slaves, as Britain had done in 1833–1834 when it freed 130,000 slaves, most in the West Indies. See, Kevin Phillips, *Wealth and Democracy: A Political History of the American Rich* (Broadway Books, 2002), 31. See also, Nicolay to Therena Bates, February 4, 1865, quoted in Burlingame, *With Lincoln in the White House,* 173.

848 The first soldiers to enter Charleston were members of the 21st Infantry Regiment of the US Colored Troops and the 55th Massachusetts Infantry, another Black regiment. See, Paul Starobin, *Madness Rules the Hour: Charleston, 1860 and the Mania for War* (Public Affairs, 2017).

849 Nicolay to Therena Bates, February 26, 1865. Quoted in Burlingame, *With Lincoln in the White House,* 174–175.

850 Keckley and Foster, 136.

851 Nicolay to Therena Bates, March 5, 1865. Quoted in Burlingame, *With Lincoln in the White House,* 175.

852 Nicolay to Therena Bates, March 5, 1865. Quoted in Burlingame, in *With Lincoln in the White House,* 175.

853 A nice description of the inaugural scene appears in Burlingame, *Lincoln,* vol 2, 425.

854 Wills, 161.

855 Foner, "The Emancipation of Abe Lincoln," A19.

856 White, *Lincoln's Greatest Speech,* 156.

857 The author's bold highlights of John Hay's notable contributions.

858 Discussed in Foner, "The Emancipation of Abe Lincoln." See also, Jackson Lears, *Rebirth of a Nation: The Making of Modern America, 1877–1920* (HarperCollins, 2009), 12.

859 John Hay, "Memorial to William McKinley to joint session of Congress, February 1902," in *Addresses of John Hay* (Books of Libraries Press, 1970), 148–49. First published 1906.

860 Donald, *Lincoln,* 568.

861 All pasted in John Hay's scrapbook, JH MSS, LCW.

862 Clara S. Hay to R.W. Gilder, November 20, 1908, in The Century Company Collection, Manuscripts and Rare Books, NYPL.

863 Domer, "John Hay," 275–331.

864 Goodwin, 702.

865 Abraham Lincoln to John Hay, March 22, 1865, document #233423, ALPL.

866 During the past year, Hay and Nicolay had talked with Lincoln and Seward about their respective wishes for foreign-service appointments if there was a second term.

Chapter 27: The Reckoning

867 Hay to Gilder, no date, c. 1889–1890, in John Hay collection, ALPL; noted in John Bigelow, *Retrospections of an Active Life,* vol. 2 (Baker & Taylor, 1909), 430. *Retrospections* totals five volumes.

868 Montgomery Meigs to father, April 1865, Washington, DC, Meigs MSS, LC.

869 Hay, "William McKinley," *Addresses,* 148–149.

870 Kevin Phillips, *Wealth and Democracy: A Political History of the American Rich* (Broadway Books, 2002), 312.

871 In the three decades between 1860 and 1890, the country's population more than doubled, from thirty-one million to sixty-three million. The urban population, too, swelled by 100 percent. See Phillips, *Wealth and Democracy,* 36–37.

872 Woodrow Wilson (1856–1924) was born in Staunton, VA, to native Ohio parents. His father, a Presbyterian pastor, was sent from Steubenville, OH, to Staunton for his first ministry, then to Augusta, GA, when Wilson was seventeen. While his parents were Southern sympathizers during the Civil War, Wilson's own allegiance ran to the Whig Party in college at Princeton University. Following his graduate education at Johns Hopkins University in Baltimore, 1883–1890, Wilson was a resident of New Jersey, as president of Princeton and governor of New Jersey.

873 Quoted in Hay, *Addresses,* 40.

874 The 5,544-acre property was located in western Virginia, now Springfield, KY.

875 In 1924, legislation permitted citizenship to Native Americans born in the United States. Through the end of the nineteenth century, The Homestead and the Pacific Railway acts of 1862, hastening construction of the transcontinental railroad, delivered substantial losses to tribal people. Forced by the federal government, they gave up land, natural resources, and even traces of their culture. Lincoln, continuing the policies of previous administrations which are now viewed as discriminatory, stripped Native Americans of their lands and forcibly relocated and concentrated them on reservations, often far from their original homes. In 1863, for example, eradicating Navajos and Mescalero Apaches from their New Mexico territory, Lincoln condemned the Navajo to march 450 miles along harsh and tough terrain. Two thousand Navajos perished on the trek. And in 1864, among several other massacres, the Union army killed hundreds of Cheyenne and Arapaho during the Sand Creek Massacre in southeastern Colorado.

876 Oliver Wendell Holmes to Hay, April 10, 1865, JH MSS, JHBU. Of America's thirty-six states, only ten lay west of the Mississippi, five bordering the great river itself. In the process of bringing the Western territories of Kansas, Texas, Nevada, California, and Oregon into the continental union during the postwar era, soon joined by Nebraska, Colorado, North and South Dakota, Montana, Washington, Idaho, Wyoming, Utah, and Oklahoma, the United States government cleared the way for American development. That is how the president and Congress sitting in Washington, DC, viewed it.

Clashing over land claims, mineral rights, and cultural differences, the US army killed tens of thousands of Native Americans in violent attacks. In 1924, Native Americans born in the US were finally offered citizenship, sixty-three years following President Lincoln's emancipation proclamation and almost six decades after the Thirteenth Amendment gave liberty and citizenship to black people.

877 Nicolay & Hay, *Lincoln* vol. 10, 277.

878 Nicolay & Hay, *Lincoln* vol. 10, 278–279.

879 Nicolay & Hay, *Lincoln* vol. 10, 285.

880 Keckley and Foster, 136.

881 Nicolay & Hay, *Lincoln* vol. 10, 281.

882 John Hay described President Lincoln's dream to George F. Hoar, the prominent Massachusetts politician who went on to serve in the United States Congress (1869–1877) and Senate (1877–1904). See, Hay to Hoar, April 18, 1865, Executive Mansion, JH MSS, Huntington Library.

883 Nicolay & Hay, *Lincoln* vol. 10, 283. This is also quoted in Gideon Welles, "Lincoln and Johnson: Their Plan of Reconstruction and Resumption of National Authority," *The Galaxy* 13 no. 4 (April 1872).

884 Nicolay & Hay, *Lincoln* vol. 10, 285–286. See, Burlingame, *Lincoln Observed,* 188.

885 Nicolay & Hay, *Lincoln* vol. 10, 287.

886 Nicolay & Hay, *Lincoln* vol. 10, 288.

887 Nicolay & Hay, *Lincoln* vol. 10, 289, 291.

888 Nicolay & Hay, *Lincoln* vol. 10, 292–293.

889 Nicolay was in Charleston for the flag-raising ceremony. See Jason Emerson, *Giant in the Shadows: The Life of Robert T. Lincoln* (Southern Illinois University Press, 2012), 101.

890 Nicolay & Hay, *Lincoln* vol. 10, 301.

891 Jim Bishop, *The Day Lincoln Was Shot* (Weidenfeld & Nicolson, 1955).

892 Nicolay & Hay, *Lincoln* vol. 10, 318, 301, 303–304.

893 Nicolay & Hay, *Lincoln* vol. 10, 314.

894 Unidentified newspaper, JH MSS, HLH.

895 Nicolay & Hay, *Lincoln* vol. 10, 315.

896 Burlingame, *Abraham Lincoln,* vol. 2, 832.

897 Quartermaster Gen. Montgomery Meigs organized President Lincoln's funeral cortege, including the funeral train from the nation's capital to the closed-casket burial in Springfield. Neither Mary Lincoln nor Robert Lincoln attended the burial. See, Meigs to father, April 18, 1865, Meigs MSS, LC.

898 Burlingame, *Abraham Lincoln,* vol. 2, 831.

899 Frederick Douglass, quoted in Burlingame, *Abraham Lincoln,* vol. 2, 830.

900 Henry Adams wrote his father, Charles Francis Adams, "I am much too strong an American to have thought for a moment that we are going to be shaken by a murder." See, HA to CFA Jr., May 10, 1865, London, Henry Adams Papers, MHS.

901 On April 25, 1865, Robert Lincoln wrote to President Andrew Johnson requesting that his family stay two-and-a-half weeks because his mother "cannot possibly be ready to leave here." The Lincolns then moved to Chicago, where Robert completed law studies at the old University of Chicago law school (later absorbed into Northwestern University School of Law). He was admitted to the bar on February 25, 1867. RTL MSS, LCW.

902 Henry Adams to Charles Francis Adams Jr., May 10, 1865, HA Papers, MHS.

903 Philip Kennicott, "Painful Lessons the Civil War Taught Us, R3. Here, Kennicott claimed that Lincoln's speeches echoed eighteenth-century philosopher Immanuel Kant.

904 Wootton, 551.

905 Wootton, 553.

906 "Hay's reverence for Lincoln was a beautiful characteristic," said Jean Jules Jusserand, the French ambassador in Washington, DC (1902–1925), who talked frequently with John Hay, Secretary of State (1898–1905). See, Jusserand, *What Me Befell: The Reminiscences of Jean Jules Jusserand* (Houghton Mifflin, 1934).

907 Interview with Marc Mytar, PhD, July 16, 2019.

908 Discussed in Burlingame, *Abraham Lincoln* vol. 1, 685.

909 Jusserand

910 Nicolay to Honorable O. H. Browning, in conversation, June 17, 1875, Leland Hotel, Springfield. Quoted in Burlingame, *An Oral History of Abraham Lincoln: John G. Nicolay's Interviews and Essays.* (Southern Illinois University Press, 1996), 1–2 .

911 Ophelia in *Hamlet said:* "There's rosemary, that's for remembrance; pray, love, remember; and there is pansies, that's for thoughts.... There's fennel for you, and columbines; there's rue for you, and here's some for me; we may call it herb of grace o' Sundays. O, you must wear your rue with a difference. There's a daisy."

912 The next stanza was crossed out in the original manuscript of the poem, presumably by John Hay, who wrote: "Will dearer scenes and older friends / Have power to chain and baid you, / And banish out of memory / The friends you leave behind you."

913 John Hay, "When you shall leave us," n.d., c. May or June 1865, JH MSS, JHBU.

914 John Hay Writing, JH MSS, JHBU.

915 Hay wrote this for the *Daily Chronicle,* Washington, DC, about the time the Freedom statue was raised upon the Capitol dome on December 2, 1863.

916 John Hay Writing, JH MSS, JHBU.

917 Written on versos of three pages of US Army Department of the South, General Order no. 16, aboard steamer *Dictator,* Atlantic Ocean off the Florida Coast, in John Hay Writing, JH MSS, JHBU. Published in *Illinois Daily Journal,* May 1864 and in *Harper's Weekly,* 1864.

918 Published in *Harper's Magazine,* replaced "wanton" with "generous."

919 Published in *Harper's Magazine,* "encinctured" instead of "encompassed."

920 On the lower right-hand corner of the page, John Hay drew a tiny palm tree.

921 Written on the choppy Atlantic Ocean along the Eastern Seaboard. JH MSS, JHBU.

922 Originally published in *Illinois Daily Journal,* c. 1861–1864; republished in *Little Breeches and Other Pieces: Humorous, Descriptive & Pathetic* (Savill, Edwards, 1871). See, Manuscripts and Archives Division, NYPL.

923 Published by Malcolm McG Dana, *Annals of Norwich: New London County, Connecticut in the Great Rebellion of 1861–65* (J.H. Jewett, 1873), 202. See, extract from "The Advance Guard" by John Hay, JH MSS, JHBU.

924 Originally published in *Harper's Weekly,* June 18, 1864. Republished during World War I, 1918. Signed "John Hay, Executive Mansion, Washington, D. C.," JH MSS, JHBU.

925 Reverie to the Mississippi River, where John Hay passed many hours throughout his boyhood and also as an adult on visits to his family in Warsaw, IL. See, the JH MSS, JHBU.

ACKNOWLEDGMENTS

Gratitude shines on the individuals who supported me in the making of this book.

First and foremost, George Hartman, my husband, now deceased, offered constant support and invaluable encouragement. In his steady and quiet way, he has been at my side, supporting me through the joys of discovery and the headwinds of disappointment. This book would not have been possible without his confidence and love. During March 2025, he read every word and page of the manuscript, forever at my side and in my heart. He died on April 13, 2025, shortly after I delivered the final manuscript to the publisher.

Michael Mungiello and Michael Carlisle of InkWell Management Literary Agency in New York City, my remarkable agents and champions, were crucial to bringing the manuscript to light. Their confidence in the book's merit and distinction, and their impressive connections with editors and publishers, were vital to this book finding its home. They are wonderful advocates. My appreciation is boundless.

Cooper Lippert, friend and gifted writer, was a true helpmate in the final creation of the manuscript. A graduate of Kenyon College's creative writing program, Cooper has both the training and natural gifts of an eloquent writer and gifted teacher. Our work together was nothing short of a miracle. Thank you!

Marc Myter, PhD, (clinical psychology), was my trusted advisor who illuminated the psychological relationship between John Hay and Abraham Lincoln, both individually and in their creative collaboration and friendship with one another. A native of Springfield, growing up just four blocks from the historic Lincoln family residence, he offered especial insights about Lincoln in his Illinois hometown.

Robert M. (Bob) Longsworth, who was a professor of English at Oberlin College from 1963–2000, a scholarly medievalist, and etymologist and is an expert in the use of words. As words are a central element in the Hay–Lincoln relationship, Bob has been a wonderful resource for this manuscript. He was also a close friend of Geoffrey T. Blodgett, my history mentor at Oberlin, where I studied as an undergraduate and earned highest honors. Thank you, Bob.

At Brown University, home of the John Hay Library, Harriett Hemmasi, who was formerly the university librarian and the dean of libraries at Georgetown University, opened doors at Brown that provided full access to the John Hay papers and rare book collections. I also thank my friend Joan Sorensen of the Brown University Corporation. At the John Hay Library, I am grateful for the assistance offered by Samuel A. Streit, Joseph Meisel, Christopher Geisler, Jennifer Braga, Robin W. Ness, Andrew Moul, Ann Dodge, Lee Anzick, and Holly Snyder.

In the Manuscript Division of the Library of Congress in Washington, DC, where I enjoyed many months of research, I am thankful for the assistance of, and conversations with, Jennifer Brathozde, Bruce Kirby, Jeffrey Flannery, Patrick Kerwin, and John R. Sellers, the former curator of the Civil War archives.

At the Massachusetts Historical Society in Boston, I was honored to hold a Mellon research fellowship. I am especially appreciative of the assistance of Conrad Edick Wright, formerly the Worthington C. Ford Editor of Publications and director of research there. He was an early sponsor of my work during my fellowship at this extraordinary archive. Others who lent their gracious support were Elaine Heavey, Peter Drummey, and Dennis Fiori.

In Cleveland, the Western Reserve Historical Society was an important resource for my early research on John Hay. I am especially grateful to Ann Sindelar for her assistance and friendship over the years. Charles P. Bolton, a true believer in John Hay's historical value, marshaled his influence to garner support for my Cleveland research. In addition to Charlie and Julie Bolton, for whom I am deeply grateful, I am indebted to later generations of John Hay's extended family that included James R. Garfield II and Kate Schofield.

Archival collections are irreplaceable treasures that demand the expertise of talented and carefully trained curators to navigate the specific details among millions of documents. At the Huntington Library in Pasadena, California; The New York Public Library's Manuscripts and Archives Division; the Clark University Archives in Worcester, Massachusetts; the Abraham Lincoln Presidential Library and Museum in Springfield; the Illinois State Historical Society, also in Springfield; and the National

Archives and Records Administration in Washington, DC, and College Park, Maryland, I am grateful to the assistance provided to manuscript collections. I also extend thanks to the private historical resources of Kathy Zimmerman of Pittsfield, Illinois, Robert Hoffman of Rochester, New York, and Corrin Strong of Geneseo, New York, the great-grandson of John Hay.

My family has been invaluable supporters. In addition to my late husband, I have infinite thanks to Sarah Hartman, my dear friend and stepdaughter, with whom I have shared this long journey. My cherished brother, James Cigliano, is an exceptional friend and wise mentor. My sister-in-law Jennifer Rosen is a true fan of the publication coming to light. To their adorable sons, my beloved nephews Jacob, Ben, and Eli Cigliano, I say thank you; the energy of your love is beyond measure. My mother, Gertrude Cigliano, deceased, loved to hear about my archival escapades. Friends who offered companionship and counsel include Robert Wilson, the long-time editor of *American Scholar* and the beautiful writer of *Barnum: An American Life* (2019), *Mathew Brady: Portraits of a Nation* (2013), and *Explorer King: Adventure, Science and the Great Diamond Hoax, Clarence King in the Old West* (2006); Jennifer Thompson, with whom I have shared so many wonderful times and enlightening conservations; Robert Brantley and Linda Mayer of New Orleans, friends and authors; as well as Stuart Kogod, Connie Krupin, Kevin Lippert, Rob Shaeffer, Darcy Snow, Walter Smalling, and Ray Rhinehart (deceased.) Each conversation and your interest helped to sustain my hope and joy for this book.

Years of writing and editing, a long and solitary business, was made easier, even joyful, by the magical place where I wrote overlooking Penobscot Bay in Maine, sitting in the light-filled house designed by my late husband, a gifted architect. The peacefulness of my writing barn, quiet as a research library, enabled me to work for hours on end. The old saying, "a room of one's own" cannot be overrated.

In closing, I would like to extend my deep gratitude to Alex Novak and Caitlin Burdette at Post Hill Press, whose eager ambition for this book and its discoveries have brought this work to light.

Jan Cigliano Hartman
Portland, Maine
October 2025

BIBLIOGRAPHY

HLH: Houghton Library, Harvard University
JHBU: John Hay Library, Brown University
LCW: Manuscript Division, Library of Congress, Washington, DC
MHS: Massachusetts Historical Society
WRHS: Western Reserve Historical Society, Cleveland, Ohio

Manuscripts

Henry Adams Collection. Adams Family Papers. Massachusetts Historical Society (HA MHS).

John Bigelow Papers. New York Public Library.

Edward Everett Papers. Massachusetts Historical Society (MHS).

Charles Graham Halpine Papers. Huntington Library.

John Hay Collection. John Hay Library, Brown University (JH MSS, JHBU).

John Hay Papers. Manuscript Division, Library of Congress (JH MSS, LCW).

John Hay Collection. Massachusetts Historical Society (JH MSS, MHS).

John Hay Collection. Mather Family Papers. Cleveland History Center, Western Reserve Historical Society (WRHS).

Robert Hoffman private collection. Scrapbook, newspaper clippings, and miscellany of John Hay (1860–1865). Rochester, New York.

John Hay material in university archives. John Hay Library, Brown University (JH MSS, BUA, JHBU).

Abraham Lincoln Collection. John Hay Library, Brown University (AL MSS, JHBU).

Abraham Lincoln Papers. Manuscript Division, Library of Congress (AL MSS, LCW).

Montgomery Meigs Papers. Manuscript Division, Library of Congress (MM MMS, LCW).

Thomas Nast Collection. John Hay Library, Brown University (TN MSS, JHBU).

John George Nicolay Papers. Manuscript Division, Library of Congress (JGN MSS, LCW).

Philermenian Society material in university archives. John Hay Library, Brown University (BUA; JHBU).

William Roscoe Thayer Papers. Houghton Library, Harvard University (WRT MSS, HLH).

Wadsworth Family Papers. Manuscript Division, Library of Congress (LCW).

Bibliography

Adams, Charles Francis. *Charles Francis Adams, 1835–1915: An Autobiography*. Houghton Mifflin, 1916.

Albers, Adelaide, Virginia van Pappelendam, and Marie Warthen, compilers. *History of Warsaw*. The Warsaw Bulletin, 1960.

Basler, Roy P., ed. *The Collected Works of Abraham Lincoln*. 9 volumes. Rutgers University Press, 1953.

Beer, Thomas. *Hanna*. Alfred A. Knopf, 1929.

Bishop, Jim. *The Day Lincoln Was Shot*. Weidenfeld & Nicolson, 1955.

Boritt, Gabor. *The Gettysburg Gospel: The Lincoln Speech that Nobody Knows*. Simon & Schuster, 2006.

Boyd, Julian P. et al, eds. *The Papers of Thomas Jefferson*. 20 volumes. Princeton University Press, 1982.

Briggs, John Channing. *Lincoln's Speeches Reconsidered*. The Johns Hopkins University Press, 2005.

Brown, Samuel R. *The Western Gazetteer or Emigrant's Directory, Containing a Geographical Description of the Western States and Territories*. E. C. Southwick, 1817.

Burlingame, Michael. *Abraham Lincoln: A Life*. 2 volumes. Johns Hopkins University Press, 2008.

__________. *An Oral History of Abraham Lincoln: John G. Nicolay's Interviews and Essays*. Southern Illinois University Press, 1996.

__________, ed. *At Lincoln's Side: John Hay's Civil War Correspondence and Selected Writing*. Southern Illinois University Press, 2000.

__________, ed. *Dispatches from Lincoln's White House: The Anonymous Civil War Journalism of Presidential Secretary William O. Stoddard*. University of Nebraska Press, 2002.

__________, ed. *Inside Lincoln's White House: The Civil War Diary of John Hay*. Southern Illinois University Press, 1997.

__________, ed. *Lincoln Observed: Civil War Dispatches of Noah Brooks*. Johns Hopkins University Press, 1998.

__________. *Lincoln's Journalist: John Hay's Anonymous Writings for the Press, 1860–1964*. Southern Illinois University Press, 1998.

__________, ed. *With Lincoln in the White House: Letters, Memoranda, and Other writings of John G. Nicolay, 1860–1865*. Southern Illinois University Press, 2000.

Carpenter, Francis Bicknell. *Six Months in the White House with Abraham Lincoln*. Hurd & Houghton, 1866.

Chapman, Charles C. *History of Pike County Illinois*. 2 volumes. C. C. Chapman, 1880.

Chernow, Ron. *Alexander Hamilton*. Penguin Books, 2004.

Cooper, Lane. *The Rhetoric of Aristotle*. D. Appleton–Century, 1932.

Dennett, William Tyler. *John Hay: From Poetry to Politics*. Dodd, Mead, 1934.

Dodge, Daniel K. *Abraham Lincoln: Master of Words*. D. Appleton, 1924.

Donald, David Herbert. *Lincoln Reconsidered*. Vintage, 1956.

Donald, David, ed. *Inside Lincoln's Cabinet: The Civil War Diaries of Salmon P. Chase*. Longmans, Green, 1954.

Douglass, Frederick. *The Life and Times of Frederick Douglass*. Park Publishing, 1881.

Edwards, Herbert J. and John E. Hankins. *Lincoln, The Writer: The Development of his Literary Style*. University of Maine Press, 1962.

Emerson, Jason. *Giant in the Shadows: The Life of Robert T. Lincoln*. Southern Illinois University Press, 2012.

Foner, Eric, ed. *Our Lincoln: New Perspectives on Lincoln and his World.* W. W. Norton, 2008.

Gienapp, William E. *Abraham Lincoln and Civil War America.* Oxford University Press, 2001.

Glaeser, Edward L. and Claudia Goldin, eds. *Corruption and Reform: Lessons from America's Economic History.* University of Chicago Press, 2006.

Goodheart, Adam. *1861: The Civil War Awakening.* Alfred A. Knopf, 2011.

Goodwin, Doris Kearns. *Team of Rivals: The Political Genius of Abraham Lincoln.* Simon & Schuster, 2005.

Harris, William C. *With Charity for All: Lincoln and the Restoration of the Union.* University of Kentucky Press, 1999.

Harrison, Lowell H. *Lincoln of Kentucky.* University Press of Kentucky, 2000.

Harvey, Eleanor Jones and Smithsonian America Art Museum. *The Civil War and American Art.* Yale University Press, 2012.

Hay, John. *Addresses of John Hay.* Freeport, NY: Books for Libraries Press, 1970. Reprint of the original from 1906.

Hay, John. "Mormon Prophet's Tragedy." *Atlantic Monthly,* December 1869.

Hay, John. *Castilian Days.* James R. Osgood, 1871.

Hay, John. *Letters of John Hay and Extracts from Diary.* 3 volumes. Privately printed, 1908.

Hay, John. *Pike County Ballads.* James R. Osgood, 1871.

Higginson, Mary Thatcher, ed. *Letter and Journals of Thomas Wentworth Higginson, 1846–1906.* Houghton Mifflin, 1921.

Hofstadter, Richard. *The American Political Tradition and the Men Who Made It.* Alfred A. Knopf, 1948.

Holzer, Harold, ed., comp. *Abraham Lincoln The Writer: A Treasury of His Greatest Speeches and Letters.* Calkins Creek, 2000.

Holzer, Harold and Joshua Wolf Shenk. *In Lincoln's Hand: His Original Manuscripts with Commentary by Distinguished Americans.* Bantam Books, 2009.

Hubbard, Charles M. *Lincoln Reshapes the Presidency.* Mercer University Press, 2003.

Kaplan, Fred. Lincoln: *The Biography of a Writer*. Harper Collins, 2000.

Keckley, Elizabeth and Frances Smith Foster, ed. *Behind the Scenes: Thirty Years a Slave and Four Years in the White House*. University of Illinois Press, 1998.

Lamers, William M. *The Edge of Glory: A Biography of General William S. Rosecrans, U.S.A.* Louisiana State University Press, 1961.

Lears, Jackson. *Rebirth of a Nation: The Making of Modern America, 1877–1920*. HarperCollins, 2009.

Lowenfels, Walter, ed. *Walt Whitman's Civil War*. Alfred A. Knopf, 1960.

McCartney, Carol. *Our Pike County: The Soul of Western Illinois*. James Stevenson Publisher, 2004.

McPherson, James D. *Tried by War: Abraham Lincoln as Commander in Chief*. Penguin, 2009.

McPherson, James M. *Abraham Lincoln and the Second American Revolution*. Oxford University Press, 1991.

McPherson, James M. *Abraham Lincoln and the Second American Revolution & the Men Who Made It*. Vintage Books, 1948.

Mearns, David. *Long Remembered: Facsimiles of the Five Versions of the Gettysburg Address*. Library of Congress, 1963.

Mitchell, Martha. *Encyclopedia Brunoniana*. Brown University Library, 1993.

Monaghan, Jay. *Diplomat in Carpet Slippers: Abraham Lincoln Deals with Foreign Affairs*. Bobs-Merrill, 1945.

Montague, ____, ed., comp. *A College Friendship: A Series of Letters from John Hay to Hannah Angell*. Privately printed, 1938.

Nicolay, John G. and John Hay, eds. *Complete Works of Abraham Lincoln*. 10 volumes. Francis D. Tandy, 1894.

Parrington, Vernon Louis. *Main Currents in American Thought*. 3 volumes. Harcourt Brace, 1927.

Perry, Joe. *Christmas in Germany: A Cultural History*. University of North Carolina Press, 2010.

Phillips, Kevin. *Wealth and Democracy: A Political History of the American Rich*. Broadway Books, 2002.

Pinsker, Matthew. *Lincoln's Sanctuary: Abraham Lincoln and the Soldiers' Home*. Oxford University Press, 2003.

Randall, James G. and Richard N. Current. *Lincoln the President: The Last Full Measure*. 4 volumes. Dodd, Mead, 1955.

Rhinehart, Raymond and Walter Smalling. *Brown University: The Campus Guide*. Princeton Architectural Press, 2014.

Sears, Stephen W. *The Civil War Papers of George B. McClellan; Selected Correspondence*, 1860–1865. Ticknor & Fields, 1989.

Starobin, Paul. *Madness Rules the Hour: Charleston, 1860 and the Mania for War*. Public Affairs, 2017.

Staudenraus, P. J., ed. *Mr. Lincoln's Washington: Selections from the Writings of Noah Brooks, Civil War Correspondent*. Thomas Yoseloff, 1967.

Stoddard, W. O. Jr., ed. *Lincoln's Third Secretary: The Memoirs of William O. Stoddard*. Exposition Press, 1955.

Stoddard, William O., and Michael Burlingame, ed. *Inside the White House in War Times: Memoirs and Reports of Lincoln's Secretary*. University of Nebraska Press, 2000.

Stowell, Daniel W., ed. *The Papers of Abraham Lincoln: Legal Documents and Cases*. 4 volumes. University of Virginia Press, 2008.

Streznewski, Marylou Kelly. *Gifted Grownups: The Mixed Blessing of Extraordinary Potential*. John Wiley & Sons, 1999.

Strong, George Templeton. *Diary of the Civil War, 1860–1865*. Macmillan, 1962.

Ticknor, Caroline. *Poe's Helen*. Charles Scribner's Sons, 1916.

Traubel, Horace. *With Walt Whitman in Camden*. Oxford University Press, 1953.

Villard, Henry. *Memoirs of Henry Villard: Journalist and Financier, 1835–1900*. 2 volumes. Houghton, Mifflin, 1904.

Wallace, David Foster and J. C. Hallman, eds. *The Story about the Story: Great Writers Explore Great Literature*. Tin House Books, 2013.

Warren, Louis A. *Lincoln's Gettysburg Declaration: "A New Birth of Freedom."* Lincoln National Life Foundation, 1964.

White, Ronald C. *Lincoln's Greatest Speech: The Second Inaugural.* Simon & Schuster, 2002.

__________. *The Eloquent President: A Portrait of Lincoln Through his Words.* Random House, 2005.

__________. *Lincoln in Private: What His Most Personal Reflections Tell Us About Our Greatest President.* Random House, 2021.

Widmer, Ted. *Lincoln on the Verge: Thirteen Days to Washington.* Simon & Schuster, 2020.

Williams, Robert C. *Horace Greeley: Champion of American Freedom.* New York University Press, 2006.

Wills, George. *Lincoln at Gettysburg: The Words that Remade America.* Simon & Schuster, 1992.

Wilson, Douglas L. *Lincoln's Sword: The Presidency and the Power of Words.* Alfred A. Knopf, 2006.

Wootton, David. *The Invention of Science: A New History of the Scientific Revolution.* HarperCollins, 2015.

Zarefsky, David. *Abraham Lincoln: In His Own Words.* Great Courses, 1999.

Zimmerman, Warren. *First Great Triumph: How Five Americans Made Their Country a World Power.* Farrar, Straus and Giroux, 2004.